THE STRUGGLE FOR SHAKESPEARE'S TEXT

Twentieth-Century Editorial Theory and Practice

We know Shakespeare's writings only from imperfectly made early editions, from which editors struggle to remove errors. The New Bibliography of the early twentieth century, refined with technological enhancements in the 1950s and 1960s, taught generations of editors how to make sense of the early editions of Shakespeare and use them to make modern editions. This book is the first complete history of the ideas that gave this movement its intellectual authority, and of the challenges to that authority that emerged in the 1980s and 1990s. Working chronologically, Egan traces the struggle to wring from the early editions evidence of precisely what Shakespeare wrote. The story of another struggle, between competing interpretations of the evidence from early editions, is told in detail and the consequences for editorial practice are comprehensively surveyed, allowing readers to discover just what is at stake when scholars argue about how to edit Shakespeare.

GABRIEL EGAN began his academic career at Shakespeare's Globe theatre in London, where, in addition to teaching theatre history and running workshops on the Globe stage, he taught students to print on a replica wooden hand-press using the methods employed in Shakespeare's time. He is the author of *Shakespeare and Marx* (2004), *Green Shakespeare: From Ecopolitics to Ecocriticism* (2006) and *The Edinburgh Critical Guide to Shakespeare* (2007). He edited the play *The Witches of Lancashire* by Richard Brome and Thomas Heywood (2002), and co-edits the journals *Theatre Notebook* and *Shakespeare*.

THE STRUGGLE FOR SHAKESPEARE'S TEXT

Twentieth-Century Editorial Theory and Practice

GABRIEL EGAN

CAMBRIDGE UNIVERSITY PRESS
Cambridge, New York, Melbourne, Madrid, Cape Town, Singapore,
São Paulo, Delhi, Dubai, Tokyo, Mexico City

Cambridge University Press
The Edinburgh Building, Cambridge CB2 8RU, UK

Published in the United States of America by Cambridge University Press, New York

www.cambridge.org
Information on this title: www.cambridge.org/9780521889179

© Gabriel Egan 2010

This publication is in copyright. Subject to statutory exception
and to the provisions of relevant collective licensing agreements,
no reproduction of any part may take place without the written
permission of Cambridge University Press.

First published 2010

Printed in the United Kingdom at the University Press, Cambridge

A catalogue record for this publication is available from the British Library

Library of Congress Cataloguing in Publication data
Egan, Gabriel.
The struggle for Shakespeare's text : twentieth-century editorial theory and practice / Gabriel Egan.
p. cm.
Includes bibliographical references and index.
ISBN 978-0-521-88917-9
1. Shakespeare, William, 1564–1616 – Criticism, Textual.   2. Shakespeare, William, 1564–1616 –
Bibliography.   3. Shakespeare, William, 1564–1616 – Criticism and interpretation – History –
20th century.   4. Drama – Editing – History.   5. Transmission of texts.   I. Title.
PR3071.E38   2010
822.3′3 – dc22   2010029485

ISBN 978-0-521-88917-9 Hardback

Cambridge University Press has no responsibility for the persistence or
accuracy of URLs for external or third-party Internet websites referred to
in this publication, and does not guarantee that any content on such
websites is, or will remain, accurate or appropriate.

Contents

Preface		*page* vii
Acknowledgements		viii
A note on references, quotations, names and pronouns		xi
	Introduction	1
1	The fall of pessimism and the rise of New Bibliography, 1902–1942	12
2	New techniques and the Virginian School: New Bibliography 1939–1968	38
3	New Bibliography 1969–1979	81
	Intermezzo: the rise and fall of the theory of memorial reconstruction	100
4	New Bibliography critiqued and revised, 1980–1990	129
5	The 'new' New Bibliography: the Oxford *Complete Works*, 1978–1989	167
6	Materialism, unediting and version-editing, 1990–1999	190
	Conclusion: the twenty-first century	207
Appendix 1: How early modern books were made: a brief guide		231
Appendix 2: Table of Shakespeare editions up to 1623		237
Appendix 3: Editorial principles of the major twentieth-century Shakespeare editions		240
Works cited		272
Index		309

Preface

The origins of this book lie in the negative response I received to a proposal for an edition of *All's Well that Ends Well* in Michael Best's series *Internet Shakespeare Editions* in the final years of the last millennium. An anonymous peer reviewer's criticisms of my wildly ambitious plan for the edition were grounded in the belief that the entire edifice of what is known as New Bibliographical editorial theory and practice had recently been overturned and that the most I might offer would be to reprint the Folio text of the play purged of its egregious errors. In making sense of this reader's report and its rejection of my proposal I felt the need for a history of the intellectual tradition of the New Bibliography and an account of the growing influence of its detractors since the 1970s. There was no such history in existence and this book fulfils my desire to write one; I hope it also fulfils a need felt by others for such a history. In the early 1940s F. P. Wilson surveyed the New Bibliographical tradition up to that point, but since then there have been only journal articles and book chapters that address particular parts of the tradition, or briefly summarize the whole of it, sometimes to defend but mostly to attack it. In this book I attempt to tell the full story from the beginning of the twentieth century to the date of writing (2010). I engage in the story to the extent of defending certain aspects and certain varieties of New Bibliography as essential to future editorial work, while acknowledging its logical weaknesses and proposing the adoption of certain parts of the critiques that have been made of it. In surveying the attacks on New Bibliography it is striking how seldom its adherents have been proved wrong on the hard facts of a case, and I have taken care to give those rare proofs the fullest possible credence. As will become clear, the main differences of opinion arise from the differing philosophical traditions that underpin the various commentators' approaches to simple questions of human agency.

Acknowledgements

Parts of the conclusion to this book first appeared in reviews of recent scholarship (1999–2008) in *The Year's Work in English Studies* and I am grateful to Lisa Hopkins, Matt Steggle, William Baker and Kenneth Womack for their editorial work on those reviews and to the publisher Oxford University Press for permission to reuse them. Other parts of the conclusion appeared in the article 'Intention in the Editing of Shakespeare' published in an issue of the journal *Style* and I would like to thank its editor Cary DiPietro for permission to reuse the material and for a penetrating critique that improved it. Parts of Appendix 3 were first presented orally at the 2007 meeting of the Society for History of Authorship, Reading and Publishing, in Minneapolis, and I am grateful for the appropriately sharp questions and comments made by members of the audience on that occasion.

For answering specific questions about their work and discussing mine, I thank T. H. Howard-Hill, Andrew Murphy, Richard Dutton, Reg Foakes, Jerome J. McGann, Andrew Gurr, Paul Werstine, MacDonald P. Jackson, Randall McLeod, Gary Taylor, H. R. Woudhuysen, Richard Proudfoot, John Jowett and Stanley Wells. Andrew Murphy also gave excellent advice on the structure and format of this book. For supporting grant applications made in connection with the research in this book I am grateful to Ian Gadd, Suzanne Gossett, Thomas L. Berger, Stanley Wells and John Jowett. Reg Foakes and John Jowett read and critiqued parts of the typescript and generously shared their thoughts on the entire project. Three anonymous readers at Cambridge University Press gave invaluable comments and suggestions regarding the structure and focus of the argument. The idea for the book first took shape over tea with Sarah Stanton in October 2001 and since then she has sustained it with dozens of emails, a series of meetings, and numerous suggestions for improvement. The fruits of all her contributions are gratefully absorbed into the present work. Damian Love's meticulous scholarly copy-editing of this book many times saved the author from embarrassing slips and improved the sense.

Acknowledgements

The Folger Shakespeare Library in Washington DC and the Huntington Library in San Marino California awarded one-month fellowships that enabled me to consult their collections while completing the typescript, and I am grateful to their grants committees. At the Huntington the early book specialists Holly Moore and Stephen Tabor were particularly generous with their time and expertise regarding such matters as the washing of books; I was not even aware such things were possible. The professionalism and expertise of the librarians at the Folger equalled that of their opposite numbers in California, and I am especially grateful to Betsy Walsh for setting up and demonstrating to me the operation of the Folger's Hinman Collating Machine.

When work on this book began in the first years of the twenty-first century, the only place it could be done was a specialist research library. The library of the Shakespeare Institute in Stratford-upon-Avon gave the ideal environment and I am grateful to librarians James Shaw, Kate Welch and Karin Brown for hundreds of responses beyond the call of duty. By the time the book was being completed in 2010, computer technology had transformed early modern literary research. The providers of the following resources enabled the work to proceed anywhere with an Internet connection. JSTOR (an archive of journal article back issues) was the brilliant idea of William B. Bowen of the Andrew W. Mellon Foundation and was piloted by the University of Michigan. Project Muse (distributing recent and new issues of journals electronically) started at Johns Hopkins University with support from the Mellon Foundation and the National Endowment for the Humanities. The Internet Archive provides full-text access to hundreds of thousands of out-of-print books. The Database of Early English Playbooks (DEEP), hosted by the University of Pennsylvania, was created by Alan B. Farmer and Zachary Lesser and combines essential performance and publication data for plays up to the Restoration, making redundant a number of expensive reference books and greatly enhancing researchers' modes of access to the information. The commercial database of page images, Early English Books Online (EEBO), is provided by the company ProQuest but its full-text searchable supplement the Text Creation Partnership is a project of the University of Michigan led by Shawn Martin. A commercial database called the Oxford University Press Journals Digital Archive was essential for early issues of the journal *The Library*.

With the exception of the Internet Archive and DEEP (which are free to all) these resources were provided to me, a state employee, via deals struck by the Joint Information Systems Committee (JISC), the United Kingdom government's provider of information technology to institutions of higher education. I would like to thank JISC Collections for having the foresight to strike such deals and for making the substantial investments required to sustain them. Without these resources this book would have been much delayed, if completed at all.

*A note on references, quotations,
names and pronouns*

References are given by parenthetical author and date, followed by page, signature or leaf numbers where relevant, keyed to the single list of Works cited; multiple references within one pair of parentheses are separated by a semicolon. The author's name is dropped from the reference if it is obvious from the context. Because many readers now have access to them via Early English Books Online (EEBO), sixteenth- and seventeenth-century editions are referenced by signature rather than the Through Line Numbering of modern reprints (such as Shakespeare 1968b and the Shakespeare Quarto Facsimiles series), which are rather less widely available. Compared to Through Line Numbering, use of signatures enables many more readers to follow up a reference at the cost of only a small loss of precision. Where the source is a manuscript a modern transcription or facsimile is cited and, for the convenience of readers consulting the originals or different editions, referenced by leaf number and side (a or b). On first mention (discoverable from the index), the current location and call mark of each manuscript is given parenthetically. Quotations of Shakespeare where no edition is identified are from the electronic version of the Oxford *Complete Works* edited by Stanley Wells, Gary Taylor, John Jowett and William Montgomery, as are the word-counts mentioned in the conclusion and the dates of composition accepted throughout (Shakespeare 1989b). Where emphasis appears in quotations, it is in all cases not mine but copied from the source.

The terms used to categorize early modern manuscripts and books are themselves the topic of considerable disagreement, and three particular choices must be explained. Although the word *prompt-book* (or *prompt-copy*) was used by the New Bibliographers with rather too strong an expectation of regularity and uniformity (perhaps by influence from nineteenth-century theatrical practice) it remains a useful label for manuscripts that are directly concerned with making things happen on time during the performance (Jowett 2007, 35) and I retain it for that reason. The adjective in the expression *bad quartos* is commonly placed in scare quotes (shorthand for the phrase *so-called*), indicating reluctance to condemn them as bad. Just which early editions belong in this category is debatable, but because there are editions with distinctly garbled versions of lines better presented in other editions the adjective need not be applied tentatively: these are bad editions by comparison with the others, and the scare quotes are not used here. Historians of print culture have not settled on a single term for the places of work where books were made. Some call them printing offices, others printing houses, and others printshops. The first of these is misleadingly suggestive of sedentary labour using desks and ledgers and the second might imply large commercial empires ('House of ...' in modern business) so the third term, printshops, is adopted here. By analogy with bodyshops and workshops, the term printshops helpfully captures the sense of practical and dirty physical labour expended to make early modern books.

When referred to abstractly or as performances (rather than as documents) the titles of Shakespeare's plays are drawn from the Oxford *Complete Works*, so what are elsewhere commonly known as *2 Henry 6*, *3 Henry 6* and *Henry 8* are here called *The Contention of York and Lancaster*, *Richard Duke of York* and *All is True*, and whereas *King Lear* is often still treated as one play it is here treated as two, *The History of King Lear* and *The Tragedy of King Lear*. Where there is disagreement about how to number the early editions of a book (do the quartos of *1 Henry 4* start with Q0 or Q1?) I have followed the numbering of the Oxford *Complete Works*'s *Textual Companion* (Wells *et al.* 1987) even where the research being described did not. The English language is notably deficient in gender-neutral pronouns and, since many years of conventional usage have established that one of the genders may stand for both, I have elected to use feminine pronouns when referring abstractly to the reader, writer or editor of a book. However, early modern printshop workers (but not stationers) and theatre personnel (with the exception of gatherers taking money from spectators) were exclusively men and this historical fact is acknowledged by use of masculine pronouns for them.

Introduction

At the height of the trial in the cinematic court room drama *The Verdict*, a nurse acting as witness for the plaintiff offers as evidence a photocopy of a hospital admission form showing that the victim of the alleged medical malpractice was known to have eaten just one hour earlier and so should not have been anaesthetized (Lumet 1982). Yet she was anaesthetized, which made her vomit into her face mask, causing brain damage from lack of oxygen. The original admission form shown to the court recorded that the victim ate nine hours earlier (and so could be anaesthetized), but the nurse claimed that she photocopied the form before the anaesthetist (realizing his error) forced her to change the numeral 1 to a 9. On an established legal preference for original documents over photocopies, the jury is instructed to forget it ever heard about the nurse and her photocopy. Happily, the jury ignores this instruction and awards damages against the hospital.

The principle that one should ordinarily prefer an original of something over its copy is central to much of our thinking about textual authenticity, although of course there are circumstances under which it should be set aside, as when one suspects that the original was altered after the copy was taken. If the original was altered, one has to ask why and make a judgement based on one's best attempt at an answer. Originals should normally be preferred to copies because copying introduces errors, some random and some predictable. We may leave aside for the moment the new technologies that allow digital copying with perfect bit-for-bit fidelity, since these at the very least blur our convenient distinction between original and copy and perhaps even undermine our notions of what constitutes property.

The means by which early modern books were reprinted made errors of transmission inevitable. For many early modern books, the second edition was a reprint of the first and the third a reprint of the second, so that errors accumulated rather as they do in the children's game that Britons call Chinese Whispers and Americans call Telephone. When the first collected edition of the plays of Shakespeare, the First Folio (F or F1) of 1623, was reprinted in 1632 (F2), 1663–4 (F3) and 1685 (F4), each edition was based on its immediate predecessor, and error was piled upon error. These reprints' publishers and printers attempted to restore sense where they could, as indeed players in a circle of Chinese Whispers do: almost unconsciously players turn the whispered sounds into words that cohere to make at least grammatical sense. But just as in the children's game, without access to the original words these attempts at improvement are overwhelmed by the corruption. The fun arises when the resulting words are grammatically plausible but wildly and comically inaccurate.

That such degeneration-by-repetition is also true of the later Folios of Shakespeare was observed by Samuel Johnson in the middle of the eighteenth century and he decried his fellow editors' complacency in basing their editions on later Folios rather than returning to the First, the ultimate source (Shakespeare 1765, l). And yet, describing this seemingly sensible complaint from Johnson, one of today's leading theorists of textual transmission sees a darker motive at work:

Because the twentieth century's dominant textual theory raises up the ideal of recovering in an edition the full authorial presence that is now believed to lie just behind some of the earliest printed texts, the eighteenth-century preference for an edition that has benefited from cumulative editorial attentions (each removing us further from the earliest printings) has been slighted by our century's textual theorists (e.g., Wells, Taylor, *et al.* 55). (Werstine 1995, 257).

Werstine implies that it is not awareness of the Chinese Whispers problem that motivates modern editorial preference for the First Folio over its reprints, but rather the delusion that the best early editions bring one fully into the presence of the author. Werstine rightly points out that Johnson did not scrupulously abide by his own counsel of perfection (he used reprints like everyone else) but in revealing this failing Werstine seems to abandon the central principle that Johnson was sketching. Werstine accuses Stanley Wells and Gary Taylor of following Johnson's precept for the wrong reason: not because it minimizes error but because it helps us commune with the dead.

THE PURPOSE OF THIS BOOK

The story of how modern textual theorists have come to hold such divergent views about the same raw materials and processes is one of the central narratives of this book. It aims to trace the debates about Shakespeare's texts as they have developed in the past century or so since the emergence of what is known as the New Bibliography. It presents a history of a set of ideas, but not impartially, for it argues that authors are the most dominant agents in the constellation of forces (personal, cultural, political and institutional) that come together in the publication of books. This does not mean that the author is sovereign, autonomous, or splendidly isolated, those being notions of authorship that modern literary theory tells us were invented by the Romantics. (Of course the theory might be wrong and the Romantics rather more subtle about authorship than they are usually given credit for; see Pechter 2001.) When it worked properly, publication in Shakespeare's time, just as publication now, invoked a hierarchy of agencies with the author at the top, supported by the labour of copyists and printshop workers. Readers unfamiliar with recent debates about the nature of authorship may be surprised to learn that this assertion is contentious and that making it opens one to a charge of conservatism, even elitism.

This book aims to help push the pendulum back from a currently fashionable dispersal of agency and insist upon authors as the main determinants of what we read. The 'struggle' of the book's title has two senses. The first alludes to the Herculean tasks of scholarship undertaken by bibliographers to extract knowledge from the surviving early editions of Shakespeare, as when Charlton Hinman compared each of the 900 pages in one exemplar of the 1623 Folio with the same page in each of fifty-four other exemplars, looking for the small differences that arose during the printing. By revealing the details of the printing process, Hinman hoped to offer editors better means for determining how it misrepresented what Shakespeare wrote, so they could undo the harm.

A second sense of 'struggle' in this book's title alludes to the arguments between scholars about how far we can hope to undo the harms of reproduction in order to recover what Shakespeare wrote. One branch of modern textual theory, identified in this book as New Textualism, accuses another, older branch, the New Bibliography, of over-optimism about seeing beyond the early editions to the manuscripts from which they were made. The hope that we might get an editorially recovered glimpse of those manuscripts (what Werstine means by 'the full authorial presence') is, according to many recent studies, delusional. According to Randall McLeod, the argument between scholars of editorial theory about how to recover what Shakespeare wrote is itself a constructive act, for it makes the very object that it would pursue. McLeod expressed this as 'The struggle for tne text *is* the text' (McLeod 1991, 279). (The *n* in *tne* was an intentional error made as part of a larger, witty argument about the ineluctability of error.) This book argues that McLeod is mistaken and that editors may reasonably pursue the objectively existing (now lost) readings of Shakespeare's manuscripts: they are not simply inventing readings from their imaginations and their struggle is worthwhile not for itself but for the recovered texts. McLeod generously agreed to the appropriation of his phrase in this book's title, knowing that its argument would oppose his.

A currently popular view is that the early editions were so collectively (rather than individually) constructed and so imperfectly printed that the connection with Shakespeare's authorial intentions is all but lost. If this is the case, we must treat the early editions as social phenomena rather than the products of a single consciousness. In terms of the children's game of Chinese Whispers, this is akin to observing that the sentence emerging at the end of the circle is the collective product of all the whisperers and that, once the game has broken up, asking each participant what she heard will produce as many answers as there were players. To continue with the analogy, a textual optimist would be someone who, undiscouraged by the collective and corruptive process of transmission, attempted to work out the order in which the whisperers sat and so differentiate the more corrupted sentences from the less. Such an optimist would give most credence to the evidence of the first whisperer without necessarily falling into an idealist delusion of perfection; she would be expressing a relative preference for better over worse reproductions.

The subtitle of this book refers to the theory and practice of editing Shakespeare, but the book contains considerably more of the former than of the latter. This is because there simply is more theory than theoretically derived practice to describe, and because a comprehensive history of the facts of Shakespeare publication in the twentieth century already exists (Murphy 2003, 208–60). What remains to be described are the theoretical ideas embodied in the most progressive editions. Although certain editions are discussed in passing as the theories develop, a full account of the relationship of theory to practice is relegated to Appendix 3, with cross-references indicating where in the main text the associated theoretical ideas appear. The reader will find that the editions impinge more noticeably upon the main theoretical narrative towards the end of the story. This happens because for most of the century the theory was so far ahead of the practice as to be virtually out of sight. There was no edition of all of Shakespeare overtly executed according to New Bibliographical principles until John Dover Wilson's New Shakespeare series for Cambridge University Press was completed in 1966, and this edition was far from the New Bibliographical mainstream. Earlier complete works editions were in part shaped by New Bibliography, but none explained its editorial principles to the reader.

Particular volumes in the mid-century Arden Shakespeare series showed the influence of New Bibliography, but only Wilson made a sustained effort to re-examine the entire textual situation for the whole canon from the new perspectives. However, theory and practice started to become contemporaneous in the 1980s, when there appeared several new editions formed along highly divergent lines.

The term bibliography derives from the self-reflexive practice of writing about books, although it is most commonly used to mean simply a list of books. The larger, but effectively the more specialist, sense of bibliography discussed in this book has two main varieties. Enumerative bibliography is concerned with establishing lists of books, such as all the works of one writer (perhaps published under various names), or of one centre of writing (say, the mediaeval abbey at Barking), or written about one subject. Analytical bibliography, on the other hand, is concerned with studying and describing books and their linguistic content, and divides into descriptive or physical bibliography (concerned with the book as a made object, including such things as its binding, its paper and the way sheets are folded), historical bibliography (concerned with the contexts for book publishing, such as the operations of various institutions that support it), and textual bibliography, also known as textual criticism, concerned with establishing the correct words of a writer by removing the errors of transmission. The bibliography with which this book is concerned is analytical bibliography in all its forms: descriptive/physical, historical and textual. Clearly, textual bibliography – establishing the words of Shakespeare – is the main concern, but as will become apparent the boundaries between the fields are permeable. Much of the early twentieth-century excitement about recovering Shakespeare's writings arose because the New Bibliographers championed multidisciplinary and interdisciplinary skills that crossed or erased these boundaries in the effort to remove errors of transmission.

EDITING SHAKESPEARE UP TO THE END OF THE NINETEENTH CENTURY

To help make sense of the developments in editorial theory and practice in the twentieth century, the following sketch of the preceding history is offered. In the seventeenth century Shakespeare was not edited in the sense that we mean today. As we shall see, certain editions of Shakespeare (most especially the 1623 Folio) were prepared with considerable care to combine manuscripts and existing print editions, but the textual principles that characterize modern editing had not been developed. (For an argument dissenting from this view, based on the objection that many editor-like interventions were made in seventeenth-century reprintings, see Massai 2007.) As well as the four Folio collections (F1 to F4, each of the last three based on its predecessor), individual plays were printed in the smaller quarto format, typically one-per-volume, and for a given play the successive quartos (whether or not reprinting a predecessor) are abbreviated to Q1, Q2, Q3 and so on. Appendix 2 lists the editions of Shakespeare up to 1623 and who made them. The first collected works of Shakespeare that was edited in anything like the modern fashion was Nicholas Rowe's six-volume edition of 1709. Margreta de Grazia's account of the developments in editorial theory and practice in the eighteenth century, and especially of Edmond Malone's groundbreaking edition of 1790, is highly polemical and brilliantly argued (de Grazia 1991), while the developments in the nineteenth century are handled by Murphy rather more drily and without contentious philosophical assumptions (Murphy 2003, 188–207).

The intellectual development of eighteenth- and nineteenth-century editions can be characterized as an increasing regard for historical context and a willingness to undertake systematic comparison of the early editions to ascertain their relative authority. For the starkest contrast in these matters we may take an early and a late example: Alexander Pope's edition of 1723–5 and the Cambridge–Macmillan edition of 1863–6. In preparation for his editorial work, Pope published a newspaper note asking anyone who had editions of *The Tempest*, *Macbeth*, *Julius Caesar*, *Timon of Athens*, *King John* and *All is True* printed before 1620 to bring them to his publisher's office. As Murphy observed, 'Tonson and Pope might have waited until doomsday for the requested texts to be delivered to them, since all of these plays had … appeared in print for the first time in the 1623 folio' (Murphy 2003, 64). Convinced that large portions of the early editions were not written by Shakespeare, Pope either cut them entirely or relegated them to the bottom of the page. According to Murphy, the greatest contribution made by Pope's edition was that in reaction to it other editors were determined to tackle the problems more systematically and to seek objective knowledge about print transmission before relying on subjective judgements about dramatic quality (Murphy 2003, 8).

One hundred and forty years later, the Cambridge–Macmillan edition was the first produced by university-employed scholars using an openly expressed bibliographical methodology arrived at after examining afresh the entire textual situation of Shakespeare (Murphy 2003, 202–6). Its editors, W. G. Clark, John Glover and W. Aldis Wright, compared each early printing with the others (a process called collating) in order to establish textual priority (which editions were reprints of which) and used this knowledge to help decide what to put in their edition where the early editions differed. Thus although their edition of *Hamlet* was mainly based on Q2 of 1604–5, the one they thought had the highest authority in general, they used the Folio text for the line 'O, that this too too solid flesh would melt' (1.2.129). In their collation notes at the foot of the page the Cambridge–Macmillan editors wrote '129. *solid*] Ff. *sallied* (Q1) Qq. *sullied* Anon. conj' (Shakespeare 1866, 16), meaning that in line 129 their reading *solid* came from the Folios, that the quartos all read *sallied* (although Q1 differs significantly elsewhere on the same line), and that the reading *sullied* has been conjectured by persons unknown. This kind of attention to detail was new in the editing of Shakespeare, and the Cambridge–Macmillan editors were explicit about their application of processes that were established and refined for the editing of classical texts in Latin and Greek (Murphy 2003, 203).

The techniques used by the Cambridge–Macmillan editors were first formalized by the German philologist Karl Lachmann (1793–1851) for his edition of the Greek New Testament. Lachmann refined the genealogical process known as recension, in which the comparison of the surviving documents (all textual witnesses to the lost original, the author's manuscript) leads to a pictorial stemma that shows the family-tree relationships between them. The making of stemmata remains common in Shakespearian textual criticism even though it was developed not for printings that followed shortly after composition (as with Shakespeare) but for manuscripts made long after composition. Shakespearian stemmata are complicated in certain cases by the printers' copy being an existing book that was annotated by comparison with an authoritative manuscript before being reprinted, which annotation injected new authority into the genetic line of an otherwise derivative reprint; several of the debates with which we are concerned here arise from this complication. The process of recension allows the editor to determine which of the surviving witnesses is the most authoritative and should be the basis for a modern edition, for which R. B. McKerrow coined the convenient term copy-text (Nashe 1904, xi). Thereafter comes emendation, the correcting of errors in this witness.

The Lachmannian approach stressed recension over emendation and encouraged editors to try to make sense of their copy-text rather than depart from it, and if departing from it was unavoidable then the next-best witness in the family tree should be consulted for its reading. This was essentially the process followed by the Cambridge–Macmillan edition, as they explained:

The basis of all texts of Shakespeare must be that of the earliest Edition of the collected plays, the Folio of 1623 ... This we have mainly adopted, unless there exists an earlier edition in quarto, as is the case in more than one half of the thirty-six plays. When the first Folio is corrupt, we have allowed some authority to the emendations of F2 above subsequent conjecture, and secondarily to F3 and F4; but a reference to our notes will show that the authority even of F2 in correcting is very small. Where we have Quartos of authority, their variations from F1 have been generally accepted, except where they are manifest errors, and where the text of the entire passage seems to be of an inferior recension to that of the Folio. (Shakespeare 1863, xi)

The Cambridge–Macmillan edition was widely received as the culmination of all possible efforts to recover Shakespeare's true words, and it spawned a single-volume edition, the Globe Shakespeare, that sold nearly a quarter of a million copies and became the standard edition for the purposes of referencing for almost 100 years (Murphy 2003, 175–7). A sense of just how successfully the Cambridge–Macmillan editors conveyed the impression that there was nothing left to be done can be had from Horace Howard Furness's comment in his edition of *Love's Labour's Lost*:

Ever since the appearance, forty years ago, of *The Cambridge Edition* of SHAKE-SPEARE, followed by its offspring, *The Globe Edition*, this whole question of Texts, with their varying degrees of excellence, which had endlessly vexed the Shakespearian world, has gradually subsided, until now it is fairly lulled to a sleep as grateful as it is deep. (Shakespeare 1904b, vi–vii)

SCOPE AND PLAN OF THIS BOOK

This book is concerned only with Shakespeare's plays and leaves aside his poetry, this being principally his early narrative poems *Venus and Adonis* and *The Rape of Lucrece* and his *Sonnets*. The founders of New Bibliography also worked on other early modern dramatists – R. B. McKerrow edited Thomas Nashe, W. W. Greg edited Christopher Marlowe, Fredson Bowers edited Francis Beaumont and John Fletcher – and its principles were later applied to eighteenth- and nineteenth-century novels and poetry. However, in order to tell a coherent story of how the editing of Shakespeare has been theorized and practised, these additional contexts can only be mentioned in passing; New Bibliography has a larger history than can be told in this book's account of its origins and development. The entire subject of editorial theory and practice is now commonly placed within the even broader context of *l'histoire du livre* (the history of the book), which emerged as a distinct academic discipline in the middle of the twentieth century and was given its initial shape by the French historians Lucien Febvre and his protégé Henri-Jean Martin. Except where it impinges directly on Shakespeare – as it does tangentially when bibliographers discuss whether they should privilege certain authors or treat all books alike (pp. 84–6 below) – these broader contexts could not be incorporated into this book's narrative without doubling its length.

Confining our attention just to Shakespeare, his poetry is excluded because it was, for good reason, subject to an almost entirely distinct set of editorial principles in the twentieth century. The major advances in Shakespearian editorial theory emerged from knowledge of the practices of the early modern theatre, and in particular the ways that scripts for performance would be copied, divided, licensed, reworked and printed. These processes simply did not apply to the poems, which were written not for public performance but private consumption and although they probably circulated extensively in manuscript copies nonetheless went into print more or less directly from authorial papers. As we shall see towards the end of this book (pp. 215–22), the assumption that plays were written for public performance rather than private reading has been challenged, but the distinction from poems still holds since the most that can be said is that plays were intended for both kinds of consumption while poems were without doubt essentially a private pleasure. Regarding the plays, the claim (first made by the New Bibliographers at the end of the Great War) that they too were printed directly from Shakespeare's papers was controversial and requires extensive consideration.

The main concern of the narrative offered here is the development of a series of arguments about how best to present the plays of Shakespeare to modern readers. To make sense of the arguments requires knowledge of how early modern books were made, and readers without this (or wanting a refresher) will find that Appendix 1 covers the essential technical details. The story begins with a group of scholars who decided in the 1890s that the Cambridge–Macmillan editors had not achieved the best texts possible, and who invented an entirely new set of methodologies for making better ones. This book will consider the debates from the inside, as it were: how they seemed to the people who were making the arguments at the time. With hindsight it is possible to contextualize such debates by considering what else was happening in society, and a certain kind of historiography would read arguments about Shakespeare editions as symptomatic of other, wider conflicts. In such readings, Shakespearians may not even be aware that they are really arguing about human sexuality, or class, or the effects of technological empowerment (Masten 1997b; Loewenstein 1998;

DiPietro 2006). Such studies are valuable, but this book pays its subjects the compliment of taking them at their word and it deals with their overt differences of opinion without trying to discern their unconscious motives. This is how most of us wish our own arguments to be taken: literally, not figuratively, nor interpreted psychologically. The book's self-denying ordinance cuts both ways, and there is no attempt to explain in political terms the reaction against New Bibliography in the 1980s, even though some of its critics were effectively pursuing a well-established left-leaning literary criticism by other means. Rather than seeking to explain the textual debates by reference to the debaters' politics, the political underpinnings enter the narrative only when they are explicitly part of the arguments being made, as when various kinds of materialism must be distinguished.

Certain people feature rather less prominently in this narrative than they might have, as a result of the economies of selection. There is a case to be made for a feminist revaluation of the work of Alice Walker, and especially her book *Textual Problems of the First Folio* (1953) that is not much represented here. The materials for a revaluation exist in the archive of Walker's papers at Royal Holloway, University of London, but in truth she did not have much impact on the actual developments of the New Bibliography and after. Certainly, she had no more effect than John Dover Wilson who likewise is essentially tangential to this narrative except in his collaborations with A. W. Pollard and in his New Shakespeare series for Cambridge University Press. This book will for the most part take as read the facts of Shakespeare's co-authorship with other dramatists of certain plays and will not chart the development of the dawning realizations about this in the second half of the twentieth century, after initial progress was retarded by E. K. Chambers's ill-judged attack upon investigation of the subject (Chambers 1924–5). The facts of the matter are well summarized by Brian Vickers (2002), although their impact on editorial practice is as yet limited, as will be discussed in this book's conclusion.

In order to capture the debates as they developed, the structure of the present narrative is essentially a chronological survey of publications about Shakespearian bibliography with minor unchronological departures as necessary. In a few cases, the significance of a particular work was not registered when it first appeared, only to be discovered years later and built upon, and these works appear in the narrative at their delayed moment of impact. To assist the reader there are forward and backward cross-references in the narrative, so she may remind herself of where a previously discussed subject or argument first made its appearance, or skip forward to the point at which it came to fruition or destruction. The aim is not to account for every study of the textual situation of every play of Shakespeare: readers wanting such a comprehensive survey will find one in the Oxford *Complete Works* edition's *Textual Companion* (Wells et al. 1987), which may be supplemented (for works appearing since then) by the 'Shakespeare Editions and Textual Studies' sections of the annual books *Shakespeare Survey* and *The Year's Work in English Studies*. Rather, this book aims to trace closely the developments in the lines of thinking, with special attention to new breakthroughs, consolidations of positions, corroborations, disruptions and reversals. As a resting point in a long story, an Intermezzo is provided that breaks the chronological sequence to tell the full story of one strand of the New Bibliography, the theory that memorial reconstruction of their scripts by actors was the origin of certain early editions. Although it impinges upon it at key moments, and was used to buttress its claims, memorial reconstruction is not integral to the New Bibliography and its eighty-year rise and fall is best traced without disruption to the main narrative.

In 1903 A. E. Housman, editing the *Astronomica* of first-century CE Roman poet and astrologer Marcus Manilius, made a withering attack on the Lachmannian approach of finding the best documentary witness and departing from its readings only where they seemed certainly in error. This method, Housman objected, relied on the implicit assumption that the 'readings of a [witness] are right whenever they are possible and impossible whenever they are wrong' (Manilius 1903, xxxii). Since this assumption was obviously faulty, Housman advocated using judgement as well as rules, and in his inspired emendations he sought to enter the mind of his fellow poet. The early New Bibliographers began from a Lachmannian position and as their methods improved and were refined they increasingly abandoned it. A central matter of dispute lurking behind all the debates that are about to be entered is the simple question of how far editors should not only combine but also depart from the surviving textual witnesses (the various quartos and Folio) in seeking to recover for modern readers the words coming from Shakespeare's mind that his contemporaries heard and read.

CHAPTER I

The fall of pessimism and the rise of New Bibliography, 1902–1942

The history of New Bibliography's rise that occupies this chapter and the next is framed by the publication of two facsimile editions of the 1623 Shakespeare Folio. One is Sidney Lee's collotype reproduction of the Chatsworth copy (owned by the Duke of Devonshire) for Oxford University Press in 1902 and the other is Charlton Hinman's idealized line-offset reproduction for W. W. Norton in 1968. Both facsimiles were widely praised for their fidelity, but they were executed along entirely different lines that usefully illustrate the fundamental change regarding our relationship to the Shakespeare texts that occurred in the twentieth century. In 1903 A. W. Pollard became J. Y. W. Macalister's assistant as editor of the journal *The Library* and published W. W. Greg's extended criticism of Lee's introductory matter that pointed out numerous errors of fact and introduced two elements of what came to be called the New Bibliography: a theory about the copyright notions of the period and an attempt to distinguish the kinds of manuscript used to make the Folio (Greg 1903a). Matters of detail Greg later changed his mind about – for example that printed texts were used as prompt-books and that there was no such occupation as playhouse scrivener (Greg 1903a, 275, 277) – but the core of what later became Greg's contribution to the field can be discerned in this article.

A. W. POLLARD, *SHAKESPEARE FOLIOS AND QUARTOS* (1909) AND *SHAKESPEARE'S FIGHT WITH THE PIRATES* (1917)

W. W. Greg's work remained merely an objection to the weakness of Sidney Lee's model of how the Folio came about rather than a new model in its own right until in 1909 A. W. Pollard provided the final element that allowed a shift from pessimism to optimism regarding our capacity to discriminate among the surviving early editions of Shakespeare. The pessimism that descended in the eighteenth century held that we cannot hope fully to recover what Shakespeare wrote because all that remain are editions that are related in ways that make it impossible to tell which has greatest authority, or, specifically, which are closest to Shakespeare's own hand. Nineteenth-century recension (especially for the Cambridge–Macmillan edition) opened up the possibility of discriminating between the surviving early editions, but since none was thought to be close to Shakespeare's own manuscripts the outlook remained gloomy.

Pollard was aware that the preliminaries to the Folio contain a problematic claim by Shakespeare's fellow actors, Henry Condell and John Heminges, who seem to have been involved in putting the collection together:

as where (before) you were abus'd with diuerse stolne, and surreptitious copies, maimed, and deformed by the frauds and stealthes of iniurious impostors, that expos'd them: euen those, are now offer'd to your view cur'd, and perfect of their limbes, and all the rest, absolute in their numbers, as he conceiued them. (Shakespeare 1623, $^{\pi}$A3^{r})

This seems to condemn all the existing quartos as bad texts that do not reflect Shakespeare's plays as he wrote them. Yet it had been clear to Shakespeare scholars for some time (and was confirmed by the Cambridge–Macmillan collation) that a number of the plays in the Folio were in fact printed from the existing quartos, because 'Undoubted errors in the quartos are repeated in the Folio in a way which defies explanation save that a copy of the quarto (usually of the latest edition) was handed to the compositors of the Folio to work from' (Pollard 1909, 1). So the Folio, which claimed to be correcting the egregious errors of previous publications, was in fact in parts a direct reprint of those previous publications. If, as Heminges and Condell seemed to claim, the existing printings were not to be trusted then their book based on those printings was also unreliable. With neither the quartos nor the Folio to trust, the possibility of a reliable Shakespeare text disappears. This was the pessimistic conclusion reached by Lee in 1902 and to which, a century later, many textual scholars have returned. What Pollard had to overturn was the conviction that the quartos were uniformly bad, as expressed in Lee's certainty that the greater number of them were 'printed from more or less imperfect and unauthorized playhouse transcripts' obtained 'more or less dishonestly' (Shakespeare 1902a, xii).

There were two key elements to Lee's model of what happened to dramatic manuscripts and he mentioned them in relation to the procuring of copy for the 1623 Folio, a process probably made more difficult in Lee's opinion because the Globe playhouse fire of 1613 destroyed part of the

King's men's collection of manuscript playbooks. Firstly, Lee considered the author's papers:

> No genuine respect was paid to a dramatic author's original drafts after they reached the playhouse. Scenes and passages were freely erased by the managers, who became the owners, and other alterations were made for stage purposes. Ultimately the dramatist's corrected autograph was copied by the playhouse scriveners; this transcript became the official 'prompt-copy,' and the original was set aside and destroyed, its uses being exhausted. (Shakespeare 1902a, xviii)

Thus no print edition could, in Lee's view, be based directly on an author's papers, for these did not survive the theatrical processes for which they were created. A second element of Lee's model was proliferation of plays by scribal copy:

> Fortunately it was the habit of actors occasionally to secure a more or less perfect transcript of a successful piece either for themselves or for a sympathetic friend. Though some private owners easily mislaid dramatic MSS., others carefully preserved them, and it was clearly through the good offices of private owners that the publishers of the First Folio were able to supplement the defects of the playhouse archives. By such means transcripts, occasionally even 'prompt-copies,' of plays that had passed out of the actors' repertory reached the printers' hands. Private transcripts were, as a rule, characterized to a greater degree than official transcripts by copyists' carelessness and by general imperfections: they rarely embodied the latest theatrical revisions; they omitted stage directions. But in 1623 they filled, as far as Shakespeare's work was concerned, an important gap in the playhouse resources. (Shakespeare 1902a, xix)

It later became essential to one strand of New Bibliography to deny that private transcripts proliferated. In Lee's view, all the quartos were essentially debased texts and the Folio was printed from three kinds of copy: playhouse prompt-copy (transcripts of the destroyed authorial papers), inferior transcripts in private hands, and the existing quartos. The cause for pessimism is clear: none of these is close to the authorial papers that might be deemed an originating and uncontaminated source for what Shakespeare actually wrote. There is a notable irony here: the more copies of Shakespeare in circulation in his own time, the greater the chances of later generations having a text to read but the less likely that it will be something we might think of as the text as its author intended it, free of corruption.

Pollard changed the prevailing climate of bibliographical pessimism to optimism at a stroke by reinterpreting Heminges and Condell's claim about 'diuers stolne, and surreptitious copies'. This did not mean all the existing quartos, as Lee reasoned, but just some of them, which were far inferior to the rest (Pollard 1909, 4). This inferior group of bad quartos was the first editions of *Romeo and Juliet* (1597), *Henry 5* (1600), *The Merry Wives of Windsor* (1602), *Hamlet* (1603) and *Pericles* (1609). None of these was used as printer's copy for the Folio and it was these alone that Heminges and Condell meant by 'stolne, and surreptitious' texts with which the reading public had previously been abused. The good quartos, by contrast, were the remaining original editions and their various reprints, many of which were used as copy for the Folio, including some, such as Q2 *Hamlet*, that were reissues of plays already existing in bad quarto form. The bad quartos, Pollard decided, were pirated editions, printed by unscrupulous publishers from scripts made by surreptitious means such as stenography, the writing down of a play's words by a spectator watching the performance. This practice was reported in the prologue to Thomas Heywood's *Play of Queen Elizabeth*, also known as *If You Know Not Me You Know Nobody*: 'some by Stenography drew | The plot: put it in print: (scarce one word trew:)' (Heywood 1637, R4^v; 1639, A2^r). In order that the explanation of piracy be limited to just the bad quartos, Pollard was obliged to argue that generally there was not as much dramatic piracy as had traditionally been claimed (Pollard 1909, 9–10).

Pollard went on to weigh the preponderant force as dramatists and pirates struggled. Having distinguished the bad from the good quartos in 1909, he produced a theory of how their underlying manuscripts were created, and after reading it as a series of lectures and publishing it as a series of articles in *The Library* (Pollard 1916a; 1916b; 1916c; 1916d) Pollard brought his ideas together as a book (1917). Stenographers attending the theatre and making shorthand notes could not have got away with it for long, Pollard reasoned, and once the practice was stopped the most likely vector of surreptitious copying for print publication was a hired man playing a small part in a play, as Greg had argued for *The Merry Wives of Windsor* (Pollard 1917, 40–1; Shakespeare 1910, xxiii–xli). The hired men, with no long-term allegiance to a playing company, would know their parts perfectly and it would not take too much effort to memorize the lines of other, larger parts in the play by listening to their fellows on the stage. In *The Merry Wives of Windsor*, Q1 (1602) scenes containing the Host are much closer to the Folio wording than other scenes, so if the Folio represents the true script it seems that the actor playing the Host memorially reconstructed his lines and the lines of those onstage with him, fairly accurately, as well as the lines spoken while he was offstage, rather inaccurately. The memorial reconstruction hypothesis explains well certain features of certain bad quartos but for other features and other editions it is a poor explanation. The merits and flaws of the memorial reconstruction theory are explored at length in the Intermezzo (pp. 100–28 below). The precise means by which the bad quartos came into being is not as important as Pollard's founding central distinction between good and bad quartos.

For Pollard the illegitimacy of the manuscripts underlying the bad quartos would have put any honest publisher off handling them; only an unscrupulous pirate could put such corrupt and debased texts into print. All publishers, printers and booksellers were members of the Stationers' Company, a guild (or more accurately a livery company) that controlled the making and selling of books in London. The Company kept a Register of manuscripts that members possessed and had the right to publish, and Pollard thought that he could detect irregularities in respect of each of the bad quartos: 'not one of the five plays ... was entered on the Stationers' Register by its publishers' (Pollard 1917, 49). On the other hand, 'all the fourteen good texts were eventually entered on the Register' (Pollard 1917, 50) and hence absence from the Stationers' Register itself is prima facie evidence for the piracy of some of Shakespeare's plays. Unfortunately, Pollard's understanding of the purpose of the Stationers' Register was flawed: entry was not needed to make a printing legitimate as it acted only as a kind of insurance policy against another stationer publishing a work on the same topic (even one based on a different text). This point was soon realized and Pollard corrected (Chambers 1923a, 186–7; F. P. Wilson 1945, 86–7; Kirschbaum 1946, 43–4).

So much for the illegitimate practices; what about the norm? Pollard decided that a dramatist would not necessarily use a scribe to copy his rough drafts into something fair for the playing company, on the evidence of a letter by dramatist Robert Daborne to theatre impresario Philip Henslowe dated 13 November 1613:

Mr Hinchlow y^u accuse me with the breach of promise, trew it is J promysd to bring y^u the last scean which y^t y^u may see finished J send y^u the foule sheet & ye fayr J was wrighting as y^r man can testify which if great busines had not prevented J had this night fynished ... howsoever J will not fayle to write this fayr and p<er>fit the book which shall not ly one y^r hands. (Greg 1907, 78)

Pollard used this letter to establish the possibility of a dramatist being his own copyist, and went on to consider other plays that have survived in manuscripts in the dramatist's handwriting (known as autographs). Pollard commented:

Unfortunately it [Daborne's autograph] has not been preserved, but several plays by other contemporaries of Shakespeare have come down to us in their authors' own handwriting, and when we examine some of these two very important points come to light: (i) that, contrary to what might have been expected, the players were able to obtain the verdict of the Master of the Revels as to whether a play might be publicly acted, or not, by submitting to him the play as written by the author, or authors, sometimes in pretty rough manuscript, and with passages written on slips and pasted in; and (ii) that, again contrary to what might have been expected, plays endorsed with the licence for their public performance might be handed over to the prompter, and by him converted into prompt copies, without the 'playhouse scrivener,' if such a person existed, being given the chance. (Pollard 1917, 58–9)

This is a substantial claim worth summarizing: author's papers, Pollard maintained, even quite rough ones, could be submitted to the state censor, the Master of the Revels, for licensing and thereafter this 'allowed book' could, by further annotation, become the copy used by the prompter to regulate performance. This is the theory of continuous copy, as E. K. Chambers termed it (1924–5, 103), in which a single manuscript begins as authorial papers and ends up as a prompt-book.

Pollard offered as evidence three manuscripts that are in their author's handwriting and have also been to the office of the Master of the Revels: *Sir Thomas More* (British Library Harley 7368), which Greg realized was in Anthony Munday's handwriting once Munday's *John a Kent and John a Cumber* (Huntington Library HM 500) appeared in facsimile (Greg 1913), Philip Massinger's *Believe as You List* (British Library Egerton 2828) and Walter Mountfort's *The Launching of the Mary* (British Library Egerton 1994) (Pollard 1917, 59–60). Pollard also noted Henry Glapthorne's *The Lady Mother* (British Library Egerton 1994), a manuscript play written by a scribe but 'corrected by the author' and bearing the Master of the Revels' licence. The manuscript of *Sir Thomas More* has many hands in it, including that of the Master of the Revels Edmund Tilney at its beginning demanding changes that the dramatists seem not to have carried out, and it is not clear whether it was ever performed. *Believe as You List* has the unconditional licence of a later Master of the Revels, Henry Herbert, written at its end, and *The Launching of the Mary* has a conditional one at its end, also from Herbert, that is worth quoting in full:

This play, called ye Seamans Honest wife, all ye Oaths left out In ye action as they are crost In ye booke & all other Reformations strictly obserud, may bee acted not otherwyse. this .27. Iune. 1633. Henry *Herbert*.

I commande your Bookeeper to present mee wth a faire Copy hereafter or and to leaue out all Oathes, prophaness, & publick Ribaldry, as he will answer it at his perill. HHerbert. (Mountfort 1933, 349b)

The second part of this licence might mean that another, fairer copy of this play, one purged of all its sins, had to be submitted to the censor – that is Greg's interpretation (p. 27 below) – but it is hard to see what force this command could have had since the licence had already been given. More likely, Herbert was demanding that in future he should get fair copy from which the sins had already been purged, which suggests that authorial copy was perhaps borderline acceptable to the Master of the Revels: only neat writers might have their own papers sent for licensing.

So, there are four clear cases of authorial papers, rather than scribal copy, being sent off to get a performance licence; the first apparently in vain (*Sir Thomas More*), the other three with success. The difficulty comes with Pollard's insistence that all three successful manuscripts, *Believe as You List*, *The Launching of the Mary* and *The Lady Mother*, are prompt-books (Pollard 1917, 60), which if true would substantiate his theory of continuous copy. The claim for *Believe as You List* is secure because of its copious notes for readying actors and properties. The evidence for *The Launching of the Mary* is a light layer of annotation in another hand that added the word 'Musicke' in the margin at five places in the play, added 'Trompete' between two scenes for no clear reason, put in two or three speech prefixes (one is dubious) that the dramatist appears to have omitted, and marked some sections for cutting (Mountfort 1933, x–xi). The textual situation of *The Lady Mother* is somewhat more complicated, later summarized by Arthur Brown using the labels S for Scribe, A for Author, C for Censor and superscripted numbers for these men's subsequent layers of revision. The sequence of events was this:

(i) play copied out by S from A's foul papers, (ii) corrections and a few additions by A (A^1); (iii) further corrections and additions of warnings by S (S^1); (iv) censorship and addition of a licence by [Assistant Master of the Revels William] Blagrave (C); (v) thorough revision of play by A (A^2); (vi) preparation of revised manuscript for the stage and execution of changes dependent on C's reformations by S (S^2). (Glapthorne 1959, xii)

This shuttling of the document between author and scribe rather blurs the process that Pollard called the making of the prompt-book. The authorial layer A^1 added four music directions – not obviously the author's job – and, most surprisingly, the scribe 'added warnings in the left margin some twelve to twenty lines before all the entrances except those following an Act interval', prior to the manuscript being sent for licensing (Glapthorne 1959, vii–viii). The appearance of anticipatory directions – advance warnings that someone is needed to enter during a scene – are a curious feature of certain playbook manuscripts. Although it might not be enough to fetch an errant actor, twelve or twenty lines' notice of an entrance could be useful to someone running a performance from the manuscript. However, in this case the warnings were added prior to the book going for licensing, whereas we would expect the making of the prompt-book to occur after licensing when it was known that the work was to be allowed.

Only *Believe as You List* and *The Launching of the Mary*, then, seem to exemplify Pollard's theory of continuous copy and the latter's layer of theatrical annotation is so light that it rather glorifies the process to call this the making of a prompt-book. Presumably sensing that his theory ought not to rest upon the surviving play manuscripts, Pollard returned to the Folio preliminaries in which Heminges and Condell claim that 'wee haue scarse receiued from him a blot on his papers' (Shakespeare 1623, $^{\pi}$A3^{r}). This, Pollard argued, shows that Shakespeare gave his company 'the text of the plays as he first wrote them down ... first drafts', since it would hardly be a boast if it referred to fair copies, which of course should be unblotted (Pollard 1917, 62). By cutting out the scribe, Pollard reasoned, a company reduced the chances of piracy, which in the early days of Shakespeare's career was a real problem. Thus, those non-piratical printings of Shakespeare we have were probably set up from the kind of continuous-copy manuscript containing author's writing, performance licence and prompter's annotations that Pollard thought was the normal result of this way of working.

Pollard believed he could discern these different layers in the different voices of Shakespearian stage directions, since a dramatist would describe what he wanted while a prompter would command those in his employ. Prompters' directions in the imperative mood should have been omitted in printing or else turned into descriptions, but occasionally, Pollard argued (1917, 66-7), they slipped through, as in Q2 *Romeo and Juliet*'s 'Play Musicke' rather than 'music plays' (Shakespeare 1599, K1^{v}) and Folio *2 Henry 6*'s 'Bed put forth' (Shakespeare 1623, n3^{v}). This attempted distinction of moods is the least persuasive part of Pollard's book and the evidence against it was all around him. *The Launching of the Mary*, for example, has directions in the author's hand using the imperative mood, such as 'Sitt' and 'Here bringe a little table, & a paper booke: for Clerke of the Checke' (Mountfort 1933, 319b, 330a). Pollard anticipated an objection to his claim that prompt-books, themselves formerly the authorial papers, were sent to the printers. Would not the company then be without a text to perform the play? In fact, he argued, printing was a way of getting a better text since there is clear evidence 'that copies of Quartos were used in the theatre as prompt-copies' and indeed were preferred over manuscripts (Pollard 1917, 68).

In support of this Pollard noted that Folio *Much Ado About Nothing*, essentially a reprint of Q (1600), departs from surviving exemplars of the quarto in having the stage direction '*Enter Prince, Leonato, Claudio, and Iacke Wilson*' where Q has '*Enter prince, Leonato, Claudio, Musicke*' (Shakespeare 1623, 16^r; 1600c, D1^r). Jack Wilson would appear to be the actor who played Balthasar, the provider of the music, and Pollard read this alteration as evidence that the exemplar of the quarto used as copy for the Folio was one that had formerly served as the company prompt-book: once the prompter knew who was to provide the music, he accordingly altered the stage direction in his quarto prompt-book. Pollard ignored other means by which a quarto used to print the Folio might have picked up the actor's name, such as its being annotated by reference to a theatrical document as preparation for serving as copy for the Folio. Similarly, the copy for Folio *A Midsummer Night's Dream*, a reprint of Q2 (1619), had 'clearly been used in the theatre' (Pollard 1917, 68–9). Pollard thought that only a prompter would, when adding directions absent from the quarto, know that there was just one ass-head in the property stock and so write '*Enter Piramus with the Asse head*' (Shakespeare 1623, N4^v) rather than '*an Asse head*', and the prompter too was the source of the musician's name in the direction '*Tawyer with a Trumpet before them*' (1623, O2^v) that precedes the entrance of the mechanicals' dumbshow.

Even if these phrasings are accepted as theatrical, Pollard's claim that their appearance in the Folio proves that its quarto copy picked them up by being used in the theatre is unconvincing; the Folio printers might simply have had access to a manuscript in which these directions appeared. Because he supposed that, as a defence against piracy, there was usually just one complete manuscript of each play – which started as the authorial papers and ended up as the licensed prompt-book – Pollard was obliged to suppose that the players were willing to entrust this unique document to the printers because in return they got an even better prompt-book, the printed quarto. This claim found few adherents, not least because the quarto format seems too small for use by a prompter who would want to fill the margins of his book with notes arising from his professional duties. One adherent, C. J. Sisson, was later able to show a clear case of quartos used as prompt-books but the circumstances were most unusual: Catholic recusant players touring Yorkshire in 1609 performed from print editions of John Day, George Wilkins and William Rowley's *The Travels of the Three English Brothers* (1607), Shakespeare and Wilkins's *Pericles* (1609) and a play about King Lear that may have been Shakespeare's (Sisson 1942). Had these players been using quartos of their own plays, and had they been more typical a company, Sisson's evidence might count as significant support for Pollard's theory.

The central, groundbreaking assertion of Pollard's book was that the good early editions were authorized by the playing company and were made directly from prompt-books that began life as Shakespeare's papers. Pollard knew that any such hypothetical chain leading from the pen of Shakespeare to the surviving early editions was only as strong as its weakest link, and he was prepared to hazard some numbers. An 80 per cent chance that printing was done from prompt-copy, multiplied by an 80 per cent chance that the prompt-copy was essentially authorial, multiplied by an 80 per cent chance that the authorial papers were actually autograph, gives about a 51 per cent chance that autograph manuscript was the printer's copy (Pollard 1917, 70). In other words, there is a slightly better than even chance that all that stands between the modern reader of a good quarto and a manuscript in Shakespeare's handwriting is the work of the early modern printer. Thus, according to Pollard, perhaps half the good quartos fall into this category and for the others the path from author's pen to type was not so convoluted as had formerly been assumed (Pollard 1917, 71).

Pollard's theory of how the early editions came about led him to suggest new principles for the editing of Shakespeare. Obviously where there is no good quarto to weigh against the Folio for a given play, a modern edition has to be based on the Folio. Where there is a good quarto, the makers of the Folio were, in Pollard's view, most likely to have used it as their copy. In such a case the original has priority over the reprint, so the good quarto would be the modern editor's preferred text. However, in many cases the Folio text of a play has readings that differ from those of the quarto on which it was based. Of these there are good (clearly Shakespearian) readings, bad (not Shakespearian) readings and indifferent variants. (This last class are variants where one word replaces another with essentially the same meaning, as with *between* and *betwixt* or *news* and *tidings*; the latter pair are semantically identical but in verse their metrical difference might be important.) Shakespearian readings have to be incorporated into the modern text where one can be certain, and bad, non-Shakespearian readings kept out, but what about the indifferent variants? What if one thought that the Q/F differences (good, bad and indifferent) derive from an authoritative manuscript used to annotate the exemplar of the quarto that was sent to the printer to be copy for the Folio? Pollard was prepared to accept that this might give the Folio greater authority than the quarto it reprinted: 'If we can find ground for believing that the text of any play first printed in quarto was revised *as a whole* by the aid of a good manuscript, then for these indifferent readings we must follow the text of the Folio' (Pollard 1917, 78–9).

In such a case Pollard did not advocate using the Folio text as copy for the modern edition, but only importing its good and indifferent variants into an edition based on the quarto. This will become a significant point of contention among New Bibliographers; the requirement that the revision was done '*as a whole*' was seized upon by Greg when R. B. McKerrow later made the same proviso (pp. 35–6 below). The reason for Pollard's caution was his belief that had there been thorough annotation of quarto copy by reference to an authoritative manuscript then the resulting Folio plays ought to be considerably better than they are. Their few good variants suggest either an annotator of extraordinary incompetence failing to copy most of the variant readings from his manuscript into the quarto, or else the readings came by another, more haphazard, vector. Pollard thought of one such alternative route: the prompter in the playhouse, working from a quarto prompt-book, heard the actors speaking their parts (derived from an authorial manuscript) and corrected his quarto prompt-book where he noticed that it was wrong and the actors right (Pollard 1917, 80–1). This process of authorial manuscript influencing printed quarto would necessarily be haphazard because it was not the prompter's job to get the words exactly right and actors do not always speak what is written for them. Indeed, wrong words that we might otherwise think are printer's errors could have arisen from the prompter mistakenly altering a good quarto reading to conform to an actor's error.

Pollard's *Shakespeare's Fight with the Pirates* was the first book-length argument for New Bibliography's key principles of editing. Its vital contribution was to raise confidence in the accuracy of the good quartos, since these Pollard argued had been printed from Shakespeare's authorial papers that had been turned into prompt-books for the company. Although the continuous copy part of the argument did not catch on, the principle that the good quartos were based on Shakespeare's papers was widely accepted and celebrated. Pollard was not dogmatic about the continuous copy principle, and when he first suggested that a quarto was printed directly from Shakespeare's papers – Q1 *Richard 2* (1597), studied by Pollard while making a facsimile of the newly discovered Q3 (1598) – he was prepared to leave open the matter. Either the authorial manuscript was sold to the publisher after it had been made into the prompt-book or else it was discarded when the prompt-book was made by copying it and it was then sold to the publisher, and an exemplar of the quarto then became the prompt-book (Shakespeare 1916, 96–9).

The first of the new editorial principles was that no printing after the first good quarto has authority unless there are sound reasons for believing that rather than being a mere reprint it was also based on a manuscript of some authority, 'And to construct such a case all the variants in the edition must be brought together and considered as a whole' (Pollard 1917, 84). Only the presence of authorial revisions in later printings could give an editor reason to break from the simple principle that one relies on the earliest authority (Pollard 1917, 90–1). The second of Pollard's stated principles was that, although printers had scant regard for the 'spelling, punctuation and system of emphasis capitals' in their copy, their reluctance to exert themselves in these things makes the earliest non-piratical printing the greatest authority on these matters too (Pollard 1917, 91). The third principle was that in as much as it was an attempt to put together a memorial to Shakespeare, the 1623 Folio itself was, for some of the plays at least, an edited edition (Pollard 1917, 98).

Pollard ended his book by observing that 'The theory that the plays must have been "multiplied by transcript after transcript" has held the field from his [Samuel Johnson's] day to our own and has not one shred of evidence to support it, nothing but an imaginative pessimism convinced that this is what must have happened' (Pollard 1917, 101). Instead of multiple complete manuscript versions of each play, Pollard insisted that usually there was just one, which began as authorial papers, acquired the censor's licence, was annotated to make the prompt-book, and was, if the desire arose, sent to the printers. The play would also exist in fragmented form as a collection of actors' parts, but there was no back-up to the single authoritative manuscript. With relatively slight adjustment, Pollard's central ideas held the field until the 1980s. Pollard began at this time a series of collaborations with John Dover Wilson, who had been recording unusual spellings found in early editions of Shakespeare, and with Edward Maunde Thompson who had become convinced by similarities of letter shapes in the signatures on his wills that Hand D in the manuscript of *Sir Thomas More* was Shakespeare's. On 16 December 1918 Pollard and Wilson presented a paper to the Bibliographical Society, and shortly after published its substance as an article and letters in the *Times Literary Supplement* that attracted several sceptical responses (Pollard 1919a; Wilde 1919a; Wilson 1919a; Bayfield 1919a; Pollard 1919b; Wilde 1919b; Wilson 1919b; Bayfield 1919b; Steele 1919; Stopes 1919). Their argument was that the orthographic and palaeographic evidence was mutually buttressing: distinctive spellings in Hand D, such as *scilens* for *silence*, *straing* for *strange* and *sealf* for *self*, appear in the good quartos, indicating that these editions were made directly from Shakespeare's papers (Pollard and Wilson 1920).

W. W. GREG, *DRAMATIC DOCUMENTS FROM THE ELIZABETHAN PLAYHOUSES* (1931)

W. W. Greg too rejected the multiple transcripts theory, but instead of a single authoritative manuscript he made the crucial, and what was to be the characteristically binate New Bibliographical, decision that there were always two: the authorial foul papers and the prompt-book. Aspects of Greg's thinking appeared in articles (Greg 1925; 1925–6), but the landmark statement was his *Dramatic Documents from the Elizabethan Playhouses: Stage Plots, Actors' Parts, Prompt Books* (1931) in two volumes. One volume was a gloriously oversized triumph of book-making that gave almost full-size facsimiles and fifteen transcriptions of manuscripts in whole or part associated with the playhouses, and the other provided commentary on these documents. The commentary shows Greg's increasing confidence that he could make sense of the playhouse documents, which confidence fed into his subsequent theorizing and practical advice to the editor wishing to convey Renaissance plays to a modern readership.

Greg began with a three-way distinction:

Generally speaking it may be said that for every piece in the repertory of an Elizabethan theatrical company there must have existed three playhouse documents or sets of documents. First and foremost was the *Book*, or authorized prompt copy. Two early examples that have preserved their original vellum wrappers are found inscribed respectively 'The Booke of Sir Thomas Moore' and 'The Book of Iohn A kent & Iohn a Cumber', while this technical use of the word is likewise seen in the term 'book-holder', as the prompter was called in the Elizabethan theatre. Next there were the *Parts* of the several characters, written out for actors on long scrolls of paper, if we may rely on the evidence of the solitary example that has survived … Last there were the *Plots*, skeleton outlines of plays scene by scene, written on large boards for the use of actors and others in the playhouse. (Greg 1931, ix)

Amongst the prompt-books Greg made a further three-way division into category A, 'prompt books proper' with clear signs of being made for, or used in, the theatre; category B, simply manuscripts 'which show no definite evidence of having been used in the playhouse, and if written there were probably prepared for some private purpose'; and category C, a 'miscellaneous collection' of manuscript plays with 'some particular interest deserving attention' (Greg 1931, 191).

Greg described what he thought were the naturally succeeding processes after a play first took form as a set of documents. 'Most authors', he wrote, 'would probably produce a rough copy or mass of "fowle papers"', a term being 'an apt enough description of the rough draft' (Greg 1931, 195, 196). Unlike 'prompt-book', the expression 'foul papers' had currency in the period, being used in a note made by the scribe Edward Knight when copying out the manuscript of John Fletcher's play *Bonduca* (British Library Additional Manuscript 36758). At the beginning of the fifth act, Knight apparently hit a gap in his copy, for he wrote:

Actus: Quinti: Scaena: pri^a:

~~Here should be a Scaene of the Solemnitye of paenius his ffunerall: mournd by Caracticus:~~

Here should A Scaene. be betwene Iunius. & petillius: (Iunius mocking petillus for being in loue wth Bonducas Daughter that Killd her selfe: to them: Enterd Suetonius: (blameing petillius for the Death of paenius:

The next scaene. the solemnitye of paenius his ffunerall mournd by Caracticus:

The begining of this following Scaene betweene petillius & Iunius is wanting. – the occasion. why these are wanting here. the booke where ~~it~~ by it was first Acted from is lost: and this hath beene transcrib'd from the fowle papers of the Authors wch were found:

pettilius: I kille me quickly suddenly.
       now kill me
(Fletcher 1951, 23a)

Knight's account of the making of the manuscript clearly contradicts A. W. Pollard's continuous copy theory in which the authorial papers become the prompt-book, since the absence of 'the book whereby it was first acted' is made good by something else, the author's 'fowle papers'. Greg built much upon this base.

    Six years earlier Greg had cited the evidence of *Bonduca* to revise his former statement that there was no such occupation as playhouse scrivener (Greg 1903a, 277), and he began to develop a theory of the characteristic differences between foul papers and fair copy that was to dominate the subject for decades (Greg 1925–6). That the author's foul papers were found by the scribe making a transcript of *Bonduca* indicated to Greg that they must have been lodged in the company archive – it is hardly likely that the dramatist's home was searched – and hence 'We can only conjecture that the company may have required authors to hand over their "fowle papers" along with the fair copy, either as a safeguard against such double sales as Greene was accused of and Heywood denounced, or merely to meet such an eventuality [loss of the prompt-book] as here actually occurred [with Fletcher's *Bonduca*]' (Greg 1925–6, 156). In the same article Greg took the opportunity to point out that Humphrey Moseley's preface to the collected plays of Francis Beaumont and John Fletcher referring to the making of transcripts for 'private friends' and 'Gentlemen' (Fletcher and Beaumont 1647, A4^r, A4^v) does not indicate that the practice was common, nor that it occurred at all twenty-five years earlier when the Shakespeare Folio was being prepared (Greg 1925–6, 148–9). Pollard's great advance had been achieved by overturning the idea that multiple manuscript copies of a play were routinely generated, and having split Pollard's unique manuscript (that started as authorial papers and then became the licensed prompt-book) into two distinct manuscripts, Greg was understandably keen not to readmit the notion of manuscript proliferation by the back door.

The crucial distinction between foul papers and fair copy is clear from a series of letters from the dramatist Robert Daborne to theatre impresario Philip Henslowe between March and December 1613, recorded as Articles 73–97 in Greg's edition of Henslowe's papers (Greg 1907, 69–82). Daborne was being pressed for delivery of dramatic material for which he had received cash advances, and he wished to extract further money as sections were completed. Daborne's language indicates that 'fair' could be an absolute or a relative term in relation to the quality of the papers: in Article 73 he promised 'J will deliver in ye 3 acts fayr written' and in Article 74 he recalled 'some papers J have sent y^u though not so fayr written all as J could wish'. Frequently syntax makes the precise meaning unclear, as in Article 78's 'J hav sent y^u 2 sheets more fayr written', in which 'more' might refer to the number of sheets or their fairness, and also in the next article's 'J have sent y^u a sheet & more fayr written'. Most interesting and ambiguous is the letter Pollard had drawn attention to (pp. 16–17 above):

Mr Hinchlow y^u accuse me with the breach of promise, trew it is J promysd to bring y^u the last scean which y^t y^u may see finished J send y^u the foule sheet & ye fayr I was wrighting as y^r man can testify which if great busines had not prevented J had this night fynished

It is clear that Daborne was transcribing his foul papers to make fair copy and sending the latter to Henslowe, and that on this occasion he wanted to prove that he had done the difficult work of composing and only the mechanical operation of transcription remained, so he sent the 'foule sheet' to Henslowe. But did he also send the fair sheet? 'J send' might govern both foul and fair, or it might govern only the foul sheet, which went to Henslowe as proof of work done, in which case his man is merely to testify that Daborne was in the act of copying out when he arrived. In any case, whatever went off to Henslowe, the copying must have been completed or else it ceased with the fair copy incomplete since Daborne could not continue writing the fair copy having given up the foul sheet.

In Article 92 Daborne promised to deliver 'one plaie fullie perfected and ended Called by the name of the Oule', which indicates that (as we would expect) the dramatists were supposed to hand over something flawless and complete, and indeed in the next letter Daborne acknowledged that £3 more would be paid to him when he had 'fynished and made perfect' *The Owl*. In Article 94 Daborne promised to stop asking for money 'till y^u hav papers in fully to y^r content', and it seems from Article 96 that Daborne sent papers that were literally incomplete in their dramatic content: 'J pray send me ten shillings & take these papers which wants but one short scean of the whole play.' Seventeen days later, Daborne wrote again to Henslowe saying 'yu hav now a full play' (Article 97). The recurrent concern with the fairness of the handwriting and the completeness of the drama shown in Daborne's letters is good reason to suppose that players set minimum standards for the manuscripts they received from dramatists.

To advance his two document (foul papers and prompt-book) theory, Greg took care to dismiss Pollard's one clear case of an author's autograph being sent for licensing and then made into a prompt-book, *The Launching of the Mary*. Greg commented 'It is true that the unlucky censor read, marked, and actually with reservations licensed this appalling stuff, but having done so he proceeded to demand a revised "fairer Copy" of the "Bookeeper"' (Greg 1931, 200). In fact, as we saw (p. 17 above), in the Malone Society Reprint edition of the manuscript, which Greg as general editor had approved, Herbert's writing was transcribed as demanding 'faire' copy, not 'fairer' as Greg here quoted him, and Herbert seems to be referring to future submissions. The most recent palaeographic examination of the manuscript quotes the word as 'fayre' (Ioppolo 2006, 78). While distinguishing foul papers from the fair copy with which it would be much easier to run a performance, Greg insisted that 'it would be a great mistake to suppose that no additions were ever made to the Book, nor a good deal of untidiness tolerated' (Greg 1931, 201) and he went on to describe additional and substitute passages being pinned and pasted in, as well as being written into margins.

Greg's greatest obstacle in proposing the existence of the manuscript category of foul papers was that we have no documents that obviously belong to it. In *Dramatic Documents from the Elizabethan Playhouses*, Greg categorized Thomas Heywood's *The Captives* (British Library Egerton 1994) as prompt-book, but with some reservations because although there is little blotting, interlining or alteration, the original handwriting is difficult to read, as are the 'prompt notes', and the manuscript lacks the censor's licence (Greg 1931, 203). Greg himself was the first to stress that *The Captives* has a confusing combination of features. Pollard insisted that stage directions written by the book-keeper, or rather the prompter in Pollard's terminology (Greg pointed out that these are synonyms for our purposes, p. 24 above), would be imperative and stage-centred (pp. 19–20 above). Yet Greg observed of stage directions that 'Diversity is the characteristic that strikes the reader most and is most bewildering to the student' because 'essentially literary directions are commonly left unaltered in prompt copies' and 'the whole question badly needs studying in relation, not to a priori expectation, but to the actual evidence of the Books themselves …' (Greg 1931, 208, 209).

Greg's foul papers/prompt-book distinction, which was to grow in importance until it utterly dominated New Bibliography, was supposed to emerge from the differing labours and purposes of the dramatist and the book-keeper. If the distinguishing features of these layers of writing could be codified, it might be possible to examine an early edition of Shakespeare and say whether its underlying copy was authorial (foul papers) or theatrical (prompt-book). However, Greg readily acknowledged that in many areas these classes of writing are hard to distinguish. For example, in answer to his own question 'What treatment did the book-keeper mete out to the author's stage-directions?' Greg offered that 'as a rule he left them alone. So long as they were intelligible it mattered little to him the form in which they were couched' (Greg 1931, 213). If the directions did not stand out clearly to someone glancing over the page, the book-keeper might highlight them or repeat their substance in larger writing and he allowed himself the left margin to add his repetitions or amplifications of what authors usually put in the right margin. When an actor's name appears in an early edition where we should expect the character's name it is difficult to say whether the dramatist or someone else who handled the underlying manuscript was responsible. Greg was cautious about inferences made from this phenomenon, but he believed that 'in every instance in which an actor's name appears in a manuscript play it is written in a different hand from the text, or at any rate in a different ink and style, showing it to be a later addition and not part of the original composition' (Greg 1931, 216). Greg went on to refine his thinking about the significance of actors' names in early editions (pp. 48–9 below), a point upon which he was to be much misrepresented by his detractors.

Also inconsistently present in printed plays, Greg noted, is the practice of moving entrance directions back a few lines so that the actors walk on stage 'a few moments earlier [than the author intended] in order that they may be able to enter into the dialogue at the correct point'; this was done occasionally, not uniformly (Greg 1931, 217). Related to these, but worth distinguishing from them, are book-keeper's notes for properties and actors to be got ready backstage before they are needed:

Now it is perfectly true that anticipations, as distinct from warnings, occur sporadically in printed texts, and it has been assumed that they imply a playhouse origin for the copy used. This is probably a quite valid inference, though it seems to have been based rather vaguely on the belief that such anticipations are normal in prompt books, which is not the fact. If we leave on one side the quite exceptional *Lady Mother*, anticipations are just as sporadic in manuscript as in printed plays. (Greg 1931, 219)

There may well be perfectly reasonable explanations for sporadic phenomena, and as we shall see (pp. 153–66 below) one of the most misleading and unhistorical claims of the recent New Textualism, inspired by Michel Foucault's belief in an epistemic shift occurring around 1800, is that such inconsistencies arise because early modern notions of orderliness differed from ours.

Greg accepted that book-keepers were not all equally 'careful and elaborate in their methods' (Greg 1931, 220), but he knew that seemingly inconsistent behaviour can turn out to have a rational basis once the full facts are known. Where a book-keeper found in the manuscript he received that something requiring his special attention occurred near the top of a page, he would probably want advance notice of it on the preceding page and mark his book accordingly. (Depending on how he held the book – open to a two-page view or folded back on itself to show only one page – the book-keeper might also give himself advance warning of things happening just after he turned a leaf but not bother for similar things at the top of a page – such as the recto of a two-page view – that he could simply glance across at.) Because the page-breaks of the manuscript would not be preserved when it was printed, this pattern of advance warnings would look bafflingly inconsistent (a mix of overzealousness and indifference) in an early print edition. Greg gave examples of cross-page anticipation and commented that 'It seems to me probable that we here have the explanation of the sporadic anticipations found in printed texts' (Greg 1931, 220). By re-examining the documentary record and systematically categorizing the materials, the New Bibliography was beginning to make sense of phenomena previously dismissed as beyond interpretation, and it was thereby generating the means for editions executed along wholly new lines.

R. B. McKERROW, *PROLEGOMENA FOR THE OXFORD SHAKESPEARE* (1939)

In 1929 R. B. McKerrow was asked by Oxford University Press to produce a new, original-spelling edition of the Shakespeare canon and, the work proceeding more slowly than he had hoped, his introduction (*Prolegomena*) was published separately in 1939. Having asserted that no edition could be definitive – since none could serve all possible readers (McKerrow 1939, 1) – he defined the ideal towards which his edition would strive:

> For scholarly purposes, the ideal text of the works of an early dramatist would be one which, on the positive side, should approach as closely as the extant material allows to a fair copy, made by the author himself, of his plays in the form which he intended finally to give them, and, on the negative side, should not in any way be coloured by the preconceived ideas or interpretations of later times. (McKerrow 1939, 6)

This might be taken to mean that the editor is most interested in the play as it stood in the author's final fair manuscript, just before it was handed over to the players. But McKerrow could see a problem there:

> Shakespeare ... would ... have been concerned with producing, not plays for the study, but material for his company to perform on the stage, and there can be little doubt that his lines would be subject to modification in the light of actual performance ... Such alterations may have been made by the author himself or, if he was not available, they may have been made by others. He may, or may not, have regarded them as improvements: he probably merely accepted them as necessary changes, and it is quite likely that he never bothered about whether they introduced inconsistencies into what was originally conceived as a consistent whole. We must not expect to find a definitive text in the sense in which the published version of the plays of a modern dramatist is definitive. (McKerrow 1939, 6)

Definitiveness thus dismissed as unobtainable, and the seeking of it as anachronistic, McKerrow's selection of a moment in the play's realization (just before the players got the script) and of a particular form it might have taken (the author's fair copy) should be seen as pragmatic, not naively idealistic.

This particular moment in the artistic process and its physical embodiment were in part dictated by McKerrow's knowledge that company practices blurred the boundary between authorial and actorly labour. Moreover, we possess so little knowledge of what a Shakespeare autograph manuscript would have looked like ('nor even a manuscript copy of such a manuscript') that 'we cannot hope to infer with any approach to certainty Shakespeare's own practice as regards such details as spelling, capitalization, the use of italics, or punctuation' (McKerrow 1939, 7). He cautiously acknowledged 'the exception of one possible fragment' of drama in Shakespeare's hand, the Hand D of *Sir Thomas More*, but McKerrow was relatively pessimistic (much more so than A. W. Pollard and W. W. Greg) about the whole endeavour of recovering what Shakespeare wrote.

In theory, McKerrow's idealized document – the one the editor should set as her goal – stood at the boundary between author and playing company and was written in the author's handwriting. In practice he accepted the primacy of the extant early editions:

As, therefore, we cannot deduce rules for normalization, the only possible course is to determine for each play separately the most authoritative text of those which have come down to us from early times, and to reprint this as exactly as possible save for manifest and indubitable errors. Such a method will no doubt give us a series of texts which are less uniform in the details of presentation than those to which we are accustomed in modern-spelling editions, but this cannot be helped. (McKerrow 1939, 7)

The most authoritative early edition must be one not derived from any other known edition (that is, it must be substantive), although of course there are a number of different ways such a thing might have been made, depending on what kind of copy the printers had before them.

Four years earlier McKerrow had published an essay, 'A Suggestion Regarding Shakespeare's Manuscripts' (1935), that gave hope of being able to tell from a print edition what kind of manuscript was used as its copy. McKerrow surveyed variations in the names used in speech prefixes in the Folio-only plays *The Two Gentlemen of Verona* and *The Comedy of Errors* and noted that in the former 'the names given to the characters are permanent labels, and are quite unaffected by the function of the character at the moment' while in the latter they depend 'on the progress of the story or on the person with whom the character is conversing' (McKerrow 1935, 460–1). Thus the Antipholi's father is '*Merchant*' in the first scene (Shakespeare 1623, H1^r–H1^v) but '*Father*' in a scene with his sons (11^v–11^r). Similarly across Q2 *Romeo and Juliet* (1599) Lady Capulet is variously '*Wife*', '*Mo*[*ther*]' and '*La*[*dy*]' of the household, depending on her function in a particular scene. McKerrow attributed the variation to the dramatist, in the heat of composition, conceiving of his characters in relational rather than absolute terms, and thus when reading such editions we are admitted to Shakespeare's mind in a way not previously thought possible.

It is likely 'that a play in which the names are irregular was printed from the author's original MS., and that one in which they are regular and uniform is more likely to have been printed from some sort of fair copy, perhaps made by a professional scribe' who would have regularized the dramatist's variations (McKerrow 1935, 464). This last sentence has had a far-reaching effect on Shakespeare editing, for until the end of the twentieth century virtually every critical edition used it to offer an opinion on the nature of the manuscripts underlying the early editions of the play being edited. McKerrow came to think that his test ought to be hedged with qualifications and he seldom showed great faith in it, but for Greg it transformed the search to identify printer's copy. Greg once declared such determination impossible – 'We lack evidence sufficient to decide the question' (Greg 1903a, 283) – but McKerrow's test strengthened the new optimism that was sweeping away such caution.

McKerrow was right to suppose that variation in speech prefixes is more likely to originate with the dramatist, who has creative reasons for thinking in variable terms, than with a scribe who has not. McKerrow recognized that a scribe might faithfully copy an author's speech prefix variations when doing his work, and noted that in general scribal practice 'may perhaps be regarded as uncertain' (McKerrow 1935, 464). But he made a fatal error in supposing that certain tendencies could be predicted:

a copy intended for use in the theatre would surely, of necessity, be accurate and unambiguous in the matter of character-names. A prompter of a repertory theatre could hardly be expected to remember that Bertram was the same person as Rossillion, or Armado the same as Braggart. Such variations would be an intolerable nuisance to him ... It is difficult to imagine a theatrical scribe, at any rate, not attending to a point of this kind. (McKerrow 1935, 464)

Were this true, speech prefix variation would be a reliable indicator of the copy underlying an edition, since its presence to any great extent would prove that the text had not been through the theatre, and its complete absence would suggest that the text had been through the theatre since even a careful dramatist might be expected to vary speech prefixes somewhat when writing a play.

Unfortunately, McKerrow was wrong: as the New Textualism was to show (pp. 155–8 below), speech prefix variation was not effaced in manuscripts used in the theatre. The most we can say is that certain features are unlikely to have originated with agent X or agent Y (because the agent had no reason to generate the feature) but we cannot directly move from this negative conclusion to positive knowledge about the nature of the underlying copy for an early edition. A faithful transcript might preserve the signs of authoriality, and use in the theatre need not efface them. Although he did not retract his claim about theatre scribes' regularizing practices, McKerrow clearly felt by 1939 that his comments on distinguishing authorial copy from theatrical copy had encouraged too much over-confident speculation and that investigations had 'become increasingly far-reaching' and in many cases dependent on 'the assumption of an extremely complicated history'. McKerrow did not identify these over-confident investigations, mentioning only that Pollard and Greg were interested in such things (McKerrow 1939, 9 n.4). Obvious targets for the accusation were John Dover Wilson's articles, written on his own and with Pollard, on the bad quartos (pp. 101–2 below) and his books on the manuscripts of *Hamlet* (Wilson 1934a; 1934b), but these all preceded McKerrow's 'Suggestion' about speech prefixes.

We should remember, he cautioned, 'that the greater part of the conclusions reached are, and must always remain, guess-work' (McKerrow 1939, 9). The problem lay in the investigators' illogical confusion of positive and negative knowledge in respect of errors and inconsistencies: 'we shall as a rule find that such errors may be explained in a number of very different ways and that there is no criterion by which we can ascertain which explanation is correct' (McKerrow 1939, 9). In determining the 'possible history of the copy used in printing any of the extant "substantive" texts of Shakespeare', McKerrow declared himself convinced of what Greg had claimed in 1903, that it is generally 'impossible to arrive at any certainty – or even at any reasonable probability' (McKerrow 1939, 10).

Thus distanced from investigations for which his own work had generated the optimistic impulse, McKerrow turned to the distinguishing of derivative from substantive printings, drawing on the principles outlined in his Appendix B that discussed the different kinds of evidence that might be used. Real knowledge was to be generated from careful use of logic, and perhaps counter-intuitively the evidence of greatest value is '*unimportant variants*' (McKerrow 1939, 106). Where variants of no literary importance are shared by two editions there is a high probability that one was made from the other, while peculiarities that are highly noticeable – especially glaring errors – draw the attention of proofreaders who might alter them even without reference to copy. McKerrow went on:

> The best of all evidence of the genetic connexion between editions is undoubtedly the persistence of misprints or of 'unnatural' typographical arrangement. If, for example, in two or more editions of a work 'though' is misprinted 'thought', or if in these editions a stage direction is found awkwardly placed when there would have been room for it in a more normal position, or if it is divided into two or more lines unnecessarily or is in any other way typographically unusual, it is highly probable that one or more of these was used as 'copy' for one or more of the others, that, in fact, we can arrange them into a genetic group; and if we find a number of similar arrangements between the texts we may take the relationship as almost certain. (McKerrow 1939, 107)

McKerrow was unequivocal on this point, yet others associated with New Bibliography disregarded it and attempted to deduce the relationships between early editions using evidence of shared good readings. Most notoriously, Andrew S. Cairncross argued from common readings that Q2 (1602) and Q3 (1619) provided copy for Folio *Henry 5* (Cairncross 1956), that Q1 (1597), Q3 (1602) and Q6 (1622) did the same for Folio *Richard 3* (Cairncross 1957), and likewise in studies of the Folio copy for *2 Henry 6* (Shakespeare 1957b, xxxii–xxxix) and *3 Henry 6* (Shakespeare 1964, xxiii–xxxiii). When J. K. Walton demonstrated the insignificance of the agreements in the editions of *Richard 3*, Cairncross simply pleaded that he had little faith in random coincidence and offered the false principle that 'identity of reading implies identity of origin' (Walton 1959, 139).

Karl Lachmann is commonly credited with formulating the principle that only agreement-in-error shows that one document is a copy of another, although others were using it around the same time (Kenney 1974, 135 n.1). Elsewhere in Shakespeare studies, the principle was employed to devastating effect in the first issue of the journal *Shakespeare Survey* when I. A. Shapiro proved from its errors that J. C. Visscher's engraving *View of London* (1616?) has no independent authority (is not substantive) and must be derived from John Norden's map *Civitas Londini* of 1600 (Shapiro 1948). The clincher is Visscher's labelling of the church 'St Dunston in the cast', which is what Norden's map also appears to read, instead of 'in the east'. Norden's *e* and *c* letter shapes were virtually indistinguishable and had Visscher had any other authority, or local knowledge, his engraving would not have contained this error. At a stroke Shapiro demolished the work of the most respected living early modern theatre historian, John Cranford Adams, whose reconstruction of the Globe (Adams 1942) was built – literally, in the form of the Folger Shakespeare Theatre in Washington DC – upon Visscher's evidence.

Like Pollard, McKerrow held that a derivative edition has no authority whatever and that the edition standing first in the genetic line has full authority. All descendent editions are unauthoritative, even when they restore what is undoubtedly a correct reading where the parent has an incorrect one; this way of thinking comes close to saying that the errors of the most authoritative edition are themselves authoritative. McKerrow stopped short of this and declared that all the readings of the authoritative edition are authoritative 'with the exception of such readings as are on the face of them miscopyings or misprints' (McKerrow 1939, 12). Thus if an editor can make sense of a suspected reading in the authoritative text, the reading should be kept; unless clearly an error it has total authority. Notice the binate and centrifugal force here: a reading is either utterly authoritative or unauthoritative. Such binate thinking is a weakness of New Bibliography that its detractors seized upon towards the end of the century.

Having covered cases in which there is a single line of genetic descent, McKerrow went on to consider what an editor should do when there are two independent lines of descent, each headed by a substantive edition that '*may* be the one which represents most accurately the author's manuscript'; that is to say when we have polygenous rather than monogenous descent (McKerrow 1939, 13). In such a case – and only then – must the editor attempt to judge the quality of the competing substantive editions to determine 'which in his judgement is most representative of the author' because it is the 'most careful copy of its original and the most free from obvious errors' (McKerrow 1939, 14). Just as in the determination of which edition is derivative and which substantive, the evaluation of substantive editions cannot be settled by such evidence as the correction of obvious error (for example, the supplying of syllables to smooth metre) since someone other than the author might be responsible for it.

Like Pollard, McKerrow acknowledged the possibility that a derivative text may nonetheless contain authoritative individual variants – perhaps because an authoritative manuscript was used to annotate the copy for the reprint – but 'in the great majority of cases, there is no means of deciding whether they [the variant readings] are authentic or not' and as ever we can be more confident about rejecting something because it is not possibly Shakespearian than we can be about including something we think must be Shakespearian (McKerrow 1939, 17). Even if an editor were sure that a reprint has authoritative readings, it would not necessarily follow that this reprint should be the copy-text for the modern edition. Without thoroughgoing correction of the whole text by the dramatist, the authority attaches only to the individual readings and not to the edition as a whole, which, because it is a reprint, probably 'will (except for the corrections) deviate more widely than the earliest print from the author's original manuscript' (McKerrow 1939, 18). It were best, then, to base the modern edition on the earliest good edition and import to it those corrections from the later edition that seem 'derived from the author'.

To distinguish this apparent eclecticism from the caprice of eighteenth-century editors such as Alexander Pope, McKerrow made clear the criteria for inclusion:

We are not to regard the 'goodness' of a reading in and by itself, or to consider whether it appeals to our aesthetic sensibilities or not; we are to consider whether a particular edition taken *as a whole* contains variants from the edition from which it was otherwise printed which could not reasonably be attributed to an ordinary press-corrector, but by reason of their style, point, and what we may call inner harmony with the spirit of the play as a whole, seem likely to be the work of the author: and once having decided this to our satisfaction we must accept *all* the alterations of that edition, saving any which seem obvious blunders or misprints. (McKerrow 1939, 18)

McKerrow was quite clear about what an obvious misprint had to be: 'any form which, in the light of our knowledge of the language at the time when the text in question was written, was "impossible", that is, would not have been, in its context, an intelligible word or phrase' (McKerrow 1939, 21). But what about 'those words and locutions which we must class as doubtful' in the derivative edition? McKerrow insisted that there is no 'infallible objective test of what is correct in the texts' and editors simply have to use their judgement (McKerrow 1939, 34, 35). If they followed McKerrow's lead they would be conservative, which is to say that they would be reluctant to change what stood in their copy-text.

If one is going to change something, McKerrow thought it reasonable to give some consideration to what subsequent reprints (derivatives) of one's copy-text had in place of the suspect word: these alternatives have at least the merit of being probably acceptable English of the period (McKerrow 1939, 37–8). In an original-spelling edition, an emended word would naturally have to be put into the spelling of the period, or better still into the spelling of the copy-text's underlying manuscript if the editor has a sense of it (McKerrow 1939, 39). For following this practice, the editors of the Oxford *Complete Works* of 1986 (which was the fulfilment of the commission that McKerrow had been given in 1929) were later mocked (pp. 187–8 below). The remainder of McKerrow's *Prolegomena* was concerned with the precise rules that he intended to follow in his Oxford Shakespeare regarding such matters as alteration of punctuation and the recording of readings in editions other than the copy-text.

We may summarize developments so far in our chronology, then, as these. First came the sudden dispersal by Pollard of pessimism about our capacity to discriminate between the early editions of Shakespeare and assess their relative authorities. Then Greg constructed precise classifications of early modern play manuscripts (surviving and lost), and he and McKerrow devised tests for determining which of the various categories of manuscript (authorial papers, fair copy, scribal transcript, prompt-book) the underlying copy for a particular edition belonged to. Finally came the beginnings of the cautious application, by McKerrow, of these new theories, categories and tests to the task of preparing an edition of Shakespeare aimed at the modern reader and deriving from fresh analysis of the original materials.

There matters stood at the outbreak of the Second World War. McKerrow died the year after the *Prolegomena* was published, and the next landmark publication was Greg's response to it, which criticized McKerrow's excessive caution. McKerrow's epistemological attitude was summarized in the preface to the *Prolegomena*: the new methods 'may be able to tell us with an approach to certainty what an author *might* have written or what, in view of his date, he *could not* have written; it can seldom give us much aid in guessing what he probably wrote' (McKerrow 1939, viii). Greg's response was that radical textual intervention could discover what Shakespeare probably wrote even if the surviving early editions give little sign of it. The early New Bibliography, as the Pollard–Greg–McKerrow school was christened by Greg (1919b, 380), blew away most of the uncertainty that preceded it, and the mature New Bibliography blew away the remaining uncertainty of the early phase. Once McKerrow made his 'Suggestion' about speech prefix variation, Greg changed his mind about the possibility of determining the nature of the manuscript underlying an early edition. The next significant developments concerned the mechanical processes of printing itself, which left evidence in early books that the Pollard–Greg–McKerrow school had not discovered how to read. With the development of the skills needed to read this evidence, New Bibliography ceased to be an exclusively British school and became primarily an American one.

CHAPTER 2

New techniques and the Virginian School: New Bibliography 1939–1968

The American advances in New Bibliography became widely known with the launch in 1948 of the journal *Studies in Bibliography* by the Bibliographical Society of the University of Virginia, under Fredson Bowers's editorship. Emerging differences of opinion about the reliability of the methods of New Bibliography were counterbalanced by the development of ever more technical means for the analysis of early books, such as investigations of compositors' spelling preferences and the evidence that running titles offer about the order in which formes were machined by the printing press. One might say that post-war confidence about the fruits of new technical developments overcame qualms about the school's foundational principles. The new procedures seemed to offer the clearest glimpse yet of the characteristics of the manuscript copy underlying early editions.

Most excitingly of all, analysis of press variants was dramatically sped up by Charlton Hinman's invention of a collating machine, which he applied to the seventy-nine exemplars of the 1623 Folio held in the Folger Shakespeare Library in Washington DC in the hope of speaking definitively about that edition's proofreading and press correction. Together with Hinman's innovative analyses of the frequency of reuse of particular pieces of type (identified by their defects) that revealed the order in which the Folio's pages were set, and the corroborating evidence provided by George Walton Williams's analyses of substitutions forced upon compositors by type shortage, the new discipline seemed to be finding a solid empirical foundation. The beginnings of the American school of New Bibliography overlapped with the last major British publications, which were career-summing monographs from W. W. Greg.

W. W. GREG, *THE EDITORIAL PROBLEM IN SHAKESPEARE* (1942) AND *THE SHAKESPEARE FIRST FOLIO* (1955)

For the Clark Lectures at Trinity College, Cambridge, in 1939, Greg extended the binate division of playbook manuscripts into foul papers and prompt-books that he had presented in *Dramatic Documents from the Elizabethan Playhouses* (1931). The other documents necessary for a performance, the playhouse plot and the actors' parts, dropped out of the argument because they cannot easily have served a purpose outside the theatre, such as being copy for a printing. (John Dover Wilson thought otherwise about parts, and Tiffany Stern restated the importance of this class of documents, pp. 225–6 below.) An obstacle to Greg's use of the term foul papers had been that we seem to possess no examples of this kind of manuscript, but Greg now decided that a fragment of Christopher Marlowe's *The Massacre at Paris* might be one (Greg 1942, 28) and that his tentative categorization in *Dramatic Documents from the Elizabethan Playhouses* of Thomas Heywood's *The Captives* as a prompt-book was mistaken: it is too untidy to serve the purpose of controlling a performance in the theatre (Greg 1942, 30). That any extant document represented foul papers, Greg thought, 'we cannot tell for certain, but we may get an idea of what the pages of rough copy probably looked like by examining the carelessly written additions that we find in some theatrical manuscripts, for instance *Sir Thomas More*, *The Faithful Friends* and Shirley's *Court Secret*' (Greg 1942, 28). Nonetheless, reflection upon two developments had given Greg increased confidence about his categorical distinctions and their application to the editorial problem.

The first development had been the publication of a study of Shakespeare's handwriting (Thompson 1916) that suggested that Hand D in the playbook manuscript *Sir Thomas More* was Shakespeare, and the subsequent confirmation of this by others (Pollard *et al.* 1923). Something like Shakespeare's foul papers seemed to be available. The other development had been two articles by R. B. McKerrow. The first addressed the question of why plays were often badly printed in Shakespeare's time, even by printers who in other work showed themselves capable of great care (McKerrow 1931–2). McKerrow's explanation was that the players would not give printers the valuable prompt-book with its censor's licence, so they handed over the author's papers; the untidiness of these created the difficulties we know from the early editions. A second article buttressed the first and was the suggestion regarding speech prefix variation that we have already seen (pp. 31–3 above). Both articles confirmed the identification of Hand D in *Sir Thomas More*, for, as John Dover Wilson had shown (Pollard *et al.* 1923, 113–31), this part of the play has a number of idiosyncratic spellings that also appear in good Shakespeare quartos. The explanation for these shared spellings was obvious: Shakespeare's own manuscripts, with his idiosyncratic spellings, were used as copy for these editions, giving further reason to trust that they reliably witness the author's intentions.

In *The Editorial Problem in Shakespeare*, Greg outlined his thinking up to that point and proposed a set of rules about how editors should proceed in the light of current knowledge. Between the delivery of the Clark Lectures in 1939 and their publication in 1942 as *The Editorial Problem in Shakespeare*, Greg wrote an article responding to McKerrow's *Prolegomena* and he sprinkled his criticism with asseverations about the recently deceased scholar's 'mature conclusions' whose 'fullest and best discussion of the subject' was merely marred by 'some signs of haste in a few curious slips' that, had he lived, McKerrow would doubtless have fixed (Greg 1941, 139). But the substance of Greg's reflection on McKerrow's *Prolegomena* was a point-by-point disagreement with its conservative principles, and Greg codified his alternative rules in the opening section of *The Editorial Problem in Shakespeare* labelled 'Prolegomena' in explicit response to McKerrow's book (Greg 1942, vii–lv). The first two of Greg's new rules were uncontroversial: 'The aim of a critical edition should be to present the text, so far as the available evidence permits, in the form in which we may suppose that it would have stood in a fair copy, made by the author himself, of the work as he finally intended it' and 'With this aim in view, an editor should select as the basis of his own edition (as his copy-text, that is) the most "authoritative" of the early prints, this being the one that on critical consideration appears likely to have departed least in wording, spelling, and punctuation from the author's manuscript' (Greg 1942, x, xii).

Thereafter subtle novelties entered the argument. Greg conceived of a potential conflict 'between the essential readings of a text and what may be called the "accidents" of spelling and punctuation', since a sloppy first-generation copy, say a printing directly from autograph, would probably preserve the general character of spelling and punctuation while mangling a number of the individual readings, and another more careful second-generation copy, say a printing based on a transcript of the autograph papers, would be further from the author's habits regarding spelling and punctuation and yet record more accurately the words he used (Greg 1942, xiii). This idea of divided authority later emerged as the basis for the distinction made in Greg's celebrated essay 'The Rationale of Copy-Text' (pp. 44–7 below) between the copy-text, the one an editor copies from to make her edition, and what has since been dubbed by Gary Taylor (1981a) the control text, the authority to be followed for substantive variants.

Having described the difference between substantive and derivative editions, Greg considered the problem of reprints that seem to have been made with the aid of an authoritative manuscript to supplement the edition being reprinted and of non-reprints that show evidence of some use of an existing edition. In theory such phenomena could change the essential nature of the printing (turning derivative into substantive and substantive into derivative) but luckily in practice, Greg claimed, the consultation only runs for short sections at a time, so for these alone is the essential nature changed. What matters with manuscript consultation used to modify an edition being reprinted is whether or not the collator was trying to make the existing edition conform to the manuscript: if he was, then the reprint becomes substantive via this manuscript consultation. Equally, where authorial changes (revisions) have been written onto an existing print edition (and not recorded elsewhere), a reprint of that edition incorporating those changes gains substantive status because of them (Greg 1942, xv–xix).

In its preference for the authorial over the theatrical manuscript, the New Bibliography can easily seem to be irrationally prejudiced against performance as an art form. This misleading impression derives from the serious concern to base modern editions upon documents at the heads of genetic lines of descent rather than on their derivatives. As Greg put it, 'If critics are correct in supposing the second quarto of *Hamlet* to have been printed from Shakespeare's autograph and the folio text to derive from the prompt-book, then no doubt the quarto is the *more* authoritative, since it would be directly derived from the manuscript which was also the source of the prompt-book' (Greg 1942, xxiv n.2). It is not theatricality per se that diminishes the authority of a prompt-book, but the simple fact that it is a copy of the authorial papers; as always, originals should in general be preferred over copies. Greg held that annotations made by those involved in first performance are worth having – he did not reject them on principle as nothing to do with the play – but thought that in practice they might well be annotations made for a revival and hence not necessarily authorially intended, or they might come from someone's faulty memory and thus 'combine conjecture with recollection' (Greg 1942, xli).

Greg was not anti-theatrically disposed but simply wanted to end the long tradition of Shakespeare being corrupted by material that had nothing to do with him; he wanted to recover and guard Shakespeare's exertions over the exertions of others, and these he believed were more likely embodied in an authorial manuscript than anywhere else. Because Greg's ideal was what Shakespeare wrote for his fellow players rather than what they accepted of what he wrote, he felt obliged to restore from a less authoritative printing those passages that the more authoritative printing entirely omits, since even bits of Shakespeare that were cut for performance were, in his view, part of the authorial intention (Greg 1942, xxxvi). As will become clear in relation to the 'new' New Bibliography of the 1980s (pp. 167–89 below), such a conception of authorial intention is contestable since if Shakespeare's primary goal was to enable performance then his intention might be said to include respecting the cuts that his colleagues advised were dramatically necessary.

Greg most clearly departed from McKerrow's conservatism regarding what an editor should do when there are two substantive editions of comparable authority. McKerrow declared that once it had been decided (even by the narrowest of margins) which has the greater authority the editor should stick to that one except where it is clearly in error, to which Greg replied 'since *ex hypothesi* the true reading may be preserved sometimes in one and sometimes in the other text, if an editor's judgement is worth anything at all, it should enable him to approach nearer to the author's original than does either of the transmitted texts' (Greg 1942, xxvii). Someone who holds herself unable to distinguish authenticity in competing readings has no business deciding which of the two substantive editions has the greater authority, since this decision is effectively a generalization made on the basis of individual readings. An editor perceptive enough to select her copy by a better means than tossing a coin must be perceptive enough to choose between the available readings and in doing so take the reader closer to the author's words. Greg did not think he was giving the editor *carte blanche* to emend wildly, and advised that when there is not much to choose between two readings the general authority of the text the editor chose to base her edition on – which authoritativeness was the reason she chose it in the first place – should swing the decision. 'This at least saves the trouble of tossing a coin!' (Greg 1942, xxix n.1).

Greg rejected the principle that there will always be one early edition that best represents the play; rather, he insisted that different editions each best represent different aspects of what the author wrote (Greg 1942, xxxii). For example, an early edition might be based on a manuscript that is generally authoritative but has undergone a process such as expurgation of its oaths (in accordance with the 1606 Act to Restrain Abuses of Players) that removed a single aspect of that authority. One might choose to do without the oaths written by the author, or to base one's edition on an inferior printing that happens to retain them, but it is better, Greg argued, to use the more authoritative printing and import to it the individual oaths as they appear in the less authoritative printing. In such a case the eclectic approach is bound to produce something closer to what was written than will the conservative approach. Editing is necessarily an act of interrogating the editions using one's knowledge of the historical context, here the 1606 censorship law.

A comparable situation arises regarding press variants within the single edition that has been found to be generally most authoritative, and here too Greg displayed his characteristic mix of conservatism and eclecticism based on reasoned argument (Greg 1942, xlviii–xlix). McKerrow had long before pointed out that when a printing press was stopped and corrections made to the type, they would be made across the whole of a forme (four pages for a quarto, two for a folio), not in individual pages (Barnes 1904, xiii–xviii). Since an entire forme is either corrected or uncorrected, one cannot choose between individual press variants but must take those of the forme as a whole, excepting only those that seem to be accidental miscorrections. This was Greg's conservatism. But what if a correction required changing other words, spellings, or punctuation on the same line to make the new reading fit into the space available? In such a case one should take the rest of the line from the uncorrected state because it was altered only for a mechanical, non-linguistic reason. This was Greg's eclecticism. As ever, knowledge of how the text came to be the way it is must be applied, and strict conservatism – which would require taking the whole line from the corrected forme – turns out to do greater violence to the author's words than reasoned eclecticism.

In *The Editorial Problem in Shakespeare* Greg devoted just a couple of pages to the characteristics by which one might determine whether the manuscript underlying an early edition was foul papers (Greg 1942, 102–3). Although interested in seeing the underlying authorial manuscript, Greg balanced his tentative exploration of this possibility with the following conclusion about that manuscript's relation to the writer's intentions:

> There seems then in general no possibility of arriving at the perfectly finished product of Shakespeare's art, for the simple reason that he never gave it a perfect finish. It is the penalty, or if you will the limitation, of the medium in which he worked – that most vital but most incalculable medium of the theatre – in which the very tools and materials of the artist are the speech, the emotions, the personalities, of actual human beings. In such an art, to the great artist at least, the written word can never be final, and he may be the less concerned to give the last polish to the script. I do not myself believe that Shakespeare, at any rate in his maturity, wrote only for the stage – he must have known and recognized and valued the enduring element of his creation – but he wrote primarily for the stage and was content that its accidents should mould the fashion of his art. (Greg 1942, 156–7)

Despite this admirable tentativeness about the textual situation of Shakespeare, in his last major work on the subject, *The Shakespeare First Folio* (1955), Greg offered a detailed checklist of characteristics by which an editor might tell whether foul papers or prompt-book were the copy for an early edition. Knowing that it is impossible for writing fully to embody Shakespeare's intentions did not prevent Greg from pursuing those intentions amongst the various extant (and lost, but inferentially recovered) documents and discriminating between classes of manuscript and print edition, the boundaries of which he knew to be blurred. He did this because he was serving an end: bibliography exists to enable editions to be made by transcending the particularities in which the scholarship is necessarily grounded.

An intervening step in Greg's thinking, a link by which he moved from the tentative conclusion of *The Editorial Problem in Shakespeare* to the relative boldness of *The Shakespeare First Folio*, is represented in his article 'The Rationale of Copy-Text' (Greg 1950–1). This short essay was the 'direct outcome' (Greg 1952, v) of trying to reconstruct Ben Jonson's masque *The Gypsies Metamorphosed* from its multiple early manuscript and print versions, which task developed fully the consequences of Greg's realization that textual authority may be divided between multiple documents. Greg argued that the choice of copy-text for a modern edition is less important than McKerrow thought, since it has authority only with regard to the accidentals of 'spelling, punctuation, word-division, and the like' (Greg 1950–1, 21). For substantive readings – that is, those 'that affect the author's meaning or the essence of his expression' – one must consider documents other than the copy-text in case they, in a given variant, provide the more authoritative reading.

Greg probably ought to have explained his decision to use the word 'accidentals' to describe features of writing such as spelling, punctuation, paragraphing and so on (all but the words chosen), for it was bound to attract criticism. Such things are not accidents in the usual sense, and I. A. Shapiro's suggested substitution of 'incidentals' has since caught on (Shapiro 1978). This question of terminology is separate from the highly germane objection that there is no sharp distinction at work here, since punctuation (supposedly accidental) affects meaning as surely as does the choice of words (supposedly substantive). Looking at this from a practical point of view, however, it is clear that Greg was distinguishing between those things that an early modern compositor would feel himself entitled to alter (which would include the author's spelling and punctuation) and those he would not (the choice of words). Although he did not announce the fact, Greg used the word accidental in the sense that Aristotle used throughout his *Metaphysics* to distinguish the attributes that are essential to a phenomenon from those that are not. All the early modern dramatists could read and write, and it would be fair to say that because of the prevailing technological conditions those skills were essential to the work. It is undoubtedly the case that they also all wore shoes, but that is just an incidental fact (an accident, as Aristotle called it) not essential to being a dramatist. Greg assumed that his readers would recognize that he had borrowed Aristotle's terminology, and did not want to have to defend the logical rigour of its application: 'The distinction I am trying to draw is practical, not philosophic' (Greg 1950–1, 24 n.1).

That spellings are accidental is generally accepted, since unless one distinguishes between the unembodied meanings of words (their essences) and their embodiment in particular writing with particular spellings, there can be no hope of modernizing the spelling of classic books; nor indeed could they be translated into other languages. This presents a limit to what in the 1980s became understood as the materialist approach, a view that classic books exist only in their embodied forms as documents. This development is taken up in Chapter 6 below. It is sometimes thought that 'The Rationale of Copy-Text' was Greg's first airing of his accidental/substantive distinction, but the terminology was active when he first discussed the problem of authority being split between two documents, in *The Editorial Problem in Shakespeare* (Greg 1942, xiii). The problem now loomed large in Greg's thinking, and he decided that an editor who refuses to distinguish the authority of accidentals from the authority of substantives shows 'undue deference to the copy-text' and is 'abdicating his editorial function' (Greg 1950–1, 28). What such editors produce are 'not editions of their authors' works at all, but only editions of particular authorities for those works' (Greg 1950–1, 29). Greg invoked an idealist distinction between the work and a particular material embodiment of it that goes to the heart of the debates that structure this book.

Having argued that an editor might use one document as copy-text (because it is the best authority for accidentals) but draw substantive readings from another document, Greg dealt with the problems arising from such a synthesis. Logical consistency required that when importing a reading from outside the copy-text it should nonetheless appear in the form it would have taken had it appeared in the copy-text. Thus if one overruled one's copy-text reading of, say, *hazard* in favour of the reading *venture* from another document, and if *venture* were habitually spelled *venter* elsewhere in the copy-text, then *venter* is the right form to use even though none of the authorities has it (Greg 1950–1, 30). Where one's choice is between two readings that are exactly balanced in apparent authority, Greg had previously argued (1942, xxix) that the copy-text should be preferred simply because it had been chosen for its generally greater authority. However, the new rationale required choosing the copy-text for its authority in the matter of accidentals alone, so its ability to break a deadlock in substantive readings is lost. Greg's binarily disposed mind had entirely split the notion of authority into two kinds that might in principle repose in each of two different documents. Fortunately the split is seldom absolute and usually when selecting one's copy-text 'the choice will be the same whichever rule we adopt', that is, whether using the rule of McKerrow (and of Greg in *The Editorial Problem in Shakespeare*) that looks for correctness of wording, or Greg's new rule that selects the copy-text solely because its accidentals are closest to – or perhaps we should say least distant from, since there is little chance of getting close in absolute terms – the authorial habits (Greg 1950–1, 31 n.18).

In the tricky matter of authorial revision being present in reprints, Greg argued that no single rule regarding copy-text could suffice because the means by which revision can be effected are highly varied and they produce individually distinct problems in each case (Greg 1950–1, 34–5). Where the Folio edition of a Shakespeare play has clearly been set from a preceding quarto that was first annotated by reference to an authoritative manuscript – as Greg believed happened with *King Lear* and *Richard 3* – the Folio is derivative, not substantive, and yet is the better copy-text for two reasons. The first is that such a process of alteration makes it 'an almost impossible task to distinguish between variation due to the corrector', the person annotating the quarto, 'and that due to the compositor' printing it. To incorporate the revisions one must use the Folio as copy-text, and this alone would be reason enough even were it not the case that for these plays – and this is the second reason – 'the quartos contain only reported texts' whose accidentals therefore have no authority, whereas the Folio texts have in parts a transcriptional connection with the author's manuscript (Greg 1950–1, 35).

The whole subject of reported and memorially reconstructed versions of plays is treated in the Intermezzo below. Although he here called *King Lear* and *Richard 3* 'reported texts', Greg did not simply follow Leo Kirschbaum (1938, 21–9), who had inflated A. W. Pollard's original group of five Shakespearian bad quartos – *Romeo and Juliet* (1597), *Henry 5* (1600), *The Merry Wives of Windsor* (1602), *Hamlet* (1603) and *Pericles* (1609) – to nine by including the first printings of *The Contention of York and Lancaster* (1594),

Richard Duke of York (1595), *King Lear* (1608) and *Richard 3* (1597). Rather, in *The Editorial Problem in Shakespeare*, Greg rejected a binate distinction and created a new category of doubtful quartos specifically to encompass *King Lear* and *Richard 3* (Greg 1942, 77–101).

Greg's essay 'The Rationale of Copy-Text' appeared in Fredson Bowers's new journal *Studies in Bibliography*, and immediately after it Bowers printed an essay of his own ending with the memorable claim that bibliography undertakes 'to pierce this veil of the printing process' to see the manuscript underneath (Bowers 1950–1, 62); later he rephrased this to 'strip the veil of print from a text' (Bowers 1955b, 87). Bowers's metaphor has attracted criticism for eroticizing bibliography, and even for encouraging editors to see themselves as rapists: 'the intellectual inquirer is empowered to ravish the object, violently tearing aside its protective covering to render the female body naked to the male observer's gaze, answerable to the male desire' (Holderness, Loughrey and Murphy 1995, 97). In an essay highly tuned to the erotic overtones of New Bibliography, Jeffrey Masten quoted Alice Walker using the veil metaphor too (Masten 1997a, 103 n.40; Walker 1955b, 9), without condemning it as a sexual fantasy.

Although he used similar language of concealment, Greg was less confident than Bowers about the chances of seeing the manuscripts behind the early printings when in his last book on the subject, *The Shakespeare First Folio*, he returned to the problem. Greg warned that the reader was entering 'a misty mid region of Weir' in which there could be nothing but 'tentative and proximate conclusions' (Greg 1955, 105). He had not abandoned the caution with which he ended *The Editorial Problem in Shakespeare*, and yet Greg was more willing than ever to codify the features to look for when trying to determine the nature of a printer's copy. Greg had become somewhat more confident that Hand D of *Sir Thomas More*, the fragment of *The Massacre at Paris* and *The Captives* might be extant foul papers (Greg 1955, 108), but little could be built on those because the first two are short extracts and the last could easily be (as Greg formerly believed) a prompt-book. Greg had to fall back on inference: 'In general, and *a priori*, we should expect an author's foul papers to show quite a lot of deletion, alteration, interlining, false starts, and the like, and the thoroughness and clearness with which corrections were made would be likely to vary much with the care and patience of the writer' (Greg 1955, 110).

Although there was little direct documentary evidence to support Greg's view that foul papers would be untidy, the claim made intuitive sense and Greg could illustrate it from print editions that seemed to show their underlying authorial papers:

One of the most interesting texts in this respect is the 'good' quarto of *Romeo and Juliet* of 1599. From this it appears that the first four lines of the Friar's opening speech of II.iii were first written as part of Romeo's speech at the end of the preceding scene, for they are printed in both positions. Again, in Romeo's soliloquy at the tomb, the four lines

> Depart againe, come lye though in my arme,
> Heer's to thy health, where ere thou tumblest in.
> O true Appothecarie!
> Thy drugs are quicke. Thus with a kisse I die

are plainly a not very happy first draft of the ensuing thirteen lines (V.iii.108–20). (Greg 1955, 110)

Thus Q2 *Romeo and Juliet* was printed from authorial papers in which we can see the dramatic mind in the heat of composition, with false starts and reconsiderations not tidied up. Greg went on:

Another possible mark of foul papers is the appearance of 'ghost' characters. At the beginning of a scene an author will sometimes write down a list of characters he is likely to require, but when it comes to the point he may not provide speeches for them all. Or he may find that he does not need a character till later, and may provide a separate entrance for him while still leaving his name standing at the head of a scene. If the dumb characters have parts elsewhere and are minor members of a group, this does not matter much, though it is theatrically extravagant and may prove dramatically clumsy. If, on the other hand, they appear nowhere else, or are inappropriate to the scene as developed, or are too important to be allowed to appear as supers, the book-keeper is likely to eliminate them from the prompt-copy. (Greg 1955, 112)

The clearest ghost appears in the 1600 quarto of *Much Ado About Nothing*, the first two acts of which begin with entrance directions including Leonato's wife Innogen who is otherwise absent from the play (Shakespeare 1600c, A2^r, B3^r).

Greg next considered the related problem of actors' names appearing where we should expect characters' names. Greg could see 'two ways in which actors' names may find their way into dramatic manuscripts and so occasionally into print' (Greg 1955, 120), from the author or the book-keeper. The questions to be asked are who would need to remind themselves and of what. The dramatist would only mention an actor if his particular skills or physique were required for the scene, and he would not normally mention minor actors (hired men) because their identities would not be known during composition; only the lead actors of the company (the sharers) would definitely be in the performance. On the other hand, the holder of the prompt-book is likely to be concerned with the casting of small roles that might easily be forgotten:

> When the book-keeper introduces actors' names into a manuscript it is as glosses upon the names of characters or the description of supers; he wishes to remind himself of the particular actor he has to be on the look-out for, and his addition usually leads to duplication. As a rule, but not invariably, it is only actors of minor parts that are noted. (Greg 1955, 117)

To help himself organize the movement of bodies backstage, the book-keeper might have made an additional note beside a character name to remind himself who was taking that part; hence duplication (character name and actor name) would be typical of a theatrical manuscript. Greg was able to cite forty examples: nine from John Fletcher and Philip Massinger's *Sir John van Olden Barnavelt* (British Library Additional 18653), eight from Massinger's *Believe as You List*, seven from the anonymous *The Two Noble Ladies* (British Library Egerton 1994), four from Heywood's *The Captives*, three from the anonymous *Thomas of Woodstock* (British Library Egerton 1994), two from Fletcher's *The Honest Man's Fortune* (Victoria and Albert Museum Manuscript Dyce 9), five from the anonymous *Edmond Ironside* (British Library Egerton 1994) and two from Robert Greene's *John of Bordeaux* (Alnwick Castle Manuscript 507) (Greg 1955, 118).

Pollard's idea (pp. 19–20 above) that a dramatist's stage directions would be phrased differently from a prompter's – the former using a literary and descriptive style, the latter a practical and prescriptive one – Greg found unconvincing: 'This *a priori* distinction is only partly borne out by examination of the manuscripts and may on occasion prove misleading' (Greg 1955, 121). Generally, plays were written by professional men of the theatre so they would use the same industry terminology as the prompter, and hence 'there is hardly a stage-direction that has been cited as characteristic of the prompter that cannot be paralleled from texts for which the author was probably alone responsible' (Greg 1955, 123). But dramatists could write stage directions that were of interest to themselves alone and of no use to anyone else, and others that have a literary quality because, as Greg pointed out (1955, 124, 167), dramatists read their plays to actors by way of sales pitch. Greg cited a number of stage directions in manuscripts and print editions that give, by way of explanation, background information on characters and their relations, such as '*enter ... Ventigius which Timon redeemed from prison*' (*Timon of Athens*, 1.2.0), and others that indicate disguises, properties required, business to be enacted once onstage, characters' demeanour and expression, sound effects and geographical location

(Greg 1955, 124–32). 'Not all these directions were necessarily written by the author', Greg wrote, yet 'there is no doubt that the great majority were, and they follow a common pattern' (Greg 1955, 132).

Whatever stage directions a dramatist wrote would probably, in Greg's view, remain in the prompt-book because 'So long as they do not actually interfere with the use of the book, the book-keeper lets them alone' (Greg 1955, 132). Not only do authorial stage directions get into the prompt-book, but also dramatists use the professional terminology of the book-keeper, so 'the great mass of stage-directions are of very little assistance in distinguishing between foul papers and prompt-copy' (Greg 1955, 134–5). Were there no kinds of stage direction that might betray their origin? Greg thought there were:

> An author shows his hand most clearly in indefinite directions and in what may be called permissive or petitory directions, neither of which could originate with or commend themselves to the book-keeper. One form of vagueness shows itself in the mention of unspecified groups: *John a Kent*, 334 'Enter Turnop wth his crewe of Clownes', 554 'Enter Turnop [and others] wth their Consort', 581 'the Bridegroomes come foorth', 648 ... (Greg 1955, 135)

A book-keeper responsible for staging a play would not think up these unspecific stage directions (how many is a crew?), but the crucial question is whether he would retain them in the book used to run the play. Greg admitted that he usually would:

> Where groups have been previously defined or are obvious from the action, such indefinite directions are, of course, sufficient. In other cases the exact composition of the groups would doubtless be settled in production and presumably noted in the 'plot', as all 'attendants' must have been; anyhow, the book-keeper very seldom interfered with them. (Greg 1955, 135)

What looked like a possible means for determining the printer's copy for an early edition by its indefinite stage directions was offered by Greg only to be retracted again, because if the book-keeper made a note anywhere of the numbers of actors needed for such a direction it would not be in the prompt-book but in the playhouse plot. These plots are summaries of the action of a play and six such documents are extant, with a seventh recorded in an eighteenth-century transcription. Their precise function is unclear: Greg thought they hung backstage as a reminder of who was to go on in which scene and what properties or effects were needed, but they might mainly have been used in casting a play (Greg 1931, 1–4; Bradley 1992).

Even more puzzling to Greg than the book-keeper's tolerance of loose phrasing was his acceptance of an author's hazily indicated numbers: '*More,*

453 "Enter [t]hree or foure Prentices of trades"; *Launching*, 1216 "Enter Lo. Ad: wth.2. or.3. attendantes"' (Greg 1955, 135–6). Another kind of vagueness found in authorial stage directions concerns the means by which an effect or action was to be realized, including such examples as: '*John a Kent*, 836 "The fourth [*sc.* Antique] out of a tree, if possible it may be" ... *Captives* ... 2432 "Eather strykes him wth a staffe or Casts a stone" ... *Launching*, 1154, "where yt must be the least man wth a long beard"' (Greg 1955, 136). Here again, the trouble is that these things apparently were tolerated in theatrical documents: 'It is little use arguing that indefinite and optional directions must have been cleared up in the prompt-book when we have reason to suppose that in fact they were often left standing' (Greg 1955, 137). In short, Greg believed that there were no kinds of stage direction whose imprecision could be used to argue authorial rather than theatrical provenance.

What about arguing the matter the other way and looking for 'directions that can only have been introduced by the book-keeper'? Greg evasively commented that 'It has usually been held that one characteristic of the book-keeper is that he tends to mark entries a few lines earlier than required by the text' and yet 'The evidence is rather conflicting' (Greg 1955, 138). Greg repeated his view given in *Dramatic Documents from the Elizabethan Playhouses* that although it is 'on the whole likely that the persistent placing of directions a few lines too early does indicate the use of prompt-copy' this should not be heavily relied upon ('the inference may not be a very strong one') because the practice is so sporadic (Greg 1955, 139). Only one kind of stage direction remained, and it provides 'perhaps the best evidence of all of the intervention of the book-keeper' (Greg 1955, 139): the warning for an actor or a property to be made ready before he or it was needed. Greg listed eight examples from Massinger's *Believe as You List*, including 'Gascoine: & Hubert below: ready to open the Trap doore for Mr Taylor', 'Harry::Willson: & Boy ready for the song at ye Arras' and 'All the swords ready', none of which could conceivably be written by the dramatist in the heat of composition. The argument was clinched (Greg 1955, 139–40) by a further five examples from Thomas Dekker's *The Welsh Ambassador* (Cardiff Central Library Manuscript 4.12), mostly of the kind 'bee redy ...' followed by a character's name, five from Henry Glapthorne's *The Lady Mother* that connect by a line the entrance direction and a point (the readying moment) between twelve and twenty lines earlier, five from the anonymous *Thomas of Woodstock* (that have since been read an entirely different way by William B. Long, pp. 155–8 below) and one from the anonymous *Dick of Devonshire* (British Library Egerton 1994).

Yet here too Greg remained cautious and insisted that 'even warnings are no infallible criterion of prompt-copy' (Greg 1955, 141) because of seven examples, including 'Fellowes ready' and 'Ink: paper ready', in, of all places, the manuscript of Heywood's *The Captives* that he had reclassified as foul papers not prompt-book. These seven warnings are in the hand of the book-keeper, forming part of his layer of theatre-minded annotations, and since the manuscript holds the author's writing and the book-keeper's it necessarily belongs to – or 'swallows up', to use Paul Werstine's powerful phrasing (1997, 490) – both of Greg's primary categories of document. A way out of this dilemma was clear to Greg, but he would not take it. Pollard's theory of continuous copy (pp. 16–19 above), accepted also by John Dover Wilson in his New Shakespeare editions (Appendix 3 below), supposed that a single manuscript began as authorial papers and ended up as a prompt-book, and this could account for *The Captives*. In *The Editorial Problem in Shakespeare* Greg considered whether *Sir Thomas More* might fall into this category, and concluded that the whole theory was 'a figment of the editorial brain' (Greg 1942, 43), and yet he was also willing to acknowledge that the problem of explaining the provenance of the copy underlying Folio *1 Henry 6* is somewhat eased by accepting the theory (Greg 1942, 138–9). In his last book on the subject, Greg would not go so far and confined himself to thrusting the blame for the mistaken continuous copy theory onto Wilson's shoulders and suggesting that Pollard advocated it only when the two worked together (Greg 1955, 102–3). As we have seen (pp. 20–4 above), Pollard was in fact fully committed to the idea.

Greg followed his cautious and tentative descriptions of the features that characterize authorial and theatrical copy with a summary that included the qualifications and caveats:

Characteristic of foul papers are, first of all, loose ends and false starts and unresolved confusions in the text, which sometimes reveal themselves as duplications in print: next, inconsistency in the designations of characters in directions and prefixes alike, and occasionally the substitution of the name of an actor, when the part is written with a particular performer in view: lastly, the appearance of indefinite and permissive stage-directions, and occasionally of explanatory glosses on the text. It must, however, be recognized that owing to the casual ways of book-keepers these characteristics may persist, to some extent at least, in the prompt-book; but in general the ordering of the text seems to have received more attention than that of the directions, which was perhaps only natural. Characteristic of prompt-copy are the appearance of actors' names duplicating those of (usually minor) characters, possibly the general appearance of directions a few lines too early, and warnings for actors or properties to be in readiness. At the same time these features may be introduced by the book-keeper into foul papers if he annotates them with a view to transcription. The possibility may not be a very serious one, but it should none the less be borne in mind. It may be added, however, that whatever deductions have to be made from the weight of these criteria, the presence of any of them in a print argues a close dependence on a playhouse manuscript of some sort, which carries with it a high degree of authority. (Greg 1955, 142)

The danger of Greg's rhetoric here should be apparent. Even though he included the qualifications and caveats that emerged along the way, this checklist of features belonging to each class of document is ripe to be exploited by editors looking for simple rules. This is precisely how it was used (Appendix 3 gives examples), which practice was rightly criticized by the New Textualism (pp. 162–6 below).

Before leaving the subject of distinguishing foul papers from prompt-book copy, Greg considered the possibility that an author's peculiar spelling preferences might help to identify the nature of an underlying manuscript, as with Shakespeare's *scilens* (for *silence*) witnessed in Hand D of *Sir Thomas More* and – sixteen times, not eighteen as Greg, following Wilson, had it (Greg 1955, 148; Pollard *et al.* 1923, 129) – found in the quarto of *2 Henry 4* (Shakespeare 1600a, F2^r, F3^r, K1^v–K3^r). Isolated examples should not count for much, Greg concluded, but if one found 'any considerable number of eccentric or archaic spellings in a print' this would add weight to a claim that it was printed from authorial papers and not a scribal copy of them, where we should not expect many such oddities to survive. Evidence from the presence or absence of oaths, and their relation to the 1606 Act of censorship, was, Greg thought, bound to be inconclusive since the legislation affected only performance, not printing, and in any case we do not know 'how far the provisions of the Act were enforced' (Greg 1955, 149–50).

The binary-mindedness of Greg is often commented upon – we shall see the New Textualists complaining of it at length (pp. 153–66 below) – and yet we have found him insisting on intermediate categories such as doubtful (rather than good or bad) quartos and hedging his descriptions with qualifications and caveats. However, he was binary-minded in as much as he denied the possibility either that a single manuscript served all purposes (the continuous copy theory) or that there were usually more than two manuscripts of any play. Before publication of Greg's *The Shakespeare First Folio* Alice Walker let him see proofs of her forthcoming book *Textual Problems of the First Folio* (1953), which explored the degree to which quartos used as copy for the 1623 Folio were first improved by comparison with authoritative manuscripts (Greg 1955, vi). Where this would require the hypothesizing of a manuscript in addition to the authorial foul papers and the prompt-book, Greg strenuously, in the teeth of private protests from Fredson Bowers, denied the existence of such documents (Greg 1955, 142, 168, 370). Of the claim that plays circulated widely in private transcripts made for patrons and aficionados Greg was sceptical: 'Since publication was contrary to the general policy of the King's men they are not very likely to have favoured' such circulation, although they might have relaxed after 1619, and noticeably all extant transcripts are later than this (Greg 1955, 153). That a third kind of manuscript might creep into the equation by the reassembly of actors' parts to make a full script Greg denied as inherently unlikely: it would be worth doing only if the foul papers and prompt-book were destroyed, and whatever destroyed them (such as a playhouse fire, as befell the Fortune in 1621) would probably destroy the parts too (Greg 1955, 157).

Rather than accept that additional copies might serve useful purposes in the textual economy of the theatre, Greg insisted that anything beyond two copies – authorial papers and prompt-book – would have been 'extremely uneconomical' (Greg 1955, 467). Perhaps only unconsciously, two was the magic number because of the logical manoeuvre it enabled. As soon as one has excluded the possibility that the copy underlying an early edition belongs in one of the two possible classes (by showing that the edition lacks the stigmata, as Greg liked to call them, of that class) one has instantly proved that it belongs to the other class. By clearing away other, complicating possibilities, Greg had implicitly set as a task for subsequent Shakespearian editors the binate determination of the underlying copy for the early editions on which theirs were to be founded, and many of them used his checklist without regard for the qualifications in it.

FREDSON BOWERS, *STUDIES IN BIBLIOGRAPHY* (1948–) AND *ON EDITING SHAKESPEARE AND THE ELIZABETHAN DRAMATISTS* (1955)

In 1940, when R. B. McKerrow died, the United States had not yet joined the European war. At a conference of the English Institute at Columbia University in September 1941 Fredson Bowers and his research student Charlton Hinman presented papers that initiated a westward shift in the centre of gravity in Shakespearian bibliographical studies, from England to America (Bowers 1942; Hinman 1942a). The two men served together in military cryptanalysis from 1942 to 1945 (Tanselle 1993, 29–34) and after the interruption caused by the war their work rapidly established an entirely new approach to bibliography. The Bibliographical Society of the University of Virginia began to publish its annual volume of papers in 1948, edited from the start by its vice-president Bowers and renamed *Studies in Bibliography* for its second volume. One new strand of research built upon a little-regarded letter to the *Times Literary Supplement* in which Thomas Satchell had pointed out that the variations in spellings of certain words in the Folio text of *Macbeth* follow a distinct pattern (Satchell 1920). For each of thirty-five words, one half of the play consistently uses one spelling, labelled A by Satchell, and the other half consistently uses an alternative spelling, labelled B by Satchell. Either the underlying copy was written by two scribes, each using his own spelling preferences that the compositor slavishly followed, or there were two compositors, each imposing his own spelling preferences when setting type.

Edwin Eliott Willoughby applied spelling tests to other plays in the Folio, focussing on 'five especially significant words' from Satchell's list and adding a sixth of his own (Willoughby 1932, 56–7). Willoughby eliminated the possibility that the contrast arose from variations in copy by showing that it is absent in the *Richard 2* quarto from which the Folio text was printed, a conclusion that stands even though Richard E. Hasker (1952–3) subsequently demonstrated that the situation was somewhat more complex than Willoughby thought and Folio *Richard 2* derives from a combination of Q3 (1598) and Q5 (1615). With the sophistications introduced by Hinman (1940–1), identification of compositors by their preferred spellings became a widespread activity of bibliographers, and one for which an independent check existed in cases where they were setting not from lost manuscripts but from extant early editions. In such cases the compositors' personal preferences might well be somewhat suppressed – their sense of professional duty being diminished by the copy having already been through a printshop – but the evidence is of the highest quality because we can directly compare copy with result. Such analyses filled the pages of *Studies in Bibliography* in its first decade, and although a number of them were by British scholars the cutting-edge work, exploiting technical resources, was American.

Looking at plays printed in Nicholas Okes's shop in 1609 and 1612, Philip Williams reckoned he could identify the spelling habits of two compositors, one of whose habits are also apparent in Q1 *King Lear* (1608): 'the absence of the apostrophe in *Ile* forms, the frequent spellings in final *ie*, and the preponderance of *doe* spellings' (Philip Williams 1948–9, 68). Toning down Bowers's metaphor, Williams saw the value of this kind of research as removing 'the varnish' of printing to reveal 'the grain of the underlying manuscripts ... in its true color' (Philip Williams 1956, 11). Using a group of spellings – *deare / dear, does / doe's / do's, beene / bene / bin, deuil / diuel, sirra(h) / sirrha / sirra, houre / hower /*

howre, *vilde* / *vile*, *power* / *powre*, *breefe* / *briefe*, *yong* / *young* and *blood* / *bloud* – I. B. Cauthen Junior thought he could show that Folio *King Lear* consistently follows the habits of Satchell's compositor B, who therefore set the play (Cauthen Junior 1952–3).

Alice Walker used the same technique to work out the parts of Folio *1 Henry 4* set by compositors A and B, and since they were essentially reprinting Q6 (1613), she was able to compare their copy with their setting and so deduce how accurate their work was; she concluded that compositor B was careless and hence editors should be more than usually keen to emend what seem like errors in his parts of other plays (Walker 1954). She repeated the analysis for the two compositors, X and Y, working in James Roberts's shop whom John Russell Brown showed (1955) had set Q1 *The Merchant of Venice* (1600) and Q2 *Hamlet* (1604–5). We do not have the printer's copy for these editions, so Walker approximated the accuracy of the compositors' stints by observing how often modern editors feel the need to emend what each of them set, assuming that across the copy the rate of error was uniform and hence any differences arise from their differing attention to detail. Roberts's compositor Y emerged the better workman, but when rushed both could be quite inaccurate (Walker 1955a). Hinman had begun to argue that the Folio (and by inference early books generally) were not thoroughly proofread, so the upshot for editors of the new compositor studies was clear: there should be more editorial intervention than hitherto practised, especially where the compositor of one's copy-text is known to have been careless, and it should be done in the light of knowledge of the compositor's characteristic slips (Walker 1956).

Roberts's compositors X and Y were examined again in Paul L. Cantrell and George Walton Williams's study of their behaviour in setting Q2 *Titus Andronicus* (1600) using Q1 (1594) as their copy. From their characteristic spellings determined by Brown, plus other habits (such as how carefully they centred stage directions), Cantrell and Williams (1956) determined their stints in Q2 *Titus Andronicus*. From the same kinds of evidence they determined that Q2 *Romeo and Juliet* (1599) was set by two compositors with distinct habits (Cantrell and Williams 1957). Walker (1951) had shown that Q2 *Hamlet* (1604–5) was set, at least in part (most obviously the first act), from Q1 *Hamlet* (1603), and Bowers applied this evidence to the problem, revealed by Brown's division of the compositor stints, that Roberts's compositor X alone set sheets B, C and D of Q2 *Hamlet* where normally we would expect X and Y to take alternate sheets (Bowers 1956). If the printshop had just one exemplar of Q1 (extensively marked up from an authoritative manuscript) then X and Y's being unable to share it would explain the mystery, but that would imply that rather than just occasionally consulting Q1 (and sharing it) the exemplar formed compositor X's primary copy; this Bowers thought he could disprove. Using the new catalogue of Roberts's compositor X's spelling habits (compiled by Brown and by Cantrell and Williams), Bowers argued that where he set against his preferred form (say, *eies* or *saies*) even though Q1 had his preferred form (*eyes* or *sayes*) he must have been setting from something other than Q1, presumably manuscript copy that he followed closely.

As should be clear from this survey of it, the new work on compositor identification emerged rapidly and was dauntingly technical. Because hypotheses were built upon hypotheses – using logic of the kind 'if a compositor did this here, he could not have done that there' – the whole edifice was vulnerable at its foundations. The growing excitement in these articles is nonetheless palpable. A case in point is Hinman's announcement of a third Folio compositor, E, to add to Satchell and Willoughby's A and B – slots C and D were reserved for later discoveries already half-suspected – which began with a celebration of the 'almost absolute certainty' of the new methods (Hinman 1957, 3). Tracking of distinctively damaged pieces of type showed that each Folio quire was set in turn starting at the inside, the forme $3^v:4^r$, and working outwards to forme $1^r:6^v$, and combined with knowledge of compositors A and B's distinctive habits Hinman began a detailed narrative of their progress through the book that culminated in a monumental study (1963a; 1963b). Compositor E emerged when it became obvious that certain pages show neither A's nor B's habits and have errors (and proof corrections) suggestive of an apprentice standing in when A and/or B were required elsewhere, and that this man was trusted with setting only from easy-to-read printed copy, as befits an apprentice.

It should have been obvious that although finding a new compositor seemed like progress it also threatened to undermine the fragile foundations of the whole subject, since Folio pages that were previously attributed to A or B (and from which habits were inferred) were now attributed to E, so confidence in the earlier attributions must have been misplaced. This was pointed out (Foakes 1958, 56–7 n.5), but caution was not the prevailing spirit in the new discipline. Ironically, the scholar who in the late 1960s was to provide a critique that brought down the entire edifice was, in the late 1950s, busily adding to it. Since Folio compositor B (about whom much was known) worked in the printshop of William Jaggard, his habits might be detectable in other Jaggard books from the period. Jaggard's printshop produced Q2 *The Merchant of Venice* (1619) from Q1 (1600), and by comparing them D. F. McKenzie found that

Walker was right: Jaggard/Folio compositor B was careless in his work (McKenzie 1959a).

To show what such knowledge of compositors' habits can do for an editor pondering an emendation, a single illustration from Walker may suffice. In Q2 *Romeo and Juliet* (1599), Juliet says that to avoid marrying Paris she would brave a night in a charnel house among 'yealow chapels sculls' (Shakespeare 1599, 13^r). Juliet means *chapless* skulls, ones without lips, but is the Q2 reading merely an error of transposition, *chapels* for *chaples*? Walker pointed out that it could not be since the compositor consistently used *-lesse* spellings in setting this edition, so if he meant to set the word *chapless* Q2 would read *chaplesse* not *chaples* (Walker 1955b, 9–10). Thus the compositor must intentionally have set *chapels*, which shows that his copy did not have one of the long forms (*chapless* or *chaplesse*) but rather something that the compositor mistook for *chapels*. Thus we get a glimpse at the spelling of the manuscript underneath the printing of Q2.

The height of optimism to which these new spelling studies brought theorists of editing can be gauged from Bowers's prediction, made at the end of the first decade of *Studies in Bibliography*:

> the bibliographical editor of the future will collect his evidence only from the pages of these texts set by the compositors in question. Moreover, these identified workmen set other plays, and their characteristics elsewhere become a part of the total evidence that will assist an editor to balance the compositors' observed treatment of the printer's copy in the play under consideration against their observed characteristics in setting other copy. Under such controlled conditions compositor-analysis may be used not only to provide an estimate as to the nature of the printer's copy, and thus to add to our general knowledge about the transmission of a text; it may be used also to apply to specific problems of transmission as represented in the question whether specific readings faithfully transmit the underlying copy. (Bowers 1959, 111)

Bowers was fond of calling this kind of work 'controlled' – the word recurs in his writing (1950–1, 58; 1975, 45) – and for him the rigour of the procedures made up for an inherent uncertainty in the material, for unlike W. W. Greg (who believed in essentially just two kinds of manuscript) Bowers held that the printers often set from scribal copies, of which there could be many for one play, and hence revealing the manuscript would not bring an editor directly into the presence of Shakespeare (Bowers 1959, 113–14).

One kind of procedural error to be avoided if the research was indeed to be properly 'controlled' was identified early on by Hinman:

'Justifying' causes variants, especially in prose and in long lines of verse in narrow columns. It probably causes variants also in lines of verse which are considerably longer than the lines immediately preceding and following, even though the long lines do not reach the margin. (Hinman 1940–1, 79 n.1)

Because a compositor might change a spelling to help justify a full line, only spellings in short lines (where the space at the end of the line makes the expedient unnecessary) should be counted for compositor identification. This principle was widely ignored until T. H. Howard-Hill reminded everyone that in texts for which there is no extant copy 'all spellings occurring in any full line must be considered suspect' and pointed out that A. W. Pollard had said as much forty years before (Howard-Hill 1963, 9; Pollard 1923–4, 6). Howard-Hill also observed that Hinman's compositor identifications were made after the discarding of allegedly 'insignificant' (because inconsistent) spellings that could not be used to distinguish between two compositors. This elimination of data, Howard-Hill pointed out, is valid only if one already knows that there were just two compositors and not a third man whose habits are generating the inconsistency (Howard-Hill 1963, 7–8).

The safest procedure for identifying a compositor's habits is to confine oneself to reprint editions for which the copy is extant, as McKenzie did in showing that to judge from his actions when setting Q2 *The Merchant of Venice* (1619) from Q1 (1600), Jaggard's compositor B tended to increase the pointing of his copy, especially by adding commas and most often at the ends of verse lines (McKenzie 1959b). If this man was also compositor B of the Folio (a qualification McKenzie neglected to make), this explains the unwanted commas in his stints on it. To be properly cautious, compositor hunters should have considered even spellings in short lines to be suspect. Greg had observed that when setting a text of mixed verse and prose a compositor might employ two composing sticks of different widths, a short one for the verse and a long for the prose, and that the bother of changing over for a short passage of prose within verse might encourage the compositor to reline the prose as verse (Greg 1936–7, 181–3). If only one stick were employed, the compositor would have to fill out the remainder of every verse line with many quadrat spaces, which would be time consuming and place a burden on his stock of spaces; for extended runs of verse it might be simpler to switch to a short stick and take up the space with furniture when the type was imposed in the chase. A corollary of this practice is that long verse lines might have filled the short stick being used, as George Walton Williams observed (1949–50), and hence spelling might be altered to make the line fit.

Through the 1940s and 1950s the stock of exciting new means to accrue bibliographical evidence grew so rapidly that incaution should perhaps be considered venial. Bowers offered a new way to detect a change of compositor by the slight change in an edition's measure caused by the two men having slightly differently spaced composing sticks (Bowers 1949–50), and Williams noticed that one can tell from certain type substitutions such as *vv* for *w* or roman letters for italic the order in which pages were set (George Walton Williams 1958). Where substitution is caused by shortage of type, we can assume that the correct settings were made before the supply ran out and then the substitutions were resorted to. In any quarto sheet set seriatim (that is, in reading order: 1^r, 1^v, 2^r, 2^v and so on) the substitutions, if any, ought to occur on pages near the end (thus 4^r and 4^v), but Williams found quartos in which the substitutions occur on pages (such as 1^r and 3^r) that are early when viewed in reading order. This makes sense only if compositors were setting by formes, meaning that instead of setting the pages in reading order they first set all the pages needed for one forme (say 1^v, 2^r, 3^v and 4^r, in any order, to complete the inner forme) and then set all the pages of the other (so 1^r, 2^v, 3^r and 4^v, in any order, to complete the outer forme). Only that way might 1^r and 3^r be among the last pages set and hence the places where substitution was resorted to.

Aside from championing compositor identification and analysis, a distinctive methodological innovation of the Virginian school – that is, the American branch of New Bibliography with Bowers and Hinman in the vanguard – was announced in two early articles in which Bowers considered those parts of a printed book that do not change from page to page such as running titles and rules that form boxes around the text columns in the Folio (Bowers 1938–9; 1942). A so-called skeleton containing this matter would be carefully placed around the type pages during imposition, and Bowers observed that slight differences between running titles show that typically two such skeletons were used alternately during a printing run. The reason was efficiency: instead of holding up printing while the skeleton was stripped from a forme just removed from the press and rebuilt around the two or four pages needed for the next forme, use of a second skeleton enabled the compositor to impose the next forme while the pressmen were still machining its predecessor. At least, it would if the compositors were keeping ahead of the pressmen in their work. If the press had to stop anyway while the compositors finished setting the type for the next forme then the advantage of a second skeleton disappears. Bowers thought he could show that the need to keep up with the pressmen often put compositors under a strain that was manifested in their rates of error.

The two-skeleton system made it possible to proof-correct printed sheets in an efficient way too, and Bowers rejected Greg's account of proof correction because it required three skeletons (Greg 1940, 40–57; Bowers 1947–8; 1948, 585–6). Greg's account arose from a consideration of the press variants in the twelve surviving exemplars of Q1 *King Lear* (1608), and in particular the curious fact that no sheet has press variants on both sides: if one side has variants the other is, across all twelve exemplars, invariant. Greg thought he could account for this by proof correction happening in the following manner. The first of the two formes for the sheet was placed on the press, one proof impression taken, and the forme immediately removed and the second forme placed on the press, a proof impression taken, and then machining of that second forme continued. (Because the two formes of a sheet, inner and outer, had to be ready at almost the same time, the compositors had to make a third skeleton to keep ahead of the pressmen.) The proofreader marked the corrections required in the first forme on the proof impression and passed it to a compositor for adjustment to the type, and while this adjustment was taking place the proofreader marked the corrections to the second forme on its proof impression. As soon as the corrected first forme was ready, it was returned to the press to perfect (impress the second side of) the sheets already printed and the remaining white paper (the entirely blank sheets), during which time the second forme of type was corrected. When machining of the first forme was completed the (by now corrected) second forme was put on the press and the remaining sheets perfected. The result is that the first forme is invariant and corrected (since only the discarded proof impression shows its uncorrected state) and the second forme is variant, some exemplars showing the uncorrected and some the corrected state. The significance for editors is clear: the discovery of a variant forme (of which the editor must determine the uncorrected and corrected states) has the compensatory benefit of proving that the other side of the sheet has been proof corrected, no matter how few exemplars are available to be examined.

Bowers was able to show from the reuse of headlines in Q1 *King Lear* that if Greg's account of proofing were correct then the press was stopped unnecessarily and the printers needlessly neglected a more efficient way of proofing, which he outlined. According to Bowers, the process started with the first forme on the press having its first impression sent to the proofreader but machining continuing while this proof impression was marked up for corrections. When this marking was complete, the first forme was removed for correction and the second forme placed on the press and a single proof impression taken and given to the proofreader. (Because the second forme did not have to be ready at the same time as the first – as Greg's method required – only two skeletons were needed for the compositors to keep ahead of the pressmen.) Ideally, the adjustments to the type in the first forme could be made in the time taken for the second forme to be fixed in the press, the press adjusted to print it (the process called make-ready), and the first impression taken, but if not the press was stopped. The corrected first forme was returned to the press and used to finish machining the white paper, while the second forme was corrected. When all the white paper had been impressed by the first forme, the corrected second forme was put on the press to perfect the sheets. The result of this method is that the first forme is variant (showing uncorrected and corrected states) and the second forme invariant.

As Bowers readily admitted, his proposed method of proofing was no more capable of being proven than Greg's, since apart from anything else the surviving twelve exemplars of Q1 *King Lear* are too small a sample. But Bowers's method was undeniably more efficient of the workmen's time, and if getting the book finished were their prime concern then the method he described was undoubtedly the best. (As we shall see (pp. 81–4), this assumption that printers wanted to get each book finished before turning to the next was a fatal flaw that vitiated much of Bowers's work, as was discovered in 1969 but never acknowledged by him.) Bowers was not the first to try to refine Greg's model of proofing. His protégé Hinman had also proposed a system that did away with the third skeleton and that would render one of the two formes almost entirely invariant and the other invariant (Hinman 1942a). Hinman went further than his mentor in trying to quantify how fast pressmen and compositors worked. The relative speed of these two teams in the printshop was crucial to the decision to use two or more skeletons, which was only worth doing if the composition was ahead of the presswork; if it was not, the press would be idle in any case and the compositors might as well use only one skeleton. The pressmen's speed was controlled by the size of the run, and Hinman calculated that for an average play quarto 1,200 exemplars was the crossover point. Below that, the press would be idle as the compositors raced to finish setting the type pages fast enough and one skeleton would do, but above 1,200 exemplars the compositors would have time on their hands while the sheets were being machined and might as well make up extra skeletons to speed their work. Thus counting the skeletons gives a guide to the size of the press run.

Edwin Wolf thought Hinman's improvement of Greg's procedure essentially correct, not least because Greg required the perfecting by the first forme of some few sheets already impressed by the second forme (done while the first was being corrected) and this surely risked transfer of still-wet ink (Wolf 1942). Since Hinman's system made both sides variant (to differing degrees), Wolf tried to work out the proportions of a print run that would show uncorrected and corrected states of each side, assuming that the heap of sheets was turned in one go for perfecting, and thus the uncorrected impressions at the beginning of the white-paper run were backed with the uncorrected impressions at the beginning of the perfecting run. Francis R. Johnson responded to Wolf by pointing out that the problem of ink transfer was illusory (Johnson 1946, 280–1), since R. C. Bald had already observed that the evidence from the earliest authority, Joseph Moxon's 1683 manual of printing *Mechanick Exercises*, contradicted McKerrow's *Introduction to Bibliography for Literary Students* and that in fact a sheet was not hung up to dry before being perfected and hence the inks normally in use were unlikely to transfer unless placed under great pressure (Moxon 1683, ss1^r, xx1^r–xx2^r; McKerrow 1927, 23; Bald 1942, 178–81). Johnson argued that with this impediment to Greg's model removed, it is the more likely procedure, especially when one considers the management of the various heaps of paper (white, half-done and perfected) that each system implies.

What was being decided in these articles was essentially the national character of future research on presswork, and Johnson's paper marks the tipping point in favour of the Americans, for despite supporting Greg on a point of detail Johnson saw Wolf and Hinman's modelling to be more advanced and declared that their refinements would be the basis for future research. The topic of proofing and heap management continued to exercise bibliographers, with Kenneth Povey detailing the tricky modelling of possibilities if all eventualities of heap-turning and differing rates of work are to be considered. Povey's tongue was doubtless in his cheek as he wrote: 'If the reader cares to draw all the thirty-five possible diagrams for combinations of formes ...' (Povey 1955, 45). What quickly became apparent was the great number of alternative practices that might upset the various calculations arising from Bowers's assumption that the printers proceeded as quickly and efficiently as possible to complete one book.

Wolf and Johnson had noticed that dinner breaks and overnight stops, or printers simply not pursuing tasks in a serial fashion, would throw off calculations of efficiency and the deductions that derive from them. Povey added another contingency arising because early modern paper was wetted with water before printing to improve its absorption of ink. A heap of paper that had dried out might need to be rewetted before perfecting and if done by handfuls this would disrupt the assumptions of bibliographers: 'Mathematical formulae lead to positive conclusions only if strict adherence to routine is postulated' (Povey 1955, 48). Thus, from its first foundations the Virginian-school bibliography was erected upon precarious assumptions about the regularity of labour practices. As we shall see, the edifice collapsed when irregularity was proven to be the norm.

In much of what he wrote about bibliography, Bowers dreamt of putting the subject on a firm methodological footing, raising it to the status of a real science, allowing it to progress towards 'the ideal of a definitive text' or an 'ideally definitive work' (Bowers 1950–1, 44, 62), the very thing McKerrow asserted could not exist (McKerrow 1939, 1). Bowers seems here to have meant by 'definitive' the best text that scholarship could achieve given the surviving materials, but elsewhere he retreated from such absoluteness. In an article that dismissed McKerrow's *Prolegomena for the Oxford Shakespeare* as essentially useless to an editor of early modern texts, Bowers asserted that 'the test of the establishment of a text is not wholly an objective factual one but partly subjective in that it rests ultimately on the reactions of the users' (Bowers 1955a, 315), which is precisely the point from which the *Prolegomena* sets out. Bowers thought that McKerrow's failing health and his inherent conservatism made him react excessively to John Dover Wilson's wilder theories that E. K. Chambers had publicly rejected (Chambers 1924–5, 102–6), that Greg gave only scattered and uncertain responses to (Greg 1942, 42, 139; 1955, 102–3), and that only Pollard seemed to accept.

In overreaction to Wilson, McKerrow cautioned that we can know virtually nothing about the manuscript copy underlying early Shakespeare editions, even though his own work (such as his 'Suggestion' about speech prefix variation, pp. 31–3 above) indicated otherwise. Bowers smelt a contradiction in McKerrow's conclusion that, because we cannot know enough about the underlying copy for early editions to pick and choose between their variant readings, the best thing is to reprint the most authoritative early edition save for its manifest errors. As Bowers pointed out, until one has done something to determine the underlying copy (at the very least determining whether it was a manuscript or an existing print edition) one cannot tell which is the most authoritative early edition (Bowers 1955a, 313).

Bowers addressed the vague way that McKerrow employed the idea of authorial final intentions. This might mean the play as Shakespeare finally wanted to give it to the actors to rehearse, or as he wanted it performed after being shaped in rehearsal, or even as he wanted the buying public to read it. McKerrow's rules for presenting the play as Shakespeare left it overlook the possibility that he never left it at all:

> what text ... are we to attempt to establish? The literary text before acting, or the acting version? Or in order not to lose from the main text of a modern standard edition one precious Shakespearian word, are we, as all editors have done, going to conflate the two texts [of *Hamlet*, *Othello*, *King Lear* or *Troilus and Cressida*] to produce some form which almost certainly never existed at any time as a unit and hence can bear no real relation to the author's hypothetical final intentions either for a literary or a dramatic text, and certainly is not going to resemble any form in which he left it, for whatever purpose? This is the text of *Hamlet* that we read, I am convinced. Are we not hypocrites when we avouch our undying devotion to Shakespeare's plays as 'theatre'? What editor would not prefer the literary, uncut version to the theatrically cut and shaped version, even if this latter could be shown to be Shakespearian? (Bowers 1955a, 318)

So long as editors were prepared to cut these philosophical Gordian knots, the outlook was bright: 'Much of what McKerrow thought to be unknowable, and subject only to speculation, is now coming within the range of evidence' (Bowers 1955a, 323). Bowers wanted editors to concentrate on making critical original-spelling editions that represented the best available knowledge about the early editions and their underlying manuscripts. There could be no halfway house between a diplomatic reprint and a critical edition, since as soon as one corrects any error the result cannot be called a diplomatic reprint; one might as well follow through and make a full critical edition, emending as necessary (Bowers 1955b, 74–5). Although the rules for a diplomatic reprint had not been codified, Bowers later offered the useful definition that it is 'an exact transcript of a document but the text run on without consideration for the original line and page endings', as distinct from a type facsimile, which gives 'a line-for-line and page-for-page reproduction of the original' (Bowers 1975, 32 n.1).

On Editing Shakespeare and the Elizabethan Dramatists (1955b) was Bowers's book-length statement of how the new thinking should affect editorial practice, and having dealt with McKerrow he marked his differences from Greg. Whereas Pollard had thought that the printer's copy for early editions was generally prompt-book (because in the continuous copy model there was just one, multi-use manuscript of the play), it was now – from the influence of Greg, itself deriving from McKerrow (1931–2) – generally assumed that the printer's copy was usually foul papers. This assumption Bowers wanted to revise, for Robert Daborne's letter to Philip Henslowe (pp. 16–17 above) indicates that he sent the foul sheet simply to prove that he had finished the composition and that only the fair copying remained to be done. Thus 'There is no evidence whatever here or elsewhere in Henslowe that an author ever submitted for payment anything but a fair copy, or that the company required a dramatist to turn over his original foul sheets along with the fair copy' (Bowers 1955b, 15). (However, as Greg pointed out – pp. 25–6 above – Edward Knight's use of Fletcher's foul papers to copy out *Bonduca* rather suggests that the company had them.) Thus for Bowers, if a printer got his copy from the company, it was probably fair copy (all they had) and if the printer got his copy from the dramatist, it was probably foul papers (all he had), and hence we cannot assume just because an edition was authorized by a company that its printer's copy was foul papers. Emendation should not, then, proceed boldly on the assumption that the printer's copy was hard to read and the resulting edition likely to be full of errors.

Much of what we might think are the distinguishing features of foul papers, such as the duplicated speeches in *Romeo and Juliet*, might well have stood also in Shakespeare's authorial fair copy and might 'show him revising lines while writing' in the course of copying out. (This insight will become important when developed further by E. A. J. Honigmann, pp. 69–72 below.) Even supposing that an author was allowed to hand over foul papers instead of fair copy, the company could have a scribe make more than one transcript, and one of these might end up with a printer. Bowers could think of at least eight different kinds of manuscript that might get made and thus disabled Greg's binate foul papers/prompt-book choice when determining printer's copy (Bowers 1955b, 11–12). Pollard had decided that a dramatist routinely gave his foul papers to the playing company on the evidence of Heminges and Condell's 'scarse receiued from him a blot in his papers' remark, which was meaningless if it referred to fair copy (which by definition is unblotted), but in fact, Bowers pointed out, *Timon of Athens* and *Romeo and Juliet* have blots of a sort in their tangles, and perhaps the papers for these were fouler (nearer the initial composition) than the clean manuscripts that Shakespeare usually gave his company and to which Heminges and Condell were referring. In any case, we should not rely too much on 'a pious literary compliment' in the Folio preliminaries (Bowers 1955b, 26).

In compensation for increasing editors' ignorance about printers' copy, Bowers added to their knowledge of what happened in the printshop. Where headline analysis reveals regular two-skeleton printing (one for all the inner formes, another for all the outer) we can be sure 'that efficient teamwork is present, that the speediest method for imposing new formes without delaying the press has been adopted, and that the compositor is setting type fast enough to keep up with the press' (Bowers 1955b, 36). If not – if one finds the same furniture and running titles on the inner and outer forme of each sheet – then the compositor was failing to keep up with the press, and we may suppose that in his hurry he made more errors than usual. In Q2 *Hamlet* Bowers detected two compositors, one falling behind the other in places, allowing an editor to decide 'the amount of emendation necessary sheet by sheet, depending on which compositor set it and on the estimate whether it was set at a normal rate or an abnormal rate of speed' (Bowers 1955b, 39–40). This was a new way to get what New Bibliography had long sought, an impression of the nature of the underlying manuscript, for if the error rate fluctuates closely (and only) with the stints of the compositors or with their states of hurriedness, we can infer that the manuscript itself was consistent, and by looking at the sheets that were not rushed we can see what the compositors could at best do with their copy; thus we get a sense of how clean the manuscript was (Bowers 1955b, 40).

As the data about particular compositors accumulated, Bowers thought it would become possible to edit Shakespeare using knowledge of just what kind of manuscript would cause a particular compositor, whose work elsewhere was known, to do what he did. In an essay appended to the second edition of his book, Bowers foresaw new technology augmenting the editorial mind:

> I have some hopes that electronic computers can be put to work to digest and to analyze much information that at present we do not have. It will be a blessed day in the future when one can press a button and give such a lordly command as 'List for me every time compositor B follows his copy in spelling *win* as *win* or *winne*, every time he changes a copy spelling *win* to *winne*, or *winne* to *win*, and distinguish in each case what he does in setting prose and setting verse. Then give me all the occurrences of *win* and *winne* in texts that he set from manuscript. (Bowers 1966, 136)

It is salutary to note that despite the availability of cheap computers roughly 3 million times more powerful and less expensive than those of 1966, we are no nearer (and according to the New Textualists somewhat further from) the masterful situation Bowers anticipated.

One way to think of Bowers's work is as a continuation of Greg's on the subject of a split authority: not only might a print edition be split between the authority of its substantives and accidentals (so that for the best of each one must draw upon two distinct editions), but it might also be split in authority between better and worse formes. This Bowers illustrated via the dependence of Q2 *Hamlet*'s compositor X upon an exemplar of Q1, which necessarily raises the status of formes set by compositor Y who could not have been using this inferior copy at the same time (Bowers 1955b, 42–4). The concomitant was obvious: a modern editor must divide into sections her copy-text (and if using a separate control text as the authority for substantives, divide that too), in each of which the amount and type of intervention she should make might vary. If two compositors set the edition upon which a modern one is to be based, the first compositor conservatively (likely to follow his manuscript copy) and accurately and the second carelessly, the parts of the modern edition based on the latter's section will be in greater need of emendation than the parts based on the former (Bowers 1955b, 56). Decisions about when and how to emend would be shaped by knowledge of compositors' habits and the order of their stints, which itself derived from spelling analysis and reconstruction of the order of presswork, predicated on assumptions about efficient working.

Essays in *Studies in Bibliography* and elsewhere through the 1960s built upon the three new technical procedures of running title analysis (from Bowers), broken type reuse analysis (from Hinman) and type shortage analysis (from George Walton Williams). A typical example using all three procedures is Robert K. Turner Junior's deduction of the order of composition and machining of formes for Q1 *A Midsummer Night's Dream* (1600), which showed that it was set by formes and that its frequent mislineation of verse was due to a miscalculation in casting off the manuscript copy (Turner Junior 1962). Casting off is the process of determining in advance which sections of the manuscript copy will occupy which pages in a printed book, as is necessary if type is to be set by formes rather than seriatim. There will be more to say on these topics in connection with Hinman's work on broken pieces of type (pp. 72–5), for he advanced the study of them more than anyone. Another fruit of the new approaches was John Hazel Smith's determination that Q *Much Ado About Nothing* (1600) was cast off and set by formes (Smith 1963) and that signs of type shortage corroborate other evidence indicating that the extra matter (on leaves E3–E6, holding scene 3.1 that would otherwise be omitted) in some exemplars of Q *2 Henry 4* (1600) was produced during a delay in the printing of Q *Much Ado About Nothing* in the same printshop, that of Valentine Simmes (Smith 1964). Along such lines, essays derived from the Virginian-school breakthroughs of the 1950s continued in the 1960s the examination of the early editions of Shakespeare, albeit at the rate of about one article a year instead of three.

Although an essay in *Studies in Bibliography* at the end of the 1960s wiped out a considerable part of this body of post-war work, a counter-example that has endured is offered here as a corrective to generalization. Povey's two-page note on an optical means for determining which of the two formes of a sheet (inner or outer) was printed first is an unassailable empirical observation, beautiful and characteristically New Bibliographical in its stark simplicity of logic (Povey 1960). The impression of paper onto inked type deforms the surface of the paper, producing hillock-like protuberances in the finished book. Raised bumps on the second-printed side would be pushed down by the inked type of the perfecting forme, so on the second-printed side the only surviving bumps will be ones that fell in the spaces of the perfecting type and hence these bumps will be uninked. A bump with ink on it can only exist on the first-printed side, since this patch of paper must already have had that ink on it when the bump was created by the perfecting side. A home-made lamp shining beams almost parallel to the surface of the paper can reveal these features and so reveal the order of machining.

E. A. J. HONIGMANN, *THE STABILITY OF SHAKESPEARE'S TEXT* (1965)

We have seen that unlike W. W. Greg, Fredson Bowers was able to contemplate Shakespeare revising his plays, perhaps as he copied them out prior to handing them over to his fellow actors. Precisely because he was a conscientious author rather than one of Philip Henslowe's hacks, Shakespeare probably reworked things, perhaps several times: 'I am not so convinced as some critics [such as Greg] that the perfection of Shakespeare's plays was achieved in only a single act of composition, and that this "original draft" was thereupon the manuscript turned over to his company' (Bowers 1955b, 107). Turning to the preliminaries of the 1623 Folio and their praise of Shakespeare's mind and hand going together, E. A. J. Honigmann understood that John Heminges and Henry Condell's claim that 'wee haue scarse receiued from him a blot in his papers' (Shakespeare 1623, ᵠA3ʳ) need not be literally true: it might only follow the fashion for praising writing that comes easily to the writer (Honigmann 1965, 23–4). But what if, asked Honigmann, it were literally true that Shakespeare's papers were unblotted, not because he did not change his mind but because he avoided crossing out during composition and chose instead to let the original and the improved word, or clause, or line, stand in his papers?

On the evidence of eye-skip, Honigmann showed that the manuscript of Thomas Heywood's *The Captives* was probably made by the author copying out fairly his own foul papers (Honigmann 1965, 200–6), as Bowers believed was usual before a script was given to the players. If Shakespeare was expecting to make his own fair copy he could afford to leave first and second thoughts together, neither crossed out, in his thus unblotted foul papers, so that when he came to the copying out he could coolly select the better version in the fresh light of a new day. The players would thus get a fair copy purged of these ambiguities. Shakespeare might well retain the foul papers which, although unblotted, had good and bad mixed together and unsifted, whence the errors and confusions in the early editions made from them. Honigmann's hypothesis would explain the ghost characters (pp. 47–8 above) in the early editions, such as Innogen in Q *Much Ado About Nothing* (1600). Shakespeare did not go back and delete the scene-opening directions featuring Innogen because he knew he would simply not copy her forward into the fair copy of the play that he would present to the players.

Picturing Shakespeare making his fair copy, Honigmann saw an inveterate tweaker: he would alter spellings and change words as he copied. We can see this from variation in the spelling of names in speech prefixes. In *Macbeth*, for which we have only the Folio edition, *Banquo* when he is first named has the unusual spelling of *Banquoh* (Shakespeare 1623, ll6^r). The historical source, Raphael Holinshed's chronicles, calls him *Banquho* so we must assume that Shakespeare is responsible for the odd spelling in the Folio; the name is too unusual for us to imagine that the compositors, having read their Holinshed, put in the *h* upon noticing that Shakespeare had omitted it. But later in the play he becomes *Banquo*, so the logical inference is that Shakespeare dithered over the spelling, settling on *Banquo* only after trying out *Banquoh*. The principle Honigmann established is important: Shakespeare dithered over details and made small changes whilst writing or between the first draft and the final fair copy. Honigmann looked at many dramatic and non-dramatic manuscripts of the period, and later, and argued convincingly that such tinkering is the ingrained habit of poets (Honigmann 1965, 47–77).

A final example clinched the argument (Honigmann 1965, 59–62). There are six manuscripts and three early printed editions of Thomas Middleton's *A Game at Chess*, and between them numerous variants. We might be able to dismiss these variants as errors in transmission, were it not for the fact that one of the manuscripts (at Trinity College, Cambridge) is in its author's hand throughout and another (in the Huntington Library, California) has the last two scenes in the author's hand. We can compare these two scenes as represented in two manuscripts written by the dramatist:

Trinity Manuscript:

Bl:K^t. Is it so uilde there is no name ordaynde for't
Toades haue theire Titles, and Creation gaue
Serpents and Adders those names to bee knowne by
———
Wh.Kt. this of all others beare's the hiddest Venom
the smoothest poyson, – I am an Arch-Dissembler S^r,
———
Bl.Kt. how?
———
wh.Kt. tis my Natures Brand turne from mee, S^{ir}
the time is yet to come that ere I spake
what my heart mean't? (Middleton 1990, Trinity 50b)

Bridgewater-Huntington Manuscript:

Bl.Kt. is it so uile there is no name ordayn'd fort,
Toades haue theire Titles, and Creation gaue
Serpents and Adders those names to bee knowen by;
———
wh.Kt. this of all others beares the hiddenst Venom
the Secretst poyson; I'me an Archdissembler, (Sir)
———
Bl.Kt..how?
———
wh.Kt. tis my Natures brand, turne from mee (S^{ir})
the time is yet to come that e're I spoke
what my heart mean't! (Middleton 1990, Bridgewater-Huntington 52b)

Here are minor differences in punctuation and spelling, such as *ordaynde / ordayn'd* and *knowne / knowen*, but alongside them are more significant differences such as *uilde / uile*, *hiddest / hiddenst* and *spake / spoke*, as well as the truly substantive variant *smoothest / Secretst* that seems connected to the metrically distinct *I am / I'me*. The inescapable conclusion is that Middleton made small tweaks as he copied out his play at different times, and that as far as he was concerned such differences between fair copies were tolerable. There was, then, no such thing as the definitive text of *A Game at Chess* even in the mind of the dramatist. Rather, in the differing early documents we read the dramatist's changes of mind over time.

Honigmann's conclusion was potentially devastating for New Bibliography as it had existed before Bowers began this train of thought, since it had rested on the assumption that while we might never find a single document containing the definitive wording of the script (since errors of transmission are unavoidable), the writer at least had in mind a single definitive version. Honigmann had uncovered direct documentary evidence for variation within the authorial mind, as it was clear that different documents in the hand of the writer might contain differences at all levels from accidentals of punctuation and spelling to indifferent and substantive variants in which the dramatist seems to be trying out word changes. That different documents might witness wholesale revision of lines and scenes could be accommodated by New Bibliography, but the idea that writers themselves might introduce variants at the level of individual word choices presented an entirely new problem.

Honigmann showed that with other writers, and therefore arguably with Shakespeare, the variants might be not only words similar in meaning or sound but also words similar in appearance such as *hulks* and *bulks*, or to take a well-known example, *Indian* (Shakespeare 1622, N2^r) and *Iudean* (Shakespeare 1623, vv5^v) in Othello's final speech. A writer so indifferent to the particular word might even 'deliberately tone down a word or line, in order to allow a neighbouring passage to gain in effect' (Honigmann 1965, 74), which is to say that the worse word might be the better choice when looked at in context. Editors have traditionally assumed that if a textual variant offers a choice of two equally plausible words, an editor should generally select the more poetical. This is called the principle of *lectio difficilior potior* (Latin for 'the more difficult reading is the stronger'), and is based on the observation that unwanted human interventions in the copying of writing by scribes and printers tend to replace difficult and unfamiliar words with easy and familiar ones rather than the reverse. Honigmann's work thus challenged core principles of textual scholarship that had long seemed utterly reliable.

CHARLTON HINMAN, *THE PRINTING AND PROOF-READING OF THE FIRST FOLIO OF SHAKESPEARE* (1963) AND *THE NORTON FACSIMILE OF THE FIRST FOLIO* (1968)

Charlton Hinman's great contribution to New Bibliography was the invention of a device that speeded up (by a factor of more than fifty) the process of collating different exemplars of a single edition to find variants caused by alterations to the type after the first impression(s) had been taken (Hinman 1947). To reveal how a single page appears in two exemplars, the Hinman Collator presents to the viewer alternating images from first one

New techniques and the Virginian School 73

and then the other (switching at about once a second) so that where the pages are identical the image appears steady but where they differ (as by small adjustments to the type) the letters appear to shift before the viewer's eyes. Hinman used the machine to collate the variants in the Folios in the Folger Shakespeare Library in Washington DC, and in the process discovered that the book was made by a method overlooked until William H. Bond drew attention to it: the manuscript copy was cast off and the pages set by formes rather than seriatim (Bond 1948). In printings by Thomas Marshe, Bond noticed that variations in the number of lines set per page do not occur randomly throughout a particular book but rather tend to occur on one forme only, usually the inner. This is hard to explain if the pages were set seriatim, but makes perfect sense if the pages were set by formes.

Some of the decisions about where page-breaks will fall that are made in the process of casting off are immutable when setting by formes, since there are limited opportunities to shift lines from the bottom of one page to the top of the next (or back the other way) when the pages are set non-sequentially. If an error in the casting off calculation emerged while setting a particular page, the compositor might nonetheless be forced to fit his predetermined amount of manuscript writing into the page because the next page was already in the press being printed, and he could do so by wasting or saving space and, if necessary, by setting a greater or lesser number of lines on the page. Casting off could involve awkward calculations and irksome limitations, and R. B. McKerrow had repeatedly claimed that the 'intricate calculations' were 'impracticable' and perhaps even 'theoretically impossible' for most kinds of work (McKerrow 1921–2, 106; 1924–5, 357). The earliest manual of printing had in fact described just how it is done (Moxon 1683, $Ll3^v$–$Mm3^r$). McKerrow believed that in any case 'The order in which the pages were set up in type leaves no evidence whatever by which we can trace it' (McKerrow 1924–5, 359), but George Walton Williams's work on substitutions forced on compositors by type shortage, Bond's on over/undersetting of lines, and most especially Hinman's on type recurrence, showed that the evidence can in certain cases be wrung from the books.

Setting by formes rather than seriatim had the special advantage of reducing the amount of type that had to be set up at any one time, and hence a printshop did not need to own as much of it to work this way. Or, to see the equation as they probably did, a printshop could do more work with a given amount of type when setting by formes. Since the press could print only from a completed forme of type (four pages for a quarto, two for a folio-in-sixes), a compositor working seriatim on a quarto sheet would have to set seven of its eight pages (1^r, 1^v, 2^r, 2^v, 3^r, 3^v, 4^r) before he had enough pages to impose a forme (the inner, 1^v, 2^r, 3^v, 4^r) that he could pass to the pressmen. For a folio-in-sixes, a compositor working seriatim would have to set seven of its twelve pages (1^r, 1^v, 2^r, 2^v, 3^r, 3^v, 4^r) before he could impose a forme (the inner forme of the inner sheet, 3^v:4^r). If, on the other hand, he cast off his manuscript he would know which parts of it would be copy for which pages and could proceed immediately to setting just the pages needed to complete any forme. Rather than cast off a whole gathering, a compositor might cast off only the pages he did not wish to set seriatim. Thus for a quarto he might cast off 1^r, set 1^v and 2^r, cast off 2^v and 3^r, and set 3^v and 4^r, thus enabling him to impose the inner forme; this procedure would have the advantage of boxing him in only in respect of the 1^{r-v} and 3^{r-v} page-breaks, the ones predetermined by the casting off.

This way of working also gave a printshop flexibility in matching the rates of work. Pressmen would take more time to finish machining all the sheets for a long print run than a short one, but it made no difference to them how many pieces of type, or pages, were in the forme being impressed. Compositors would take more time to set and impose a forme consisting of many pages in small type than they would a forme of a few pages in large type, but it made no difference to them how many impressions the pressmen would pull from the forme. On a short print run of a book with lots of type on each page, the pressmen would tend to get ahead of the compositors and on a long print run of a book with little type on each page, the compositors would get ahead of the pressmen. Because it allowed the pages to be set in any order, casting off copy gave the printshop the option of putting additional compositors on to a job if this would help balance the workload and keep both teams busy. If two compositors were working simultaneously on the pages for one quarto sheet then the casting off need not be highly accurate since miscalculations could be fixed by moving lines from one page to another even across formes. Two compositors working on a gathering for a folio-in-sixes printed from the inside out could cast off the first six pages (1^r–3^v), then share the setting of the forme 3^v:4^r by taking a page each. Then one compositor could work backwards through the cast-off pages of the first half of the gathering (from 3^r to 1^r), enjoying the advantage of being able to make minor adjustments between pages so long as he began 1^r in the right place, while the other compositor completed the second half of the gathering (4^v–6^v) seriatim.

Hinman showed that the 1623 Folio has just the features of space saving and space wasting that are consistent with casting off and printing by formes (Hinman 1955, 261–9), and, from other evidence, that in fact it must have been printed this way (Hinman 1955, 269–73). The absolute proof arose from considering how often a particular piece of type might be set in a gathering of a folio-in-sixes. If set seriatim, no piece of type could appear twice in the first seven pages, since these pages would have to be in type at once for printing to commence with $3^v:4^r$. Ordinarily one cannot tell apart the pieces of type (collectively known as the sort) that form the stock of one letter or symbol in a typecase, but the high-powered lenses on Hinman's collating machine allowed him to spot pieces of type that had received peculiar injuries that made them distinctive, and these he could identify upon their reuse in the book. Listing the ones that are most easily spotted in printed facsimiles of the Folio, Hinman concluded that most of them 'recur scores of times throughout the Folio; none ever appears twice in the same forme; all are found in pages where they could not possibly appear if the Folio had been set by successive pages' (Hinman 1955, 270–1). He apparently gave no advance notification of this remarkable discovery to W. W. Greg, whose book on the Folio published the same year described its being set seriatim with seven pages of type kept standing (Greg 1955, 434), although Greg kept up with Hinman's published output. Understandably, Hinman did extend to his old supervisor advance notice of his discoveries (Bowers 1964, viii–ix).

Hinman published preliminary findings of his collation of the Folger Folios before the mammoth task was completed (Hinman 1942b; 1947; 1950; 1953; 1953–4; 1955; 1957), but the definitive statement of his investigation of press variants and recurrent damaged type was the two volumes of *The Printing and Proof-reading of the First Folio of Shakespeare* (1963). This remains one of the enduring monuments of New Bibliography, although Peter W. M. Blayney subsequently revised certain of Hinman's conclusions (pp. 258–9 below). In his groundbreaking article of 1955, Hinman confined his list of examples of broken type to those that could be seen with ease even in the 'far from reliable' new Yale facsimile of the Folio (Hinman 1955, 270 n.13; Shakespeare 1954b). Fredson Bowers gave this facsimile a scathing review under two heads: the quality of its reproduction and the accuracy of Charles Tyler Prouty's introduction (Bowers 1955c).

The Yale facsimile reproduced a single exemplar, owned by the Elizabethan Club of Yale University, in reduced size and, it claimed, 'as faithfully and accurately as modern techniques permit' (Shakespeare 1954b, v). Bowers objected that its line offset reproduction was not the most faithful or accurate method but rather the cheapest and that because this method does not capture shades of grey (let alone colour) the images had to be extensively reworked for the text to be readable. The reworking gravely harmed the accuracy. Bowers described other ways of making a facsimile, the most expensive and accurate being collotype (as used in Sidney Lee's 1902 facsimile) and the less good but still respectable fine-screen offset system that produces an illusion of shades of grey by varying the size of tiny dots of purely black ink. While still engaged in his collection of primary evidence Hinman announced his hope to produce a new facsimile of the 1623 Folio (Hinman 1953, 288) and in 1968 it appeared, using the fine-screen offset process.

Hinman believed that the proof correction of the 1623 Folio was not as thorough as that later described by Joseph Moxon, on the evidence of 'far too many obvious errors of all kinds in far too many Folio pages' (Hinman 1963a, 228 n.2). Of William Jaggard's proofreader, Hinman wrote: 'Such obvious substantive errors as he noticed he tried to eliminate; but he ordinarily did so without referring to the copy and the result was sometimes (as can and presently will be demonstrated) rather a further corruption than a restoration of the true reading' (Hinman 1963a, 239). This conclusion has a bearing on what should appear in a facsimile edition, for, as Bowers had pointed out, the introduction of substantive errors during correction (especially correction made without reference to copy) can easily result in a technically corrected sheet that is actually less correct, in the sense of faithful to copy, than its uncorrected predecessor (Bowers 1952).

Allied to his view of the relatively poor printing work in the Folio was Hinman's belief that rather than reproducing just one particular exemplar of the book (as the Lee and Yale facsimiles did) he could use his knowledge of its manufacture to provide a facsimile that encapsulated the entire edition:

> The primary aim of the present facsimile is to furnish a reliable photographic reproduction of what the printers of the original edition would themselves have considered an ideal copy of the First Folio of Shakespeare: one in which every page is not only clear and readable throughout but represents the latest or most fully corrected state of the text. It is sought, that is, to give concrete representation to what has hitherto been only a theoretical entity, an abstraction: *the* First Folio text. For such an ideal representation of the Folio is not now, and almost certainly never has been, realized in any actual copy of the edition: and no previous facsimile has attempted to offer one – nor could possibly have succeeded in doing so, indeed, if only because the most fully corrected state of each Folio page was not yet known when the most recent predecessor [the Yale] of the present facsimile was published. (Shakespeare 1968b, xxii–xxiii)

In this statement of purpose, Hinman began with an ideal: what the printers would have considered a perfect book. Alterations to the type after the printing started improved certain pages, but the uncorrected sheets were not discarded; rather they were mixed with the corrected. This exigence was forced on the printers by economic necessity, and Hinman saw himself able to realize the goal the printshop workers strove towards but did not attain. (We know that they held an idealized goal in their minds, else there were no point in making corrections at all.) Hinman intended to realize the printers' ideal by bringing together the best pages from different exemplars, since 'almost certainly' the 'latest or most fully corrected' sheets had never previously come together in one book. The qualification was needed because a lost exemplar might, by slim chance, have had exactly the combination of sheets that Hinman considered to be ideal, as might a lost exemplar made up from fragments by a bookseller in the intervening centuries. Hinman's ideal, then, would seem to be something firmly grounded in reality: his preferred selection (and the printers') could have come into existence when the book was made or at any time since, and it was merely misfortune that it probably had not until now.

Hinman's notion of idealizing printers was perfectly reasonable and new evidence uncovered by James Binns (p. 96 below) proves that they did so idealize. Moreover, he quite reasonably aimed to produce what the printers could in theory have made but did not, rather than – as some of his detractors have claimed (pp. 192–3 below) – to produce something belonging only to the unembodied realm of thought. However, Hinman departed from this otherwise respectable materialist doctrine in choosing to select individual pages for fine-screen offset reproduction, rather than selecting by forme. For his 1904 reprinting of Barnabe Barnes's *The Devil's Charter* (1607), McKerrow had established the principle that since the unit of press correction was the forme, not the page or the sheet, one should use this unit when selecting what best represents the ideal intention imperfectly embodied in an edition (Barnes 1904, xiii–xviii). For his reprint, McKerrow worked out which of his four exemplars of the 1607 quarto represented the most corrected state of each forme and switched between them as necessary.

For his Folio facsimile, however, Hinman selected the best page in every case. The reason for this was that Hinman believed that the unit of proofreading was the page, not the forme:

the reader used one impression of the forme as proof for one page and then another impression for the other. Thus the press could be stopped and a compositor could begin correcting the type for the forme being printed immediately one of its pages had been proofed. The proof for the second page could then be marked while the compositor was making the required changes in the first. No labour would be saved by this method of working; but such a procedure would have the obvious advantage of permitting the compositor to correct his forme sooner than if he had to wait until both its pages had been marked by the reader – and so of reducing the number of impressions made from the uncorrected state of that forme. (Hinman 1963a, 234–5)

That this way of working cut down on the uncorrected impressions corroborates Hinman's assertion that they idealized a goal of perfection even as they failed to achieve it. It is important to notice that the unit of correction remains the forme, not the page, because the press was not restarted with one page corrected and the other uncorrected: rather, the proofreading and marking of the second page of the forme was undertaken in (and perhaps hurried by) the time it took to make the alterations of type in the first page. On this fine distinction Hinman hung his claim to be perfecting the printers' labour by choosing the most corrected state for each of the pages in his facsimile.

It would be fair to object that in choosing his images by page rather than by forme Hinman weakened his facsimile's materialist credentials, since he created something that the printers could not have produced. Hinman was attempting to wield potentially conflicting criteria for selecting his pages, since he had to balance a desire for the most corrected state of each page with a need to choose pages that would photograph well. In the event he was able to find amongst the thirty Folger Folios that he used a clear-enough corrected page in every case (Shakespeare 1968b, xxiii). Yet in choosing by pages he brought together from different exemplars pages sharing the same forme (Shakespeare 1968b, 925–8). For example, for pages $A1^r$ and $A6^v$ Hinman photographed different Folger exemplars despite the fact that these pages occupy one side of a single sheet (the outside of the outer sheet of a gathering) and thus are forme-mates. Hinman's selection is analogous to the printers choosing to have these pages bound from different sheets in the A heap, and since that would have been impossible (each $A1^r$ was physically joined to a particular $A6^v$) his claim to be reproducing what the printers might have made with their own technology is misleading. No mixing of the sheets could produce Hinman's pairings from different exemplars, and the same is true of his selection for all the forme-mates in this gathering ($A1^v$:6^r, $A2^r$:5^v, $A2^v$:5^r, $A3^r$:4^v and $A3^v$:4^r) and so on in gatherings B, C and D, whereafter by chance a run of forme-mates from a single Folger exemplar was photographed. The same objection applies where Hinman brought together from different exemplars pages that shared a leaf, as with $A2^{r-v}$, $A4^{r-v}$, $A6^{r-v}$, $B1^{r-v}$, $B3^{r-v}$, $B4^{r-v}$, and so on for about half the leaves in the facsimile.

It is possible that binders in the intervening centuries might have made up perfect exemplars of the Folio by combining individual leaves to bring together pairings that Hinman was later to select, although such patchwork could not produce a leaf bearing recto and verso pages from different Folio exemplars, as Hinman's photographic process did. Hinman's pairings could not have occurred in the printing house and hence cannot represent the printers' ideal, although much hinges on what we mean by that word. Had Hinman detached his notion of the printer's ideal from the practicalities of their actions – had he, for example, simply claimed that their ideal was to reproduce Shakespeare's plays as perfectly as possible – then the problem would disappear. It is strange that, having determined that there was little proofreading and correction, Hinman chose to base his facsimile on 'what the printers of the original edition would themselves have considered an ideal copy' (Shakespeare 1968b, xxii) when he might have chosen the publishing consortium's, or John Heminges and Henry Condell's, more abstract ideals. Yoking ideals to physical possibilities is apt to cause entanglement in philosophical paradoxes when one sets out to produce a facsimile and must decide just what is meant by the new object being an imitation (Latin *similis*) of the original.

Hinman's Folio facsimile of 1968 represents the high-water mark of a certain kind of idealization about early modern printing. It coincided with the publication of two essays in French introducing new literary-theoretical ideas about knowledge that had an almost immediate effect on Shakespeare criticism and a somewhat belated one on bibliographical theory. They were Roland Barthes's 'La mort de l'auteur' ('The Death of the Author') (1968) and Michel Foucault's responding 'Qu'est-ce qu'un auteur?' ('What is an Author?') (1969). Of immediate impact in bibliographical studies, however, was D. F. McKenzie's 'Printers of the Mind' (1969) that indicated the gap between the reality of early modern printshop practices and the idealized and simplified models of those practices in the work of the postwar Virginian school.

Two essays by William S. Kable sounded early warnings of what was to come. In an analysis of how Folio/Jaggard compositor B behaved, Kable (like McKenzie) used his work in 1619, for which the printed copy is extant, to determine that he would depart from his preferred spellings not only to justify a line but also to avoid setting a long verse line that stood out noticeably from its neighbours (Kable 1967). By Hinman's rules (1940–1) a short line would not normally fall under suspicion of having its spellings shaped by the needs of justification, but Kable pointed out that such a line might be short precisely because its spellings had been so shaped.

In a second article, Kable turned to the neglected matter of the spellings about which a compositor was indifferent and would just follow his copy (Kable 1968). Again using compositor B's work from known copy in 1619, Kable tabulated not his preferences but his indifferences, and pointed out that this knowledge would enable one to be tolerably certain of the copy spelling whenever the same word occurs in something else he set in type, for it will be whatever he set. This insight (often latent in compositorial studies but seldom addressed) opened up the possibility, later explored by Paul Werstine (pp. 208–9 below), that strong spelling preferences in the manuscript copy might coincide with compositorial indifference (that is, willingness to follow copy in respect of these spellings), which might easily be misinterpreted as strong compositorial preference.

As these cautions were being sounded, Robert K. Turner Junior came up with a new way for bibliographers to pile inference upon inference and so mislead themselves. Turner argued that when one has ambiguous evidence (say, from spelling preferences) for identifying how many compositors worked on a book, the recurrent type technique developed by Hinman might fill the breach (Turner Junior 1966). Where the reuse of pieces of type is not evenly spread across a book but clusters on certain pages that fall into two heaps, we can be tolerably certain that this is because two typecases (or sets of typecases) were being used, with the type not moving from one to the other when distributed back into the typecases after printing. This suggests that two compositors, each with his own typecases, were at work. In such a situation, there might be a page that yields no clear evidence of its compositor in its distinctive spellings (perhaps the words one is looking for happen not to occur on this page), but does contain a distinctive piece of type that one has seen before in an earlier page for which the compositor can be identified. According to Turner, this gives indirect evidence about the compositor of the uncertain page, since so long as the compositors did not share typecases this will be the same man. Such indirect evidence was increasingly wielded in the 1970s, with predictably unreliable results.

CHAPTER 3

New Bibliography 1969–1979

The 1970s may fairly be characterized as the heyday of New Bibliography, as there emerged a highly specialized and technical branch of work that attempted to build upon the breakthroughs of the 1950s and 1960s in order to provide what Fredson Bowers had declared (pp. 66–8 above) to be within reach: a comprehensive tabulation of the identities of the compositors of the early editions, their identifying habits, the order of their work and that of the pressmen, the nature of each edition's underlying copy and the kinds of correction introduced during the print run. Knowing what kinds of errors may creep in (as from compositors' misreadings, or miscorrection) would enable a modern editor working from the early editions to better decide upon the kind and the degree of emendation needed to restore the authorial meanings.

D. F. McKENZIE, 'PRINTERS OF THE MIND' (1969)

The objections to the Virginian-school approach to bibliography made in 'Printers of the Mind' did not come entirely out of the blue. Bowers argued that hurried compositorial work can be detected by the pattern of headline reuse, on the principle that if the compositors fell behind the pressmen there was no advantage to making extra skeletons (pp. 60, 67 above), and Alice Walker (1953) thought she could detect haste in the rate of errors made by compositors. Time-and-motions engineer Norman Nathan rejected the logic of these approaches and observed that in explaining errors in the execution of fiddly work one has to consider all sorts of factors other than haste: 'was the weather favourable or hot or cold or muggy? was the work done on a Monday, a Wednesday, or a Saturday? did A or B have any personal problems on a given day?' and so on (Nathan 1957, 135). Since these questions are unanswerable, there can be no hope of correlating rate of work and rate of error.

'Printers of the Mind' arose from D. F. McKenzie's study of what actually happened at Cambridge University Press from 1696 to 1712, a period for which substantially complete records exist, and the most devastating news was that concurrent working was the norm. Rather than see one book to completion as quickly as possible, printers kept different projects going at the same time in order to most efficiently utilize the capital and labour in a printshop. Without an assumption that each book was completed as quickly as possible many of the methods of the Virginian-school New Bibliography could not be applied, for concurrent working invalidated deductions about who was ahead, the compositors or the pressmen. The Cambridge records showed that one man's daily rate of work – judged by his income, since they were paid for piece-work – could vary enormously over the days and weeks. Concurrent printing adds further uncertainty, for if the working rates of compositors and pressmen were highly variable, and if underused men could be put to work on other books, then the relationship between skeleton formes and edition size breaks down. Rather than having to match the time taken to distribute one forme and set the next with the time taken to machine however many impressions of the forme were needed, the printshop master could simply shift people between different books being worked upon simultaneously in order to maximize efficiency.

McKenzie found that where compositors shared the setting of a book, they tended not to divide the work by sheets but rather one took over wherever the other left off and continued for a while before he himself was reassigned. Rather than a norm of two compositors setting different parts of the same book at once to keep up with the press, the pattern of work was shaped simply to keep the printshop busy and not to finish any particular book. Likewise with presswork: it was not normal for a book of more than a couple of sheets to be done on one press alone. Rather any free press in the shop might be used for different parts of the book. In a printshop where a compositor might rapidly switch between tasks, a change in the compositor's measure in a particular book would not necessarily indicate a change in compositor, as Bowers thought it did (p. 60 above), because one man's stick was constantly being adjusted as he worked on different books and it might not be returned to precisely the original measure when he resumed a particular task.

McKenzie's discoveries invalidated Charlton Hinman's claim, calculated from supposed rates of working, that the 1623 Folio had a run of 1,200 copies. Hinman and Robert K. Turner Junior had shown bibliographers how to track the recurrence of distinctive pieces of type in order to make arguments that infer that because type from the outer forme of a quarto sheet, say B(outer), appears on the next sheet, say C, but type on the inner forme B(inner) does not, B(outer) must have gone through the press before B(inner). Such deductions were valid only if the press were working continuously to complete the book, proceeding alphabetically through the sheets, and McKenzie showed that this cannot be assumed: any order of sheets was technically possible. The only sure way to detect the order in which sheets were printed is to find progressive deterioration in types, rules, headlines and ornaments, and within a single sheet one can sometimes tell which forme was machined first by use of the Povey lamp (p. 69 above).

Hinman and Bowers were sceptical that the extensive proofing pulls and correction phases described by Joseph Moxon were used in the 1620s, since surviving books are full of errors. McKenzie pointed out that evidence of proof correction would not normally survive and we are left only with evidence of stop-press correction that caused variant formes. We must not assume that preceding stages of proofing did not happen just because we have no record of them. After all, 'The existence of some formes in three or more states indicates that at one or more stages of correction errors were missed which were later thought serious enough to alter' (McKenzie 1969, 45–6). What Hinman called proofs might easily be understood as revises: subsequent checks after the main work of proofing had been done, for which the evidence is lost. If so, Hinman was (despite his own mistaken hypotheses) after all quite right to choose particular pages rather than formes for his Folio facsimile, since Moxon indicated that for revises the forme was kept on the bed of the press and attended to as separate pages.

According to McKenzie bibliography could not be a science because it does not engage in exploratory experiments or make hypotheses that it checks with replicable tests. Bibliography relies on inductive reasoning, the kind that says 'I have seen hundreds of swans, none of them red, so there probably are no red ones', which is inherently weaker than the logic of deduction, which would say 'This swan is red, so there are red swans.' Either bibliographers must undertake extensive historical work to validate their assumptions about normal printshop practice, or else they must 'confess outright the partial and theoretic nature of bibliographical knowledge, proceed deductively, and at the same time practise a new and rigorous scepticism' (McKenzie 1969, 6). The new ignorance that McKenzie brought to the subject – especially his demonstration that the order of presswork cannot be deduced from running title and type reuse – was in the service of furthering genuine knowledge by removing spurious certainties. He was no part of the literary-theoretical movement, born at the same time, that would on principle deny the existence of certainties and dismiss as illusory the advance of human knowledge.

RESPONSES TO McKENZIE: A SCHISM IN NEW BIBLIOGRAPHY

For a certain kind of bibliographical study, the late 1960s were an endpoint. New knowledge continued to be generated regarding which printers used which founts and paper stocks and about the sharing of jobs between printshops, and following Charlton Hinman's lead new portable mechanical collators were developed. But no bibliographical procedures as wholly new as those introduced by the Virginian school were subsequently invented, and D. F. McKenzie presented limits upon what could be asserted with the existing procedures. (A new class of tests for identifying compositors was invented in the 1970s – the so-called pyscho-mechanical tests developed by T. H. Howard-Hill – but in a companion piece to 'Printers of the Mind' McKenzie showed in 1984 that they could be unreliable too.) Yet certain principles of bibliographical analysis remained untouched by McKenzie's essay. It was still true that a particular piece of type could not appear in two formes that were standing in type at the same time, and that the use of four skeleton formes in a book makes better sense if there was more than one compositor. McKenzie limited the application of such knowledge by insisting that bibliographers take a wider purview than the individual book: the work of the whole printshop must be examined. This development can be paralleled with the literary theory that arose at the same time, for Roland Barthes's and Michel Foucault's influential essays (1968; 1969) also called for widened purviews. According to Barthes, any particular piece of writing is shot through not only with the phrases of other works but also the habits of thought of the culture in which it was created – hence it is a 'tissue of quotations' (Barthes 1977, 146) – and likewise for Foucault there could be no proper analysis of an individual work without consideration of the wider social, cultural, scientific and literary conditions, what he called the discursive formations, that give it meaning.

McKenzie's introduction of the complicating factor of concurrent printing called for a kind of dispersal, a diverting of the bibliographer's attention away from the singular object to a collection of related objects, which dispersal mirrored the printers' own dispersal of attention in concurrent printing. Even before McKenzie, bibliographers were aware that concurrent printing in the eighteenth century vitiated the value of studies focussed upon a single book (generally, by an important author) considered in isolation from the other books produced in the same printshop at the same time (generally, by authors considered not so important). An exchange in the *Times Literary Supplement* of July–September 1966 indicates that the benefits of decentred, author-indifferent scholarship were known to bibliographers; the question was where to cease the dispersal of attention. The exchange began with a review by J. D. Fleeman of William B. Todd's *A Bibliography of Edmund Burke*, which commented:

Historical studies in bibliography may be likened to a web in which the careers of the various authors form the parallel threads of the warp, interlacing themselves with the cross threads which represent the activities of the printers and publishers of authors' works ... from a strictly bibliographical point of view one book, considered as the physical product of a particular process carried out by particular persons in a particular place, is as interesting and significant as another. It may be that the days of the author-bibliography are already numbered. (Fleeman 1966b)

Fleeman's particular objection was that Todd gave more attention to – provided more detailed descriptions of – the early editions of Burke (ones that could be associated with the author's preferences and revisions) than he gave to the later, posthumous ones, which sliding scale of priorities is called the degressive principle in bibliography. For Fleeman, later editions were just as deserving of attention, since a book is a book is a book.

Fleeman's attack on the centrality of authors did not go unchallenged. In a letter to the editor, John Carter defended the degressive principle as necessary to prevent bibliographical descriptions inflating to absurd proportions (Carter 1966a) and in the same issue Fleeman responded that this practical necessity should not be the excuse for avoiding hard bibliographical work. Moreover, Fleeman pointed to McKenzie's and Hinman's early studies on concurrent printing as showing the importance of putting the printshop, not the author, at the centre of one's attention (Fleeman 1966a). After one more shot from Carter (1966b), Todd himself weighed in a witheringly sarcastic offer to complete the 192 volumes of bibliography needed to do for Burke's various printers what McKenzie had done for Cambridge University Press, as well as the three-quarters of a million pages needed to do for Burke's books what Hinman had done for the 1623 Folio (Todd 1966). This, then, was the practical cost of giving up the author-centred view of bibliography. Just as in criticism, according to Foucault, the author (or what Foucault called the author-function) serves as a 'principle of thrift', a brake upon proliferation (Foucault 1994, 352). In an extended consideration of this exchange of letters, Fredson Bowers commented that without an author at the centre of bibliography 'it would become a branch of the study of the craft of printing, not of literature' and that he shared

W. W. Greg's view that literary study is 'the final goal of bibliography' (Bowers 1969, 98).

The first explicit response to McKenzie's 'Printers of the Mind' came from Peter Davison, who objected to its inconsistent characterization of the work ethic of the early modern printing shop, where apprentices were driven hard but other workers were allowed to slack off (Davison 1970). From his own research on Q1 *1 Henry 4* (1598) Davison reported that Peter Short's printshop used two skeleton formes, but not (as Bowers would have us expect) one for all inner formes and one for all outer, which would maximize the work-rate, but rather one for the inner and outer formes of one sheet, the other for the inner and outer formes of the next sheet. Thus, although they were not doing what we would expect, the compositors were nonetheless working systematically: we need not abandon analyses of skeleton forme reuse, only modify them (Davison 1970, 139–40). In a second, longer response to McKenzie, Davison cast the matter in terms of the social conflicts of the late 1960s and early 1970s, and in relation to science. At the turn of the decade, 'basic assumptions' were 'being challenged' in society and in the academy, whose 'nature and purposes' were up for question (Davison 1972, 1). It is not hard to hear in this the echoes of Paris 1968. There was revolution in the air, or at least 'uncertainty', and it was no less fruitful when it arose in connection with art and printing rather than sociology and politics (Davison 1972, 2). Tennyson and Marx were of an age, were they not?

According to Davison, the history of science offered a way of understanding what McKenzie had initiated: it was a Kuhnian paradigm rejection, the kind of readjustment of the intellectual spectacles that seems to undermine all certainties but in fact makes new discoveries possible. The analogy from science was central to Davison's argument, because in the woolly world of English Literature and its criticism, bibliography's obsessive and recondite empiricism gives it a spuriously scientific air. McKenzie had objected that bibliography could not be a science because it could not use the scientific method of deduction – drawing conclusions from what is already known – but in truth, responded Davison, science often cannot use deduction either and falls back on the inductive method of inferring general principles from limited facts in the hope that they were typical rather than anomalous (Davison 1972, 5–10). Davison quoted the physicist Werner Heisenberg, discoverer of the Uncertainty Principle, and suggested that the uncertainty introduced by McKenzie, and by E. A. J. Honigmann's *The Stability of Shakespeare's Text* (pp. 69–72 above), showed bibliography following the lead of science, departing from singularity, originality and reason, and discovering the inherent multiplicity, reproducibility and irrationality of the universe. Bibliography, like science, was going postmodern.

Returning to the problems of 'our agonized society', Davison saw the dusty empiricism of 'the school of Bowers and Hinman' as out of step with real science as much as with real politics and with the most advanced artists. McKenzie's upsetting of the apple-cart should be relished:

> My concern here is ... the change since Einstein, Heisenberg, and Gödel pronounced The Special Theory of Relativity, The Principle of Uncertainty, and the Theory of Incompleteness, respectively. No longer is the world within the atom to be understood in terms of the laws of cause and effect ... It is surely not mere coincidence that those in the forefront of physics and mathematics, and those in the avantgarde in the arts, are concerned in their very different ways and to very different purposes, with uncertainty, incompleteness and irrationality? In this at least, and most excitingly, science and art are related. (Davison 1972, 26–7)

The abuse of Kurt Gödel's name confirms this as a piece of protopostmodernism (Franzén 2005). Like Relativity and the Uncertainty Principle, Gödel's Incompleteness Theorems have a name that suggests that twentieth-century science was abandoning reason, but they have no connection to subatomic physics. Moreover, on the very question for which Davison invoked their names – the question of how knowledge relates to objective reality – the other two men, Einstein and Heisenberg, were locked in lifelong disagreement, the former never accepting the latter's Copenhagen Interpretation of quantum mechanics because it abandoned scientific realism (Kumar 2008). According to Davison, Virginian-school New Bibliography is like Newtonian physics in giving not quite the full answer – for that Relativity and quantum mechanics are necessary – but providing one good enough for most tasks in the world. Where they fail, 'we ought not to be afraid of irrationality and infinite coincidence', meaning 'imagination and taste' (Davison 1972, 27–8). As Alan Sokal and Jean Bricmont complained, likening quantum mechanics to creativity comes dangerously close to suggesting that scientists just make things up (Sokal and Bricmont 1998, 49–95, 167–72).

Davison's celebration of indeterminacy anticipated the New Textualism that emerged in the 1980s but it was markedly anomalous at the time; a reviewer in the *Times Literary Supplement* thought that Davison had simply stated the obvious in denying that bibliography could be an objective science (Anonymous 1972). However, within New Bibliography there were emerging significant differences on points of principle, and McKenzie's work became embroiled in them. Paul Baender rejected Greg's claim in

'The Rationale of Copy-Text' (pp. 44–7 above) that the printing closest to the authorial manuscript has greatest authority in respect of accidentals and should, for that reason, be the preferred copy-text (Baender 1969). Baender thought that this would not apply when there exists an authorial manuscript purposely left incomplete because the writer expected the printer to make final decisions about the accidentals. Two significant books agreed with Baender regarding such completion of authorial intentions in the printshop. In *Principles of Textual Criticism* James Thorpe wrote that

> In many cases, probably in most cases, he [the writer] expected the printer to perfect his accidentals; and thus the changes introduced by the printer can be properly thought of as fulfilling the writer's intentions. To return to the accidentals of the author's manuscript would, in these cases, be a puristic recovery of a text which the author himself thought of as incomplete or unperfected: thus, following his own manuscript would result in subverting his intentions. (Thorpe 1972, 165)

The same year, in his successor to R. B. McKerrow's classic *Introduction to Bibliography*, Philip Gaskell agreed:

> Most authors, in fact, expect their spelling, capitalization, and punctuation to be corrected or supplied by the printer, relying on the process to dress the text suitably for publication, implicitly endorsing it (with or without further amendment) when correcting proofs ... It would normally be wrong, therefore, rigidly to follow the accidentals of the manuscript, which the author would himself have been prepared – or might have preferred – to discard. (Gaskell 1972, 339)

Using the extreme example of Shakespeare's inconsistently spelled and largely unpunctuated contribution to *Sir Thomas More*, Gaskell exhorted editors: 'Let us carry out the author's intentions wherever we can, but not to the extent of taking pride in reproducing the manifest inadequacies of his accidentals' (Gaskell 1972, 359). Greg would prefer the accidentals of the author's manuscript if only we had it, although he harboured no illusion that the early edition most authoritative for accidentals came close to the author's accidentals; rather he was concerned with not settling for accidentals even more distant. Gaskell's retort was that we might very well know what would have been in the manuscript and consider it not fit to print.

Gaskell's *A New Introduction to Bibliography* was dedicated to his former student McKenzie and cited 'Printers of the Mind' ten times in its first half. The very existence of Gaskell's book indicated that McKenzie's work did not mark the end of bibliography itself, even though in a review of 'Printers of the Mind' Gaskell declared that it 'demolishes the greater part of the theory of skeleton formes' and that

Equally devastating assaults are made on received theories of proof correction and of press figures, and in every case the message is the same: all the primary documentation shows the actual working of real printing houses to have been both complex and inconstant, and therefore also shows much of the 'scientific' bibliography of the past twenty or thirty years to have been simplistic or mistaken. (Gaskell 1969)

Instead of getting despondent about analytical bibliography, Gaskell pointed to the 'great increase in our knowledge of the printing procedures of the past' that McKenzie had provided, which would in time 'enable bibliographers to formulate new and more soundly based hypotheses'.

Bowers saw where McKenzie's influence was leading and published a heavily critical review of Gaskell's book. Although also condemnatory regarding matters of scope (Gaskell's account went up to 1950 whereas McKerrow had stopped at 1800) and means of documentation, the thrust of Bowers's objection was Gaskell's dependence upon his former student:

> [McKenzie's] attempt in his controversial 'Printers of the Mind' to argue that the detailed conditions he has recovered from this special case [Cambridge University Press after 1695] apply substantially point for point with competitive London job printing of a hundred years before is much more conjectural than is generally recognized, and often demonstrably ill founded. That, in fact, analytical bibliography largely disproves his [McKenzie's] case is responsible for much of his attack on that discipline. 'Printers of the Mind' ... is not a safe foundation on which to rear the structure of a *New Introduction*. (Bowers 1973, 115)

The book was particularly galling in that as an eighteenth-century specialist Gaskell ought to have started with the Restoration rather than, as Bowers saw it, dabble earlier where his expertise was weak. To try to show this weakness Bowers repeated without substantiation Hinman's claim that the 1623 Folio was only scantily proofread and gave a list of Gaskell's supposed misrepresentations and errors (Bowers 1973, 118–20), mostly concerned with what can be determined from skeleton forme analysis. In this and his denial of concurrent printing – a 'fantastic assertion' (Bowers 1973, 119) – Bowers's real target was, in every particular, McKenzie's 'Printers of the Mind'.

Bowers's attack on McKenzie via Gaskell's book was motivated by a realization that a great proportion of his life's work was at stake. Like Gaskell, Peter W. M. Blayney saw McKenzie as a necessary corrective to New Bibliography, not an enemy of it. Blayney reassessed William S. Kable's essays on Folio/Jaggard's compositor B (pp. 79–80 above) and disagreed with his counts regarding the compositor's spelling preferences, as evidenced in the work for William Jaggard in 1619 and again for him in the 1623 Folio (Blayney 1972). Methodologically, it is reasonable to separate out contrasting habits in a long text suspected of being set by more than one man (as with the 1623 Folio), but it is unreasonable, Blayney argued, to use these habits to identify one of these men's work in a book set at another time, as when Folio compositor B is 'detected' working in Jaggard's printshop setting the quartos published by Thomas Pavier. After all, might not any number of men share those habits?

Blayney worked out from their watermarks the likely order of printing of the Pavier quartos and tabulated the skeleton forme reuse: essentially, sheets A(inner and outer), C(inner and outer) and E(inner and outer) used one skeleton, and B(inner and outer), D(inner and outer) and F(inner and outer) used a second skeleton (Blayney 1972, 196–9). But in the light of McKenzie's 'Printers of the Mind', is not skeleton forme reuse meaningless? No, Blayney argued, we just have to be careful about its value as evidence. While we cannot prove a break in printing from an irregularity of skeleton formes – because irregularity can arise from other causes if presswork and composition were not being balanced for each book – such a break might nonetheless be the cause and further evidence should be sought. In quartos it is safe to say that if a single skeleton is used throughout, the setting was essentially a one-man job. Even if different compositors took turns being that man, the single skeleton suggests that work was concentrated on one forme at a time: it is not that one compositor could not set two formes simultaneously, but if he was using one skeleton there would be no point to it. If two skeletons were used it is more likely that the copy was cast off into alternate sheets and that two compositors were setting in parallel. If we divide the Pavier quarto of *A Midsummer Night's Dream* (1619) by skeletons, there seem to be distinct habits that follow the skeletons (Blayney 1972, 200–3). So, Kable's claim that Folio/Jaggard compositor B alone set the Pavier quartos cannot be trusted, since it seems that two men set this one. But was Folio compositor B one of the two men? We cannot tell, for there is insufficient evidence: different men might have the same habits in respect of a given test and thus be indistinguishable by its means and yet behave distinguishably on other tests. Habits change, so that a single man might, over time, look like two, and equally two men might over time become indistinguishable.

Identification of compositors' habits in individual Shakespeare quartos was bound to be more speculative than identification of compositors in the 1623 Folio, because for the latter there had accumulated a significant body of knowledge about the underlying copy, printed and manuscript. Certain quartos are reprints of extant preceding editions, allowing bibliographers to compare the printer's copy with the resulting text (and so derive the compositorial habits), but precisely because they are reprints rather than substantive editions these quartos are of minor interest to editors. (Exceptions exist where Q2 is based in part on Q1 and elsewhere based on a manuscript, as seems to be the case with *Romeo and Juliet*, since compositorial habits determined from the section of Q2 that is merely a reprint can illuminate the section that is substantive, if the same man set it.) Identification of compositors in the 1623 Folio, on the other hand, is highly germane to the editorial task because it is the substantive early edition for many of the plays, and even for those for which it is merely a reprint it contains matter that an editor may well want to use because missing from, or more poorly presented in, the preceding quarto. Grounded in Hinman's monumental study, Folio compositor identification seemed blessed with reliable knowledge, and further advances were made by T. H. Howard-Hill while completing two doctoral theses (1960; 1971) that combined study of the writing habits (especially spellings) of the King's men's scribe Ralph Crane with compositorial analyses of the Folio comedies thought to have been set from Crane transcripts, *The Tempest, The Two Gentlemen of Verona, The Merry Wives of Windsor, Measure for Measure* and *The Winter's Tale*. Howard-Hill's confirmation that Crane transcripts were indeed the bases of these Folio plays appeared in a small book that had little immediate impact but was to become important to later work (Howard-Hill 1972) and in an immediately groundbreaking article in *Studies in Bibliography* (Howard-Hill 1973).

Howard-Hill's second thesis was supervised by Alice Walker, then still technically contracted to finish the original-spelling complete works of Shakespeare for Oxford University Press begun in earnest by McKerrow (Murphy 2003, 221–9). Howard-Hill found that his ends, in compositor study of the Folio, and Walker's could both be served by the production of original-spelling concordances to the early editions upon which Walker would base her project. Oxford University Press contracted Howard-Hill to produce such concordances for publication and the university made available computer facilities to mechanize the work (Howard-Hill 1969). These printed concordances continue to be used by editors and for specialist bibliographical studies, most prominently by Howard-Hill himself. Although at the time he thought their value small for his own work (1969, 163), Howard-Hill was still drawing useful conclusions from them four decades later (2006, 26). More significantly, long after they were produced the concordance project's computer tapes became invaluable to the purpose for which they had been originally created because their highly accurately keyboarded texts of the early editions formed the basis of the Oxford *Complete Works* of 1986 (pp. 167–89 below). To get the Folio texts keyboarded, Howard-Hill supplied his own copy of Sidney Lee's 1902 collotype facsimile (Howard-Hill 1969, 160), the introduction to which had stimulated the reaction from Greg with which the present narrative began (pp. 12–14 above).

Howard-Hill's article announced that Folio compositor A of the comedies section and compositor A of the histories section were not the same man: there was a new compositor F to be allowed for (Howard-Hill 1973). F was the next letter because A and B were identified by Thomas Satchell (1920) and Edwin Eliott Willoughby (1932) and Hinman added C, D and apprentice E (1957; 1963a; 1963b). Howard-Hill took the view that identifying compositors from their spellings alone is unreliable where we do not know how far they were affected by the spellings in their copy. He offered new habits to distinguish compositors: the presence or absence of spaces around commas in short lines and at the ends of lines, styles for turning over long verse lines and ways of dealing with *'ll* and *th'* elisions, and he added new spelling preferences to supplement the other tests. Howard-Hill acknowledged McKenzie's point that since compositors sometimes shared cases the identification of them by the appearance of their distinctive pieces of type alone was invalid (Howard-Hill 1973, 64), and he hoped to put identifications on a firmer footing. A new distinction was that compositor B was most likely to add a space after a comma, and this test corroborated evidence from spelling preference, after taking into account the possibility that Crane's preferred spellings in the copy he provided for the comedies might also affect the compositor (Howard-Hill 1973, 84–7).

The bifurcation in New Bibliography can be seen clearly by contrasting Howard-Hill's attempt to find new, more reliable methods of compositor identification with Alan E. Craven's attempt to develop further previous studies based upon the old and discredited methods. Building on W. Craig Ferguson's (1959) and Hinman's (Shakespeare 1966) identification of a single workman they called Simmes's compositor A, Craven attempted to sketch his habits as witnessed across Q1 *Richard 3* (1597), Q1 *Richard 2* (1597), Q *Much Ado About Nothing* (1600), Q *2 Henry 4* (1600) and Q1 *Hamlet* (1603), all made, in part at least, in Valentine Simmes's printshop and set, in part at least, by this man (Craven 1971; 1973a; 1973b; 1974). In constructing this career within the context of Simmes's business, Craven assumed (against all recent exhortations not to) that over the best part of a decade the compositor's habits were essentially unaltered, that for the purpose of allocating stints in a shared book it can be assumed that compositors did not share typecases (so recurrence of distinctive types can settle attribution where other evidence is lacking) and that from the variants within an edition the extent of its proofreading can be inferred. Because on some jobs Simmes's compositor A was setting from extant printed copy, Craven was able to quantify his rate and habitual types of error and so offer to any editor of a play set by him guidance about where and how to emend.

With rather more reliability, the same approach could be taken with Folio compositors. Howard-Hill had revised Hinman's attribution of Folio compositors, enlarging the share of compositor C (Howard-Hill 1973, 74–5) and MacDonald P. Jackson set about comparing this man's work with that of Folio compositors A, B, D and E (Jackson 1974). The evidence is compositor C's setting of Folio *Much Ado About Nothing*, which was essentially a reprint of Q (1600), and by looking at the Q/F differences Jackson decided that, rather like compositor B, compositor C was prone to omitting words, phrases and even whole lines, and hence an editor working on something set by him ought to be more than usually willing to emend possible error. Next Jackson turned to Folio *Love's Labour's Lost*, essentially just a reprint of Q1 (1598), to confirm this man's unreliability (Jackson 1978). Hinman's attributions of the sections of Folio *Love's Labour's Lost* set by compositors B, C and D had been confirmed by Howard-Hill and John O'Connor, and Jackson was able to derive a table of how often these men introduced trivial errors, omissions, interpolations, substitutions and transpositions in their work. The overall error rate was around six such slips per Folio page and the three men were about equally likely to err.

O'Connor attempted to refine Howard-Hill's identification of a new Folio compositor, F, and found new ways to distinguish him from compositor D with whom he shared habits (O'Connor 1975). Rejecting as sloppy Andrew S. Cairncross's work on compositor identification (Cairncross 1971; 1972), O'Connor used Howard-Hill's new psycho-mechanical tests, finding that compositor D made overflowing verse lines start at the left side of the line below (indented somewhat), while compositor F preferred right-flushed turnover or turnunder. The difference in habits, however, was not as marked as Howard-Hill thought and O'Connor added new tests based on spelling, and, relying upon compositor D's preferences as determined from what he did when setting from known quarto copy, O'Connor refined the attribution of their stints by using the absence of those traits to determine sections set by compositor F.

By the mid-1970s the field of compositorial studies looked like it had recovered from the shock of McKenzie's 'Printers of the Mind' and was finding ways to overcome its cautions. The least troublesome procedure was to footnote McKenzie's essay and then proceed as though it did not exist. Millard T. Jones did this when arguing that the 1622 quarto of *Othello* has so many gross errors that it cannot have been proofread (Jones 1974, 183), and so did Jackson when applying knowledge acquired from George Eld's printing of Shakespeare's *Sonnets* (1609) to *Troilus and Cressida* produced the same year in the same printshop (Jackson 1975, 3 n.7). McKenzie thus noted, Jackson went on to find evidence of 'composition ... comfortably ahead of press work' (1975, 12 n.30), indicating that he had not taken McKenzie's point at all. Perhaps sensing vulnerability, Jackson made a prediction: the compositor assignments he had deduced would match the results of psycho-mechanical comma-spacing tests that Howard-Hill had introduced. Eld's compositors A and B whom Alice Walker identified setting *Troilus and Cressida* put a space after 25 per cent and 11 per cent of their commas respectively, while for Jackson's compositors A and B working on *Sonnets* the rates are 19 per cent and 9 per cent respectively. The chance that these closely matching pairs of numbers were just coincidence, rather than the unconscious signatures two men left on two jobs, Jackson calculated at less than one in a thousand (Jackson 1975, 15).

The acknowledge-and-ignore approach to McKenzie was more prevalent in studies of early quartos than of the 1623 Folio and one more illustration may stand for many. George R. Price surveyed Q1 *Love's Labour's Lost* (1598) and established from apparent errors in casting off and the pattern of type shortage that it was set by formes (Price 1978). Price codified the habits of spelling, capitalization and indentation of three compositors who set the edition, without noticing that the same phenomena could be parcelled into a smaller number of less self-consistent men or a greater number of more self-consistent men, and he made no attempt at the kind of statistical analysis that Jackson advocated to firm up compositor assignments. Inferring the order of presswork from running title reuse, Price acknowledged McKenzie and Gaskell's warnings about 'the fallacy of thinking in terms of an uninterrupted process' only to ignore them: 'The order of formes through the press ... suggests a retarded movement and may reflect the compositors' difficulty in setting the text' (Price 1978, 426–7). A rather more subtle approach was taken by Thomas L. Berger in refuting Jonathan H. Spinner's (1977) claim that Q1 *Henry 5* (1600) was set by two compositors. The recurrence of type, including a distinctive italic V appearing on the inner and outer forme of one sheet, shows that one compositor was at work and that composition and presswork proceeded, for this sheet at least, at 'a relatively leisurely pace'. Either that or else (and this kept Berger on the windy side of McKenzie's law) 'printing [was] concurrent with another job' (Berger 1979, 117).

In an article that revised his initial responses to McKenzie's 'Printers of the Mind' (pp. 86–7 above), Davison showed that Greg, Hinman and Craven had occasionally selected bibliographical evidence to suit their arguments (Davison 1977). Characterizing the habits of Simmes's compositor A (pp. 92–3 above), Craven had presented as hard-and-fast his distinctions of such things as where stage directions are placed within the measure (flush-left, flush-right or centred) when in truth the phenomena are rather indistinct (a bit to the left, a lot to the right, or roughly central). The compositor's habit of omitting the period at the end of an unabbreviated speech prefix, which Craven relied upon, was also not consistent. Scepticism of the kind promoted by McKenzie would require rejection of these habits as inadmissible evidence, but Davison argued that they could be put to the cautious uses an editor might find for them. Inconsistent practices, Davison explained, might arise when a compositor moved from one printshop to another, taking with him his habits and perhaps spreading them to his new co-workers. Davison ended by considering the final editorial purpose of compositor identification, which is to establish how reliable each man's work was, so that an editor might, page-by-page, apply more or less emendation depending on the relative likelihood of error in the early edition on which her edition was based. This he thought reasonable, if the appropriate checks on the evidence were applied.

Doing much as others had done for Folio compositor B, O'Connor argued that we can work out the kinds of error that Folio compositors C and D habitually made, using the evidence of the quarto copy for their work, and that knowledge of these habits would help editors emend cruces (O'Connor 1977). He started by acknowledging that compositorial analysis had not yet given editors what was hoped for: clear guidance about when and how much to emend. But we know fairly well who did what and could now, O'Connor announced, say what kind of work they produced and to what level of fidelity. Under the headings of substitutions, omissions, interpolations and transpositions, O'Connor tabulated compositor C's and D's departures from known quarto copy in setting Folio comedies (O'Connor 1977, 59–65), and using the discovered habits he suggested what to do with certain cruces in pages set by these men from unknown or lost copy. Stanley Wells's Oxford *Complete Works* team drew on just this kind of work to make the bold emendations in their edition (pp. 167–89 below and Wells et al. 1987, 43).

Towards the end of the decade an entirely new and hitherto neglected class of evidence was brought into the discussions of early modern printing: books in Latin printed in England. James Binns collected and translated examples of where such books have notes from the author or the printer regarding the book's printing, which showed that in general they characterized it as a careful and methodical practice and wanted to acknowledge and rectify error (Binns 1977; 1979a; 1979b). One example quoted by Binns showed that printing could be done directly from autograph, and another (on the same page) showed, sixty-six years before Moxon wrote the same, that accidentals were considered the printer's and not the author's responsibility, and also that marking off another's words from one's own was considered an important means of assigning ownership of not only ideas but also the forms in which they were expressed (Binns 1977, 7). Thus although there were no notions of copyright in the sense that we mean it today, early moderns recognized the moral right of authors to ownership of their thoughts and words.

McKenzie found concurrent printing in the late seventeenth-century printshop and inferred that it was normal in the earlier period, which inference got empirical support when Philip R. Rider illustrated a case from the 1630s (1977). The catchwords '*Cla.* The' in the edition of James Shirley's *The Bird in a Cage* printed for William Cooke by Bernard Alsop and Thomas Fawcett (Shirley 1633a, G4^v) must be wrong because there is no such character in the play. The same year Alsop and Fawcett also printed Shirley's *The Wittie Faire One* for Cooke and at the top of one page Mr Clare has a speech that begins 'The old humour ...' (Shirley 1633b, F3^r). The obvious conclusion is that the plays were 'on the imposing stone at the same time', where the catchwords belonging to *The Wittie Faire One* got accidentally added to *The Bird in a Cage* (Rider 1977, 329).

In one of his first published papers, Paul Werstine returned to Walker's 1950s work on Folio compositor B (p. 56), which had determined that he was sloppy by showing that when setting Folio *1 Henry 4* from Q6 (1613) he made many more errors than his co-worker on the same play, compositor A (Walker 1954). Werstine wanted to see if Folio compositor B's work on *1 Henry 4* was typical of what he did when setting F from known quarto copy, so he considered the cases of *Much Ado About Nothing*, *Love's Labour's Lost*, *A Midsummer Night's Dream*, *The Merchant of Venice*, *Titus Andronicus* and *Romeo and Juliet* (Werstine 1978a). Folio compositor B's stints in these plays add up to about 133 per cent of the number of lines he set in Folio *1 Henry 4*, so if the latter was typical of his behaviour we ought to find in these six plays about 133 per cent of the number of errors found in *1 Henry 4*, making 215 errors in all. In the event, Folio compositor B made fewer errors than expected, and far fewer of the most serious types, so his reputation as a man who took liberties with his copy was undeserved. After considering, only to reject, the possibility that we are not examining the work of one man here – that is, the possibility that there might be yet another unidentified compositor who accounts for the differences in error rate – Werstine decided that what was anomalous was Folio *1 Henry 4* itself.

Large sections of prose accounted for errors in the casting off of the quarto copy for Folio *1 Henry 4*, and rather than redo the casting off compositor B decided to cram text into the existing allocations, departing from copy to do so. The evidence for this is that his errors do not occur evenly through his work, but are clustered in locations where he was setting prose copy in reverse order of pages (Werstine 1978a, 257–8). But even allowing for this, and for the greater effort of justification in setting prose (which may prompt departure from copy), Folio compositor B seemed to make too many mistakes in *1 Henry 4*, and Werstine pondered whether this showed that we cannot really discover the essentials of how the Folio was printed. Might we not in fact be deluding ourselves about something as basic as our capacity to tell one compositor's stint from another? This 'rather desperate' conclusion that compositor identification is 'useless' Werstine shied away from: 'Compositor identification remains a useful editorial tool' (Werstine 1978a, 260). On this fundamental, Werstine was later to change his mind and the minds of many others. Werstine here decided that with no reason to doubt Folio compositor B's general competence and fidelity to copy, editors working on plays he set should not lightly reject Folio readings. Werstine's research led him to counsel editorial conservatism: 'suspicion of error ... must be grave indeed, if emendation is to be acceptable' (Werstine 1978a, 261).

CODA

At the very start of the New Bibliography, W. W. Greg had amused himself and readers of *The Library* by baiting anti-Stratfordians who found in early books concealed evidence that Francis Bacon wrote the plays of Shakespeare (Greg 1902; 1903b; 1909). The Baconians' evidence was the presence of encrypted forms of their hero's name hidden inside other works or in pictures, and Greg had special fun showing that by the acrostic method of decoding employed by William Stone Booth he (Greg, that is) could uncover Bacon's 'ante-natal' work signed in early editions of the poetry of

Geoffrey Chaucer and John Lydgate (Greg 1909, 436–41). The problem, of course, was that Booth's method of discovering acrostics used rules so varied and flexible that almost any desired message could be uncovered from any substantial body of writing. For all its serious endeavour, the hunting of compositorial traits in the early editions of Shakespeare was in danger of falling into the same trap.

Andrew S. Cairncross re-examined the evidence from which Folio compositor E had been spawned by Charlton Hinman and, adding some refinements of his own, found that E set a couple of hundred pages formerly thought to be by compositor B (Cairncross 1972). T. H. Howard-Hill was moved by the extensive distortions of Cairncross's scholarship to publish privately two small monographs on them (1976; 1977), and an article setting the record straight on the extent of compositor E's work on the Folio. Cairncross's evidence and methods just had to be wrong, since by adopting them for testing purposes Howard-Hill discovered that 'E's hand could be found in every page in the Folio hitherto assigned to compositor B' (Howard-Hill 1980, 158). As with Greg's mockery of Baconians, the unacceptable conclusion invalidated the procedure. Howard-Hill suggested that Hinman's work on compositor E was skewed by the apprentice compositor setting type from two typecases and then distributing it without regard for which case it came from. In general type recurrence is not a good indicator of compositorial stint, and nor is spelling since compositors could be influenced by their copy in ways that are hard to predict. Howard-Hill criticized studies that assumed that each man's habits were fixed, this being as bad as assuming that 'a printer had only one job on hand at a time' (Howard-Hill 1980, 171). Thus D. F. McKenzie was acknowledged and the discipline could proceed using the best kind of evidence: the psycho-mechanical habits of spacing, methods of justification, style of turnovers and turnunders, layout of stage directions and the forms of catchwords and dashes.

By the end of the 1970s New Bibliography was over half a century old and had only just begun to generate from empirical principles new knowledge that might help an editor of Shakespeare make decisions at the level of the individual emendation. This help took the form of estimating the general level of fidelity to copy that could be presumed in an early edition (or part thereof) that would form the basis of a modern edition. Although the body of knowledge was growing, there was as yet little unanimity even regarding such basic facts as how many compositors set each early edition. The detailed studies that emerged in the 1970s had been technically feasible since the breakthroughs in headline analysis and type reuse of the 1940s and 1950s (pp. 54–64 above), but until the 1970s there were simply too few people engaged on the work for much headway to be made. Once the body of work grew, however, the singularity (and hence presumed certainty) of the bibliographical interpretations disappeared and it became clear that the basic data were available to widely different interpretations.

A second weakness of New Bibliography that began to be felt in the 1970s was its anti-theatrical prejudice. The focus upon early books and the frequently avowed desire to recover the script as it left the author's hands smacked of a disdain for drama as a performance art. Scott McMillin published two articles that showed just what could be brought to the debate by a proper consideration of recent research on theatrical practicalities (McMillin 1970; 1972). The second article also formed the first stage in a growing reassessment of the bad quartos and their relationship to the good editions, which led to one long-standing (but not integral or essential) strand of New Bibliography being widely discredited: the theory of memorial reconstruction. As we shall see, the essential principles of New Bibliography were not inherently antithetical to the treatment of Shakespeare as a theatre artist, and a synthesis called here the 'new' New Bibliography culminated in the most original and daring complete works edition of the century. First, however, it is worth surveying how the memorial reconstruction theory came about and how it collapsed.

Intermezzo: the rise and fall of the theory of memorial reconstruction

As we saw at the beginning of this narrative (pp. 12–15 above), the foundational act of the New Bibliography was A. W. Pollard's 1909 reinterpretation of the 1623 Folio preliminaries' reference to 'stolne, and surreptitious copies' as denoting not all the preceding quartos but only the bad ones produced by piracy: *Romeo and Juliet* (1597), *Henry 5* (1600), *The Merry Wives of Windsor* (1602), *Hamlet* (1603) and *Pericles* (1609). The following year W. W. Greg identified a possible vector for piracy when he established that the quarto of *The Merry Wives of Windsor* has scenes containing the Host that are much closer to the Folio text than the rest, suggesting that the journeyman actor who took this role had a hand in making the quarto's copy by recalling his lines (Shakespeare 1910, vii–lvi). Necessarily, an actor's recollection of lines (especially his own) from scenes in which he was onstage and speaking would be better than his recollection of lines overheard from somewhere offstage, which would explain why the quarto becomes like the Folio, the authoritative text, when the Host enters and drifts away from it when he exits. At this early point in the life of the new hypothesis the other bad quartos stood in an unknown relation to the good versions that appeared in subsequent quarto and Folio editions, but over time all of them (and more) were claimed by adherents of memorial reconstruction.

Greg was not the first to suggest that a Shakespearian bad quarto was created by the memorial reconstruction of the play by an actor who had performed in it. In the middle of the nineteenth century Tycho Mommsen claimed that Q1 *Hamlet* (1603) was so created, with the gaps in the actor's memory being filled by a hack dramatist (Mommsen 1857), and Henry David Gray revived this forgotten claim (Gray 1915). Gray advanced his case as Greg had his, by identifying the part played by the actor supposed to be responsible for the memorial reconstruction, in this case Marcellus. Gray gave a full list of the mistakes in the Q1 part of Marcellus, showing that they are far fewer than the mistakes in other parts and that when Marcellus is onstage the reporting improves in quality. This last claim

Gray did not drive home and it is the crux of the matter, since to make a case parallel to *The Merry Wives of Windsor* requires that the quality of the memorial reconstruction drops off as soon as the actor supposed to be doing it leaves the stage. This Gray failed to show. To get around the problem that the play-within-the-play is well reported in Q1 even though Marcellus is not in it, Gray suggested that the actor of Marcellus doubled as one of the Players. To account for the bad verse of Q1 *Hamlet*, Gray followed Mommsen in supposing that a hack dramatist stitched together the actor's recollections with joining material of his own devising. While working on *The Merry Wives of Windsor* Greg had wondered whether a 'reporter' was also responsible for the corruption of Q1 *Hamlet* (Greg 1910, 197), which term leaves unsettled the matter of whether an actor recalled his lines or a stenographer took shorthand notes during a performance. The difference between these two vectors might be impossible to detect. Both rely upon actors' memories, although a stenographer's report ought to be more even than one by a single actor, who would likely recall his own lines more accurately than others'. A shorthand stenographer's report relies upon a further operation of memory since the potentially ambiguous symbols have to be expanded in the light of what the stenographer recalled the actors saying.

John Dover Wilson published a pair of articles on the topic, and they were republished as a stand-alone pamphlet (Wilson 1918c; 1918a; 1918b). He argued that the bad quarto of *Hamlet* was based on a transcript of the play as it was performed in the early 1590s, which original play by Thomas Kyd was subsequently worked upon by Shakespeare. However, just before it was printed this transcript (now a decade behind what was being performed under this title on the London stage) was altered by the actor who had played Marcellus and Voltemand (and others) in the recent performances, who used his memory and his actor's part to bring the old transcript into general conformity with the play as currently staged. Wilson's tortuous argument received a lukewarm review from Percy Simpson, who objected that 'the element of conjecture enters largely into it' (Simpson 1919). Simpson was more sceptical of the part of Wilson's narrative concerning the transcript than of the presence of memorial reconstruction. In his review of the pamphlet, Greg described the body of recent textual research that Wilson drew upon as the 'New Bibliography' (that term's first appearance in print), and characterized it as 'practically a new science' (Greg 1919b, 380, 382). Wilson had not established a second clear case of a bad quarto being created by memorial reconstruction and his wilder conjectures led to a pair of volumes on the 'Critical Bibliography' (as his subtitle put it) of the *Hamlet* manuscripts (Wilson 1934a; 1934b). These books lie outside the mainstream tradition of New Bibliography because their sound technical investigations (such as systematic collation of press variants in early editions) were mixed with unsubstantiated speculations of bewildering complexity.

In 1919 Wilson collaborated with A. W. Pollard on a series of articles that extended his early-1590s-transcript hypothesis to cover not only Q1 *Hamlet* (1603) but also Q1 *Romeo and Juliet* (1597), Q1 *Henry 5* (1600) and Q1 *The Merry Wives of Windsor* (1602) (Pollard and Wilson 1919a; 1919b; 1919c; 1919d; 1919e). These plays, they claimed, were particularly vulnerable to piracy because they had been shortened for touring in May 1593 when plague closed the London theatres. Pollard and Wilson pointed out that stenography could not be the source of these bad quartos, for it produces evenly bad results and in these plays the badness clearly varies by role. Memorial reconstruction, Pollard and Wilson argued, was resorted to only where the purloined transcript lacked what had been recently performed in London, and they attempted to show moments where the bad quarto seems a garbled version of the Folio text. Pollard and Wilson's unsubstantiated historical narrative about theatres and touring was clearly meant to compensate for their lack of textual data, and nowhere did they show that the bad quartos had writing that could come only from an actor's memory. The best they could do was point to garbled meanings and the occasional phrase or line that seemed like an echo or anticipation of material from elsewhere, arguing that these are the kinds of textual corruption that human memory generates.

T. M. Parrott published an article on Shakespeare's authorship of *Titus Andronicus* and its early stage history (Parrott 1919) that mentioned in passing Greg's narrative about the circulation of the text among the theatre companies of the early 1590s (Greg 1908c, 159–62). Responding to Parrott, Greg added a new example to the list of claimed memorial reconstructions: the so-called 'fly scene' (3.2) in *Titus Andronicus* that is absent in Q1 (1594) and its reprints Q2 (1600) and Q3 (1611) and present in the 1623 Folio printed from Q3 (Greg 1919c). Their own copy lost in the Globe playhouse fire of 1613, Greg argued, the King's men bought the most recent edition, Q3, and observing that it lacked the 'fly scene' (due to its Q1 copy being made before Shakespeare revised the play) they 'succeeded in reconstructing it from memory'. Greg offered no evidence for this conclusion, other than that it fitted the scant facts available from theatre history, and he did not pursue the point in his later work. Other ways that scene 3.2 could have got into the Folio include its Q3 copy being compared to the prompt-book just before printing, and the missing 84 lines being inserted. Thus, although Laurie Maguire included the Folio's printing of this scene as one of her 'suspect texts' in a revaluation of the theory of memorial reconstruction (pp. 119–23 below), it was only incidentally associated with the theory and can be disregarded without consequence.

Hereward T. Price opposed Wilson and Pollard's view that Q1 *Henry 5* derives from an early 1590s version of the play, and used P. A. Daniel's evidence that the version of the play represented in the Folio was shortened (rather badly) to make the version in Q1 (Price 1920, 5). Daniel pointed out that in Q1's scene 1.2 the bishop outlines Henry's claim to France using the phrases 'Hugh Capet also' and 'the foresaid Duke of Loraine' with no grammatical antecedents, and having explained only Capet's case the bishop sums up with 'So ... King Pippins title and Hugh Capets claime, | King Charles his satisfaction all appeare' (Shakespeare 1600b, A2^v), despite his having said nothing about Pépin and Charles. Daniel argued that unless a dramatist intentionally wrote this nonsense and the necessary antecedents were added later to make the perfectly sensible wording of the Folio (a rather implausible hypothesis), Q1 must represent an imperfect shortening of a fuller version, already in existence, that later supplied the Folio copy (Shakespeare 1877, xi–xii). This, Daniel realized, disproves the theory of eighteenth-century editors that Q1 represents an early version of the play that Shakespeare improved upon to make the one represented in F. Daniel anticipated by nearly half a century the evidence and logic by which Peter Alexander would demonstrate the same relationship between Q1 *The Contention of York and Lancaster* (1594) and Folio *2 Henry 6* (Alexander 1924a). Seeking to explain how the version of *Henry 5* underlying F became the version underlying Q1, Price found variants that shorthand abbreviation (that is, stenography) might produce (Price 1920, 13–18). He had to admit, though, that Gower's part is so well reproduced in Q1 that the actor playing him must have had a hand in the process, either by recalling his lines or supplying his part containing them (Price 1920, 19).

R. Compton Rhodes declared himself of the opinion that the bad quartos of *Romeo and Juliet* (1597), *Henry 5* (1600), *The Merry Wives of Windsor* (1602) and *Hamlet* (1603) were memorial reconstructions by 'former hired men of the Lord Chamberlain's Company, who had prepared the versions for performances not in London, but round the country' (Rhodes 1923, 73). Rhodes's work was imperiously free of references to preceding scholarship, so it is difficult to tell how much of it was fresh thinking of his own; he acknowledged in prose (without an explicit reference) Greg's work demonstrating that the Host in *The Merry Wives of Windsor* is implicated in the making of the quarto. On the crucial matter of how memorial transmission might be distinguished from other modes of transmission, Rhodes had nothing new to offer. Using much the same arguments as Price made for *Henry 5*, B. A. P. van Dam argued that Q1 *Hamlet* was produced by stenography (Dam 1924). To account for the obvious errors in the text, van Dam supposed lapses of a hurried shorthand, exacerbated by the kinds of transposition, repetition and interpolation with which actors habitually mangle a text when speaking it (Dam 1924, 1–72). This innovative claim has been revived by a scholar of the transmission of folk narrative, for whom performers' alterations are more a kind of benign streamlining than a mangling, and it deserves further investigation (Pettitt 2001). Although the idea was clearly catching on, no-one had presented a case for memorial reconstruction anything like as strong as the case Greg made for *The Merry Wives of Windsor*.

New hard evidence came when Peter Alexander published an article claiming that Q1 *The Contention of York and Lancaster* (1594) could only have derived from a memorial reconstruction by actors of the play later printed in the Folio as *2 Henry 6* (Alexander 1924a). The clinching evidence is a bungled account of his ancestry spoken by the character York. In Q1 York says that Edmund of Langley (Duke of York) was the second son of Edward 3, which if it were true (it is not) would make the rest of his argument, claiming the throne via the third son Lionel Duke of Clarence, entirely pointless (Shakespeare 1594, C4^r). The problem is not merely that the account is unhistorical, but that it makes no sense on its own terms, and hence, Alexander reasoned, the text cannot closely represent what any competent author could have written. Only actors, recalling their lines, could get this complex but crucial genealogical claim so badly wrong. Alexander's argument has yet to be convincingly refuted, although as we shall see there have been strenuous attempts. Having established that memorial reconstruction was the main source for Q1, Alexander sought the agents and settled on the two men playing Warwick and Suffolk/Clifford. Their lines, like those of the Host in *The Merry Wives of Windsor*, are well reported, if we judge by how closely they match the corresponding lines in the Folio.

Alexander was careful to qualify his claim with the observation that a Q1 stage direction ('Enter at one door the Armourer and his neighbours … drinking to him', Shakespeare 1594, D1^v) is so close to the corresponding direction in F (*'Enter at one Doore the Armourer and his Neighbors … drinking to him'*, Shakespeare 1623, n1^r) that Q1's printers must also have had a transcript of the play. Because actors memorize actions rather than the words used to describe them, their recollections could not be the source of the precisely phrased direction in Q1, and on the evidence of the sole surviving actor's part from the period (Edward Alleyn's in the title role of Robert Greene's *Orlando Furioso*) even the actors' cue-scripts being available to the printer could not account for Q1's stage direction being verbally identical to F's. In a second article the same year, Alexander claimed that memorial reconstruction also underlies O (for octavo) *Richard Duke of York* (1595), which imperfectly reports the play that was later printed in the Folio as *3 Henry 6* (Alexander 1924b). The logic of the argument was the same – only actors' faulty memories could produce the errors discovered – but the evidence was not quite so secure. The first key moment was Richard Gloucester's line 'And that I loue the fruit from whence thou | Sprangst, witnesse the louing kisse I giue the child' (Shakespeare 1595, E7^v), which is a mangling of F's 'And that I loue the tree fro<m> whence y^u sprang'st | Witnesse the louing kisse I giue the Fruite' (Shakespeare 1623, q4^v). The problem, of course, is that the 'fruit' should be the outcome (as in F), not the source (as in O), of the new young bud being kissed. Perhaps, Alexander conceded, 'the accepted theory might be stretched to cover this corruption' so that the lines were said to have been mangled in theatrical adaptation and/or printing.

Alexander had a second example that was more convincing. In O, Clarence complains:

> *Cla.* For this one speech the Lord *Hastings* wel deserues,
> To haue the daughter and heire of the Lord *Hungerford*.
> *Edw.* And what then? It was our will it should be so?
> *Cla.* I, and for such a thing too the Lord *Scales*
> Did well deserue at your hands, to haue the
> Daughter of the Lord *Bonfield*, and left your
> Brothers to go seeke elsewhere, but in
> Your madnes, you burie brotherhood.
> (Shakespeare 1595, D3^v–D4^r)

This makes reasonable sense on its own, but much better sense is made by the version that appears in F:

> *Clar.* For this one speech, Lord *Hastings* well deserues
> To haue the Heire of the Lord *Hungerford*.
> *King.* I, what of that? it was my will, and graunt,
> And for this once, my Will shall stand for Law.
> *Rich.* And yet me thinks, your Grace hath not done well,
> To giue the Heire and Daughter of Lord *Scales*
> Vnto the Brother of your louing Bride;

> Shee better would haue fitted me, or *Clarence:*
> But in your Bride you burie Brotherhood.
>   *Clar.* Or else you would not haue bestow'd the Heire
> Of the Lord *Bonuill* on your new Wiues Sonne,
> And leaue your Brothers to goe speede elsewhere.
>   (Shakespeare 1623, p6ʳ)

As Alexander pointed out, F matches what the chronicle source says: Scales's heir and daughter was married to the new queen's brother, and Bonville's heir and daughter married to the new queen's son. These favours being resented by Richard and Clarence, the Folio is properly motivated. O has Richard and Clarence pointlessly objecting to Scales himself marrying the heir and daughter of Bonville, with no mention of the crucial fact that it is the new queen's relations (brother and son) being honoured in this way that is so resented by Edward's brothers who helped him to the throne.

Memory is used to hold a few words at a time during transcription and printing, but Alexander pointed out that whereas a scribe or printer always has the correct phrasing in front of him and can refer to it if words drop from his memory, an actor recalling his lines has nothing but memory to go on and is likely to transpose whole scenes or speeches in a way that scribes and printers could not. Having established one clear example of memorial garbling, Alexander offered other moments that can best be explained by this hypothesis, and pondered how and why the reconstruction was executed. Such extra-textual matters regarding the circumstances that might drive actors to make a memorial reconstruction were thought to bolster the new theory and Greg used them extensively in his argument (1919a; 1922, 333–57) that the 1594 edition of Greene's *Orlando Furioso* was also a bad quarto in which memorial reconstruction (as well as actors' interpolation and theatrical cutting) had played a part.

Alexander repeatedly attempted to expand the category of Shakespearian bad quartos to bring in early editions hitherto unsuspected (Alexander 1926). The 1594 edition of *The Taming of a Shrew* had long been held distinct from the play printed in the 1623 Folio as *The Taming of the Shrew*: its plot differences, its place names (Athens instead of Padua for the main action, Sestos instead of Verona for the hero's home) and its verbal differences are sufficient to see these as two plays instead of one. However, Alexander argued that *A Shrew* is a debased version of *The Shrew*, principally on the evidence that the latter is closer to the source play, Ludovico Ariosto's *I Suppositi*. Either Shakespeare turned *A Shrew* into *The Shrew* by making the play more closely follow Ariosto's version, or *A Shrew* derives from *The Shrew* and its greater distance from Ariosto is explained by corruption. Alexander's argument that the latter scenario is inherently more likely is not especially convincing.

Alexander attempted to bolster his weak claim with an example that 'beyond dispute' showed the quarto version to be a garbling of lines that were later printed in the Folio version:

> *San.* thou hast braued
> Many men: braue not me.
> Thoust faste many men.
> *Taylor.* Well sir.
> *San.* Face not me Ile nether be faste nor braued.
> (Anonymous 1594, E2^v)
>
> *Gru.* Thou hast fac'd many things.
> *Tail.* I haue.
> *Gru.* Face not mee. thou hast brau'd manie men,
> braue not me (Shakespeare 1623, T4^v)

For Alexander, the Folio shows Grumio rightly beginning with the tailoring sense of the verb 'to face' to get the tailor's assent, then switching to the everyday meaning and extending it with 'to brave'. The garbled quarto ruins the pun by putting 'to face' after the open aggression of 'to brave', and it would be extraordinary, argued Alexander, for someone to have found the quarto's mess, its latent pun in ruins, and fixed it up to make the Folio's lines.

Although Alexander's is indeed 'the obvious explanation', he had not proved his point decisively, as he did with the Henry 6 plays, by showing that the early edition contains something virtually impossible for a skilled dramatist to write. Two years later Alexander added another (also relatively weak) claim of garbling to the case, and made much of the fact that fragments of Christopher Marlowe's writing are embedded in *The Taming of a Shrew* (Alexander 1928). These are by either Marlowe or someone recalling or copying his work. Since so much of *The Taming of a Shrew* is poorly written, Alexander held that neither Marlowe nor Shakespeare could be responsible. Would not someone else familiar with the period's drama (say, an actor) who was in the act of reconstructing what was spoken in performances of *The Taming of the Shrew* be likely to interpolate garblings of Marlowe where his memory or other resources failed him? Simultaneously, John Semple Smart made precisely the same claim on the same evidence (Smart 1928, 201–5).

The theory of memorial reconstruction gained adherents rapidly, and became an attractive research topic for higher degrees. Before Alexander presented his full findings in book form, Madeleine Doran published her Master of Arts degree thesis, which corroborated his view of the relationships between the 1590s editions and Folio *2 Henry 6* and *3 Henry 6* (Doran 1928). She found evidence of adaptation (that is, theatrical revision) as well as memorial reconstruction separating the 1590s editions and the Folio, just as Greg found when comparing Alleyn's part in *Orlando Furioso* with the play's 1594 quarto. Like Greg, Doran could see good (non-piratical) reasons for a theatrical company to recreate a full text of a play from the actors' recollections of their lines, such as being on tour and wanting to perform a play for which the authorized book has been left behind in London. Thus an edition derived from memorial reconstruction need not be surreptitious. There was increasing awareness in the 1920s that A. W. Pollard erred in interpreting non-entry of a play in the Stationers' Register prior to publication as evidence of wrongdoing by a publisher (pp. 15–16 above), and Doran commented that the non-registration of *Richard Duke of York* (1595) might have been 'merely an attempt on [publisher Thomas] Millington's part to save the fee by running it through under the license of the entry for the *First Part of the Contention*' (Doran 1928, 82). For Alexander, however, memorial reconstruction was virtually synonymous with 'Theatrical Piracy', as he called it in his book summarizing his position (Alexander 1929, 53–73). Introducing Alexander's book, Pollard implicitly distanced himself from this view by commenting that: 'for such [pirated] texts the money would have been so small as to make their construction hardly worth while' (Alexander 1929, 4).

Alexander and Doran offered their analyses of Q–O/F relationships as alternatives to the narrative presented by Edmond Malone in which the 1590s editions of the Henry 6 plays represent versions by Robert Greene and George Peele that Shakespeare revised to make the plays presented in the Folio as *2 Henry 6* and *3 Henry 6* (Shakespeare 1821, 555–96). Thus an additional attraction of the memorial reconstruction theory was that it restored a sense of Shakespearian wholeness: the textual fragmentation is merely a consequence of faulty transmission in the first editions rather than inhering in the dramatic material itself. At just this moment, E. K. Chambers powerfully and influentially insisted on the integrity and wholeness of the Shakespearian canon (Chambers 1924–5), and his concern to resist others' hands in the work can be understood in relation to the ways that early twentieth-century literary criticism developed in response to the experiences of those who had lived through the 1914–18 War (Grady 1991, 47–63; Egan 2006, 4–16; King 2006). In such a climate, an attractive theory can seem to operate almost by stealth. In his introduction to

Alexander's book, Pollard claimed that it was 'if not generally, at least very widely accepted' that as well as the proven cases of *The Merry Wives of Windsor*, *The Contention of York and Lancaster* and *Richard Duke of York*, the bad quartos of *Romeo and Juliet* (1597), *Henry 5* (1600) and *Hamlet* (1603) were also at least in part created by 'reconstruction from memory and actors' parts' (Alexander 1929, 5). It is not clear why these additional plays were sliding over to the memorial reconstruction category, for hard evidence had not been offered. But they were sliding.

In 1930 appeared Chambers's monumental *William Shakespeare: A Study of Facts and Problems*, the title and structure of which gave the impression that anything not presented as a problem had been established as a fact. Chambers wrote that Q1 *Romeo and Juliet* (1597) 'is certainly a reported text ... from an original more closely resembling Q2' and that 'Most evidential of a reporter are transpositions of lines and phrases from one place to another' (Chambers 1930, 341, 342). To make this a convincing argument Chambers should have established the direction of transposition, showing why the lines' and phrases' locations in Q1 could have arisen only by corruption of the writing underlying Q2. Chambers scarcely bothered to argue the case for Q1 *Henry 5* (1600), beyond observing its 'perversion' of F: 'This corruption is far beyond what can be attributed to errors of transcription and printing, and can only be explained by some process of reporting' (Chambers 1930, 391). Q1 *Hamlet* (1603), Chambers wrote, is 'generally accepted' to be based on a report and again he gave examples of echoes and anticipations that show material that later appeared in Q2/F being dispersed across Q1 (Chambers 1930, 415). Within twenty years of Greg's proving the presence of reporting in Q1 *The Merry Wives of Windsor* (1602), the memorial reconstruction theory was being used to explain all the bad quartos that Pollard offered as the referent of the Folio's 'stolne, and surreptitious copies'. The inflation of the new theory's range continued apace and brought yet more early editions into the bad quarto category. Chambers was hesitant about the copy for Q1 *King Lear* (1608), but declared 'I think that the characteristics of Q point to a reported text' and wondered if it 'was produced ... by shorthand and not memorization' since 'it does not misplace bits of dialogue within a scene, or bring in bits from other scenes or other plays' (Chambers 1930, 465).

In the published version of the argument of her Ph.D. thesis, Doran resisted this characterization of Q1 *King Lear*, pointing out that the edition is much too good to be the result of memorial reconstruction and that its few errors typical of mishearing (by stenographer or actor recalling another's lines) – such as 'a dogge, so bade in office' for 'a dog's obeyed in office' (Shakespeare 1608, 14ʳ) – could also be explained by dictation of copy in the printshop or by a compositor misremembering a line as he set it (Doran 1931, 122–37). In an analysis that anticipated by half a century a celebrated upheaval in the discipline, Doran argued that the greatest differences between Q1 and F *King Lear* were created by Shakespeare's substantial revision of his work (Doran 1931, 136). Responding to Doran, Greg gave qualified support to Chambers's view: 'the quarto *Lear* emphatically is not [an actors' memorial reconstruction]. If it is indeed a reported text it must have been taken down by shorthand' (Greg 1933, 256). Amplifying this argument about stenography, Greg went on to respond to Edwin Hubler's objection that the mislineation in Q1 *King Lear* saves space, and hence must be a compositor's doing rather than a reporter's (Greg 1936–7). Greg asserted that in fact the mislineation does not save space but nonetheless is a compositor's doing: he was trying to make sense of copy that lacked division into verse lines, which is the kind of copy one gets from a stenographer. In passing, Greg mentioned that the case of Q1 *King Lear* is rather like the case of Q1 *Richard 3* (1597), which gave him reason to doubt the theory of stenographic transmission, since the system capable of producing such good quality texts was introduced in 1602, too late for *Richard 3*. Greg was cautious about memorial reconstruction in general, and was not proselytizing for his new explanation of the provenance of the bad quartos. Others were proselytizing. In the published version of his Ph.D. thesis, David Lyall Patrick made the case for Q1 *Richard 3* being 'memorially transmitted' (Patrick 1936, 146) although he was unwilling to commit himself on whether this was done by actors recalling their lines or by stenography. Patrick presented examples of transposition and substitution of words that he considered conclusive evidence of memory at work; they read now as uncompelling evidence that is merely compatible with his theory (Patrick 1936, 35–104).

There was one final addition to the bad quarto category. In 1916 Pollard published a facsimile of Q3 *Richard 2* (1598), recently distinguished from another edition in 1598, and commented upon the appearance of the play's abdication episode for the first time in Q4 (1608). This newly printed episode had, Pollard thought, 'too many omissions and too many mistakes in line arrangement to allow us to believe that it was obtained for cash from the King's servants as a body, or transcribed from an acting part', so it was 'probably procured by means of shorthand writers sent there [the playhouse] for the purpose' (Shakespeare 1916, 64). Chambers took the same view (1930, 350), and thus when Leo Kirschbaum came to write a census of bad quartos towards the end of the 1930s the tally for Shakespeare stood at nine-and-a-bit: *The Contention of York and Lancaster* (1594), *Richard Duke of York* (1595), *Romeo and Juliet* (1597), *Richard 3* (1597), *Henry 5* (1600), *The Merry Wives of Windsor* (1602), *Hamlet* (1603), *King Lear* (1608), the abdication episode scene of *Richard 2* (1608) and *Pericles* (1609). Kirschbaum took Greg's likening of the case of *King Lear* to *Richard 3* as support for the latter being a memorial reconstruction (Kirschbaum 1938, 27), although Greg had in fact been outlining the evidence that gave him doubts: Q1 *King Lear* and Q1 *Richard 3* are alike, yet the former is too good to be a memorial reconstruction by actors and the latter preceded the invention of a system of stenography good enough to make it.

In Kirschbaum's census, the term bad quarto was synonymous with memorial transmission, whether directly by actors or by stenographers who had to expand shorthand notes using their recollection of what the actors remembered of their lines when performing the play. The memorial theory had taken on a life of its own, yet only two substantial arguments had been made for it: Greg's foundational claim for *The Merry Wives of Windsor* based on Q and F locking together and drifting apart as the Host enters and exits, and Alexander's observations about York's absurd genealogy in *The Contention of York and Lancaster* and the absurd complaints about the marriages of the daughters of Scales and Bonville in *Richard Duke of York*. Wilson's student George Ian Duthie set out to strengthen the claim for Q1 *Hamlet* (Duthie 1941). Although he provided an exemplary history of the development of the theory of memorial reconstruction, and gave powerful reasons to reject the wilder theories of his tutor, Duthie was unable to adduce evidence proving that Q1 *Hamlet* is a memorial reconstruction.

The following year, Greg produced one of his monumental statements of where the discipline stood, *The Editorial Problem in Shakespeare* (1942), and in respect of the quartos he was unwilling to approve a simple binate split between the good and the bad, inventing an additional category for the doubtful cases. Those he declared bad quarto memorial reconstructions were *The Contention of York and Lancaster* and *Richard Duke of York* (on the basis of Alexander's arguments), *Romeo and Juliet* (with disquiet about the evidence, and nothing new to offer), *Hamlet* (with disquiet about which actor could have done it, and suspicion that it was not piracy at all), *Henry 5* (confidently, but with no hard evidence offered) and *The Merry Wives of Windsor* (for the reasons he gave in 1910). At the end of this list of bad quartos (Greg 1942, 52–76) he put *The Taming of a Shrew* and *Pericles*, but in each case he gave his reasons for thinking the edition not really bad, not essentially a memorial reconstruction. By placing them at the end of his bad quarto list, Greg implied that they might easily pass over to the next category, the doubtful quartos, to join *Richard 3* and *King Lear* (Greg 1942, 77–101). Greg declined to call the first editions of these two plays bad because they are of generally high quality, and the variations they show from their authoritative counterparts are mostly indifferent.

Regarding *Richard 3* Greg declared himself convinced by Patrick's arguments about the memorial nature of the underlying manuscript (p. 110 above), and especially the point (rather more tentatively offered by Patrick than Greg made it seem) that the occasion for its manufacture was an entire troupe recalling their lines to overcome the lack of an authorized book. That is to say, for Greg the collaborative theatrical nature of the memorial reconstruction explains its high quality when compared to other reconstructions made by one or two actors, and also removes suspicion of piracy. Although his critics have not credited him for it, Greg here showed that he regarded the theatre as a legitimating force, not a corrupting one, in relation to early editions. Likewise with *King Lear* not only the quality of Q1 but also its legitimate theatrical provenance set the play apart from the bad quarto memorial reconstructions. Greg believed that the underlying manuscript came from a stenographer using a powerful new system (Willis 1602) who was attending a private or court performance, the special venue accounting for the play being much longer than other reported texts, which reflect the relatively short duration of public performance. Although Greg refused the simple good/bad quarto distinction, insisting on a middle category, the New Bibliographical tradition he did much to create tended to wield this binary as freely as it wielded his foul papers/prompt-book distinction. At their most careful, the New Bibliographers combined a claim of memorial reconstruction with one of revision, so that both authorized variation and corruption was said to separate the bad edition from the legitimate. This often overlooked synthesis of hypotheses is essential, since it would be absurd to imagine that someone simply forgot all the choruses of *Henry 5* when making the bad quarto of 1600.

His admission about the 'fly scene' (3.2) in *Titus Andronicus* notwithstanding (pp. 102–3 above), Greg was opposed to the idea that Shakespeare revised his plays, so wherever alteration for performance seemed to arise Greg had to find unauthorized agents. Alfred Hart, however, thought that alteration for performance might be a routine procedure fully accepted, even anticipated and welcomed, by Shakespeare. His prime evidence was that Shakespeare and Ben Jonson wrote plays longer than everyone else's, and that given what we know of the duration of performances they would routinely have had to be cut (Hart 1932a; 1932b). Thus when he came to consider the bad quartos, Hart treated their relative shortness (compared to their Folio counterparts) as merely a sign that they had undergone the cutting necessary for performance and not evidence of mutilation (Hart 1942, 119–49). If Hart was right that any play over about 2,400 lines would be cut for performance, then two of the bad quartos, Q1 *Richard 3* (1597) and Q1 *King Lear* (1608), could not be acting versions for the simple reason that they are too long.

Work on the bad quartos continued from the 1940s to the 1960s, with only minor details of difference about particular cases, as when Duthie argued that *The Taming of a Shrew* was a memorial reconstruction not of Folio *The Taming of the Shrew*, but of a lost early play that was reworked by Shakespeare to make the Folio version (Duthie 1943). The published version of Harry R. Hoppe's Ph.D. thesis attempted to strengthen the case for Q1 *Romeo and Juliet* (1597) being a memorial reconstruction. Under the now traditional headings of transpositions, anticipations, recollections, borrowings, repetitions, mishearings, paraphrase, summary, expansion, non-Shakespearian verse and equivalent expressions, Hoppe collected the internal evidence that showed Q1 to be consistent with the presumed characteristics of memorial reconstruction (Hoppe 1948, 126–90). But he failed to find evidence that could be explained by no means other than memorial reconstruction. In 1949 Duthie showed that Q1 *King Lear* (1608) could not have been made by one of the three methods of stenography available at the time, because the differences from F are not the ones that any conceivable misreading or faulty expansion of symbols could generate, and moreover the misreadings and faulty expansions to which the systems are prone are generally absent (Duthie 1949). This substantial achievement Kathleen Irace later mistook for proof that no bad quarto could have been made by stenography (Irace 1994, 189 n.2).

By the 1950s the theory of memorial reconstruction was firmly established as an orthodoxy that accounted for the bad quartos, and although small pieces of evidence consistent with the theory continued to turn up there were to be no new compelling proofs of the kind with which Greg and Alexander had founded the hypothesis. For plays other than *The Merry Wives of Windsor*, *The Contention of York and Lancaster* and *Richard Duke of York*, the memorial reconstruction explanation was vulnerable to critique. Yet when the attack came it was directed towards the two history plays. The first fully worked denial of part of the received opinion – the part that made memorial reconstruction and bad quarto virtually synonymous – did not appear until 1972. Scott McMillin set out to answer the pertinent question 'how good are the "bad" quartos' of the Henry 6 plays and *The Taming of a Shrew* (McMillin 1972, 143)? A theatre historian, McMillin approached the problem by thinking in terms of a playing company's human resources and practices. *The Taming of a Shrew* (1594) and *Richard Duke of York* (1595) name Pembroke's men on their title pages, and although *The Contention of York and Lancaster* (1594) does not, it is so closely connected with *Richard Duke of York* (1595), the pair of them being printed together as the *Whole Contention* as early as 1619, that Pembroke's men presumably performed it as well. So Pembroke's men's resources and practices were the issue.

One of the supposed signs of memorial reconstruction is the transposition of material from its proper place to elsewhere in the play, and McMillin noted that Q1 *The Contention of York and Lancaster* and O *Richard Duke of York* have whole scenes in different places from their Folio counterparts. This, he argued, could not happen by actors' misrecollection of their scripts since that would suppose them 'deficient in a basic requirement of playing in ensemble' (McMillin 1972, 146). This was not entirely fair, for the significant transpositions claimed by adherents of memorial reconstruction were fragments of dialogue not whole scenes, and they generally accepted that large-scale revision (as would move whole scenes) was an additional factor separating the memorial reconstruction and the authoritative edition. This is why they often associated bad quartos with regional touring, which would provide the occasion for such adaptation. More pertinently, McMillin caught Doran attributing to actors' error a reordering of scenes that produces in Q1 *The Contention of York and Lancaster* a thematic contrast – two fathers fight one another, then their sons fight one another – that improves upon Folio *2 Henry 6* (Doran 1928, 67–8; McMillin 1972, 146). More significantly still, McMillin was able to show that Q1 improved upon the Folio version by reducing from thirteen to eleven the number of adult actors needed, and eleven actors are also needed for the most populous scenes in *Richard Duke of York* and *The Taming of a Shrew*. By approaching the problem with the practicalities of performance in mind, McMillin showed that the allegedly bad quartos were rather better than they were commonly held to be by critics whose primary criterion was the quality of the poetry. As scripts, they were not so bad at all and embodied intelligent reworkings for improved doubling throughout.

Also stage-centred was Michael Warren's attack on the idea that Q1 and Folio *King Lear* are two witnesses to a single, lost ideal version of the play (Warren 1978). As Warren noted, Chambers resisted the idea that Shakespeare revised his plays, for this would force us to accept that differing early editions might accurately reflect distinct versions, whereas the work of poetic-artist Shakespeare should, by Chambers's critical criteria, display wholeness and integrity (Warren 1978, 97; Chambers 1924–5). Dismissing

Doran's claim (1931) that Q1 and Folio *King Lear* are separated by authorial revision, Greg commented that 'we have no evidence whatever that such persistent and wholesale revision was anything but exceptional in Elizabethan dramaturgy, and further ... it appears particularly unlikely in the work of so fluent a writer as Shakespeare' (Greg 1942, 89). Warren pointed out that many respectable writers are known to have revised their work, and he demonstrated that separating Q1 and Folio *King Lear* is a clear set of systematic artistic changes that weaken Albany and turn Edgar from 'a young man overwhelmed by his experience' to one who 'has learned a great deal, and who is emerging as the new leader of the ravaged society' (Warren 1978, 99). Much as McMillin claimed for the Henry 6 plays, Warren argued that a coherent set of theatrical changes could not have emerged merely by textual corruption. Warren's argument, taken up and extended by others, has been entirely successful and most professional readers of Shakespeare avoid treating Q1 and Folio *King Lear* as one play (pp. 133–46 below). However, as with McMillin's argument, establishing that revision separates two early editions does not of itself dismiss the memorial reconstruction hypothesis, for its adherents had largely accepted that revision might also be at work.

Steven Urkowitz was the first directly to attack memorial reconstruction as a fundamental mistaking of the nature of dramatic writing. He warmed up with an argument that the three editions of *Hamlet*, Q1 (1603), Q2 (1604–5) and F (1623), are separated by conscious artistic revision, much in the manner of the two early editions of *King Lear* (Urkowitz 1986b). In one detail, however, Urkowitz demonstrated that memorial reconstruction was positively the weakest explanation for a variation. In Q1 Gertrude learns from Horatio of Claudius's plot to kill Hamlet, which is also how the play's sources tell the story, whereas Q2 and F have Gertrude ignorant of her husband's guilt. As Urkowitz pointed out, it is hard to see how memorial reconstruction by actors would bring back material from the sources that the dramatist had dropped, but easy to imagine that the first version of the play, underlying Q1, contained this detail from the sources that was lost in the revision that made the versions underlying Q2 and F (Urkowitz 1987b, 48). The same logic had been used to show that authorial revision separates Q1 and Folio *King Lear*: in certain details Q1 is closer than F to the source play *King Leir*, which is hard to explain if Q1 derives from a corruption of the play underlying F (Jackson 1983, 332).

In a second article, Urkowitz attacked David Lyall Patrick's claim – accepted by Antony Hammond for his Arden edition (Shakespeare 1981) – that Q1 *Richard 3* (1597) is a memorial reconstruction of the play that ended up in the Folio (Urkowitz 1986a). Urkowitz used essentially the same means as McMillin, but argued his cases more trenchantly. According to Urkowitz, the adherents of memorial reconstruction were insufficiently aware of stage practice, getting wrong such matters as casting economy, and in truth the allegedly bad quarto is perfectly good. Like McMillin and Warren, Urkowitz convincingly demonstrated that the memorial reconstruction hypothesis was not the only, or necessarily even the best, way to account for the bad quarto's differences from the authoritative edition, but he failed to prove that it was definitely the wrong explanation.

In the title of a third article, Urkowitz went to the heart of the problem in seeking to prove that memorial reconstruction cannot exist where its presence had been thought indisputable, naming his target as Peter Alexander (Urkowitz 1988b). Urkowitz began with curiously vehement praise for Alexander's silencing of 'the noxious voices' (Urkowitz 1988b, 232) of disintegrators who would give 'Greene, Peele, Marlowe, and many less worthy others' a hand in *The Contention of York and Lancaster* and *Richard Duke of York*. Regarding the problem of York's bungled genealogy in Q1 *The Contention of York and Lancaster* (p. 104 above), Urkowitz accused Alexander of misrepresenting its consequences: 'In neither the Quarto nor the Folio does York in the dialogue mention his own lineal descent from Edmund of Langley' (Urkowitz 1988b, 237). The problem would not exist for an audience member, thought Urkowitz, unless she knew the true genealogy, since York's stumble (saying that Edmund Langley was Edward 3's second son) has no consequences within the play. No-one would spot the problem because 'an audience will inevitably lose track of the argument' while York recites his family tree. Urkowitz here perhaps underestimated the capacity of an Elizabethan theatre audience to follow an oral history lesson, and he wondered whether Shakespeare, away from his prose chronicles, made the genealogical mistake himself and fixed it later.

Regarding O *Richard Duke of York*'s version of the complaint by Edward's brothers of favouritism towards the queen's relatives (pp. 105–6 above), Urkowitz defended it as merely different from the Folio version but equally plausible dramatically. Urkowitz had one last strand to his argument that he thought 'terminally embarrassing to Alexander's case' (Urkowitz 1988b, 253). This was the observation that the phrasing of stage directions in Q1 *The Contention of York and Lancaster* is suspiciously close to the phrasing of stage directions in Folio *2 Henry 6*, which ought not to happen since the wording of stage directions is not committed to memory by actors. In fact, Alexander himself had pointed out the most arresting such case regarding the drunken armourer (pp. 104–5 above) and acknowledged that it proved a transcriptional link between Q1 and F in addition to the memorial link. Urkowitz made no mention of R. B. McKerrow's suggestion that in places the Folio texts of *2 Henry 6* and *3 Henry 6* were set up from exemplars of the 1590s editions (McKerrow 1937). He did, however, respond to Andrew S. Cairncross's wild speculations on the matter and rightly drew attention to the problem that if F was in places set from these editions then the difficulty becomes explaining the small differences between Q1 and F and O and F in these places (Urkowitz 1988b, 254 n.17). Again, McKerrow had anticipated the objection, commenting that 'We should ... not be at all surprised if we find these scraps of bad quarto text inserted into the Folio somewhat tidied up, punctuation and metre improved and occasionally a better word substituted' (McKerrow 1937, 70). The terminal embarrassment Urkowitz thought he had uncovered had been fully anticipated.

Kathleen O. Irace (1994) undertook to re-examine the cases of what she counted as the six most eligible candidates for the memorial reconstruction hypothesis: *The Contention of York and Lancaster* (1594), *Richard Duke of York* (1595), *Romeo and Juliet* (1597), *Henry 5* (1600), *The Merry Wives of Windsor* (1602) and *Hamlet* (1603). As well as the usual discursive analysis of such matters as staging requirements and revision, Irace performed statistical tests to try to put hard numbers on the likeness of each character's part as represented in the alleged memorial reconstruction and the authoritative edition. If the grouping of characters on the stage were figured into this analysis, it would provide a means for distinguishing between transcription and recollection, for

if a character's lines are very similar in the two texts, the role might have been simply copied from a player's manuscript containing his lines. But if lines spoken by others when a particular character is on stage correspond in the two versions, along with the character's own lines, this would suggest that the actor playing the role reconstructed the segment from memory. (Irace 1994, 116)

Necessarily, a degree of subjectivism entered even such an apparently objective analysis, since the distribution of speeches among speakers is not identical in the bad quartos and the good editions. For example, in the excerpt from O *Richard Duke of York* given above (pp. 105–6), Clarence makes the complaint about Lord Scales's marriage, but in the Folio the complaint is made by Richard. Irace tried to distinguish between cases where a change in speaker seems artistic and those where it looks like a printing error (Irace 1994, 201 n.3). Since the stage directions in all early editions are imperfect to a greater or lesser extent, Irace had to make judgements in supplying necessary entrances and exits. Clearly a character who speaks must first be given an entrance direction, but how far in advance of the speech to place it can be hard to decide, as can the moment to send off a character who has no more lines. The placing of these directions bears upon a key variable that Irace was trying to isolate: who might overhear whom (Irace 1994, 201–2 n.4).

Also fallible was Irace's way of measuring the similarity between a line from a bad edition and its counterpart in a good one, which allowed five degrees of likeness: *all*, *most* or *some* of the words were the same (irrespective of word order), one line was a *paraphrase* of the other, or the line was *exclusive* to one edition. Irace did not discuss whether or by how much she discounted articles, conjunctions and prepositions when making the comparison. If they are not discounted, her method would detect that *most* of the words (four out of seven) are shared between 'For a cat sat on the mat' and 'For on the hour a lifetime froze', whereas most readers would declare these utterly unalike and not linked by memory. Irace added one more rule: a reporter would remember his own lines more accurately than the lines of those onstage with him, so the candidates for reporter could be only characters whose own lines in the bad quarto are better reported than the lines of those onstage with them. Irace tabulated her results, and for *The Merry Wives of Windsor* the outcome was clear: the Host's lines in Q1 and the Folio are especially close, followed in order of closeness by the lines of Falstaff and Pistol in Q1 and Folio *Henry 5*. Irace repeated the analysis for the other plays, and in general confirmed the identifications of reporters made by previous scholars (Irace 1994, 118).

However, Irace was not able to confirm the central hypothesis since her results did not show that memorial reconstruction must have occurred. According to her Appendix C the accuracy of bad quarto lines is high for the likeliest reporter-candidates – the Host and Falstaff in *The Merry Wives of Windsor*, Marcellus and Voltemand in *Hamlet*, Exeter in *Henry 5* and Romeo, Paris and Mercutio in *Romeo and Juliet* – but in general the lines of those onstage with these characters are no better reported than the lines of those who are not. Thus a traditional assumption of the memorial reconstruction hypothesis could not be validated by Irace's method. To account for this Irace was forced to fall back upon the familiar additional hypotheses of adaptation/abridgement, lapses of attention by the reporter, and patterns of doubling that make it impossible to determine just who might have overheard whom. Irace thought that she had at least established that 'the reporters must have been working from their knowledge of performances based on scripts very similar to those preserved in the Folio – an important finding of this study' (Irace 1994, 124). This claim arose from the suspected reporters' parts in the reported editions being nearly or fully as large as their corresponding parts in the Folio, whereas 'an intermediate abridgement would presumably have reduced the [reporter's] role along with the rest of the play' (Irace 1994, 123). This was an unsafe assumption, since certain parts in any play are more necessary to the plot than others and will be cut by less, if at all, in an abridgement, as Lukas Erne pointed out (2003, 207–8).

The whole subject of bad quartos and memorial reconstruction was taken up in Laurie Maguire's *Shakespearean Suspect Texts* (1996). Maguire looked for hard evidence to support the claim that plays could in principle be reconstructed from memory. The little evidence available was strongest regarding systems of stenography, their use in the recall of sermons and practices in the Spanish theatre; new evidence from the heart of the Shakespeare performance tradition could not be found. A fresh re-examination of all the alleged signs of memorial reconstruction in extant early modern drama ought to reveal what else, apart from the operations and lapses of memory, could cause the phenomena. If the alleged signs of memorial reconstruction are real, they ought to be largely absent in the non-suspect plays, and Maguire used as a 'control ... all the dramatic texts in the Malone Society Reprint series, and a comprehensively random reading of the printed works of ... Anon., Beaumont, Brome, Chapman, Dekker, Fletcher, Greene, Heywood, Jonson, Kyd, Lodge, Lyly, Marlowe, Marston, Middleton, Munday, Nashe, Peele, Shirley, Tourneur, and Webster' (Maguire 1996, 155).

The outcome was that many of the alleged symptoms of memorial reconstruction are present in the non-suspect texts, so either there was greatly more memorial reconstruction than previously suspected, or the tests were giving false positives. Maguire took in turn each symptom of memorial reconstruction that had been alleged since the theory was first presented:

1 under 'Repetition': External echoes/recollection; Internal repetition; Paraphrase; Connective repetition; Formulae; Banal and stereotyped exit lines
2 under 'Insertion': Extra-metrical connectives; Local/topical references; Expanded clowning
3 Omission
4 Transposition
5 Submerged or wrecked verse
6 Aural error
7 Length of speeches (that is, failure to develop long ones)

8 Fractured allusions and Factual errors
9 Unevenness
10 Character vignette (that is, overly blunt statements in place of development)
11 Poor jesting
12 Plot unconformities
13 Reduced casting
14 Staging requirements
15 Brevity
16 Under 'Stage directions': Descriptive stage directions; Vestigial characters; Massed entries
17 Mislined verse
18 Punctuation

Symptoms 1 to 11 Maguire considered as aspects of 'The Poem', meaning 'that which the audience hear and the actors speak', symptoms 12 to 14 were aspects of 'The Play', meaning 'that which an audience would see and/or the actors would perform', and symptoms 15 to 18 were aspects of 'The Text' meaning the extant 'material entity' in as much as this contains 'material features which are neither seen/acted nor heard/spoken, such as punctuation, stage directions, and mislining' (Maguire 1996, 155–6).

This somewhat debatable taxonomy (are not stage directions seen in performance?) did not detract from the core of the research, which was that virtually every phenomenon claimed as a symptom of memorial reconstruction is present in editions no-one had suspected (Maguire 1996, 159–223). Rather than abandon these symptoms altogether, Maguire used the evidence of non-suspect texts to refine her criteria. For example, when locating the recollection of an external text in a given suspect, she would exclude phrases that are short and/or merely commonplace, and likewise with internal repetitions (Maguire 1996, 161–75). The use of repetitive formulaic language is common in dramatic writing of the period and counts for nothing as evidence, whether in dialogue or as means of giving characters a reason to leave the stage (Maguire 1996, 176–80). Insertions, especially pleonastic ones that spoil the metre, would at first seem a good indicator of memorial reconstruction, but Maguire was able to show that they too are common in non-suspect editions (Maguire 1996, 181–6). Something redundant when spoken in the London theatres, such as mentioning that a certain place is near London, might not be redundant when playing to a provincial audience, and Maguire excluded 'Local/topical references' as too weak a support on which to rest an argument (Maguire 1996, 186). Passages of low comedy that have been castigated as too poor to be the dramatist's own Maguire rejected on the grounds that actors' improvisations might work their way into an authorized document, and in any case the whole distinction was too subjective (Maguire 1996, 186–90). An obvious objection to the claim that actors' improvisations got into authorized documents is the apparent pointlessness of recording them, although Eric Rasmussen made the ingenious argument that those of the clown playing Ralph Betts in the original performances of *Sir Thomas More* had to be remembered and written down (in the surviving manuscript) for a revival in the early 1600s, when improvisation had fallen out of fashion (Rasmussen 1991).

In order to put all the editions 'on an equal footing' (Maguire 1996, 155), Maguire did not look at the good quartos or Folio of Shakespeare when searching for the symptoms of memorial reconstruction in the bad quartos, so necessarily it was difficult to detect omission except where there is glaring discontinuity in dialogue or action (Maguire 1996, 190–3). In any case, as Maguire observed, once we discount the unfounded association between provincial performance, shortened texts and memorial reconstruction (Maguire 1996, 54–5), the omission of material of itself gives no cause for suspicion. The local transposition of words and clauses can occur just as easily in transcription and printing (by eye-skip) as in recollection, so Maguire gave this evidence no credence at all (Maguire 1996, 193–4). Seriously wrecked verse, however, is hard to attribute to copiers or to dramatists themselves – bad writers of verse are, if anything, more metronomic than good ones – so for Maguire this textual condition, while not weighty on its own, could corroborate other evidence (Maguire 1996, 194–6). Aural errors of the kind 'a dogge, so bade in office' for 'a dog's obeyed in office' (Shakespeare 1608, 14^r) can occur in transcription and printing, so they count for nothing in diagnosing memorial reconstruction (Maguire 1996, 196–8). Faulty classical allusions and other factual errors (such as getting from Verona to Milan by ship) Maguire thought just as easily assigned to authors as reconstructors, and hence of 'little diagnostic' value (Maguire 1996, 201). Where there is a noticeable unevenness in the literary/dramatic quality of a play, this can just as easily be due to various kinds of adaptation or even replacement of lost sheets of a manuscript as it can be due to variations in the quality of recollection of a reconstructor, and hence Maguire was willing at most to accede that it is only 'a symptom of some hiccup in textual transmission' (Maguire 1996, 204).

Another subjective criterion is the under-development of a character, as when stereotypical or mechanically unhuman in relations with others. In performance such things can produce powerful artistic effects, and in any case some suspect editions have extremely subtle characterization, so this symptom counts for little (Maguire 1996, 204–5). 'Poor jesting' (unfunny material and fragments of humour where we would expect whole episodes) is likewise subjective, and a fragment in the writing might have been the cue for extended improvisation in performance. Plot inconsistencies and discontinuities are found in non-suspect editions and hence are not symptomatic of misrecollection (Maguire 1996, 205–11). Having dismissed the association of memorial reconstruction with touring performances by reduced casts using shortened scripts, and showing that in any case suspect editions need large casts, Maguire dismissed as useless the criteria of cast size and staging requirements. A play might be short because someone could not recall all the lines, but equally it might have been intentionally shortened, so length proves nothing (Maguire 1996, 211–16).

Evidence from the tone and descriptive nature of stage directions should never have been taken seriously and for each example from a suspect edition an analogue from a non-suspect one could be found by Maguire. The presence in stage directions of ghost characters (named but having no role in the play) and mutes (named but having no lines in the scene where named, although active elsewhere in the play) Maguire took together under the heading 'Vestigial characters'. There are examples in non-suspect plays and in any case the ordinary behaviour of dramatists, such as a change of mind during composition, and the exigencies of adaptation can produce ghosts and mutes (Maguire 1996, 216–21). Where an edition masses in a scene-opening stage direction all the characters in the scene, one might construct plausible hypotheses about the utility of this within an act of memorial reconstruction – perhaps the playhouse plot was available to aid memory, or the reporter was recalling everyone needed for the scene – but the symptom proves nothing for it is also the demonstrable habit of the King's men's scribe Ralph Crane (Maguire 1996, 221). Similarly, mislining of verse occurs in non-suspect editions and since we know it can be created by non-suspicious means it counts for nothing (Maguire 1996, 221–2). Finally, Maguire turned to light punctuation and admonished New Bibliographers for setting aside their knowledge that, on the evidence of Hand D in *Sir Thomas More*, Shakespeare's own manuscripts were virtually unpointed; moreover, she quoted Joseph Moxon describing punctuation as the compositor's responsibility (Maguire 1996, 222–3). As we saw (p. 96 above), James Binns showed that, long before Moxon wrote about it, printers took responsibility for punctuation in their books.

Maguire's book is worth close inspection because it is to date the most systematic study of the memorial reconstruction hypothesis, and was executed with rigour. Its main conclusion is that almost all the tests used to diagnose memorial reconstruction give false positives and that the short-term memory failure of a compositor or scribe misrecalling a line he had just read from copy is easily confused with the long-term memory failure that is properly a sign of memorial reconstruction (Maguire 1996, 223). Maguire tabulated her verdicts on forty-one plays suspected of being memorial reconstructions, including fourteen that she deemed 'Shakespearean' (Maguire 1996, 154). These fourteen comprise the nine-and-a-bit bad quartos identified in Kirschbaum's census (pp. 110–11 above), rounded up to ten, plus the 'fly scene' (3.2) in Folio *Titus Andronicus* (identified by Greg, pp. 102–3 above, omitted by Kirschbaum), plus *The Taming of a Shrew* (identified by Alexander, pp. 106–7 above, omitted by Kirschbaum), plus two quartos, *1 Troublesome Reign* (1591) and *2 Troublesome Reign* (1591). These last two Maguire included because she thought that E. A. J. Honigmann had identified them as memorial reconstructions (Maguire 1996, 13). In fact, Honigmann observed only that they seemed bad and were perhaps based on foul papers (Shakespeare 1954e, 174–6), as Maguire acknowledged elsewhere in her book (Maguire 1996, 315). In a list of how each play fared with her tightened-up rules, none came out as definitely memorial reconstruction. For *The Taming of a Shrew* (1594) 'A Strong Case Can Be Made' while *Hamlet* (1603) and *Pericles* (1609) fell into the 'A Case Can Be Made' category and the remaining Shakespearian candidates were 'Not' memorial reconstructions (Maguire 1996, 324–5). Of course, Maguire noted, it is easier to show that the script underlying an early edition need not have been a memorial reconstruction than to prove that it must have been (Maguire 1996, 323), and for the cases that cannot be proven it remains an 'ingenious ... and attractive possibility', not a fact (Maguire 1996, 338).

We have seen the New Bibliography's blurring of the distinction between a bad quarto, simply a member of the category invented by Pollard to explain the Folio preliminaries' apparent hostility towards earlier editions, and a memorial reconstruction. At the close of the twentieth century, Paul Werstine examined that process in respect of *Romeo and Juliet* (1597), *Henry 5* (1600), *The Merry Wives of Windsor* (1602) and *Hamlet* (1603) to show that memorial reconstruction alone could not 'provide a full account' of their origins (Werstine 1999a, 311). (There is an element of straw-man argument here, since memorial reconstruction was in any case usually combined with an hypothesis of theatrical revision.) Werstine applied Greg's original exacting standard – good and bad versions should lock together when the reporter enters and break apart when he leaves – to show that the one clear example in *The Merry Wives of Windsor*, the Host's first entrance, is unique: never again in that play, and never in other plays, does an entrance by the alleged reporter make such a noticeable difference. When the Host leaves in 2.1, Q1 and Folio break apart, Werstine admitted, and hence Greg's claim about the Host's agency in the reporting is corroborated.

The inadequacy of the memorial reconstruction hypothesis is revealed, according to Werstine, when we notice that the Host's presence does not always make Q1 and F snap into agreement, even for his own speeches, and that occasionally Q1 and F lock together when he is offstage. Werstine mockingly dismissed Greg's explanation that this occurs because F represents a revised script, later than the Host's performance recalled to make Q1. This explanation struck Werstine as special pleading brought in to explain what 'prevented the Host from knowing his lines' (Werstine 1999a, 315 n.12). For the other plays, Werstine rightly complained that the snapping together and breaking apart of the supposedly memorial and authoritative versions is never consistently associated with any potential actor-reporter's entrances and exits. In Q1 *Hamlet* (1603), the usual suspects Marcellus and Voltemand are absent from the second half of the play, and in the first half the correlation between their presence and the quality of the reporting is inconsistent. Some times their entrances make the versions lock together and their exits make them break apart, but at others they are onstage when the reporting is bad and off when it is good. Wilson thought up a doubling assignment for one actor that he hoped would save the memorial reconstruction hypothesis: Marcellus, Voltemand, a Player, Second Grave-digger, Churlish Priest and English Ambassador, and non-speaker in other scenes, but unfortunately for several of these roles Q1 does not noticeably converge with Q2/F although they are present when others' lines do converge, so they cannot be the reporter's roles (Werstine 1999a, 322).

The case of Q1 *Henry 5* (1600) is even harder for the supporters of memorial reconstruction, Werstine argued, because there is little agreement even about the basic matter of where the correspondences with F lie. Exeter is the best candidate for a reporter, but some of his lines are so badly reported that this is hard to sustain. More difficult still is the case of Q1 *Romeo and Juliet* (1597) and Werstine thought that only Harry R. Hoppe argued for its being a memorial reconstruction (Werstine 1999a, 326). In fact the argument was made by Pollard and Wilson in 1919 and Rhodes in 1923, was declared by Pollard to be generally accepted in 1929, was repeated by Chambers in 1930 and Kirschbaum in 1938, and reiterated by Greg in 1942, before Hoppe's Ph.D. thesis, published in 1948, made what Werstine thought the lone claim (pp. 102–13 above). Hoppe proposed the actors of Romeo and Paris as the reporters, but needed considerable special pleading to get around extensive poor reporting while these men are onstage and good reporting while they are offstage. As we saw with Irace's work (pp. 117–19 above), there is no agreed quantitative way to measure the quality of reporting and numbers can be precise yet inaccurate. Gary Taylor's work on Q1 *Henry 5* – considered below (pp. 170–1) in the context of the Oxford Shakespeare – looked for the scenes with the least number of the errors that happen in reporting, and within these scenes (in which the reporter must have been onstage) looked for errors in each candidate's part: the man with the least errors in the least erroneous scenes is the reporter. The problem with this last-man-standing quantitative analysis, Werstine pointed out, is that in a rank ordering after any kind of corruption (even just random garbling) someone has to come out on top; ranking the disparate effects of corruption gives no indication of its cause (Werstine 1999a, 328).

Roger Warren returned to the originary problem of the Duke of York's bungled genealogy in Q1 *The Contention of York and Lancaster* (1594) and Urkowitz's attempt to set it aside. York wrongly says that Edmund Langley (Duke of York), his ancestor, was the second son of Edward 3 when in fact he was the fifth son (Shakespeare 1594, C4^r); were he the second son York need hardly continue justifying his descent via his mother, a descendant of the third son of Edward 3. Urkowitz saw no serious dramatic problem here since York does not draw attention to Edmund Langley (Duke of York) being his ancestor, so an audience will not notice the error, but Warren countered that an audience would make the historically correct assumption that one York was descended from the other and hence Q1's version is dramatic nonsense (Warren 2000, 194). Warren went on to detail a collection of moments (none as clinching as the genealogy) in which Q1's wording is just a garbling of F's, not a viable dramatic alternative. He also made a subtle and complex argument about revision separating Q1 and F, the latter being essentially the later version. If we accept the principle that a pair of early Shakespeare editions might be separated by revision and by memorial reconstruction, rather than only one of these agents, the number of potential explanations for a particular textual difference is multiplied and the chances of pinning down the correct one are greatly reduced. All that remains is the opportunity to demonstrate that in particular cases one or other of these agents of change cannot be operating.

This more limited aim John Jowett brilliantly achieved in an analysis of Q1 *Richard 3* (1597) showing that its underlying manuscript could not have been made by memorial reconstruction since it follows F's erratic stage direction and speech prefix alternation between Stanley and Derby as names for one man (Jowett 2000). Actors do not memorize speech prefixes and stage directions in the way they memorize dialogue, so the link must be transcriptional. Folio *Richard 3* was printed from exemplars of Q3 (1602) and Q6 (1622) – both reprints in a monogenetic line descending from Q1 – annotated by reference to an authoritative manuscript. This annotation produced regularity in speech prefixes such as Lady Anne's that are variable in Q1 (*Lady An.*, *La.*, *Lady*, *Lad.*) but consistent, with abbreviation, in F (*Anne* or *An.*). However, the character of Lord Stanley is inconsistent in a special way. Q1 and F have other characters refer to him as Derby until scene 3.1 when they switch to calling him Stanley. In speech prefixes and stage directions, however, the play from 3.4 to the end has a peculiar pattern of inconsistency in both editions. In 3.4 he is Derby in speech prefixes and stage directions even though he has become Stanley in dialogue, in 4.1 he goes back to being Stanley in speech prefixes and stage directions (just as he is in dialogue), and from 4.5 to the end of the play he switches again to Derby in speech prefixes and stage directions even though he is Stanley in dialogue.

If the manuscript used to annotate the Folio's quarto copy had contained these changes in Stanley's name then the annotator would have let them stand, but if it did not we can be sure he would have annotated the quarto to reflect the manuscript, making the Folio's copy, and hence the Folio, consistent regarding this name. We know this because the annotator introduced such consistency for other names and for other details in the scenes containing the variation. Indeed, he even did it for Stanley's name elsewhere in the play, overruling the quarto. Since the Folio has this variation in Stanley's name, the inescapable conclusion is that it was present in the manuscript used to annotate the Folio's quarto copy. The variation was also present in the manuscript from which Q1 was printed (which is how it got into Q1) and hence these two manuscripts are related by a process of transcription, not memorial reconstruction, since no actor could possibly remember such a pointless system of variation in the forms of a single character's name. Could not the manuscript underlying Q1 have been based on a memorial reconstruction but later annotated by reference to an authoritative manuscript (in the line that led to F) in which the variation in Stanley's name was present? No, because other speech prefix names in Q1 do not match their Folio counterparts (for example, *Bish*[*op*] versus *Ely* and *Glo*[*ster*] versus *Rich*[*ard*]), which they should do if someone attempted to bring Q1's underlying manuscript into line with the Folio's.

There, with a negative proof, we must leave the topic of memorial reconstruction. There seems little hope of new positive proofs demonstrating that only memorial reconstruction can explain a particular early edition of Shakespeare, although Adele Davidson attempted to overturn Duthie's widely accepted argument that no system of stenography sufficient to the task was available when the manuscript underlying Q1 *King Lear* (1608) was written (Davidson 1992; 1996; 1999). Davidson showed that there was more stenography in use than has been thought, that Henry Chettle provides a link between the world of the theatres and those using stenography to record sermons for publication, and that some of the Q1/F variants in *King Lear* could emerge from ambiguities arising in shorthand. She was unable to show, however, that only stenography could explain the state of Q1. Following up a suggestion by Maguire, Jesús Tronch-Pérez showed that in the Spanish theatres of Shakespeare's time a renowned master of memory, Luís Remírez, was able to write down an entire Lope de Vega play after hearing it three times in performance, and that the resulting manuscript differs from the authorized version much as Q1 *Hamlet* (1603) differs from the good editions (Tronch-Pérez 2002; 2004). Again, this keeps open the possibility of an explanation of memorial reconstruction without proving it. Also inconclusive is William Davis's argument that Q1 and Q2/F *Hamlet* are separated by a pattern of subtle authorial revision in which complex chiastic structures in the former were returned to later and reworked (Davis 2006).

The memorial reconstruction hypothesis alone cannot explain the existence of the bad quartos. Allied with a hypothesis of revision, memorial reconstruction is persuasive for some of the plays (for example in Warren's account of *The Contention of York and Lancaster*) but sceptics are entitled to complain that this looks like special pleading: where one explanation fails, the other can fill the breach. Arguments such as McMillin's and Urkowitz's that the bad quartos are theatrically competent have encouraged writers to surround the adjective with inverted commas ('bad' quartos) to signal scepticism. The bad quartos are now often put on an equal footing with the good editions and published as alternative versions of the same plays (pp. 190–206 below). Just one remaining bad quarto, Q1 *The Merry Wives of Windsor* (1602), has features that even sceptics such as Werstine accept as proof that it is not a distinct version in its own right but rather must derive by corruption from the good version (Werstine 1999a, 313 n.9); the decisive evidence is the impact of the Host's entrances and exits on the closeness of Q1 and F.

We seem to be back where we started at the beginning of the twentieth century, with the theory of memorial reconstruction having followed an almost circular trajectory. In the light of other developments in the 1980s and 1990s called the New Textualism, it might look as though the whole field of Shakespearian bibliographical study has followed such a trajectory. This Intermezzo has treated memorial reconstruction separately from the larger chronological account in order to forestall such projection from the smaller narrative to the larger. The fall of the memorial reconstruction hypothesis is sometimes made to stand as synecdoche for the fate of New Bibliography in general (for example, Weingust 2006, 78–136), which is imagined to have been so comprehensively unpicked that we are returned to the late Victorian state of ignorance about how well the early editions reflect what Shakespeare wrote. The critiques and revisions of New Bibliography in the 1980s show that the truth is somewhat more complex than that.

CHAPTER 4

New Bibliography critiqued and revised, 1980–1990

> ... it is not inconceivable that in the future we can make better texts of Shakespeare than we have today. I do not see any drastic or sensational changes. As long as the current consensus of opinion about the authority of the texts is substantially correct, as I believe it is, there is no possibility of a drastic shake-up; that would follow only the upsetting of our notions of authority.   (Shaaber 1947, 108)

PRECURSORS OF NEW TEXTUALISM

In 1935, C. S. Lewis initiated an exchange of letters in the *Times Literary Supplement* by suggesting that Shakespeare's primary artistic intention was to create performances rather than write a definitive manuscript, and so modern editors seeking to recover from the early editions the words of the lost definitive authorial manuscript were chasing something that never existed (Lewis 1935a; Bateson 1935; Wilson 1935a; Lewis 1935b; Lawrence 1935a; Wilson 1935b; Ridley 1935; Greg 1935; Lawrence 1935b; Wilson 1935c). Any manuscript Shakespeare created would at best be only the 'embryo' of his final object, Lewis argued, requiring others to work upon it and merge their creativity with his in order to produce Shakespeare's intended outcome, the performance. In his contribution W. J. Lawrence cited similar objections to editorial method made in 1917 and 1928. W. W. Greg agreed with Lewis that scripts are not fixed but change over time as they are reworked by their authors, by scribes and (in the case of plays) by theatre practitioners. That is to say, Greg affected to have already accepted the central point and never have believed otherwise, although the default New Bibliographical assumption, which Greg did most to foster, was that early editions of a play vary from one another by corruption in transmission from a single authorial archetype rather than by authorized revision. To admit revision would entail giving up the editorial desire to represent a play *in toto*, since an edition necessarily arrests the motion of revision, showing a play as it existed at one moment in time.

Lewis had raised a theoretical objection in principle, without demonstrating that authorized revision actually does separate early editions of a Shakespeare play. But a year before E. A. J. Honigmann demonstrated that variants of little or no semantic importance might be introduced by authorial tinkering when copying out fairly (pp. 69–72 above), Lewis's fellow Inklings club member Nevill Coghill showed that Q1 (1622) and Folio *Othello* are distinct versions that cannot be conflated without artistic damage (Coghill 1964, 164–202). Coghill approached Shakespeare from the point of view of performance, the post-war academic study of which began to undermine New Bibliography. The theatre historian G. E. Bentley's reading of Henslowe's Diary and other surviving scraps from contracts and lawsuits led him to conclude, in his book *The Profession of Dramatist in Shakespeare's Time* (1971), that collaborative writing and revision for revival were normal practices in the theatre and hence are present but undetected in many of the surviving plays' early editions. Bentley considered Shakespeare typical in these matters but he did not explore the consequences for editorial theory. Stephen Orgel did, and bringing in Honigmann's persuasive claim for authorial revision when making fair copy, he decided that authorial fixity had been overstated: dramatists changed their minds, the plays belonged to companies not authors, and were altered without their consent and turned into performances by a team (Orgel 1981). The image of a solitary dramatic author making a singular output was mistaken and needed to be replaced with a social and collaborative model of creation in which the script is unfixed and endlessly reshapeable. Once we realize that writing plays was like this, Orgel argued, New Bibliography (what he called 'Modern scientific bibliography') is revealed to be fundamentally mistaken in its assumptions and anachronistic in its practices.

Orgel's critique of New Bibliography was acute yet weakened by overstatement of the post-structuralist insights, such as the claim that the author becomes 'a curiously imprecise, intermittent and shifting figure' when Christopher Marlowe's last name is misspelled 'Marklin' on a quarto title page for *Doctor Faustus* (Orgel 1981, 6; Marlowe 1616, A1^r). A full appreciation of the collaborative nature of dramatic performance should certainly make us see the dramatist as one locus of authority among several, but Orgel muddied the waters by insisting that publication too diminished the writer's control over the words. It is true that once a manuscript was sold to a playing company or a publisher the author's legal rights largely ceased, as Orgel pointed out, yet there is considerable evidence that moral rights were thought to remain with the author as the source and authority for a performance's or a book's contents. James Binns uncovered fresh evidence for this (p. 96 above), and Brian Vickers collated the ample evidence that an author's moral rights were generally accepted and respected (Vickers 2002, 506–41).

Nonetheless, there is a sense in which publication, like performance, is a collaborative venture between the writer and others. Paul Baender, James Thorpe and Philip Gaskell argued that a writer might expect a printer to provide the spelling, capitalization and punctuation of the text (pp. 87–8 above), and D. F. McKenzie extended this idea (1981). McKenzie rejected as meaningless Greg's distinction between substantives and accidentals (pp. 44–6 above): there simply is no dividing line between the two. Decentring the author, McKenzie argued that all aspects of a book's design, including layout (sometimes called *mise en page*) and typefaces, are as important to its meaning as the words chosen by its author. To illustrate his claim, McKenzie considered Jacob Tonson's 1710 edition of the works of William Congreve, designed by master printer John Watts, which made extensive use of typographic distinctions to embellish scene divisions (Congreve 1710a; 1710b; 1710c). According to McKenzie this edition must be seen as an active collaboration between author, publisher and designer, and hence only a notion of the book as a social object can account for its meanings; he called for a 'new and comprehensive sociology of the text' (McKenzie 1981, 118).

Randall McLeod brought McKenzie's socialized approach to the attention of Shakespearians, and likewise argued from the facts of typography (McLeod 1979; 1982b; 1983). Certain letters such as italic *k* and italic long *s* have tails, called kerns, extending beyond the body of the type, and compositors had to insert something to separate combinations in which these tails would otherwise clash. It might well be that an italicized word like *amongst* was printed as *amongest* simply to prevent the backward-leaning tail of the long *s* fouling the lower bowl of the *g*, in which case the *e* that parts them is not a spelling preference but a mechanical necessity. As well as single letters, compositors could use ligatures (multiple-letter pieces such as *ssi* and *st*), so we cannot study their spellings on the assumption that there were just twenty-four letters in the alphabet to choose from. (The pairs *i/j* and *u/v* were each counted as one letter with two shapes.) A compositor's spelling choice each time he came to set Cressida's name would be shaped by the availability of ligatures for *si*, *ssi*, *ssei* and *sse* in his typecase, and when choosing between variants in early editions, McLeod argued, editors must think of the material realities of typesetting. In *King Lear* the storm is described in Q1 as 'that dearne time' (Shakespeare 1608, H1ʳ) and in F as 'that sterne time' (Shakespeare 1623, rr4ʳ). By lexical criteria alone this variant seems unlikely to have arisen from compositorial error and an editor would focus on the words' meanings, but when it is realized that the typecase compartment for the ligature *st* was near the one for the letter *d* the variant looks more likely to be a slip of the compositor's hand (McLeod 1983, 160).

New Bibliographers who want to retain their copy-text's original spellings should also, in McLeod's view, preserve such typographic features as ligatures, else crucial evidence is lost. Taken to its logical limit, this approach leaves no room for editorial mediation and the works of Shakespeare and his contemporaries must be presented to the reader in unedited photofacsimile. The term 'unediting' from the title of McLeod's 1982 essay became the standard shorthand for the opposition, made popular by him, to editorial interventions that regularize such things as speech prefix variation, actors' names in place of characters' names and typographic evidence. Even photographs are mediations, and McLeod championed them as merely the least intrusive medium by which early editions can be widely and cheaply disseminated. To show the illogic of mainstream Shakespeare editing, McLeod attacked Brian Gibbons's Arden edition of *Romeo and Juliet* (McLeod 1982a; Shakespeare 1980b). Gibbons thought he could tell that Q1 (1597) is bad and Q2 (1599) good even though we do not have the underlying manuscripts from which to judge either edition's fidelity, but McLeod pointed out that the latter, supposedly printed from foul papers, contains elements that an editor might easily decide are bad, such as the repetition of certain lines. (Greg gave examples from this edition to illustrate the untidiness of foul papers, pp. 47–8 above.) Gibbons tried to work out in each case which was the author's first attempt and which the second thoughts, but McLeod objected that once you start doing that there is no obvious place to stop. Friar Laurence is a long-winded and repetitious man and could easily be made taciturn, to the destruction of Shakespeare's character.

Repeating ideas that had been aired in connection with memorial reconstruction (pp. 113–17 above), McLeod argued that by privileging Q2 *Romeo and Juliet* the editor loses sight of what is perfectly good in Q1, if only that version were taken on its own terms. If Q2 was indeed printed from foul papers as Gibbons believed (hence it was his copy-text), then the repetition of certain lines was in those foul papers and their deletion requires setting one's sights upon something else, a supposed fair copy in which these tangles had been sorted out. But we have no proof that a fair copy was made, so Gibbons's editorial preference for what Shakespeare wrote should oblige him to retain the repetitions. To do otherwise is 'setting art above its material manifestation' (McLeod 1982a, 425). McLeod's argument is undoubtedly right on its own terms, although it bears an unacknowledged debt to E. A. J. Honigmann's *The Stability of Shakespeare's Text* (pp. 69–72 above). However, where Honigmann saw these problems as a challenge to editing, McLeod saw them as an insuperable barrier. Moreover, there is a whiff of antiquarianism in McLeod's rejection of the desire to set art above its material manifestation. As McKenzie put it, the purpose of an edition of a literary work is 'to draw its readers into a literary experience and not to distract them into admiration of the author's editorial indecisiveness' and howsoever limited are the things we can say about an author's intention in a work, we can be tolerably sure that 'it was not that a reader should study its genesis' (McKenzie 1981, 87).

McLeod complained that the reader is misled by editors turning multiplicities into singularities, refusing to 'allow multiple textual authorities to rest as a simultaneous set of existential entities to be encountered absurdly by the reader' (McLeod 1982a, 422). Yet McLeod's essay 'Spellbound' (1979) was itself revised and reprinted as a chapter in a collection (1984), and a McLeodian reader would presumably have to spend as long encountering absurdly these versions' differences as she spent considering the core idea that is invariant between them. McLeod's account of the act of reading seems on principle to privilege difference and fragmentation over singularity and wholeness, and thus is as ideologically prejudiced as New Bibliography. His rejection of New Bibliography arose not from its inherent flaws, contradictions or blindness to the raw materials – as we saw, Greg quoted the same repetitions in Q2 *Romeo and Juliet* as McLeod – but from his post-structuralist preference for dispersal, contradiction and multiplicity. It is by no means clear that readers are better served this way.

THE SPLITTING OF *KING LEAR*

The arguments that quarto and Folio editions of a single Shakespeare play ought to be treated as distinct versions, their integrity and distinctiveness preserved, acquired particular urgency in the early 1980s as it became clear that the differences between Q1 (1608) and Folio *King Lear* (1623) could best be explained by post-performance revision by Shakespeare. Working independently, three scholars reached this conclusion in the late 1970s, with Michael Warren the first into print (1978) and the others publishing shortly after (Urkowitz 1980; Blayney 1982). A fourth, P. W. K. Stone, was thinking along similar lines, but his theory that the revision was non-authorial received little credence (1980). The key evidence needed to substantiate a two-version theory is that something in one replaces, in a conscious and artistic way, something in the other. It is essential that mere corruption could not produce the difference between the two editions. Warren's celebrated paper argued that the characters of Albany and Edgar were substantially altered:

> the part of Albany is more developed in Q than in F, and in Q he closes the play a mature and victorious duke assuming responsibility for the kingdom; in F he is a weaker character, avoiding responsibility. The part of Edgar is shorter in F than in Q; however, whereas in Q he ends the play a young man overwhelmed by his experience, in F he is a young man who has learned a great deal, and who is emerging as the new leader of a ravaged society. (Warren 1978, 99)

Looking at the differences in the speeches for each character in each edition, Warren plausibly argued that the Folio deliberately omits Albany's speeches towards the end and builds up, by the provision of extra lines, Edgar's part. The chief weakness of this argument is its reliance on literary-critical interpretation of dramatic characters, a subjective matter notoriously open to dispute.

Steven Urkowitz's book, the first on the subject, picked up the same reshaping of the character of Albany and added further evidence of revision, the most compelling being Kent's account of the French invaders learning of the abuse of Lear. In Q1 Kent instructs a gentleman to bring this news to them (Shakespeare 1608, F3^v) while in F he reports that their spies have learnt of the abuse and conveyed this news to their leader (Shakespeare 1623, rr2^v). This alters the motivation of the French, who come on in Q1 not knowing of, hence not motivated by, the abuse of Lear. Moreover, on this matter the two versions are incompatible and cannot sensibly be conflated: Kent cannot send the gentleman to tell the French something that he thinks their spies have already told them (Urkowitz 1980, 67–74). Peter W. M. Blayney's research on *King Lear* had also led him to the two-version hypothesis, although his book on the play was concerned primarily with the facts of the quarto's publication and is best considered in the context of the decline of Virginian-school New Bibliography (pp. 158–9 below).

The two-version hypothesis for *King Lear* achieved dominance with the publication of a collection of essays wittily entitled *The Division of the Kingdoms* (Taylor and Warren 1983b), likening the textual division to the territorial division in the play. Commonly thought to be the major expression of the hypothesis, the essays were not meant to prove the division but only examine 'several outstanding issues pertinent to' it (Taylor and Warren 1983a, v). In the event, most of the essays adduced fresh evidence to bolster the hypothesis, as when Randall McLeod argued that the *Gonorill* of Q1 and *Gonerill* of F can be distinguished (McLeod 1983), Thomas Clayton argued that the dramatization of Lear's death is markedly improved in F (Clayton 1983), and Roger Warren argued that the mock trial present in Q1 is absent from F because Shakespeare and his company realized, as modern practitioners often do, that for all its merits it slows the pace at a crucial point and creates an unhelpfully 'generalized sense of chaos' (Warren 1983, 46). According to Warren the Fool's jokes and Edgar's ravings blunt the scene's inversion of ceremonial norms that is meant to convey serious points about reason-in-madness and the iniquities of official justice.

In the first of his two essays in the collection, Gary Taylor's main concern was to demolish the argument that the Folio's omission of material present in the quarto is due to censorship (Taylor 1983c). Taylor worked through each alleged example of censorship in Folio *King Lear* and with one exception showed that either too much had been omitted (including material that could not give offence) or too little so that the remaining matter ought to have gone too, and that in any case there was no single historical moment when all the material could have caused offence. The exception was a part of 1.4 in which the Fool directly calls Lear a fool, complains about aristocratic monopolies, and puns on fool meaning custard, which is present in Q1 (Shakespeare 1608, C4^v-D1^r) and absent in F. Taylor was sure that the Master of the Revels, George Buc, would not have allowed this in 1605–6 when so many other plays had caused offence to James I (Taylor 1983c, 102–9). If Q1 derived from the version underlying F, say by memorial reconstruction, it should not contain these offensive remarks as Buc's censorship would have prevented them getting into the first performances. Their presence in Q1 is consistent with its being printed from authorial papers.

John Kerrigan's contribution was concerned with the two styles of revision found in early modern drama. Authors revising their own work tend to tinker with everything at a roughly uniform rate, making 'small additions, small cuts and indifferent word substitutions' as well as larger changes, while authors revising another's work tend to insert or remove sizeable sections of text without touching the surrounding material (Kerrigan 1983, 195). Kerrigan's detailed evidence came from Thomas Kyd's *The Spanish Tragedy*, given additions and substitutions, possibly by Ben Jonson

(Kyd 1592; 1602), Christopher Marlowe's *Doctor Faustus* with additions and substitutions by William Birde and Samuel Rowley (Marlowe 1604; 1616) and someone's adapting of Edward Sharpham's *The Fleire* (1607), with minor evidence from other plays. In these cases, the revisers worked with substantial runs of continuous dialogue. Turning to plays altered by their own authors, Kerrigan found here too the addition or deletion of substantial blocks of texts, but also localized tweaks in the detail of readings (most amply evidenced in Jonson's rewritings), which is something non-authorial revisers almost never do. This discovery provides a simple test: if the revision includes local tweaking, the reviser is the author; if it does not it could be anyone (including the author). The Q1/F differences in *King Lear* fall into the former camp: the tweakings implicate Shakespeare as the reviser. But could someone else have done the major surgery that separates the editions? Kerrigan observed that the commonest kind of non-authorial revision was to expand the jesting and clowning parts of a play (as with the Rafe and Dick material in *Doctor Faustus*), and in this regard Folio *King Lear* is no advance upon the quarto.

Paul Werstine's contribution to *The Division of the Kingdoms* was an essay showing that alteration in the printshop, either by an editor or a compositor, cannot account for the differences between Folio *King Lear* and its printer's copy, whether that copy was Q1 or Q2 (Werstine 1983). As we shall shortly see, W. W. Greg offered evidence that the Folio copy was an exemplar of Q1 (1608), and the only other possibility (argued here by Taylor) was that it was an exemplar of Q2 (1619). Werstine dealt with both possibilities although he agreed with Taylor in favouring Q2, and pointed out that it would make no difference to his overall conclusion (Werstine 1983, 292 n.73). If a single authorial archetype underlies Q1 and F then their differences are due to errors of transmission from that archetype, and Folio compositor B's careless setting of *1 Henry 4* from Q6, as argued by Alice Walker (p. 56 above), would be relevant since he set *King Lear*. Werstine had already shown that Walker was wrong about Folio compositor B: his reputation for carelessness was undeserved and his poor performance in setting *1 Henry 4* can be explained by the nature of his copy (pp. 96–7 above). Werstine found that interference by a printshop proofreader might also have created some of the departures from copy that Walker counted against compositor B (Werstine 1983, 257–9). Shortly after Walker published her research, Charlton Hinman discovered apprentice compositor E, and with T. H. Howard-Hill's adjustment of the attribution of pages (p. 98 above) he became responsible for about half of Folio *King Lear*. With a refined sense of just what departures from copy these two compositors were likely to make, Werstine showed that they could not account for Folio *King Lear*'s differences from its quarto copy. Authorial variation rather than compositorial or editorial intervention was the more plausible agent, not least because many of the changes have since been accepted into critical editions and justified artistically (Werstine 1983, 277–81).

MacDonald P. Jackson's essay applied statistical analysis to the prevailing explanations of Folio *King Lear*'s reliance on quarto copy that had been annotated by reference to an authoritative manuscript and found them inadequate (Jackson 1983). The problem is clearest in scene 4.2, where Q (either Q1 or Q2) and F share a string of errors and yet F omits a series of passages present in Q and adds one line absent in Q (Jackson 1983, 322). If the exemplar of Q used as Folio copy had first been annotated by reference to an independent authoritative manuscript, it is hard to see how the annotator could so carefully attend to the deletions and additions needed to make Q conform to the manuscript while at the same time failing to fix Q's faulty readings that presumably were correct in the authoritative manuscript. Jackson endorsed Stone's solution to this conundrum: the authoritative manuscript itself was derived from Q1 and contained these errors (made when Q1 was printed), so that when the exemplar of Q2 (a reprint of Q1) that was to be used as Folio copy was compared with this manuscript it was clear what needed to be cut and added in 4.2 but the errors were not apparent because they were shared by the Q1-derived manuscript and Q2 (Stone 1980, 100–12; Jackson 1983, 329). A plausible explanation for this manuscript being based on Q1 is that Shakespeare revised the play, especially the beginning and end, by taking an exemplar of Q1 and writing his alterations on it. In Stone's view this revision was not by Shakespeare but 'another dramatist ... an experienced writer' (Stone 1980, 114), but this does not affect the main point. Gross errors in Q1 Shakespeare would have been corrected, but smaller ones might easily have escaped his notice, especially if the revision occurred years after composition and the Q1 readings made reasonable sense.

Precisely one-quarter of *The Division of the Kingdoms* was taken up with Taylor's bibliographical argument that Folio *King Lear* was printed from an exemplar of Q2 (1619) that had first been annotated by reference to a playhouse manuscript that was itself derived from Q1 (1608). The nub of the argument appeared simultaneously as a journal article (Taylor 1983a) and drew upon Greg's observation that certain readings in Folio *King Lear* seem to derive from Q1 (Greg 1933, 258–9; 1940, 138–42). F seems to get the following readings from an exemplar of Q1 that had the first two press variants in the corrected state (marked *c*) and the third in the uncorrected state (marked *u*):

Q1u after	Q1c hasten	Q2 after	F hasten
Q1u alapt want	Q1c attaskt for want	Q2 alapt want	F at task for want
Q1u retention	Q1c retention, and appointed guard	Q2 retention, and appointed guard	F retention

According to Greg, Q1c's 'attaskt for want' (Shakespeare 1608, D2ᵛ) was a miscorrection of 'alapt want' (itself a compositor's mistake for the manuscript's 'ataxt for want'), and Q1u's omission of 'and appointed guard' (1608, K4ᵛ) was also an error, corrected during the run. F's 'at task for want' (Shakespeare 1623, qq5ᵛ) essentially agrees with Q1c's miscorrection, and F follows Q1u's omission of 'and appointed guard' (1623, ss2ʳ), so the agreement-in-error principle (pp. 33–5 above) shows that F was set from an exemplar of Q1 containing this mix of errors. That conclusion was disputed by Stone (1980), Howard-Hill (1982) and Taylor, who showed that the Folio compositors must have had an exemplar of Q2 in their hands (Taylor 1983b, 356–7). The strongest argument that Q2, not Q1, was F's copy was Taylor's observation that Folio compositor E's setting of the play follows the accidentals of Q2 at his usual, conservative rate, whereas if setting from Q1 he was departing from his copy's accidentals most uncharacteristically (Taylor 1983a, 47–53). We may leave aside for the moment (because we will return to it) the possibility that compositor E set Folio *King Lear* from printed copy while his partner on this play, compositor B, set it from manuscript copy. The problem is to explain how Folio *King Lear*, printed from Q2, ended up containing readings from Q1 that were not in Q2.

Taylor focussed on how the phrase 'and appointed guard' came to be absent from Q1u and F and present in Q1c and Q2. Madeleine Doran argued that this was because the phrase was ambiguously placed in the margin of the manuscript underlying Q1 (which manuscript was also the source of the prompt-book) and hence left off Q1u and off the prompt-book that was, in her view, the source for F (Doran 1931, 101). As Taylor pointed out, if this were true then both Q1 and F were printed from authoritative manuscripts, in which case one would need the revision hypothesis to account for their being so unalike (Taylor 1983b, 359–60). If, on the other hand, Q1 were a memorial reconstruction of performance then it would have no direct connection with an authoritative manuscript, with its allegedly ambiguous placing of the missing three words, and hence it becomes hard to explain their shared omission in Q1u and F. One might suppose a prompt-book that went on to influence F omitted these three words and hence that the actors recalling their performances were not aware of them, but this would not account for Q1c having the three words. The only way to account for the omission of these three words in Q1u and F is for F to be getting the omission indirectly from Q1u, as if the good manuscript against which Q2 was collated (prior to its being used as copy for F) itself followed Q1u in this omission. Why would this good manuscript follow Q1u? Once the revision hypothesis itself has been accepted, the explanation is simple: someone revised the play after the publication of Q1, writing their revisions on an exemplar of Q1 that had this forme in its uncorrected state, while Q2 was printed from an exemplar of Q1 showing this forme's corrected state.

Why would Shakespeare begin his revision of the play on an exemplar of Q1 instead of the prompt-book, assuming that the foul papers were destroyed to make Q1, or at least sold to the publisher? Perhaps because near the end of his career he was away from London a lot and Q1 is easy to carry. Probably the players would not let him take away the prompt-book, since they could not be sure they would like his changes (Taylor 1983b, 365). His core argument established, Taylor set out to remove every possible objection (Taylor 1983b, 366–426). Q1 is closer to the sources than F is, as we would expect if F represents a revised script; there are some exceptions to this claim and Taylor explained them by Shakespeare rereading certain books late in his career. Indeed, not one of the F-only passages relies on the sources for the rest of the play, which itself is good evidence that Q1 is not based on a memorial reconstruction, since actors could hardly fail to recollect just the passages that do not rely on the sources. Although the F-only passages have no definite sources of their own, Taylor found a few things that might be influenced by Shakespeare's reading and writing near the end of his career, when he wrote the plays from *Coriolanus* (around 1608) to *Cymbeline* (around 1610).

Vocabulary tests confirm that the F-only passages are either later than the composition (around 1605) of the play printed in Q1 or are by another writer. If by Shakespeare, the traffic is two-way. That is, the rare words in Q1 *King Lear* – rare in the sense of being seldom used by Shakespeare – turn up in *Cymbeline* and the plays after it, suggesting that when he reread Q1 to revise *King Lear* Shakespeare was self-influenced to start using these words again. Style tests point the same way too. But what if someone else wrote the F-only passages? Taylor pointed out that this would be hard to reconcile with the Q1 *King Lear*'s rare words cropping up in *Cymbeline* and after. Moreover, there are images in the F-only passages that seem to pick up words from the preceding material (shared with Q1) and use them to build distinctly Shakespearian image clusters such as geese/bitterness/seasoning/restraint and stew/brothels/sweat/disease. The known habits of John Fletcher, Philip Massinger, Thomas Middleton, Ben Jonson, George Chapman, Nathan Field and John Webster, the likeliest authors for the revision if it was not by Shakespeare, are not found in the F-only passages, but the rare words found in Shakespeare are.

Stone argued that where F shows someone trying to make sense of a corrupt reading in Q1, that person could not be Shakespeare because he would have known the good reading obscured by Q1 (since he wrote its underlying manuscript) and would have restored it rather than try to bend the corruption back to goodness. Taylor showed that in fact Charles Dickens and James Joyce executed corrections on proofs in precisely the fashion that Stone denied was possible: rather than restoring the manuscript reading they built upon the printer's error to make something else. Moreover, quite often F does restore a good reading corrupt in Q1, and that is hard for Stone to explain but easy if we think that by and large Shakespeare remembered what he had originally written and restored it, but the occasional corruption in Q1 got the better of him (Taylor 1983b, 401–2). Regarding the date of the revision, Kerrigan argued (1983, 221–3) that the Folio line 'No Heretiques burn'd, but wenches Sutors' (Shakespeare 1623, rr2^v) is unlikely to have been written in 1612 or after when there were, for the first time in James I's reign, burnings of heretics. Since the revision was begun on a copy of Q1, this limited the period in which it was done to within 1608–11.

Taylor was at this time about halfway through editing a complete works edition of Shakespeare, so just what an editor should do with the new discoveries was no abstract question. Since Q1 was apparently printed from foul papers it might well omit staging details that got put into the lost prompt-book of the first performances. Where F has such details they might not be part of the revision but simply reflect what happens to any script in rehearsal as the staging is worked out, although in this case F's source would be the prompt-book of the revised version. Thus an edition based on Q1 might reasonably insert these details from F on the grounds that they are what the first prompt-book would have contained; the same argument could be made for small details of dialogue too (Taylor 1983b, 404–5). The remainder of Taylor's essay brushed aside certain common but trivial objections to the revision hypothesis, such as F's differences from Q1 being largely actors' interpolations, or that F shows the play as cut for less lavish performance conditions or because it was too long. Anticipating a more general objection that was indeed later made, Taylor acknowledged that much of the argument for two versions of the play was based on subjective character criticism.

The Division of the Kingdoms and the preceding works that underpinned it were mostly well received by reviewers, and the revision hypothesis was broadly accepted. A recurrent objection to Urkowitz's foundational book on the topic, however, was its author's refusal to admit the presence of textual corruption as well as revision separating Q1 and F (Edwards 1982; Werstine 1985a). Passionately trying to dispel the myth that only corruption separates the editions, Urkowitz overstated his case and made revision account for everything. The most sustained engagement with the core bibliographical case for the revision hypothesis was mounted by Howard-Hill (1982), who thought F was set from a manuscript. Tabulating Folio compositor E's and B's departures from unusual quarto spellings when setting F, Howard-Hill found them more frequent than when these men set other Folio plays from extant quarto copy. The departures did not quite rule out F being set from a quarto (in which case it was probably Q2), but Howard-Hill noticed errors that look like misreadings of handwriting, such as F's 'strangenesse' (1623, qq6^r) where Q1 (1608, D4^r) and Q2 (1619, D1^v) have the correct 'strange newes'. Howard-Hill concluded with two hypotheses that fit the facts. The first was that someone annotated an exemplar of Q2 by looking at the prompt-book, but thereby made the exemplar too untidy to be used by a compositor, so it had to be copied out again. If so, this person failed to correct the quarto's errors (which is why they persist in F) even though he had the prompt-book's correct readings in front of him. The second hypothesis, which Howard-Hill preferred, was that someone used an exemplar to help make sense of the prompt-book as he transcribed it.

An article by Taylor published the same year as *The Division of the Kingdoms* showed that Folio *Hamlet* was not set from printed copy, that Folio *Othello* was not set from Q1 (1622), and that compositor E's part of Folio *King Lear* was set from Q2 not Q1, to judge from his conservatism when setting from printed copy (Taylor 1983a). Unless Folio compositor E was being most uncharacteristically adventurous in his departures from copy spellings, his copy was Q2 rather than Q1 *King Lear*. Responding directly to Howard-Hill's essay, which argued for Q2's indirect influence upon F when used as an aid in transcribing the prompt-book to make F's copy, Taylor thought such a transcript unnecessary. Why not just give the printers the manuscript and an exemplar of Q2 to consult if they needed it? Howard-Hill argued that there are not enough of Q2's unusual spellings in F for Q2 to have been the printer's copy, but Taylor countered that Q2's unusual spellings are just the ones likely to be changed when it was annotated, which invalidates Howard-Hill's analogy with other Folio plays set by compositors E and B from quarto copy that was not annotated so comprehensively (Taylor 1983a, 52–3). Taylor noticed that when compositor B went against his customary spelling of a word in setting Folio *King Lear*, he significantly often followed neither Q1 nor Q2, so presumably he was setting from a manuscript and being influenced by its spellings. This did not affect the central argument Taylor advanced in *The Division of the Kingdoms*, since this manuscript could be the prompt-book for the revised version of the play (based on Q1) that was used directly for setting Folio *King Lear* by compositor B and used to correct the exemplar of Q2 that was compositor E's copy.

In a substantial review article, Howard-Hill took issue with the bibliographical bases for Taylor's argument in *The Division of the Kingdoms*, starting with the existence of Q1/F disagreement-in-error (Howard-Hill 1985, 170–1). The supposed errors in Q1 that got into F without passing through Q2 (pp. 137–9 above) are not, he argued, errors at all, and hence do not show dependence. Greg thought that Q1's compositor set 'alapt' where his manuscript had 'ataxt' (Shakespeare 1608, D2^v), which the proof corrector – without consulting copy – improved to 'attaskt', which word thereby came into existence (Greg 1933, 258). Howard-Hill and Taylor agreed that since 'task' and 'tax' are cognate the press corrector might have considered 'attaskt' equivalent to 'ataxt' and hence he was essentially restoring the copy's reading (Howard-Hill 1982, 21–2; Taylor 1983b, 357–8). Likewise, F's reading of 'hasten' (Shakespeare 1623, qq5^v) need not derive from Q1c since it makes perfect sense in context ('hasten your returne') and the Q1u reading of 'after' (1608, D2^v) could have arisen because these words would have looked alike in Shakespeare's handwriting if a blot made the 'h' unclear. If 'attaskt' and 'hasten' are not errors, then F's sharing of Q1's readings does not prove dependence. (Taylor had in fact argued that 'after' in Q1u was right, but the corrector was misled into remedial action because the compositor erred later in the line, setting 'after your returne' instead of his copy's 'after your retinue' (Taylor 1982a, 123; 1983b, 358).)

Taylor laid the greatest stress on F's omission of 'and appointed guard' despite its being in F's copy, Q2 (Shakespeare 1619, K4^v). Howard-Hill objected that if Shakespeare omitted these words from the revised version of the play, because he began that version with an exemplar of Q1 that omitted them, someone would have reinserted them into the prompt-book from memory or the original's actor's part. If present in the revised version prompt-book, there was no reason for them to be deleted from the exemplar of Q2 annotated from that prompt-book, and hence their absence from F is not explained by Taylor's hypothesis. Perhaps, Howard-Hill suggested, in the prompt-book of the revised play the words were underlined for emphasis (Shakespeare having accidentally omitted them), but then deleted from Q2 when it was annotated from this prompt-book because the underlining was misread as a call for deletion, and hence the words were omitted from F (Howard-Hill 1985, 172). Howard-Hill did not accept Taylor's claim that Q1 influenced F by being the base upon which Shakespeare constructed his revision of the play, and thought it inherently implausible that novice compositor E set Folio *King Lear* from Q2 while compositor B used the manuscript prompt-book of the revised play (Howard-Hill 1985, 174–5). A prompt-book would be too valuable to leave in the hands of a printer (who would normally destroy a manuscript in setting type from it), and in any case the marked-up Q2 would have been more untidy than the clean prompt-book and not suitable copy for a novice. Howard-Hill was scathing of the idea that similar rates of departure from usual practices of spelling in different jobs indicate use of similar copy, commenting pithily that 'In short, all Taylor can argue logically is "*if* E was setting from Q2 he was behaving consistently", not "*because* E was behaving consistently, he was setting from Q2", for other copy with unknown characteristics could have produced that consistency' (Howard-Hill 1985, 176).

Taylor's last major publication on this topic appeared the same year as Howard-Hill's review and attempted to show that like Folio compositor E, compositor B set *King Lear* from Q2 copy (Taylor 1985a). Stone argued that misreadings cluster in compositor B's stints, showing that he had the more difficult, manuscript copy. Taylor whittled Stone's list of errors by showing that some are indifferent variants from Q1 and others might well be authorial revisions after Q1 was printed. Seven errors remained, and Taylor added a couple that Stone missed, and overall the errors were almost evenly split between compositors B and E. The manuscript used to annotate Q2 before it was used as Folio copy was a prompt-book, so these misreadings might have occurred when that was made by copying authorial papers; they do not prove that F itself was set from a manuscript. Taylor realized that the trouble with his own method of tracking how often F follows Q2's indifferent variants and seeking to determine printer's copy from the pattern of agreement is that the annotator's varying attention to his work also produces patterns. Three passages comprising just 271 lines contain more than a third of the occurrences of F following Q2's indifferent variants. This could easily be because the annotator's attention wandered: he missed differences, so F follows Q2 (Taylor 1985a, 22).

Taylor found mislineation in F that would be just what we would expect if its copy was an exemplar of Q2 that had been marked up with line-endings. His strongest example was the speech that in Q1 appears as:

>   (thy goodnes,
> *Cord.* O thou good *Kent* how shall I liue and worke to match
> My life will be too short and euery measure faile me.
>   (Shakespeare 1608, k1ᵛ)

To remove the turn-up, Q2 reset the lines as:

> *Cord.* O thou good *Kent*,
> How shall I liue and worke to match thy goodnesse,
> My life will be too short and euery measure faile me.
>   (Shakespeare 1619, k1ʳ)

This is tidier than Q1, but metrically wrong. Editors concur that the proper lineation is:

> CORDELIA
> O thou good Kent, how shall I live and work
> To match thy goodness? My life will be too short,
> And every measure fail me.
>   (*Tragedy of King Lear*, 4.6.1–3)

To show the correct lineation the annotator of Q2 would mark breaks after 'worke' and 'short'. F's lineation is exactly what we would find if compositor E idiotically followed both Q2's line-endings and such break marks:

> *Cor.* O thou good *Kent*,
> How shall I liue and worke
> To match thy goodnesse?
> My life will be too short,
> And euery measure faile me.
>   (Shakespeare 1623, ss1ʳ)

It is hard to explain F's lineation any other way, but this example is from compositor E's stint. Taylor adduced more examples where something in F is most easily (but not clinchingly) explained as misreading of annotation upon an exemplar of Q2, from both compositors' stints (Taylor 1985a, 27–9).

To establish that Folio compositor B used Q2 copy, Taylor turned to his habits of spelling. Using just the first page of Folio *King Lear*, Taylor looked at all of compositor B's spellings that deviate not only from Q2 spellings but also from his normal spellings elsewhere in the Folio. By excluding spellings that he seems unparticular about, Taylor isolated compositor B's four notable departures from his habits on this page. This gives a baseline anomaly rate, and it matches the rate for one page each from Folio *Titus Andronicus*, *1 Henry 4*, *Richard 3* and *Troilus and Cressida*, all set by compositor B from quarto copy (Taylor 1985a, 30–7). When compositor B set Folio *Hamlet* and *Othello* from manuscript copy, he showed a much higher anomaly rate, far more often setting spellings against his habits (Taylor 1985a, 38–51). In both compositors' stints, F consistently has the spelling *Gonerill* although Q2 overwhelmingly prefers *Gonorill*. To get around this, Taylor used the parallel alteration of *Falstalffe* to *Falstaffe* in the Folio setting of *1 Henry 4* from Q6: thirty-one times an annotator struck out the second *l* in *Falstalffe*, so an annotator could easily have altered every second *o* to *e* in *Gonorill* (Taylor 1985a, 52–5). The anomaly rate test also confirmed Taylor's previous conclusion that compositor E had printed copy for setting Folio *King Lear* (Taylor 1985a, 57–69). None of this proved that Q2 was F's copy for both compositors, but it is the simplest explanation. Yet Howard-Hill's objection still applies: similarity of compositorial behaviour need not be caused by similarity of copy. Taylor ended with his discoveries' consequences for editors (Taylor 1985a, 71–4). For *Othello* and *Hamlet* we should assume that F/Q agreements are correct readings, not errors. Q1 (1622) and F *Othello* were each printed from a transcript that was not derived from the other transcript (because they bring in authoritative matter) and hence both descend independently from an ancestral text; where they agree, the likeliest reason is that they correctly witness that ancestor. Q2 (1604–5) *Hamlet* was printed from foul papers and F from a transcript, so again both editions descend independently from an ancestor (those foul papers) and are unlikely to erroneously agree. By contrast, because Q2 was copy for Folio *King Lear* they might agree on a Q2 error, so what matters is one's view of Q1 (the copy for Q2): if a memorial reconstruction then editors should emend freely but if authorial papers then not.

Howard-Hill came around to Taylor's view that Folio *King Lear* was set from Q2 but not that Q1 was an influence via the authoritative manuscript against which the exemplar of Q2 used as Folio copy was first annotated (Howard-Hill 1986). If the words 'and appointed guard' were written in the margin of the original foul papers, that could explain Q1u missing them and the corrector spotting them to make Q1c. It could also explain their being missed when the first-performance prompt-book was made, only to be added in later as an underlined insertion. As Howard-Hill previously argued, this underlining could have been misunderstood as a deletion mark, so that when an exemplar of Q2 was annotated against this first-performance prompt-book (not a revised-version prompt-book, as in Taylor's narrative), the words 'and appointed guard' were struck out of Q2, and hence are absent from F. Thus Howard-Hill accounted for the bibliographical facts without hypothesizing a revised-play prompt-book originating from Q1, and so he held that the entire revision hypothesis must stand or fall on its other merits. The problem comes down to a comparison of likelihoods, since Howard-Hill's narrative requires that each of two manuscripts, the foul papers and the prompt-book, had the phrase 'and appointed guard' written in each of two distinct ways that both made it look like it did not belong, and that for this reason each of two agents (the compositor of Q1 and the scribe making the prompt-book of the first performances) independently omitted it.

The extraordinary burst of work on *King Lear* in 1978–86 had a permanent effect: no longer will the quarto and Folio editions of the play be treated as two descendants of one archetype. New Bibliography was not inherently antagonistic to the idea of revision, nor to the concomitant need for two-text editions: Greg himself produced such an edition of Marlowe's *Doctor Faustus* (Marlowe 1950). The sometimes acrimonious struggle to overcome editorial and readerly conservatism and establish the two-version status of *King Lear* overshadowed an important corollary of Shakespeare initiating his revision of *King Lear* on an exemplar of Q1. Practical constraints such as the players' reluctance to let him work on the prompt-book might have played a part in this, but clearly the quarto was close enough to what Shakespeare considered to be the play itself that it could form a fresh starting point. As we have seen (pp. 87–8 above), Paul Baender, James Thorpe and Philip Gaskell argued that in principle a writer might well accept a publisher's completion of a work by providing the forms of dress (especially spelling and punctuation) that the reader expected to find it in. If Shakespeare revised *King Lear* using an exemplar of Q1, he clearly was happy enough with the printer's work to feel like the owner and originator of the result. Q1 must have been close to what he considered the original play.

THE SOCIALIZED TEXT: JEROME J. MCGANN, *A CRITIQUE OF MODERN TEXTUAL CRITICISM* (1983)

In the midst of the work on *King Lear* appeared *A Critique of Modern Textual Criticism* (McGann 1983), concerned with the question of how much difference needs to exist between two texts for them to be considered distinct and unconflatable versions, and with the contribution that publishers make to the creation of literary works. The first of these matters was to become the key issue of 1980s New Textualism, once *King Lear* was split and the bad quartos exonerated, and the second fed an emerging concern among Shakespearians with the degree to which the authority for plays derives from sources other than the dramatist. McGann began with the application of New Bibliographical principles to modern American writers for whom, unlike most early modern dramatists, the authorial manuscripts survive. Applying New Bibliography here required hedging it with caveats and qualifications about authorial revision in second and subsequent editions and the possibility of multiple equally authorized versions (McGann 1983, 1–8). There had been disquiet about the application of New Bibliographical principles beyond sixteenth- and seventeenth-century drama (Tom Davis 1977), but it was fairly muted. Once scholarship on *King Lear* established that it exists in multiple, equally authorized versions, objections against New Bibliography went to its core principles and not simply its misapplication to later periods.

According to McGann, the result was an intellectual crisis in critical editing generally (McGann 1983, 4–5). The problem stemmed from the foundational assumption that the author is a kind of Romantic loner, whereas in fact literary production is social: we need 'a socialized concept of authorship and textual authority' (McGann 1983, 8). McGann observed that literary theorists interested in instability and the nature of *textualité* were starting to look at textual variants and versions that formerly were of interest only to editors and textual critics, and he approved of this development: the problem was editors' and textual critics' ignorance of literary theory (McGann 1983, 10). Literary theorists were coming into textual studies rather than textual scholars turning to theory. (As we shall see, some of the theorists were moving in only in the hope of finding a scientific gloss for their essentially trivial ideas.) Because Fredson Bowers was one of the advocates of New Bibliography's application to modern literature, McGann allowed him to explain at length why the printer's accidentals should not be followed by editors of Nathaniel Hawthorne's *The House of Seven Gables* even though the author checked and approved the proofs, which departed extensively from the manuscript's accidentals. Bowers argued that Hawthorne had acceded to but not accepted the printer's accidentals; he did not adopt them in the manuscript of his next novel, *The Blithedale Romance* (McGann 1983, 18–22).

W. W. Greg thought an early modern dramatist's accidentals worth preserving because printers modernize and he wanted to avoid that. Thus, according to McGann, 'The Rationale of Copy-Text' should not apply after

1650, when orthography became considerably more standardized (McGann 1983, 28–9). The New Bibliographical practice of going back to the earliest text in a monogenetic line made sense if that line began with a printing after the author had finished revising the work, but what if there survives a manuscript from the period when the author was still working on it, one that predates final authorial intentions that are perhaps best represented in the first or even a subsequent printing? Might there not even be multiple, conflicting intentions spread over time? McGann made clear that all who entered the debate were aware of these hypothetical problems, and he quoted G. Thomas Tanselle defending the use of the pre-publication form of a work rather than the published form on the grounds that while one might retain the occasional intention that the author went on to discard (or miss an intention later conceived, he might have added) these would at least be the author's intentions and not someone else's, say the printer's, as one is likely to get by following the first published form (McGann 1983, 32–3).

This is a powerful argument, and in rebuttal McGann used the point made by Paul Baender, James Thorpe and Philip Gaskell (pp. 87–8 above): an author's intention might itself include the assumption that the printer would add fresh intellectual labour and thereby complete the work. After all 'the production of books, in the later modern periods especially, sometimes involves a close working relationship between the author and the various editorial and publishing professionals' (McGann 1983, 34). This is McGann's notion of the socialized text, much like D. F. McKenzie's (p. 131 above), with printers not contaminating but completing authorial intention. Such enlightened printers should not, McGann argued, be tarred with the same brush as the 'historically belated' scribes transmitting classical texts, nor the printers of Shakespeare's books, who overrode the author's intentions to apply their own ideas and whose interference must be undone (McGann 1983, 35). A limitation of McGann's argument is that it seems to apply only to such printers as could be said to complete the work, those of the 'later modern periods' where New Bibliography ought not to apply. As such, McGann seems concerned merely with a border dispute, the need to confine New Bibliographical principles to works from the sixteenth and seventeenth centuries, where they belong. This was not, however, how his book was received.

The idea that a manuscript is inherently better than the book printed from it is deeply ingrained but not logically coherent, McGann argued. After all, the modern critical edition seeks to decontaminate the writing – that is what it exists to do – so it must be accepted that in certain circumstance printing improves upon its raw materials. Moreover, authors actually intend printed books, not manuscripts (which are only a means to an end), and underlying the preference for manuscripts is 'a Romantic ideology of the relations between an author, his works, his institutional affiliations, and his audience' (McGann 1983, 42). McGann agreed with Thorpe: like plays, books 'are fundamentally social rather than personal or psychological products, they do not even acquire an artistic form of being until their engagement with an audience has been determined' (McGann 1983, 43–4). Using examples exclusively from post-seventeenth-century writers – George Gordon Byron, William Blake, Mary Shelley, Alfred Tennyson – McGann established that the 'arrangements' for publication (copying, editing, typesetting) are thoroughly imbricated in the creative process, and that rather than contaminations they may be thought of as 'a process of training the poem for its appearance in the world' (McGann 1983, 51). Whither authority for the work? According to McGann, final authority resides neither with the author nor the institutions that make publication possible, but rather is in 'the actual structure of the agreements which these two cooperating authorities reach in specific cases' (McGann 1983, 54).

Towards the end of his book, McGann introduced the ideas and language of high French literary theory, so that the 'structure of agreements' that enables publication became a 'dialectic between the historically located individual author and the historically developing institutions of literary production' (McGann 1983, 81). A Foucauldian/Barthesian outlook (pp. 84–5 above) is evident in McGann's claim that 'In cultural products like literary works the location of authority necessarily becomes dispersed beyond the author' (McGann 1983, 84). McGann illustrated such dispersal by Edward Bulwer-Lytton changing his novel *Pelham* in subsequent editions in response to readers' and critics' objections. More complexly, Marianne Moore edited one of her thirty-line poems down to a three-line version that referred back to the long one, which the reader was expected to remember; so was it a new poem? Moore seems to have considered the three-liner the final, streamlined version of the long one (McGann 1983, 85–6). W. H. Auden played similar games by moving his poems to new contexts, and for McGann the Greg–Bowers eclectic approach is here defeated because there is nothing definitive to return to, only versions. A critical edition is supposed to 'transcend the historical exigencies to which all texts are subject', but it necessarily fails (McGann 1983, 93). Tanselle argued that one must present texts either as historical documents (in which case one must not regularize or modernize) or as finished works (in which case one must regularize and modernize), but for McGann this distinction was meaningless since all editions are mediations, are efforts at historicism (McGann 1983, 111–12). This social aspect is lost in the narrow rules of New Bibliography, and McGann called for editors to consider 'the history of the text in relation to the related histories of its production, reproduction, and reception' (McGann 1983, 122–3.)

In an appendix dealing with a possible objection to his position, McGann offered a convenient summation of the difference it would make to editors in their choices of copy-text:

> My critique of the rule of final intentions throughout this essay has been tied to a series of counter examples, the most important of which are brought forward to argue the collaborative or social nature of literary production. The issue here involves the rule developed by Bowers that when a choice is to be made between author's manuscript and first edition, the presumption will be in favor of the manuscript, since it contains what we know to be the author's (rather than someone else's) intentions towards accidentals and so-called indifferent readings. My argument has been that the presumption should lie with the first edition since it can be expected to contain what author and publishing institution together worked to put before the public. (McGann 1983, 125)

McGann ignored the problem that for literary production to be treated as a social phenomenon one must accept harm done to the work by the printer as part of the work's genesis. To accept socialization only when it does no harm – when the publisher has acted as the author would wish – is to smuggle authorial intention back in, as Tanselle soon pointed out (1987, 131).

This point was amply, but unintentionally, illustrated in McGann's next book, a collection of essays entitled *Textual Criticism and Literary Interpretation* (McGann 1985), which appeared with a publisher's errata sheet promising to correct its many errors in 'the next printing of the book'. Ninety-five errors were listed, together with corrected readings that 'the contributors would like to call to the reader's attention'. Having just argued that authorial intention must be subordinated to a social model of textuality that disperses authority, McGann found that living authors prefer to have their faulty readings corrected. Rather than sharing responsibility, as the social model would require, the errata sheet assured the reader that its own existence came about 'Through no fault of the contributors of this volume'. To date there has been no subsequent edition, and unless the loose errata sheets survive (which rarely happens even in the most careful libraries), the only sources by which such an edition could correct the errors would be the contributors' manuscripts and typescripts, if these survive. By McGann's own argument, however, these sources have no greater authority than the error-ridden first edition. The gaiety of this textual situation is enhanced by the errors themselves, which are Barthesian in their apparent celebration of the *jouissance* of sliding signifiers: where Shakespeare's Ulysses speaks of 'work' read 'word', for 'The Political Works' read 'The Poetical Works', where lines are attributed to 'Keats' read 'Yeats' and do not attribute to Randall McLeod the loss of the hyphen, so beloved of anti-Stratfordians, in the title of his 'Un*Editing* Shak-speare'.

It is possible to keep faith with even the unwelcome consequences of a socialized conception of literary production, and to argue that printers' errors are fruitful points of fresh departure in the circulation of ideas. For the first of the British Library's Panizzi Lectures, McKenzie argued that a printer's error in the edition of William Congreve's *The Way of the World* used by W. K. Wimsatt and M. C. Beardsley for their celebrated essay 'The Intentional Fallacy' (1946) was part of their wider misrepresentation of the dramatist's purposes (McKenzie 1986, 9–20). According to Wimsatt and Beardsley the project of recovering the dramatist's purposes is mistaken and futile (that is the fallacy of their title) and the proper object of the critic's attention is not the author but the writing itself. McKenzie pointed out, however, that Wimsatt and Beardsley's quotation of Congreve's prologue altered not only accidentals but also a substantive in making the dramatist claim that he 'wrote' the play when in fact Congreve claimed he 'wrought' it. McKenzie charted the consequences:

[Wimsatt and Beardsley's] misreading has become an historical document in its own right. By speaking to what they perceived in 1946 to be the needs of their own time, not Congreve's in 1700/1710, they have left a record of the taste, thought and values of a critical school which significantly shaped our own choice of books, the way we read them and, in my own case, the way I taught them. (McKenzie 1986, 13)

McKenzie was not advocating indifference to error. To make the assessment of how and why Wimsatt and Beardsley misrepresented Congreve required that McKenzie's scholarship had to take an Olympian position above all three and diagnose their behaviour in historical terms.

Under the explicit influence of Michel Foucault and Roland Barthes, McKenzie ultimately sided with the reader over the author: 'a poem *is* only what its individual readers make it' and 'the misreading of Congreve in 1946 may be seen as almost a matter of historical necessity' (McKenzie 1986, 17). McGann's experience of printer's error shows that this approach cannot always be taken with living authors, who are apt to demand that they, not the printer or the readers, are the source of authority in writing. The socialized conception of authorship would seem suited only to writers who are literally dead and unable to object to it. For the editor this raises the ethical question of why dead authors are not entitled to the same rights as living ones. As articulated by McGann, the socialized approach treats the material objects created by writers, actual books, as more authoritative than the intentions that preceded them. The New Bibliography, by contrast, was predicated on the conviction that an editor might extrapolate from the material objects their preceding intentions, which will be of greater interest to the modern reader, and then mediate those afresh. The successor to Greg and Bowers against whom McGann defined his approach was Tanselle, who popularized the use of the terms *work* for the immaterial creation that a writer (living or dead) intends and *text* for the documentary object(s) in which it is embodied. The latter is what readers encounter as a physical object, and they habitually infer from it the immaterial *work* that it was constructed to carry.

Tanselle's was essentially a Platonic-idealist view of art, and it made for a strong distinction between the plastic arts, in which the work is tangible, and the literary arts, in which it is not:

The painting exists at a single location, and one has nowhere else to go to find the work except that one place ... In contrast, a piece of paper with a text of a poem written on it does not constitute a work of literature, and therefore any alterations one makes in the manuscript do not automatically alter the work. If one cleans a dirty spot on a manuscript and reveals a word not legible before, the word is unquestionably a part of the text of the document, but it is not necessarily a part of the literary work ... (Tanselle 1989, 27)

Being made of thoughts and language, the literary work may be represented by a document but it is always somewhere else. The point of origin is the intention considered as an historical event, a thing that once happened, even if only in someone's mind. McGann's view, by contrast, is that in literature just as in painting or sculpture, the *work* is the object made, is the *text*.

Perhaps surprisingly, Tanselle's idealist model is not inherently antagonistic to the social conception of intention:

Authorially intended texts, which have been the goal of almost all critical editions in the past, cannot be expected to reside, in perfect accuracy, in surviving documents – or perhaps, for that matter, in any documents that ever existed. But the fact that they are not – and possibly never were – fully available in physical form does not deprive them of the status of historical events. (The same could of course be said of texts as intended by publishers or any of the other individuals that had a hand in the production process.) (Tanselle 1994, 5)

Tanselle was a vigorous defender of Greg, returning to 'The Rationale of Copy-Text' many times to show that even Bowers failed to appreciate that it contains virtually all that is necessary to regulate the operation of subjective judgement in editing so that the *work* may be recovered from the surviving imperfect *texts*. When the New Bibliography came under fierce attack from post-structuralists in the 1980s and 1990s, its overt Platonic idealism was routinely and unthinkingly denigrated as a regressive habit of mind to be jettisoned in favour of an allegedly materialist approach. In these critiques, Platonic idealism was denounced for entailing a Romantic conception of the writer as a soloist whose intentions were only ever sullied by the engagement with others such as actors or printers. It was felt necessary to sweep aside these conservative notions to reveal the writer (quintessentially Shakespeare) as a sociable creature working in a collective.

NEW TEXTUALISM: THE SOCIALIZED TEXT GOES POST-STRUCTURAL

For Jonathan Goldberg, the division of *King Lear* illustrated that textual criticism was founded on a Platonism that post-structuralism had dispelled, and that with this insight 'post-structuralism and the new textual criticism coincide, historically – and theoretically' since these discourses detach 'the supposed sovereign author from texts' and authorize 'the dispersal of authorial intention' (Goldberg 1986, 213–14). Yet the new alignment remained imperfect, he thought, because textual critics had not entirely done away with the author, who still reigned supreme over both *King Lear*s. Randall McLeod had argued that Gonorill and Goneril are two distinct characters without realizing that their essential character is their difference from one another, since all signification is based on differentials, or as Ferdinand de Saussure put it 'In language, there are only differences ... *without positive terms*' (Goldberg 1986, 215). With Jacques Derrida's notion of *différance* Goldberg hoped to unite bibliography with the latest mode of criticism, New Historicism, and slay essentialism with the revelation that 'character is construction, a social and textual production' (Goldberg 1986, 217). Marion Trousdale also appropriated the division of *King Lear* to a post-structuralist model of textuality, with similar caveats about the divisionists' reliance upon old-fashioned notions of coherence (Trousdale 1986). The trick, it seems, is not stopping at two of anything: on principle, post-structuralists dislike binaries almost as much as they dislike unities. Repeating a familiar objection to Charlton Hinman's facsimile of the 1623 Folio, Trousdale saw its idealism (the desire for a perfect Folio that never existed) at work in the dividers of *King Lear* seeking 'an ideal, if divided, *Lear*' (Trousdale 1986, 223).

The complaint that *The Division of the Kingdoms* did not go far enough in overturning existing notions of textuality was indicative of an emerging fissure. Four of its contributors, Steven Urkowitz, Randall McLeod, Paul Werstine and Michael Warren went on to form the core of New Textualism's bibliographical wing – Goldberg and Trousdale representing its politico-theoretical avant-garde – while Taylor refined conventional New Bibliographical thinking by redirecting editorial attention away from authorial papers and towards the collective authority of first performances, to create the 'new' New Bibliography. A key contribution to the emerging New Textualism was Margreta de Grazia's 'The Essential Shakespeare and the Material Book' (de Grazia 1988). She began with the objection that New Bibliographers portrayed themselves as materialists concerned with the book as object, but were really idealists, as is shown by their dissatisfaction with the surviving material texts of Shakespeare (the various quartos and Folio) and their pursuit of the pure, unsullied authorial manuscripts, those 'hypothetical or inferential' documents that 'exist only as imagined rarefications of the physical constructs we have at hand' (de Grazia 1988, 71). De Grazia had to be careful in the tenses of her verbs, because these now lost documents certainly had an existence at one time else there could be no quartos or Folio derived from them.

New Bibliography's 'anti-materialist strain' was, in de Grazia's view, a form of idealism:

If its examination of the book's physical properties and the processes that produced them is conducted with the end of extracting the pure Shakespeare, it follows that a good deal of the physical book will be discarded. In theory at least, the material form to which Shakespeare was consigned, in order to be produced as performance and as book, must be cast aside to reveal the underlying manuscript. Like the disintegrationists, New Bibliographers are intent on preserving the authentic Shakespeare, undefiled by the material operations they suffered in the process of being realized as public performance and published book. (de Grazia 1988, 80)

This became a central tenet of New Textualism and was reworked, for example, in Leah S. Marcus's claim that E. K. Chambers's monumental study of *The Elizabethan Stage* was anti-historicist because he researched the material conditions of Shakespeare's dramatic art – the theatres, the companies, the procedures – precisely in order to remove them from the equation. Chambers 'advocated the study of history in order to discount it' (Marcus 1996, 21), meaning that he attended to the minute details of

material influence in order to subtract this from the drama of the period in the hope of revealing the transcendent art. In fact, de Grazia's characterization of New Bibliography and Marcus's account of Chambers's motivation are particularly clear illustrations of what materialism and historicism really mean: the study of how ideas emerge from material reality and historical conditions rather than descending from a realm of pure thought to which we have no access.

De Grazia's concern for the portion of 'the physical book ... discarded' and 'cast aside' by New Bibliography is antiquarianism, a fetishistic concern for objects in and for themselves. New Textualists habitually used the term materialism to mean such an abiding interest in matter, in things that can be touched, and a disdain for ideas simply because they are intangible. This debased conception of materialism, misappropriated from Marxist theory, Jean E. Howard dismissed as the 'thingafication' of Shakespeare studies (2003, 34). De Grazia mocked Werstine's contribution to *The Division of the Kingdoms* as a 'demonstration of how compositor study remains mystified by faith in an immanent authorial manuscript' (de Grazia 1988, 83 n.7). Ironically, Werstine was at this point moving towards de Grazia's view, at least in its scepticism towards the practices and categorizations of New Bibliography. Part of what drove him in this direction was a pair of articles about stage directions published by William B. Long (1985a; 1985b).

In the first, Long argued that contrary to New Bibliographical assumptions prompt-books could be irregular and untidy: actors did not fix permissive or inconsistent stage directions in the scripts they received, so we cannot tell whether the manuscript copy underlying an early edition was authorial or theatrical simply from its stage directions. Long promised that his characterization of prompt-books – he preferred the term 'playbook' since prompting in the modern sense seems not to have occurred – was based on 'the only detailed investigation of this material since Greg' (Long 1985b, 122). Yet he was spare with illustrations, quoting half a dozen scholars misled by New Bibliographical assumptions originating with W. W. Greg but none of the early modern manuscripts themselves, whose raw evidence he claimed contradicted them. Because the book-keeper did not need to alter much, Long inferred that there was no routine practice of creating a fair copy to make a prompt-book: the author's papers would do perfectly well for use in the theatre, being marked up in a desultory fashion as needed. Thus Long revived the theory of continuous copy proposed from within the New Bibliographical tradition by A. W. Pollard and John Dover Wilson and rejected by Greg (pp. 16–30 above), which theory dissolves

Greg's binarism of either foul papers or prompt-book underlying an early edition.

Long's second article focussed mainly on one play manuscript, *Thomas of Woodstock*, and provided the detailed evidence missing from the first. He reported that playbook manuscripts have the features that New Bibliography claimed for them, but with not nearly enough regularity to support the New Bibliographical assertion that routine practices gave rise to these features and hence that they could be expected in manuscripts of this class. Long noted that book-keepers did not attempt to improve precision by making specific such things as the dramatists' directions for indeterminate numbers of supernumeraries, of the kind 'Enter two or three …'. Marginalia that have been interpreted as notes reminding someone to have ready at the right moments the people or properties needed for the performance might in fact, Long decided, simply be records of roles to be cast and properties to be made, bought or borrowed for the production. Long listed the sixteen manuscripts he thought showed signs of theatrical use, of which half were in the dramatists' hands (hence his adherence to the continuous copy theory), and they show no 'demonstrable pattern of regular marking or adaptation for the stage' (Long 1985a, 92). Long was unconvinced that the marginal notes in *Thomas of Woodstock* necessarily fulfilled the playhouse purposes usually ascribed to them. Thus Greg called the marginal note 'Shrevs Ready' (Anonymous 1929, 179b) an advance warning, but Long suggested that it might arise from the players noting in the manuscript that they needed to cast actors and acquire properties for the parts of the shrieves (Long 1985a, 95). (Would not 'Shrevs needed' be a likelier phrasing?)

Long interpreted the various layers of annotation in *Thomas of Woodstock* as the records of three distinct productions (Long 1985a, 109–11). The excising of anti-French lines struck Long as the sort of thing that would happen in 1592–5 when Elizabeth's dealings with the French king Henry 4 were at a tricky stage, so that gave Long the date of the first performance. A revival about ten years later was evidenced by the presence in annotations of a hand that appears also in the manuscript of the play *Charlemagne* (British Library Egerton 1994) '*ca*. 1600–04' (Long 1985a, 111), and Long dated a second revival to the 1630s by the presence of a hand also found in the manuscript of Walter Mountfort's *The Launching of the Mary* licensed by Henry Herbert in 1633. The crucial feature of *Thomas of Woodstock* that gave Long his essay's title is the annotation 'A bed | for Woodstock' (Anonymous 1929, 180b), which cannot be an advance warning because it occurs just eight lines before the bed is needed – although there might have been an intervening act interval – and there is nothing reminding anyone to check that Woodstock is actually in the bed as he should be (Long 1985a, 107–8). The bed being so important to an action involving half the cast, Long thought it inconceivable that it might otherwise be forgotten during performance, and he decided that the annotation was made to remind someone to procure a bed for this play.

Another annotation that Long reinterpreted was the apparently anticipatory 'Booke' occurring eighteen lines before Richard asks Bushy 'what readst thou?' (Anonymous 1929, 166b). This cannot be a backstage reminder to have a book ready because Bushy is onstage from the start of the scene fifty-three lines earlier and no-one enters in the meantime. Either Bushy brought the book on with him, or it was already onstage at the start of the scene, so either way the annotation is not anticipatory but thirty-five lines too late. The same objections apply to supposedly anticipatory notes for 'Paper', 'Blankes', and '3: B[lanks]' (Anonymous 1929, 168a, 170b, 174b). The notes appear where the objects are first spoken of, not where they are needed to remind someone to have the objects ready in advance (Long 1985a, 112). Long pointed out that for revivals the bookkeepers did not delete anything in the manuscript, not even the names of actors of the past productions. Thus the New Bibliographical assumption that a prompter demanded a clean book to use backstage is not borne out by this manuscript. This untidiness, and the lack of anticipatory notes, Long offered as correctives to 'glib generalizations about what players did and did not do to manuscripts' (Long 1985a, 114). In a third essay arguing along the same lines, Long found that the playbook manuscript of *John a Kent and John a Cumber* also showed that little was done in the theatre to alter the dramatist's text, and that none of the things proposed by New Bibliography as the preparation of a prompt-book was done with regularity (Long 1989).

With the exceptions of 'Shrevs Ready' (which sounds like a readying note) and 'A bed | for Woodstock' (which is sufficiently anticipatory if it preceded an act interval), Long's claim that what look like readying marks in *Thomas of Woodstock* must be something else was secure, but his theatre-historical claims were not. Dating a revival to 1602–4 from a hand shared with *Charlemagne* implies that hands change rapidly over time (they need not) and that *Charlemagne* can be confidently dated. For the date, Long relied on Wilhelmina P. Frijlinck's hunch that George Chapman wrote *Charlemagne* (an attribution later rejected by the Malone Society editor of the play) and her subsequent reasoning that since Chapman began to write for this company around 1600, *Charlemagne* might be one of his first plays for them (Anonymous 1929, xxvii–xxviii; Anonymous 1938 for 1937, x–xi). Neither the Malone Society edition of *Charlemagne* (the most recent) nor Alfred Harbage's *Annals of English Drama* made an attempt to identify the playing company, the latter assigning its first performance to the period '1584–*c.* 1605', and Lucy Munro's history of the playing company made no mention of this play either (Anonymous 1938 for 1937; Harbage 1964; Munro 2005). Later, Long offered a date of '*ca.* 1600' for *Charlemagne* on the somewhat different ground of E. K. Chambers's sense of its 'style' (Long 1985a, 112, 118 n.37; Chambers 1923b, 5). The most recent analysis gives good reason to think Samuel Rowley wrote *Thomas of Woodstock* after 1605 (Jackson 2001b), in which case there was no revival in 1602–4. Dating the second revival by the presence of a hand also seen in Walter Mountfort's *The Launching of the Mary*, licensed in 1633, is unreliable because one man's handwriting may stay the same for many years. Most importantly, Long's failure to find more than the slightest hints that the manuscripts were marked up for stage use might simply indicate that these particular documents were not used to regulate performances. If two revivals were evidenced in the manuscript of *Thomas of Woodstock* it would have to be counted as something like a prompt-book, and its failure to conform to the New Bibliographical characterization of that class of documents would be compelling. But Long's evidence for those revivals was slight.

THE END OF VIRGINIAN-SCHOOL NEW BIBLIOGRAPHY

As the New Textualism was emerging, bibliographical studies along mainstream New Bibliographical principles continued at the same time as a 'new' New Bibliography was developed by the Oxford Shakespeare project, discussed in the next chapter. The most ambitious of the mainstream work was Peter W. M. Blayney's analysis of Q1 *King Lear* (printed by Nicholas Okes in 1608) that put into practice what D. F. McKenzie counselled in 'Printers of the Mind' (pp. 81–4 above) by examining all the books Okes printed around that time (Blayney 1982). This is necessary because, contrary to Fredson Bowers's assumption, printers routinely worked on multiple books concurrently and they could affect one another. What is more, Okes shared work on individual books with other printers, so Blayney had effectively to examine the entire output of the London printing industry between 1605 and 1609 (Blayney 1982, 9–10) to discover all the books that might have impinged on Q1 *King Lear*. In reconstructing the printing of Q1, Blayney attacked Bowers's very notion of a skeleton forme: if anything was transferred as a unit from forme to forme, it was the furniture that holds the type in the chase and does not print; the skeleton leaves no evidence of itself. The headlines might also be transferred in a regular fashion with the skeleton, but it cannot be assumed that they were: 'Four loose bones do not make a skeleton' (Blayney 1982, 125).

Although he disposed of the early Virginian-school approach of analysing headline reuse, as developed by Bowers, Blayney remained firmly wedded to the later Virginian methodology developed by Charlton Hinman of analysing the recurrence of distinctive pieces of type. Blayney empirically confirmed McKenzie's claim about concurrent printing but decided that Okes himself did not work on other books at the same time as Q1 *King Lear*. As Paul Werstine pointed out in a review (1985b, 122), this was not a certain deduction from the evidence presented, and if mistaken – if another book went through the printshop at the same time as Q1 *King Lear* – then Blayney's type reuse analysis, from which he determined the order of presswork and the compositorial stints, was invalid. More damagingly, Antony Hammond faulted Blayney's failure to examine three exemplars of Q1 together in order to distinguish letters that had been poorly inked or impressed from real examples of damaged type; Blayney had instead worked on single exemplars at a time (Hammond 1984). Checking Blayney's evidence, Hammond found himself agreeing with as few as one in three of the alleged recurrences of damaged type. Hammond praised Blayney for demonstrating that there was a layer of proofing, for which evidence has disappeared, before the stop-press corrections (which are really revises) that appear in early books. Indeed, the evidence of Q1 is that 'most hypotheses constructed to account for press-variants are likely to be grossly mistaken, and that as many as a third of such "corrections" are likely to be miscorrections' (Hammond 1984, 93).

While the claims of 'Printers of the Mind' were being confirmed by Blayney, McKenzie was invalidating the psycho-mechanical tests for compositor identification developed by T. H. Howard-Hill and refined by Gary Taylor and MacDonald P. Jackson (McKenzie 1984). Cambridge University Press's archives record payments to compositors for setting a book in 1701–2, and by comma-spacing tests it falls into two kinds of page: one in which spaces before commas are avoided (in a ratio of 1:5) and one in which they are favoured in ratios as high as 8:1. The text is verse so justification is not a significant factor and the copy (another book) could not be the cause of the patterns as it had no unspaced commas. The tests suggest two compositors with distinct habits, and from their derived stints it would follow that the space-favouring compositor set roughly three pages in every forme for nine consecutive formes. This knowledge could buttress other evidence from skeleton forme reuse that would reveal the relationship between presswork and compositing. Yet all such 'deductions' would be wrong, for the payments show six compositors who never shared a forme. Each of them was highly inconsistent, so 'the assumptions, and therefore the inferences, are nonsense' (McKenzie 1984, 114).

The crisis in compositor attribution studies is clear from S. W. Reid's attempt to explain away, rather than confront, the mounting evidence that the foundational assumptions were invalid (Reid 1985). Hinman identified five Folio compositors, A–E, and after Howard-Hill added F (pp. 92–3 above) Taylor added H, I and J (pp. 171–2 below). Reid tried to firm up J's stints using comma-spacing tests, despite his awareness of McKenzie's proof of their unreliability, and a sign of his despair is the remark that certain pages 'must be assigned to B, if only by a process of elimination' (Reid 1985, 134). Had that logic applied in previous studies, there would be fewer than nine compositors at this point. The sound of a methodology collapsing can be heard in Reid's deduction that 'his copy could induce B to set generally eschewed spellings like "here" and "young"' and 'he was not incapable of departing from his strongest spelling preference (for "do"), even when his copy contained his favoured form'. Whereas Reid attempted to explain away inconsistencies, Susan Zimmerman followed them to necessarily destructive conclusions, choosing as her examples Q2 *1 Henry 4* (1598) and Q1 *Richard 3* (1597), the former printed by Peter Short and the latter by Short and Valentine Simmes (Zimmerman 1985). Peter Davison argued that Q2 *1 Henry 4*'s alternation of skeletons by signature (one for sheets A, C, E, G and one for B, D, F, H) made no sense as the work of one man, so there were two compositors (Shakespeare 1968a, 250–2). Zimmerman countered that the book's extraordinary consistency in capitalization, punctuation, speech prefixes, spelling and lineation/layout indicated just one.

Type recurrence showed Zimmerman either one compositor using one typecase, or else two compositors with a case each (not sharing type), but the latter possibility was ruled out by evidence of type shortage (substitutions of wrong font): two normal cases would not be exhausted by the job. Evidence from distinctive types indicated which formes could not have been set up simultaneously, but Zimmerman refused to infer the order of presswork and insisted that headline analysis does not reveal it. At best the evidence 'suggests that the press or presses began with sheet A and moved consecutively to sheet K, that the outer forme of individual signatures was wrought off before the inner, and that each skeleton was used twice in one signature before being transferred to the next (alternating) signature' (Zimmerman 1985, 231). From signatures themselves, catchwords and patterns of spacing Zimmerman was prepared to infer nothing. The printing of Q1 *Richard 3* sheets H–M was done by Short and sheets A–G by Simmes. Jackson reckoned that in Short's printshop one compositor, N, set pages H1^r, H2^v, I1^r, I2^v, K1^r, K2^v, L3^r, L4^v, M3^r, M3^v and another, O, the other 19 pages (Jackson 1982). Zimmerman noticed that *do / doe* spellings break along just this division of pages, but the reappearance of distinctive type showed only one typecase (and hence one compositor) in use. Other standard tests showed inconsistencies within Jackson's two stints or consistencies across them, so the tests could not all be valid.

McKenzie's and Zimmerman's essays might easily have marked the end of the standard approaches to compositor identification, but fresh attempts (such as Ferguson 1989) were made to refine Shakespearian compositor identification by their psycho-mechanical habits. Jackson tried to refute McKenzie and vindicate the techniques in a study of Q1 *Pericles* (Jackson 1987). Sheets B and F–I of Q1 were printed by Thomas Creede, and commaspacing habits gave Jackson two compositors' stints. The evidence was hazy. The supposedly comma-favouring compositor set three pages, B4^r, F3^v and H2^r, in which he left out the space about as often as he put it in, in ratios of present-to-absent of 5:5, 2:2 and 6:5 respectively. The supposedly commaavoiding compositor inserted one about one-third to one-half of the time, with present-to-absent ratios of 4:7 on B1^r, 5:10 on B2^v, 3:2 on G1^r and 4:8 on H4^v. Jackson's division of compositor stints nearly matched Philip Edwards's division made from unrelated data (Edwards 1952). Perturbed by the 'slightly anomalous' (Jackson 1987, 22) page G1^r where his avoider of spaces put in three and left out two, Jackson switched to spaces before question marks, found them equivocal, and so derived a new compositor whose behaviour explained the evidence. He concluded that his article's main value was its 'vindication of evidence of spacing as an aid in the determining of shares of compositors' (Jackson 1987, 23).

In a final manoeuvre, Jackson belatedly responded to Zimmerman directly, offering new tests that corroborate his division of compositorial stints in Q2 *1 Henry 4* (Jackson 2001a). Jackson pointed out that 'oo' is set as a single ligature in 28 per cent of compositor X's pages but 44 per cent of compositor Y's pages, which would be an unlikely difference if, as Zimmerman argued, these stints are imaginary and only one man were at work. Also, where pieces of damaged type reappear in the book (eight times in all), they always come up in the stint of the man who, in Jackson's division, first set them; this too is most unlikely to be chance. It would be reasonable to conclude from all this that corroborating results from several different psycho-mechanical tests, each of which relies on premisses and evidence unconnected to the others, can indeed, as Jackson argued, establish compositorial stints to a reasonable degree of certainty. On its own, however, each test is relatively weak. Few researchers have the tenacity and statistical knowledge to combine the tests in ways that put the results beyond refutation.

NEW TEXTUALISM CONSOLIDATED

William B. Long's claim that theatrical manuscripts are more like foul papers than New Bibliographers thought (pp. 155–8 above) cleared the way for sceptical revaluation of the determination of printer's copy for early editions of Shakespeare. Paul Werstine challenged the idea that untheatrical and permissive stage directions and irregular speech prefixes show that Folio *The Comedy of Errors* was set from foul papers (Werstine 1988a). The speech prefix inconsistencies do not follow the stints of the compositors (B, C and D) so they must come from copy, but why not theatrical copy? After all, Werstine reasoned, editors today can follow the action without much trouble, so presumably early moderns could. The prefixes do not distinguish the two Antipholi when one is onstage without the other (and there is no danger of confusion) but when they meet in the last scene they are consistently distinguished as '*E[phesian] Ant[ipholus]*' and '*S[yracusan] Ant[ipholus]*' (Shakespeare 1623, 11^v–12^v). This seemed to Werstine like the practical concern of a theatrical mind. The few errors that would trouble a theatre person but not an author in the act of composition Werstine found he could explain as printshop error, and compared to the manuscripts that W. W. Greg designated prompt-books, the alleged indeterminacies of stage directions and speech prefixes are slight (Werstine 1988a, 240–2). What then was the printer's copy for Folio *The Comedy of Errors*? According to Werstine the right answer is that we cannot tell: nothing replaces Greg's strict binarism of untidy foul papers versus tidy prompt-book.

Werstine's growing scepticism was apparent too in his study of the differences between the Q2 and Folio *Hamlet*s, which generate contradictions when conflated (Werstine 1988c). What makes Hamlet apologize to Laertes for his graveside behaviour (Shakespeare 1604–5, N3^v; 1623, pp6^v)? In Q2 a lord tells Hamlet that Gertrude wishes it (1604–5, N3^v), whereas in F this lord is absent and instead Hamlet tells Horatio that he regrets insulting Laertes, who like him is grieving for a lost father (1623, pp6^r). Conflation doubles up the motivations for the apology. By chance Gary Taylor hit upon this insight at the same moment as Werstine (Wells *et al.* 1987, 400).

Only in Q2 does Hamlet mock Osric's mode of speaking about Laertes (1604–5, N2^v; 1623, pp6^v), which necessarily also mocks Laertes, so conflation with F produces a Hamlet who feels sorry for Laertes and then mocks him. Q2 and F show different, and internally consistent, versions of Hamlet's attitude towards Laertes, and in F Laertes is more mature and deserving of Hamlet's regard than Q2's Laertes, who is given royal permission to return to France only after Polonius recounts how hard he pleaded for paternal leave to do so (1604–5, B4^r; 1623, nn5^v). Werstine convincingly multiplied examples of Q2's and F's distinctiveness, but would not ascribe it to authorial revision. Indeed, he did not believe that authorial revision separated Q1 and Folio *King Lear* either, nor had he when contributing to Taylor and Warren's *The Division of the Kingdoms* (Werstine 1988c, 2 n.4).

Werstine refused to ascribe the Q2/F *Hamlet* differences to the author because he had become convinced by Michel Foucault's 'characterization of the search for origins as ultimately futile and misleading' (Werstine 1988c, 26). The 'genealogist', as Foucault styled himself, 'listens to history' and eschews such essentialist metaphysics as authorial agency. Although Foucault's followers were supposed to reject it on principle, unacknowledged binarism structured Werstine's closing remarks. Attributing the Q2/F differences to the author meant falling for the fallacy of 'a timeless and essential secret' rather than acknowledging the 'realm of history'. Admitting authorial agency meant admitting 'Shakespeare's agency alone' as opposed to the collaborative agencies of theatre and publication. Privileging the author meant imagining him as a 'timeless and tireless genius' with a pristine text (or rather two of them) instead of acknowledging that writing exists as 'alien forms [put together] through accident and succession'. The fashionable late 1980s postmodern caricature of authorship disabled Werstine's interpretation of his own facts, and he sounded aware of the disjunction between evidence and theory. Other New Textualists just let theory trump evidence every time.

Almost alone among the advocates of the emerging New Textualism, Werstine used hard-won empirical data – the habits of compositors – to undermine the rigid strictures of New Bibliography. The others either adduced primary sources for examples to counter specific claims of New Bibliography but without a systematic study of them all (Long and Randall McLeod exemplify this approach) or else looked at them afresh through the lens of post-structuralism. The latter mode generated Margreta de Grazia's essay 'The Essential Shakespeare and the Material Book' (pp. 154–5 above) that ended, like Werstine, with a Foucauldian preference for the 'collective and extended contributions and transformations' provided by non-authorial agencies of theatre and printshop (de Grazia 1988, 82). Indeed, had not Long (pp. 155–8 above) shown that Foucault was right and that around 1800 human nature changed and the modern systematic mind was born? This was claimed by Marion Trousdale, who found that the fifteen manuscripts Greg identified as prompt-books in *Dramatic Documents from the Elizabethan Playhouse* are in fact a varied bunch. The early moderns were not regular, consistent people like us: 'method itself does not appear to have been anything about which the Elizabethans in the ordering of their social processes seem particularly concerned' (Trousdale 1990, 91). Rather than simply contrast disorderliness then with orderliness now (which would recreate the very binarism from which French high theory was supposed to be a deliverance), Trousdale used the jargon of avoidance: 'the very concepts of order and disorder are mutually dependent, and, in a very Derridean way, one generates the other' and 'It is only from an idea of method that one can talk of randomness, only with an idea of orderliness that one can talk about its lack' (Trousdale 1990, 93). The incoherence of these statements was the price Trousdale paid for having her cake and eating it.

Werstine's next article pointed out that no extant document fits the New Bibliographical category of foul papers and that memorial reconstruction alone can account for none of the bad quartos (Werstine 1990). New Bibliography was built upon dyadic distinctions so that when an edition formerly called a bad quarto is shown to have authorial characteristics it is instantly redefined as a good quarto and assumed to have been based on foul papers. The taxonomy, Werstine objected, cannot accommodate the shades of grey evident in the documents. As a critique of New Bibliography this is sound, but Werstine overstated his case by suggesting that Greg utterly revised his view of the origins of Q1 *The Merry Wives of Windsor* (1602). In 1910 Greg concluded that the actor playing the Host produced the manuscript underlying the quarto by recalling his lines and those of the other actors (pp. 100–1 above), and Werstine found him 'disavowing his 1910 argument' (1990, 77), first elliptically when replying to a response to a book review he had written (Greg 1928b; Albright 1928; Greg 1928a) and then definitively in *The Editorial Problem in Shakespeare*. This implied that Greg abandoned memorial reconstruction altogether, although Werstine meant only that he gave up the 'single actor-reporter' part of the hypothesis. Even this is an exaggeration, for in *The Editorial Problem in Shakespeare* Greg clung to the possibility of just one actor being responsible ('It may be so ...') before concluding that 'Perhaps it would be safer to assume an independent reporter relying generally on mine Host's assistance' (Greg 1942, 71). Werstine's suggestion that Greg knew the memorial reconstruction hypothesis to be false but failed to abandon it proliferated. Reviewing the same sources, Laurie Maguire referred to 'Greg's *volte face*', his 'hesitant and rejected proposal' and his 'chang[ing] ground again' (Maguire 1996, 70, 75), when all Greg wavered about was whether the Host worked alone. Greg had always been unsure: 'mine Host has a main finger' (hence not the only one) in Q1, he wrote (Shakespeare 1910, xli).

According to Werstine, our collective love of unity makes us seek in the pre-Folio editions of Shakespeare a single agent (the author, embodied in his foul papers, or the lone rogue actor) and a single vector of transmission (into print directly from the author's papers or an actor's recollection). We need instead a 'narrative that includes post-structuralist differential readings of multiple-text works' (Werstine 1990, 86). Just what such a narrative would mean for bibliographical taxonomies was unclear, because New Textualism inherited from post-structuralism an ambivalent attitude towards binary opposites. Building on structuralism (and in particular the structuralist linguistics of Ferdinand de Saussure), post-structuralists wanted to retain the idea that meaning is differential rather than absolute, but were wary of the cut-and-dried distinctions (black/white, wrong/right) that structuralism defined as the basic units of meaning. Werstine's criticism of New Bibliography's taxonomical pigeon-holing – if a manuscript is not foul papers then it is prompt-book, if a quarto is not bad then it is good – is equally a critique of the *Course in General Linguistics* (Saussure 1916) and so saws off the branch on which it sits.

Long's dissolution of the binarism of foul papers/prompt-book in the study of manuscripts was also potentially self-defeating. A year before Long's article on *John a Kent and John a Cumber* (p. 157 above), T. H. Howard-Hill's account of John Fletcher and Philip Massinger's *Sir John van Olden Barnavelt*, a scribal transcript by Ralph Crane containing a bookkeeper's annotations, found it to be a theatrical document used for making the actors' parts but not for running the play in performance. Although the manuscript has clearly been marked up with theatrical concerns, 'further decisions about casting, parts, and stage movement would have been essential before the play could have been staged' (Howard-Hill 1988, 154). Crucially, chairs are brought in so the French ambassadors may sit while pleading with the Prince of Orange for Barnavelt's life, but nothing is provided for the Prince and his train to sit on; that they remain standing is impossibly indecorous and cannot reflect the final staging (Howard-Hill 1988, 166). The document did not fit Greg's binate taxonomy of foul papers/prompt-book, but it might find a place within Fredson Bowers's eight categories of manuscript (pp. 65–6 above).

Long's work on the surviving manuscript playbooks was widely received as a successful attack upon New Bibliography, but Greg and Bowers were both New Bibliographers and their incompatible ideas could not be undermined at once. As a critique of Greg's account of the making of a prompt-book, Long's interpretation assumed that the surviving documents represent the full extent of what was done in readying a play for the stage. Even Greg would admit that the making of a prompt-book might not be completed (as it almost certainly was not in the case of *Sir Thomas More*), so, without further evidence that Long was looking at documents ready to be used to run a performance, his claim that (contrary to Greg) prompt-books could be irregular and untidy is unproven. Long's critique itself relied on the binary notion that a document is either entirely untouched by theatrical annotation or entirely ready to be performed. If Bowers was right and there were many different kinds of play manuscript in existence, rather than just two, Long might have mistaken for prompt-books documents of another kind. Howard-Hill's reinterpretation of the manuscript of Fletcher and Massinger's *Sir John van Olden Barnavelt* as an intermediate theatrical document, used to make the parts but not to run the performances, gives a concrete illustration of the vulnerability of Long's logic. Greg's binarism of foul papers/prompt-book might be too rigid and yet, as Howard-Hill believed (1988, 154 n.26), Bowers's proliferation of transcripts might have gone too far the other way; the truth could lie somewhere between them.

CHAPTER 5

The 'new' New Bibliography: the Oxford Complete Works, 1978–1989

After nearly half a century of glacial progress on an edition of the complete works of Shakespeare, by 1978 all Oxford University Press had to show was R. B. McKerrow's *Prolegomena* (pp. 30–7 above), a few proof pages (Wells 1984, v) and the spin-off research by Alice Walker. In January of that year the Press appointed Stanley Wells to start the project afresh with a series of single-play volumes edited by different editors under Wells's general editorship and a complete works edition (Murphy 2003, 221–9). Guidelines for editors of the series of single-play volumes, known as the Oxford Shakespeare, were ready by the end of 1978 and do not embody the 'new' New Bibliography that was developed for the Oxford *Complete Works* discussed here (Wells 1991a). Wells had served first as associate editor under T. J. B. Spencer, and later as general editor, for the New Penguin Shakespeare since the 1960s (Wells 2006, 39–45), and was steeped in the new stage-centred approach fostered by the Shakespeare Institute in Stratford-upon-Avon, where for his Ph.D. he edited two of Robert Greene's prose narratives in 1961. The Institute was founded in 1951 by Allardyce Nicoll to build a scholarly relationship with the Shakespeare Memorial Theatre (now the Royal Shakespeare Company), and Nicoll chose as his first three fellows E. A. J. Honigmann, R. A. Foakes and John Russell Brown. They all agreed that Shakespeare wrote for a company of players whose professional and economic interests he shared, happily initiating his own and accepting others' revisions of his plays after passing them to the company.

The first fruit of Wells's employment on the Oxford *Complete Works* was a small book on *Modernizing Shakespeare's Spelling*, an attempt to think through its motivations and limitations to derive a consistent set of principles for modernization (Wells and Taylor 1979). The topic was underexamined, because the New Bibliographers favoured original-spelling editions, as exampled by McKerrow's complete works of Thomas Nashe (1904–10) and Fredson Bowers's complete plays of Thomas Dekker (1953–61). W. W. Greg argued that an editor should retain an early book's original spelling if that would preserve 'some trace, however faint, of the author's individuality' (Greg 1942, li), but John Russell Brown argued that this would give readers information they cannot make use of without specialist knowledge or else mislead them by implying that all the spellings are authorial (Brown 1960, 60–4). Brown insisted that generally the words' meanings have not changed (early modern *murther* just means *murder*) and writers placed no special value on spellings, expecting them to change in transmission, so only where the usage is special – where the modern word has not the same meaning – should original spellings be retained. Wells disposed of the argument that original spelling aids the reader's understanding of early modern pronunciation: since we cannot recover it wholly the retention of certain original spellings and not others makes an anachronistically composite text that represents no particular stage in the history of the language. With a tricky case like *travail* where the early modern word meant both wearisome toil and journeying, the best an editor can do is use the modern spelling for the primary sense active in the context (*travail* or *travel*) and footnote the other sense as available. That ambiguity was possible does not mean it was used in every case, and words unambiguous to us could be ambiguous for early moderns. Wells decided that the plays should be presented to readers in critical editions modernized in spelling and punctuation, and, accepting Jürgen Schäfer's argument on this point (1970), even in the names of people and places.

Wells's ideas on spelling had no effect in establishing Shakespeare's texts for the Oxford *Complete Works* because he decided to first produce an original-spelling edition of each play and only when the text was settled to apply the modernization. This separation of activities precluded the error of letting anticipated needs of the modern reader cloud judgements about variants and emendations, and it was enabled by a piece of luck: the publisher had digital transcriptions of early editions made for T. H. Howard-Hill's original-spelling concordances (pp. 91–2 above; Wells and Taylor 1990, 9–11; Ragg 2001, 78–9). These saved the editors rekeying the base texts. An early indication of Wells's editorial approach appeared in his study of *Much Ado About Nothing*, which accepted Greg's conclusion that Q (1600) was printed from authorial papers and F is a reprint of Q based on an exemplar that had first been lightly annotated by consultation of the company prompt-book (Wells 1980; Greg 1955, 279–81). Wells listed the quarto's signs of foul papers, but admitted that not all of them would have to be tidied for performance. When editing a foul-papers play the trouble is knowing how far to go since at the point at which these papers were written the dramatist might not have settled the details in his own mind.

It is not the editor's job, Wells argued, to finish the play for Shakespeare but rather to preserve its openness.

The Folio's layer of annotation from the prompt-book gives, nevertheless, a glimpse of how matters were resolved in the social process of rehearsal. Q brings on '*the Prince, Hero, Leonato, Iohn and Borachio, and Conrade*' to meet Benedick onstage (Shakespeare 1600c, c1ᵛ), and yet the ensuing conversation involves just Benedick and Don Pedro. At the same point, F has only '*Enter the Prince*', which seems more correct (Shakespeare 1623, 15ʳ). For Wells this showed that the author's papers recorded characters that Shakespeare, at the moment of composition, thought he might use to develop this scene, and the prompt-book showed the stage direction after it was shorn of unnecessary names (Wells 1980, 5). Although Q is the main authority for this play, where F reflects a decision made in the readying of the play for performance a stage-centred editor such as Wells would probably prefer it. Although he found moments where post-rehearsal F remedies the deficiencies of authorial Q, Wells did not, at this stage in his thinking, insist upon F every time. For the entrance of Balthasar in 2.3, Q and F represent alternative stagings and Wells commented that 'An editor has the choice of representing Shakespeare's original intention, in which case he should, I think, adopt Q's later entry for Balthasar, or of following the practice of Shakespeare's company as witnessed by F' (Wells 1980, 14). In the event, the Oxford *Complete Works* did not follow F even though 'no doubt this represents theatre practice' (Wells *et al.* 1987, 372 2.3.35.2n).

A similar situation obtains in the relationship between Q1 (1598) and Folio *Love's Labour's Lost* (Wells 1982). Q1 is generally thought to be based on foul papers because it has an apparent confusion about which of two women, Rosaline and Katharine, is wooed by Berowne and which by Dumaine. Or to put it another way, which woman had which name was not yet settled. The Folio was clearly printed from Q1, but with revisions, and John Dover Wilson and Greg agreed that these were not authoritative. Wilson held that an exemplar of Q1 was marked up in the theatre when it was being used as a prompt-book (Shakespeare 1923a, 186–91), while Greg thought F's departures from Q1 were within the capacity of a printshop editor (Greg 1955, 223). Prompted by John Kerrigan's work for a New Penguin Shakespeare edition of the play (Shakespeare 1982c), Wells sought fresh evidence that an authoritative manuscript was consulted to annotate an exemplar of Q1 to make copy for F, and found it in certain indifferent variants. Whereas Q1 does not refer to Armado as Braggart in dialogue, stage directions, or speech prefixes until 3.1, F uses an abbreviation of the label Braggart in his speech prefixes in 1.2. It is hard to see why anyone in the printshop would make this change, but a scribe marking up an exemplar of Q1 by reference to a manuscript that he has been told is authoritative might well not realize that Armado and Braggart are the same person and would, upon seeing speeches attributed to Braggart in his manuscript, 'correct' his Q1 accordingly (Wells 1982, 143).

Wells also found substantively variant speech prefixes in which F improves upon Q1 by reducing a casting inefficiency regarding a pair of lords that accompany the French princess. Unfortunately, such streamlining was not necessarily completed in the manuscript used to annotate Q1 (which Wells reckoned authorial fair copy, not a prompt-book) and the annotator's wavering attention to duty made the resulting Folio edition only partially conform to that manuscript (Wells 1982, 146–7). For Kerrigan this presented an 'editorial paradox' since giving the pair of lords the lines they probably had in the foul papers would be contrary to the authorial intention to cut them, yet their cutting probably included other changes (such as redistribution of lines) that the early editions do not record and can only be guessed at (Shakespeare 1982c, 245–6). Wells and Kerrigan agreed that while a theatre director might take such liberties as cutting the lords, an editor should not. As with *Much Ado About Nothing*, this suggests a conservatism not present in the final Oxford *Complete Works*, which executed the company's inferred collective intentions even where they are imperfectly witnessed in the early editions. Apparently, the project became bolder as it progressed.

Gary Taylor joined Wells as assistant (later joint general) editor in 1978 (Wells and Taylor 1990, 7) and his publications during the project convey a fresh approach that reinvigorated New Bibliographical thinking. To accompany Wells's essay on *Modernizing Shakespeare's Spelling* Taylor provided three studies on *Henry 5* that give a flavour of his editorial innovation (Wells and Taylor 1979, 38–164). The first dealt with Andrew S. Cairncross's failure to distinguish agreement-in-error as the key characteristic needed to prove that one book reprints another (pp. 33–4 above), and in particular his claim that Q2 (1602) and Q3 *Henry 5* (1619) provided copy for the Folio. (Part of this criticism Taylor later withdrew, realizing that he had overlooked five cases of F's agreement-in-error with Q3 that prove some influence, probably in the form of sporadic consultation by the Folio compositors (Wells *et al.* 1987, 376).) The second study argued that Q1 (1600) differs in staging from F in ways best explained by abridgement to enable performance by just eleven actors. The third study explored the implications of the realization that as a memorial reconstruction (albeit of the play as abridged for performance by eleven actors) Q1 might record decisions made in the readying of the play for performance, and hence be a more fully realized form of Shakespeare's intentions than the Folio edition based on foul papers. If the corruptions attendant upon memorial reconstruction and printing could be taken away, and Taylor was boldly optimistic they could, what remained would be the script as performed. An editor could thus recover from a memorially reconstructed edition evidence, unavailable in otherwise better editions, for the socialized form of the play.

In an important development of the ideas in Greg's 'The Rationale of Copy-Text', Taylor proposed that where the authority for accidentals and substantives is split between two early editions, the familiar term copy-text be retained for the authority for accidentals and a new term, control text, be used for the authority for substantives (Taylor 1981a). Taking *Richard 3* as his example split-authority play, Taylor pointed out that where F departs from its Q3 (1602) and Q6 (1622) copy and returns to a reading found in Q1 (from which Q3 and Q6 derive monogenetically) but not in Q1's spelling, an authoritative manuscript must have been consulted, so an editor must follow F's reading. For such a reading, F's spelling (from the authoritative manuscript) is likely to be closer than Q1's to Shakespeare's own spelling. However, where manuscript consultation resulted in only a letter or two added or deleted the annotator probably marked just those letters on the quarto rather than striking out the whole word and writing it afresh in the spelling of the manuscript. This minimal intervention would make F's spelling derived from Q3 or Q6 inferior to Q1's, the ancestor of them all. Probing the problematic boundary between accidentals and substantives, Taylor decided that variants such as *pray thee / prithee* appear substantive but bear no difference in meaning, so they count as accidentals. The Folio compositors had, in any case, a preference for one or other phrasing and consistently set it regardless of copy.

To the growing list of Folio compositors, Taylor added three more: H, I and J, whose stints so reduce the work attributable to compositor A that he no longer could be assumed highly reliable (Taylor 1981b). Howard-Hill had invented what Taylor thought a 'near-infallible' (Taylor 1981b, 97) test for compositor C: the insertion of a space before a comma at the end of a short line (pp. 92–3 above). Using spellings and his own comma-spacing test based on Howard-Hill's, Taylor compared the existing compositors' habits – including those sections where Charlton Hinman could not decide between two men – and found mutual incompatibilities. Either the compositors were behaving differently on different days, or there were other compositors throwing off the tests, whom Taylor called H1, who put spaces after medial commas, and H2 who did not. With Howard-Hill's digital transcriptions loaned to the Oxford project, Taylor was able, as no manual study had been, to check all the spelling preferences of H1 and H2. They were identical, so H1 and H2 were one man. This proved the comma-spacing test unreliable, since H was inconsistent about it. Thus Taylor inadvertently anticipated D. F. McKenzie's exploding of such tests (pp. 159–60 above), but he dismissed his discovery: 'the evidence of medial spaced commas, usually so reliable, is not reliable here' (Taylor 1981b, 103). Repeating the flawed procedure with other Folio plays, Taylor 'discovered' two more compositors, I and J. The three new men set pages formerly attributed to compositor A, leaving him no simple reprints from quarto copy, and without evidence of his fidelity to copy he could no longer be considered uniquely reliable and exempted from emendation by editors.

In a revaluation of *Troilus and Cressida*, Taylor argued that Q (1609) was printed from foul papers and F from an exemplar of Q annotated from the company prompt-book, which contained revisions made when the play transferred from the Inns of Court to the Globe playhouse (Taylor 1982b). The orthodox view was that the manuscript used to annotate Q was foul papers, since F has features associated with foul papers (such as repetitions showing first and second thoughts and anomalies of staging) that are absent in Q, and to overturn it Taylor argued that these features were deliberate choices or the consequences of revision in staging for the new venue (Taylor 1982b, 101–4). The core evidence was twenty-eight variants where, by editorial consent, F is wrong and Q right. If the manuscript used to annotate Q were foul papers, this would mean that the annotator twenty-eight times overruled Q's correct reading in order to favour not the manuscript reading (also correct, being foul papers) but his own misreading of it. Since the foul papers could not be both the copy for Q and the manuscript used to annotate Q – because the annotation makes F differ from Q – the obvious alternative hypothesis is that Q was set from foul papers and the manuscript used to annotate it was theatrical papers. This makes the annotator's behaviour easier to understand: twenty-eight times he followed the manuscript's reading (where its scribe had erred in copying the foul papers) rather than Q's reading, because it was clearly written in fair copy and so looked certain (Taylor 1982b, 107). If Q is based on foul papers and F on an exemplar of Q improved by reference to a prompt-book, F's substantive differences from Q will include improvements made in readying for performance, and hence for a stage-centred editor Q should be the copy-text for accidentals and F the control text for substantive variants.

Explaining what would be one of the most controversial decisions of the Oxford *Complete Works*, Taylor showed why an editor should give the character Sir John the last name of Oldcastle in *1 Henry 4* even though he is clearly the same character as Sir John Falstaff in *2 Henry 4* (Taylor 1985b). There is overwhelming evidence that when *1 Henry 4* was composed and first performed, the name Oldcastle offended the historical figure's living descendants, who forced Shakespeare to rename him Falstaff. An edition aiming to represent the plays as first performed would simply have to revert to Oldcastle. (That this was the aim of the Oxford *Complete Works* had not been publicly announced, but it was implicit in the independent publications of its editors.) Those who later objected to the name Oldcastle probed the complexities and paradoxes of authorial intention. David Scott Kastan accepted that the name restored Shakespeare's intention, but observed that the central tenet of the edition's 'new' New Bibliography was that 'dramatic production ... was never an autonomous authorial achievement' (Kastan 1998, 219). Thomas A. Pendleton made the same point more pithily: if people objected to the name Oldcastle, then renaming him Falstaff was a way of being sociable, and the edition was meant to capture the socialized play (Pendleton 1990, 66–7). Taylor defended the decision on the grounds of authorial intention, but could have argued more simply that Oldcastle was undoubtedly in the first performances (else his descendants would not have known to complain) and these were the arbitrary goals the project aimed towards.

Aside from an article on the manuscripts of Shakespeare's *Sonnets* (Taylor 1985–6), Taylor's only other significant article before publication of the Oxford *Complete Works* was a study of *Richard 2* co-written with John Jowett, who joined the Oxford *Complete Works* team in 1981 (Jowett and Taylor 1985; Wells and Taylor 1990, 8). They concluded that Folio *Richard 2* contains over forty readings more authoritative than those in Q1 (1597), even though F was printed from Q3 (1598), itself derived from Q1. These readings, 'sprinklings of authority', came from a prompt-book used to annotate an exemplar of Q3 that was F's copy. The first problem was that although, as Richard E. Hasker had established (1952–3), the main printer's copy for F was Q3, this lacks the abdication episode, so either Folio compositor A set the episode from Q5 (1615), which Hasker had shown also supplied the Folio's ending of the play, or else he set it from a transcript drawn from the manuscript prompt-book. Which is it? Jowett and Taylor looked at compositor A's departures from copy spellings and from his own preferences when setting Folio *Richard 2* from Q3. In 172 lines around the abdication episode he departed from Q3 much less often than the 160-line episode departs from Q5, so the odds were against Q5 being his copy for the episode (Jowett and Taylor 1985, 154–5).

Turning to Hasker's argument that Q5 was Folio copy for 5.5.19 to the end, Jowett and Taylor accepted that the evidence was of the weakest sort – F and Q5 agreeing against Q3 on indifferent variants – but argued that the agreements are so clustered, six agreements in fifty-three lines, that cumulatively they are beyond coincidence (Jowett and Taylor 1985, 156). Curiously, though, these lines follow Q3's accidentals rather than Q5's. Hasker thought that in the exemplar of Q3 used as F's copy the last two leaves were missing and it was patched from Q5 (which is how Q5 affected F's ending), but confining the dependence to just the fifty-three lines holding six indifferent agreements of F and Q5 against Q3, Jowett and Taylor were able to discard some of the evidence from accidentals that seems to speak against F's dependence on Q5. Yet there remained accidentals pointing to Q3 while substantives pointed to Q5. Jowett and Taylor reached the ingenious conclusion 'that one page was missing from the original theatrical manuscript which was collated against Q3, and that this single missing page had been supplied (at some earlier date, by someone other than Jaggard) by a transcript of the relevant portion of Q5' (Jowett and Taylor 1985, 157–8). Thus for this section of the play, where the exemplar of Q3 used as copy for F was annotated by reference to a theatrical manuscript it picked up the substantive readings of that manuscript, derived from Q5, but not Q5's accidentals.

Since annotation was done to improve the exemplar of Q3 prior to its being used as Folio copy, F's differences from Q3 are likely to be authoritative manuscript readings that overruled Q3. Q1, from which Q3 derives, was based on foul papers, so the theatrical manuscript used to annotate an exemplar of Q3 must (on Greg's binate principle) have been a prompt-book, and in Jowett and Taylor's socialized conception of Shakespeare's theatrical art its readings were to be preferred, if possible, to the pre-theatrical readings of Q1. Previous editors (including Wells for the New Penguin Shakespeare edition) ignored F's potentially authoritative readings, but Jowett and Taylor sought criteria for discerning (in order to admit) the genuinely authoritative ones. Plotting F/Q1 agreements against Q3 (signs of annotation) alongside F/Q3 agreements against Q1 (signs of non-annotation) showed that the annotation went in runs where it was done assiduously and runs where it was neglected (Jowett and Taylor 1985, 164–73). Having established where consultation occurred, Jowett and Taylor invented a rule for joining the dots:

a run of two or more indications of correction may be regarded as an area of correction. Such an area may be allowed to extend over single indications of non-annotation, but ends when two such opposing items occur consecutively. The same rules therefore apply for the uncorrected areas. (Jowett and Taylor 1985, 174)

The procedure is much like the one performed by William Montgomery – who joined the Oxford team around this time (Wells and Taylor 1990, 8) – in his doctoral dissertation when trying to work out where Folio *2 Henry 6* was based on consultation of Q3 (1619) *The Contention of York and Lancaster* (Montgomery 1985, 2: xxxvii–xlix; Egan 2008, 131–4).

When Jowett and Taylor started looking beyond dialogue to stage directions and speech prefixes, the situation seemed murky. The stage directions were added to or changed in areas of uncorrected dialogue just as often as in areas of corrected dialogue and throughout the speech prefixes for Richard and Bolingbroke were altered from Q1's system (which makes perfect sense of its own) to a wholly different one, which presumably came from the prompt-book. It seemed, then, that the annotation of stage directions and speech prefixes was done separately from the annotation of dialogue variants. This could make sense: Q3 was known to derive from authorial copy, hence reliable in dialogue but unreliable in those things that would have got fixed or developed in rehearsal and performance. Thus the collation of dialogue variants was sporadic but speech prefix and stage direction variants were attended to more closely (Jowett and Taylor 1985, 179–81).

What would all this mean for an editor of the play? Jowett and Taylor worked through the Q1/F variants to see if their discovery of which sections of F are from manuscript-corrected copy helps to pick which variant is right (Jowett and Taylor 1985, 187–91). Quite a few variants they thought were Shakespeare's own tweakings reflected in the authoritative manuscript, as would be expected if Honigmann's *The Stability of Shakespeare's Text* were right (pp. 69–72 above). Other cases seemed to show F recovering from the manuscript good readings that Q1 corrupted. Alan E. Craven's work on Valentine Simmes's compositor A, who set most of Q1 *Richard 2* (1597) and all of Q2 (1598) from Q1, gives an idea of his habitual errors (pp. 92–3 above), and these would not create the Q1/F variants. Likewise, the known habits of compositor B, who set most of Folio *Richard 2*, would not generate them. With compositorial agency discounted as their cause, the variants are important evidence of what stood in the authoritative theatrical manuscript. The extensive and minute labour of compositorial analysis from the 1950s to 1970s was finally paying an editorial dividend.

Jowett and Taylor's study of *Richard 2* threw light on one of the most famous variants in the canon: the absence of an abdication episode in Q1 (1597), Q2 (1598) and Q3 (1598), and its presence in Q4 (1608) and the 1623 Folio (Jowett and Taylor 1985, 194–8). The episode might have been newly written when it appeared in Q4. Or was it rather suppressed as politically unacceptable in the early performances and Q1–Q3 and later became acceptable? Perhaps the latter, but there is no reason to assume that F's abdication episode is what is missing from Q1, for there may have been a different one. A stage direction in Q1's scene 4.1 has '*Enter Bagot*' (Shakespeare 1597a, G4^r) just after the line 'Call forth Bagot', but F has him enter at the start of the scene with a herald who is not needed (Shakespeare 1623, d1^v). This suggests that the prompt-book, the source of F's direction, was preparing for something, including a speaking part for a herald, not in F. This something may have been an abdication episode now lost, and perhaps more censorable than the one we know. If so, when a revised episode was written (to get the play past the stage censor) the introductory stage direction was not changed to dispense with the herald. The episode in F contains little that might offend a censor, yet its absence in Q1–Q3 is most easily explained as censorship. The revision hypothesis would account for this: the first three quartos represent the authorial papers with the unacceptable episode omitted, and the Folio represents the toned-down acceptable version from the prompt-book.

Aside from this study of *Richard 2*, Jowett published two articles while editing the Oxford *Complete Works*. In the first he argued that the scribe Ralph Crane sophisticated the stage directions of *The Tempest* while making printer's copy for F by transcribing the foul papers, and that we can to some extent distinguish his words from Shakespeare's (Jowett 1983). Jowett collated the evidence from Crane's scribal work on other plays that showed him sophisticating as he copied, adding details from his own recollections of the play in performance. Listing words in the stage directions of *The Tempest* that are new to Shakespeare's language and do not arise from dramatic necessity, Jowett argued that these are the likeliest to be Crane's. In several cases the invented wording does not quite suit the moment, as with the opening direction '*A tempestuous noise of Thunder and Lightning heard*' (Shakespeare 1623, A1^r), which rather mixes up the effects (since thunder is the noise of lightning). Another odd direction for sound is the '*confused noyse*' (1623, A1^r) of the frightened sailors, whose dialogue cries are actually in verse. The word *had* in '*They all enter the circle which* Prospero *had made*' (1623, B2^v) suggests a prose narrative concern for consecutiveness which is never found in the writing of a dramatist concentrating on describing the necessary action in the here-and-now. That Crane felt the need to flesh out the directions suggested to Jowett that he was working from foul papers, which (as New Bibliography teaches) are characterized by relatively fewer and less complete directions than a manuscript used for performance.

Jowett's other article from this period was concerned with the doubly told death of Portia in *Julius Caesar*, which had been commonly attributed to the accidental presence of Shakespeare's first and second attempts at telling the news (Jowett 1984). Brents Stirling argued that because Cassius's speech prefix is usually '*Cassi.*' but becomes '*Cas.*' or '*Cass.*' in the section thought to be the second attempt (Shakespeare 1623, ll3ʳ) the revision hypothesis is confirmed: the compositor changed his habit under the influence of a change in the copy (Stirling 1962). Jowett got the hint that ligature shortage might instead be the cause when he noticed that '*Cass.*' appears as a catchword even though it anticipates the speech prefix '*Cassi.*', which had already been set because the compositor was working backwards through the first half of the quire. Using Charlton Hinman's deduction of the order in which the pages were set and distributed, Jowett counted the flow of type into and out of the *ssi* box in the typecase. This showed that the compositor changed his spelling prefix to avoid the ligature at just the point when his box was likely empty, reverted to the ligatured version when twenty-three pieces of type replenished the box (counted from the pages being distributed), and then switched back to the non-ligatured version after setting exactly twenty-three ligatured prefixes. This could not be coincidence nor the influence of copy: the speech prefix variation was due to ligature shortage, not authorial revision. Editors who want to mark one of the two tellings of Portia's death as a first shot, or delete it, would have to make the claim on non-bibliographical grounds.

Fredson Bowers had thought that Stirling's work on the double telling of Portia's death undermined the binarism of Greg's view about the paucity of manuscript copies of a play. It is hard to see where in Greg's 'rigid dichotomy' (Bowers 1978, 26) of foul papers/prompt-book the revision of the telling of Portia's death might stand. Folio *Julius Caesar* has stage directions for music and sound effects that are uncharacteristic of authorial papers, as is the care taken to enable the roles of Ligarius and Cassius to be doubled even though this generates plot inconsistencies. However, a prompt-book (the only other manuscript in Greg's dichotomy) could not contain the original and the revised version of the announcement of Portia's death. Thus, reasoned Bowers, F's copy was an intermediate transcript of the kind useful to have available for rehearsal where such details might yet be changed. Jowett's disposal of Stirling's argument for revision removed the impediment to F's copy being the prompt-book or a transcript of it (Wells *et al*. 1987, 386–7). The Oxford *Complete Works*'s editors thought Greg was right: in general and for most plays 'probably only two manuscripts ever existed' (Wells *et al*. 1987, 14).

Articles published during the Oxford *Complete Works* project indicated the outlines of its editorial approach, and the edition was accompanied by a *Textual Companion* (Wells *et al*. 1987) providing the fine detail, including which parts of New Bibliography it accepted and which it overturned. Taylor's familiarity with the emerging New Textualism was clear from the tone of his General Introduction, but he chose to use Randall McLeod's verb 'to un-edit' (Wells *et al*. 1987, 6) not in the sense of minimizing editorial mediation but of undoing previous editors' errors. (Before McLeod used it in print and popularized it, David Bevington used 'unediting' in this limited sense to describe his edition's undoing of the Globe text he inherited, and attributed it to McLeod (Shakespeare 1980a, 'Preface'); McLeod's wider sense, used by his articles, was by 1987 the dominant one.) Greg's binarism of foul papers/prompt-book was retained even though additional transcripts were found to underlie a number of early editions, since these were made from the foul papers or prompt-book for the purpose of printing rather than made between them for theatrical ends. Taylor acknowledged William B. Long's essays on theatrical manuscripts (pp. 155–8 above), but treated his examples as exceptions to the general rule that prompt-books were tidier than foul papers. The stage-centred preference for prompt-books over foul papers was expressed in terms of socialization, explicitly credited to Jerome J. McGann's *A Critique of Modern Textual Criticism* (Wells *et al*. 1987, 15) where the idea arose in relation to print publication, not performance (pp. 146–50 above). Taylor accepted Kerrigan's claim (pp. 135–6 above) that minor revisions throughout a play (as in *King Lear*) are characteristic of the author, whereas non-authorial revision/adaptation was a matter of large-scale additions and excisions, as in *Macbeth* and *Measure for Measure*, where it is detectable but not 'magically' reversible (Wells *et al*. 1987, 15). Twenty years later Taylor and Jowett attempted such magic for these two plays (Middleton 2007; Taylor and Lavagnino 2007; pp. 270–71 below).

To represent the plays as first performed, the Oxford editors put back profanity that was removed from old plays being revived after the 1606 Act to Restrain Abuses of Players, even where there was little or no evidence which oaths had been used (Wells *et al*. 1987, 16): any kind of profanity would bring Folio *2 Henry 4* and *Othello* closer to their first performance texts. A similar line was taken with early editions containing act intervals imposed for revivals after 1608, when the King's men started using breaks at their open-air as well as their indoor theatre (Taylor 1993c). Where these later-imposed act divisions co-exist with other extensive revisions (as in Folio *Measure for Measure* and *Macbeth*) the Oxford *Complete Works* retained them (as too hard to undo), but unartistic mechanical breaks were removed so as to reflect the first performances (Wells *et al.* 1987, 16). The editors' audacity in departing from the early editions was called hubris by many reviewers, some perhaps regretting that they had not been so bold in their own editions. The treatment of authorial revision stands out in this regard. For twenty-one plays we have only one substantive printed edition, but for *2 Henry 4*, *Hamlet* and *Othello* we have, as J. K. Walton established by showing that F was set from a manuscript (Walton 1971, 124–227), two substantive editions which differ in hundreds of readings. For another three, *Richard 2*, *Troilus and Cressida* and *King Lear*, the Folio was prepared by 'marking up a first edition quarto with readings from an independent manuscript' (Wells *et al.* 1987, 17). Thus six major works survive in two independent substantive sources, both apparently authoritative. The differences cannot be attributed to errors of compositors and scribes and hence must be Shakespeare's choices. Honigmann (pp. 69–72 above) showed that revision need not produce blotting and in the Folio preliminaries Ben Jonson referred directly to Shakespeare revising: '*strike the second heat | Vpon the* Muses *anuile*' (Shakespeare 1623, ᵖA6ᵛ). Editors have long denied Shakespearian revision, Taylor argued, because their training tends to make all differences seem like errors in transmission (Wells *et al.* 1987, 18).

Eleven Folio plays were printed from annotated exemplars of earlier editions, the annotation ranging from sparse (in *Much Ado About Nothing*, *A Midsummer Night's Dream* and *The Merchant of Venice* only stage directions and speech prefixes were checked), through *Richard 2* where dialogue readings were sporadically altered, to *Richard 3* where dialogue and stage directions were systematically collated. The amount of annotation seems dependent upon whether the right to print the play was owned by a Folio syndicate member: extensive annotation would maximize the Q/F differences and frustrate objections from the quarto's rights holder (Wells *et al.* 1987, 51–2). Thus the project essentially adopted the findings of Walton's study of quarto copy used to make the Folio (Walton 1971, 280–1). As well as consulting theatrical manuscripts to improve existing editions to be used as Folio copy, the reverse occasionally happened: a compositor baffled by his manuscript copy might consult a print edition for help. Probably this occurred with *Henry 5*, *The Contention of York and Lancaster* and *Richard*

Duke of York, and it makes trouble for an editor since rather than providing corroboration 'any reading shared by the two editions might result from contamination' (Wells *et al.* 1987, 52). Q2 *Romeo and Juliet* (1599) and *Hamlet* (1604–5) were set in part from their respective Q1s (1597 and 1603), and since this proves the presence of these editions in the printshop it must be suspected that elsewhere these good quartos had been contaminated by sporadic consultation of the bad ones. Theatrical manuscripts could also be contaminated by print editions, as when the prompt-book of *Richard 2* was repaired by transcription from Q5 (1615) and the revision of *King Lear*, leading to a new prompt-book, was begun by Shakespeare writing on an exemplar of Q1 (1608) (pp. 133–46 above). The Oxford editors did no fresh collation of press variants in the early editions, nor historical collation of variant readings in early editions or significant post-1709 editions. What they achieved was to develop new practices in modernizing spelling and punctuation, apply a socialized model of Shakespeare's dramatic intentions, determine the nature of the copy for all substantive editions, and for the first time give due place to revision and collaboration (Wells *et al.* 1987, 62).

Despite extensive signs of authorial and non-authorial revision elsewhere, only for *King Lear* did the Oxford *Complete Works* give two fully edited versions. For thirteen other plays they used appendices showing in edited form material that they thought a reader would want to see but which did not meet their criteria for inclusion in the main text. These were mainly passages that appear in one or more early editions deriving from authorial papers but did not, on the evidence of other early editions, reach first performance. In some cases the deleted material was replaced by something else – alternative material that the Oxford editors used for the main text – and in others it was simply discarded. A few of the appendices attempted to show the state of a play before authorial or non-authorial revision. Thus, what John Dover Wilson had decided, on the basis of mislineation, was material written up the margins of a manuscript of *A Midsummer Night's Dream* (p. 249 below) was in an appendix removed to show Shakespeare's original version of scene 5.1. *Measure for Measure* as we know it was an adaptation by Thomas Middleton in the early 1620s, so in appendices the Oxford editors conjecturally restored the most affected scenes to their pre-adaptation states.

In most cases the appendices were a compact way to convey textual difference, but *Hamlet* had sixteen of them totalling 217 lines from Q2 (1604–5), based on authorial papers, jettisoned before first performance. In collaboration with G. R. Hibbard who was independently editing the play

(Shakespeare 1987), the Oxford editors found evidence (from Q1/F agreement against Q2) that F derives from a document used in performances, but thought its major differences from Q2 arose from authorial revision probably made, *à la* Honigmann (pp. 69–72 above), when Shakespeare copied out his foul papers fairly (Wells *et al.* 1987, 399–402). Wells and Taylor soon wished they had treated *Hamlet* like *King Lear* and simply printed two complete versions, had the publisher permitted it (Wells and Taylor 1990, 16–17). The traditional author-centred preference is for Q2 over F, illustrated by Harold Jenkins's Arden Shakespeare edition in which he commented that 'In seeking to present the play as Shakespeare wrote it rather than as it was shortened and adapted for performance I do no more than follow tradition' (Shakespeare 1982a, 75). Jenkins was mentored by the central figures of New Bibliography, Greg and McKerrow, whom he met through his tutor at University College London, Charles Jasper Sisson, for whose complete works of Shakespeare Jenkins supplied an edition of *Sir Thomas More* (Honigmann 2001, 554–5, 561; Shakespeare 1954c). Jenkins was not expressing disdain for the theatre, but (as he put it to Honigmann) indicating that *Hamlet* is 'much more than a stage play' (Honigmann 2001, 570). Stanley Wells too was mentored by Sisson at University College London and later at the Shakespeare Institute (Wells 2009), and mostly differed from Jenkins in that under the influence of the stage-centred Institute he developed a new form of New Bibliography, encouraged by Taylor's (and later Jowett's) enthusiasm for following a revised set of editorial premises to their practical conclusions.

The successor to Jenkins's Arden Shakespeare in the same series followed the Oxford editors' instinct in offering fully edited versions of Q2 and F (as well as Q1) in the shared belief that F probably contains Shakespeare's changes made when copying out fairly (Shakespeare 2006b, 506–9). However, these Arden editors treated differently from the Oxford editors the consequences of there being two distinct Shakespearian holographs of the play, arguing that each early edition should be edited as though the others did not exist: 'once Taylor and Hibbard have decided F has a *new* manuscript behind it, why do we think we need Q2's readings in the argument?' (Shakespeare 2006b, 515). The answer to this rhetorical question is that the situations are not symmetrical: when F was made Q2 was in existence, but not vice versa. In the case of Folio *Hamlet*, contamination by printshop consultation of one of Q2's reprints cannot be ruled out, whereas the reverse (contamination of Q2 by F) is impossible. Moreover the very presence of authorial revision must alter the questions to be asked. A parallel with *King Lear* can help illustrate the editorial effect of this asymmetry.

As Jowett explained, when making a two-text *King Lear* the question to be asked of a suspect reading in Q1 (1608) is whether Shakespeare could have written it, and there is no need to look to other editions, but where there is a suspect reading in F one has to ask whether Shakespeare could have turned Q1's reading into F's (Jowett 1999, 68–70). In Q1, Cordelia asks if Lear's face should be 'exposd against the warring winds' (Shakespeare 1608, K2^r), which is plausibly Shakespearian. The corresponding phrase in F is 'oppos'd against the iarring windes' (Shakespeare 1623, ss1^r), and it must be asked not whether F is acceptable on its own but, since Q1 and F differ by authorial revision, whether Shakespeare could have turned *exposed* into *opposed* and *warring* into *jarring*. Taylor answered yes to the first and no to the second (since it is the weaker reading) and so the Oxford *Complete Works* edition of *The Tragedy of King Lear* (the Folio-based version) reads 'To be opposed against the warring winds' (4.6.29).

The editorial logic that led to such a conflation of editions was not explained to the satisfaction of all reviewers of the project. An extreme case was Shakespeare and George Wilkins's play *Pericles* that survives as a bad quarto with no good quarto or Folio companion (Shakespeare and Wilkins 1609). Taylor thought the bad quarto was based on a memorial reconstruction made by the boy playing Lychorida and Marina and a hired man playing Fisherman and Pandar, supplemented by the actor's part for Gower (Taylor 1986b). Before the bad quarto appeared, George Wilkins published a prose novelization of the story that is clearly dependent on the stage version (Wilkins 1608), and for the Oxford *Complete Works* Taylor and MacDonald P. Jackson treated this novelization as an indirect authority for the play, using it to patch the bad quarto. This required versifying Wilkins's prose and inventing matter from hints in his novelization, and the resulting 'Reconstructed Text' received special handling in the *Textual Companion*. In a book published near the end of the Oxford project, *Re-Editing Shakespeare for the Modern Reader*, Wells signalled his impatience with the timidity of editors unwilling to use their honed imaginations to restore Shakespeare by judicious emendation (Wells 1984, 32–56), and although Taylor and Jackson's *Pericles* was at the far end of the spectrum of editorial inventiveness it was within the project's avowed principles.

Taylor published an article picking up Wells's argument about the need for creativity, justifying the editorial invention of missing words and phrases from knowledge of Shakespeare's habits of metre, literary style and characterization (Taylor 1986a). In his book Wells indicated his philosophy on stage directions, which should indicate to the reader the likely stage action, with a special editorial duty to clarify what might otherwise be baffling if early editions are not supplemented (Wells 1984, 57–78). Since the Oxford *Complete Works* was constructed first as an original-spelling edition and subsequently modernized, spelling principles from the first wave of New Bibliography were appropriate. Greg pointed out in 'The Rationale of Copy-Text' (pp. 44–7 above) that where an editor imports a substantive reading from an edition that is not the copy-text for accidentals it should appear in the form it would have taken had it appeared in the copy-text (where this can be determined), and the principle applies to emendations too. Since editorially invented stage directions are emendations, the Oxford editors put their invented stage directions in the spelling of their copy-texts for accidentals, where possible.

A final principled innovation that drew attention was the project's new names for plays and characters. There is good reason to suppose that the name Imogen in *Cymbeline* arises from a misreading of Shakespeare's minims: she is Innogen in the sources and an eyewitness account of the play in performance, so she has that name in the edition. (John Pitcher later responded with the best arguments, mainly thematic, for retaining F's Imogen (Pitcher 1993).) A couple of other names got altered along with the restoration of Sir John Oldcastle in *1 Henry 4*, as we shall shortly see. The plays that the 1623 Folio calls *2 Henry 6* and *3 Henry 6* were published in the 1590s as *The Contention of York and Lancaster* and *Richard Duke of York*. Since the Folio is a posthumous publication that clearly aimed to impose generic distinctions and tidiness upon the canon – not least by putting the English history plays in the order of their kings' reigns – the titles from the 1590s are preferable. The publishers would hardly have used these titles if they were not recognizable labels for what got performed. The last of the English history plays the Folio calls *Henry 8*, but accounts of the burning of the Globe playhouse in 1613 consistently report its title as *All is True*, so that is the one the Oxford *Complete Works* used.

Reviewers of the Oxford *Complete Works* typically objected in principle to its extensive interventions in the received texts, and then focussed on particular points of detail. Thomas L. Berger doubted that when reprinted in F the quartos not owned by the Folio syndicate were annotated heavily to 'circumvent the copyright' of the prior publisher (Wells *et al.* 1987, 52). Berger thought that Matthew Law (owner of the rights to *Richard 2*, *1 Henry 4* and *Richard 3*), Nathaniel Butter (owner of the rights to *King Lear*) and Richard Bonian and Andrew Walley (owners of the rights to *Troilus and Cressida*) were not stupid enough to get cheated this way (Berger 1989, 147). Moreover, preference for F over Q arising solely from the annotation risks admitting to the play the annotator's errors. This

Berger saw as part of a larger danger in the socialized conception of text, which risks promoting scribes and compositors to the rank of co-authors with Shakespeare (Berger 1989, 144–6). Indeed, were not socialization and collaboration fundamentally at odds with the edition's concern to identify the canon and chronology of Shakespeare (Berger 1989, 149)? David Bevington complained that even where two essentially independent early editions agree on the words, in Gloucester's mockery of Simpcox's claim to have been cured of blindness in *The Contention of York and Lancaster* 2.1, the Oxford editors imposed metrical regularity and, to achieve it, added and removed pronouns, prepositions and conjunctions (Bevington 1987, 506–7). Ironically (since he was just then turning against editorial interference in general), it was Paul Werstine's research on lineation that prompted this: he demonstrated that compositors routinely relined verse, not only to save or waste space but also to make lines and clauses end together – a feature G. B. Harrison (1948) and Paul Bertram (1981) thought authorial – and occasionally for no discernible reason at all (Werstine 1984). Werstine advised editors to restore Shakespeare's regular metrical lineation since its absence is frequently compositorial.

The plays where 'new' New Bibliography made a significant difference from New Bibliography are:

Titus Andronicus
Love's Labour's Lost
A Midsummer Night's Dream
Romeo and Juliet
Richard 2
The Merchant of Venice
1 Henry 4
Much Ado About Nothing
Troilus and Cressida
Richard 3
King Lear

2 Henry 4
Othello
Hamlet

The Contention of York and Lancaster
Richard Duke of York
Henry 5

Pericles

These eighteen plays comprise nearly half the canon. For the first eleven of them (*Titus Andronicus* to *King Lear*) F is a reprint of an existing quarto that was annotated, to varying degrees from play to play, by reference to a theatrical manuscript, and hence each of F's departures from its quarto copy must be considered as possible authorial or collective (socialized) revision. For *2 Henry 4*, *Othello* and *Hamlet*, F was printed from a scribal transcript of a document – probably a prompt-book in the cases of *2 Henry 4* and *Hamlet*, probably not for *Othello* – containing a version of the play closer to performance than the foul papers upon which the preceding quartos were based. For *The Contention of York and Lancaster*, *Richard Duke of York* and *Henry 5*, socialization enters because although F was printed from foul papers there is also a preceding bad quarto (or octavo for *Richard Duke of York*), based upon memorial reconstruction, from which to salvage evidence of how the play developed in rehearsal. Thus in *Richard Duke of York* Clifford enters wounded 'with an arrow in his neck' (2.6.0) as recorded in O (1595) but not in F that is otherwise the edition's control text. The bad quarto of *The Merry Wives of Windsor*, by contrast, is otiose because F itself seems to derive from a prompt-book. *Pericles* exists in a class of its own because of the unique procedures used to reconstruct it from the bad quarto and Wilkins's novelization.

The Oxford *Complete Works*'s endpoint is conveniently marked by its *Textual Companion*'s publication in 1987, with its editors' articles and books from the late 1980s and early 1990s delivering goods invoiced as 'forthcoming' in the *Companion*. Some merely expanded upon arguments already made, but Jowett's reasons for using in *1 Henry 4* the names Russell and Harvey for characters commonly known as Bardolph and Peto made an innovative discrimination regarding a complex set of inter-related authorial revisions (Jowett 1987). Q1 (1598) survives in just one sheet, so the earliest complete edition is Q2 (1598), where Poins proposes that 'Falstalffe, Haruey, Rossill, and Gadshil' (Shakespeare 1598b, B1^r) commit the robbery. Q2 also has three speech prefixes in scene 2.4 for '*Ross[ill]*' to describe how the robbery went (1598b, D4^r), which suggests that when the play was first written Bardolph and Peto were called Russell and Harvey. The names Bardolph and Peto also appear in Q2, so it seems that when Oldcastle became Falstaff his companions' names changed too, but Shakespeare failed to alter every occurrence. Jowett identified historical figures who might have objected to the names Russell and Harvey. However, the robbery scene (2.2) in Q2 has staging problems that disappear if we assume that references to Bardolph should be to Gadshill. Was Gadshill once called Bardolph? F (Shakespeare 1623, e4^r) gives to Gadshill the three speeches describing the robbery that are given to '*Ross*[*ill*]' in Q2, so along with renaming there is a layer of speech reassignment. Jowett deduced that in the original composition the minor thieves were not individuated in Shakespeare's mind: Russell was to be the setter of the robbery in scene 2.2 and the describer of it in scene 2.4. While writing scene 2.4 Shakespeare realized he wanted not only a setter but also a clownish follower of Oldcastle, so he created Gadshill (taking his name from where he robs) and gave him Russell's role in the robbery so as to keep Russell as the clownish follower. In going back to what he had already written, Shakespeare altered just the first occurrence of Russell's name in scene 2.2 (making it Gadshill), much as a modern writer will mark on her proofs a singular change that means 'and so on throughout'. Jowett gave plausible illustrations of how the confusions in Q2 and F could arise from relatively minor, misreadable foul papers alterations to scenes 2.2 and 2.4. Thus, Jowett concluded, there are two distinct kinds of change for an editor to deal with. The first is the invention of Gadshill as a character during composition, which an editor must respect, and second is the imposition of a forced name change of Russell to Bardolph, part of the round of adjustments arising from objections to the name Oldcastle, and these an editor must undo.

Jowett and Taylor explained why they included Folio-only material in their text of *2 Henry 4* (Jowett and Taylor 1987). Q (1600), the only edition prior to F, exists in two states: in Qa the gathering E is a regular one of four leaves, but in Qb the leaves E3 and E4 were replaced by a new sheet, E3–E6. This expansion allowed for the inclusion of a scene (that F calls 3.1) absent from Qa. How could the printers omit exactly one scene, unless by coincidence it happened to occupy exactly one manuscript leaf that was misplaced? Scene 3.1 is removable without great theatrical harm, bringing the play closer to its source, Samuel Daniel's *Civil Wars*. This suggests that it is an afterthought, written (before the foul papers were finished) on a separate loose leaf, with a marker midway down the preceding manuscript page showing where it should be inserted. Qa's compositor might easily have passed the insertion point without realizing it. Even if he then spotted the extra leaf he would not have known where to put its contents. Without scene 3.1 the play is not obviously incomplete, but the whole central section is comic and the rebellion all but forgotten. If Qb reflects the play after Shakespeare had strengthened the political plot, then F takes the process even further: four of the eight F-only passages are, like 3.1, detachable, unlikely to have been omitted from Q by press censorship, and best explained as afterthoughts that appeared only in authorial fair copy. Of the other four F-only passages, probably two were censored from Q, leaving editors to decide on the last two. One of them, the rebellious archbishop's speech on the fickleness of the multitude, 'Let vs on ... *things Present, worst*' (Shakespeare 1623, g2^v–g3^r), is followed in F by a line from Mowbray, 'Shall we go draw our numbers, and set on?', that is spoken by the archbishop in Q (Shakespeare 1600a, c1^r). Unless we imagine a censor deleting the archbishop's speech and then compensating by giving him the next line, this looks like artistic alteration. At the point in Q corresponding to the last of the F-only passages there is the slightest of wrinkles, perhaps the effect of censorship, but Jowett and Taylor decided against it. Thus of the nine passages (eight F-only and one Qb-only) absent from Qa, two were left out by censorship and seven were authorial additions made as Shakespeare worked on the play. Thus, even though F is distanced from the authorial papers by at least a literary transcript (adding act divisions), and by the excision of profanities in performance, it has material that belongs in the play. Including scene 3.1 from Qb but not F's material that continues what Qb begins would 'leave the text in a state Shakespeare himself found unsatisfactory' (Jowett and Taylor 1987, 50). Jowett took this argument further to argue for preferring F's 'minor cuts, and adjustments to staging' (Jowett 1989, 276).

The Oxford *Complete Works* made extensive use of the habits of compositors derived from tests for determining stints that were starting to seem unreliable (pp. 158–62 above), and Jackson's review defended the practice. The expressions 'neither ... nor' and 'nor ... nor' were equally acceptable early modern English, although the former was more modern and occurs forty-seven times in the canon where the first word has to be disyllabic, but three times, all in Folio compositor B's stints, where the first word ought to be monosyllabic. It is a fair guess then that compositor B unconsciously modernized *nor* to *neither* and, on that assumption, the Oxford editors put it back to *nor* (Jackson 1989, 236). From Howard-Hill's digital transcriptions (pp. 91–2 above) were created concordances for each Folio compositor's stints, so in their original-spelling version (Shakespeare 1986) the Oxford editors were able to put emendations of dialogue and stage directions into the preferred spellings of the compositor who set their copy-text. As Wells remarked, this could have been done (but was not) with the quartos (Wells 1984, 16). Although the aim of the original-spelling edition was Shakespeare's spelling (Wells *et al.* 1987, 155), there was little confidence that, except for a few isolated instances, his preferences appeared in early editions (Shakespeare 1986, xlii–lvi). By using compositors' spellings, which would in any case predominate in early editions, words could be imported or invented without creating artificial unevenness in the orthographic texture of the original-spelling edition.

When the Oxford *Complete Works* was published, the emerging New Textualism gained momentum by opposing its editorial principles. Werstine saw a contradiction between 'new' New Bibliography's stage-centred thinking and dependence upon McKerrow's suggestion (pp. 31–3 above) that variable speech prefixes show an author in the heat of composition thinking in relational rather than absolute terms, which for Werstine betrays a 'single-minded concern with the author' (Werstine 1988b, 155). Wells followed Greg in concluding from the ghosts of Innogen and Leonato's kinsman generated by the stage directions in Q *Much Ado About Nothing* (Shakespeare 1600c, A2^r, B3^r) that the printer's copy was not theatrical, but Werstine claimed that bad quartos create ghosts too and yet the Oxford *Complete Works* treated these as theatrical texts. This point hinges on just what we mean by a ghost, for Innogen and Leonato's kinsman have no part in the play, but Werstine included characters who, having a part elsewhere in the play, are brought on when not needed, or not brought on when needed, in specific scenes; only then do bad quartos look like editions printed from foul papers. Taylor's technique for working out from bad quartos the changes made in rehearsal (pp. 170–1 above) is invalid, Werstine argued, because New Bibliographical categorization of editions is inconsistent. Q1 *Romeo and Juliet* (1597) is either wrong or indefinite in numbers of characters indicated in all the stage directions for large entrances, so it cannot be used for casting. Q1 *The Merry Wives of Windsor* (1602) is the best of the supposedly bad quartos but gives a worse indication of its casting needs than the supposedly foul-papers derived Q *Much Ado About Nothing*. For Werstine, the 'new' New Bibliography was built on New Bibliography's false premisses.

The New Textualism and the 'new' New Bibliography began on common ground and shared a rejection of the author-centricity of the New Bibliography. In the early 1980s those who ended up in distinct camps such as Paul Werstine, Steven Urkowitz and Randall McLeod on the one side and Gary Taylor and MacDonald P. Jackson on the other were able to collaborate on the splitting of *King Lear*. The publication of the Oxford *Complete Works* in 1986 seems to have divided them. The boldness of the project smacked of intellectual hubris to those who went on to champion New Textualism. Hitherto, theoretical developments in New Bibliography were always far in advance of their practical application – Appendix 3 traces this in relation to specific editions – and not until the Oxford *Complete Works* could it be said that editorial theory and practice coincided. Indeed, the theory was not fully worked out before the project started and the project got bolder as it progressed; in places the theory seems generated on-the-hoof as the plays were worked upon. Michael Dobson detected a Janus-faced quality to the Oxford *Complete Works*: if it was, as some feared, 'the first culturally relativist, post-structuralist edition' then it seemed to be 'visibly dragging its heels ... over the death of the author' (Dobson 1990, 96). What emerged after it was a new conservatism in editing. Paradoxically it arrived wearing a shining postmodern coat.

CHAPTER 6

Materialism, unediting and version-editing, 1990–1999

By the early 1990s the New Textualism was unmistakably a movement across a broad front. Uniting scholars of criticism and textual study and drawing upon post-structuralism's confrontation with traditional criticism, the movement aimed to raise the status of early editions that New Bibliography had denigrated, the non-substantive ones and especially the bad quartos. There was an underlying political element to the movement, but it was seldom more overtly expressed than in Leah S. Marcus's use of the term levelling to draw an analogy between on one hand the recent critical interest in the lower classes, the marginalized, and the radical seventeenth-century Leveller movement, and on the other New Textualism's impatience with hierarchical distinctions between substantive and non-substantive editions. The expression *equal-but-different* from gender politics of the 1970s was adapted: the previously derided editions should be thought of as 'different instead of debased' (Marcus 1991, 168). She sought to show that there is no need to rank the early editions of a play because – as argued by Steven Urkowitz in connection with the bad quartos of *The Contention of York and Lancaster* and *Richard Duke of York* (pp. 116–17 above) – each is a distinct and internally coherent version. In an argument she expanded for her book *Unediting the Renaissance* (Marcus 1996, 68–100), Marcus argued that the Folio and quarto editions of *The Merry Wives of Windsor* are separated most fundamentally not by textual corruption but, rather like Q and F *King Lear*, by conscious artistic reshaping. New Textualists argued that most readers are unaware of the differences between early editions of Shakespeare because they are available only in specialist publications. That could be remedied.

BRITISH MATERIALISM: SHAKESPEAREAN ORIGINALS

When British Cultural Materialists Graham Holderness and Bryan Loughrey echoed American New Historicist Jonathan Goldberg's claim that textual studies and criticism had come into a new and auspicious alignment (pp. 153–4 above), they used terms from Marxist cultural theory. Drama is by nature 'over-determined' and the Oxford *Complete Works* had an unspoken 'Ideological commitment' to a 'totalizing authorial project', since despite its acceptance that as a working dramatist Shakespeare revised his plays the Oxford editors 'silently reinscribed [the plays] within the ideological problematic of an authoritarian cultural apparatus' (Holderness and Loughrey 1993, 181, 182). That is to say, as Michael Dobson observed, the editors still believed in authorship. Holderness and Loughrey's article launched a series of reprints of first editions, whether quarto (bad or good) or Folio, under the title Shakespearean Originals: First Editions. The idea was to put into the hands of readers, especially undergraduates, rough-and-ready diplomatic reprints of early editions that Holderness and Loughrey thought textual theory had occluded. Janette Dillon raised the pertinent objection that preserving certain typographical features of the early editions but not others would mislead at least as much as it would elucidate (Dillon 1994). Without contextual material to explain that spellings might be varied for justification or verse set as prose to save space after a miscalculation in casting off, retaining the early editions' spellings and roughly their layout (most lineation but not pagination) is simply baffling. Holderness's defence was that for all the faults, which he acknowledged, the series had the virtue of providing cheap access to early editions (Holderness and Loughrey 1994; Holderness 2003, 86–114).

The first of the Shakespearean Originals series was Holderness and Loughrey's edition of Q1 *Hamlet* and it was unfavourably reviewed by Brian Vickers under the headline '*Hamlet* by Dogberry' and the standfirst 'A perverse reading of the Bad Quarto' (Vickers 1993). This led to an exchange of letters in the *Times Literary Supplement* focussing on Vickers's adherence to, and Holderness and Loughrey's rejection of, the theory of memorial reconstruction accounting for Q1 *Hamlet* (Sprinchorn 1994a; Holderness and Loughrey 1994; Vickers 1994a; King and Alexander 1994; Vickers 1994b; Sprinchorn 1994b; Holderness 1994; Jenkins 1994; Vickers 1994c; Godshalk 1994; Vickers 1994d). Vickers explicitly and Harold Jenkins implicitly relied on George Ian Duthie and Alfred Hart's work of fifty years before (pp. 111–13 above), and the entire debate was conducted with no reference to recent arguments, such as Steven Urkowitz's, against the theory of memorial reconstruction, nor to a recent collection of essays on Q1 *Hamlet* (Clayton 1992).

The Shakespearean Originals series' merit of supplying cheap reprints of early editions was rapidly undercut by three unconnected developments.

In 1994 Cambridge University Press's Early Quartos series (a subseries of the New Cambridge Shakespeare) began to offer edited texts of most of the Shakespearean Originals' early editions. The third series of the Arden Shakespeare began in 1995 and for plays existing in a bad quarto as well as an authoritative early edition an exemplar of the former was reproduced in a full and remarkably clear photofacsimile. In paperback these two rivals were as cheap as the Shakespearean Originals and better quality. In 1998 the publisher Chadwyck-Healey offered universities digital images of its microfilm series Early English Books, making virtually everything printed in English prior to 1700 free at the point of access to students and scholars. As a practical implementation of the democratizing impulse of the New Textualism, Shakespearean Originals was rapidly overtaken by new technology, just as a Marxist would predict.

When Margreta de Grazia repeated the claim that the New Historicism and the New Textualism share core concerns she grounded the observation in a philosophical distinction between a play and its embodiment in pieces of paper (de Grazia 1993). This distinction, she argued, serves to keep literary scholarship apart from historical scholarship and to enforce a separation between pure art, conceptualized as disembodied and ideational, and the grubby realities of history, politics and economics. The New Historicism had rejected this separation and insisted that historical documents and literary works can be understood using the same interpretative strategies, and according to de Grazia parallel insights underlay the New Textualism. As with the records of historical events, scholarship should deal with works of art as documents and not concern itself with the abstracted Platonic Ideals derived from, or imagined to precede, them. De Grazia developed this point in an influential article co-written with Peter Stallybrass called 'The Materiality of Shakespeare's Text' (de Grazia and Stallybrass 1993). The New Bibliographers, de Grazia and Stallybrass acknowledged, had 'scrupulously examined' the materiality of Shakespeare's text but 'only as a means of discovering an idealized Shakespeare' (1993, 256 n.4). De Grazia and Stallybrass reassured their readers that a concern with early documents is 'no exercise in antiquarianism' (1993, 257), but since examining unembodied ideas was ruled out as idealist, it is hard to see what is left to discuss. By these rules, the aspirations of working dramatists would be idealist, as would discussion of the papers in which these aspirations took physical form if they happen not to survive. For de Grazia and Stallybrass, the lost authorial foul papers are 'imaginary and idealized' and in an elegant aphorism they called for early editions to be 'looked *at*, not seen *through*'

(1993, 277, 257). Their use of the term 'New Textualism' (1993, 276) helped popularize this name for the movement.

De Grazia and Stallybrass thought that stop-press correction made a mockery of the New Bibliographical search for a stable text because 'it is highly probable that no two copies of the Folio are identical' (de Grazia and Stallybrass 1993, 260). The word 'probable' is necessary because Charlton Hinman collated in full only fifty-five of the Folger Shakespeare Library's Folios (Hinman 1963a, 243–8) and there are at least 228 surviving exemplars (West 2002). Moreover, the exemplars are more alike than the New Textualists supposed. Strictly, no two objects of any kind are perfectly identical, but de Grazia and Stallybrass cannot have meant their claim in an absolute sense since they qualified it with 'highly probable'. Hinman overstated the results of his collation, reporting differences arising from variations in the density and take up of ink and random shifting of type during machining. Peter W. M. Blayney found that once these, and such simple errors as the accidental omission of whole lines, are excluded from the count in order to focus on 'variants that might conceivably affect editorial procedure' (Shakespeare 1996b, xxxii), there are just five significant stop-press corrections witnessed in the Folios collated so far. There are only thirty-two (2^5) ways for an exemplar to combine these five variants, so it is a mathematical certainty that at least twenty-four of the fifty-five Folios collated by Hinman have at least one twin, another exemplar with the same combination of variants. (This assumes the most unbalanced distribution of variants in which thirty-one of the combinations appear in one exemplar each and the thirty-second combination appears in the remaining twenty-four exemplars; the real distribution is probably more even and gives most of the fifty-five exemplars a twin.) The familiar New Textualist claim that stop-press correction renders unique each exemplar of a book such as the Folio is overstated unless we think Blayney's criteria too stringent and want to count differences that for most purposes are meaningless.

Like Marion Trousdale (pp. 163–4 above), de Grazia and Stallybrass thought the early modern mind more attuned to plurality and fluidity than the modern mind. Authors seldom worked alone, they noted, and even the material fabric of books had multiple lives, first as rags and later as wrappers. On early modern variability, Michel Foucault was recurrently cited (de Grazia and Stallybrass 1993, 272 n.69, 276 n.88, 279, 279 n.102) and de Grazia was convinced by his claim that between us and the early moderns lies an epistemic rupture around 1800 that established the norms of consistency and coherence that comprise the Enlightenment. Shortly before 'The Materiality of Shakespeare's Text', de Grazia published a study of Edmond Malone's 1790 edition showing its Enlightenment construction of the Shakespeare we now know, made by suppressing the instabilities and variabilities in his works (de Grazia 1991). Writing, she argued, had to be editorially tamed, and where it showed a troubling disregard for logical coherence – as when one character after another reads aloud a written document but with different wording – Malone fell back upon the notion of a single authorial consciousness (which according to Foucault the Enlightenment had just invented) that was careless about such details. Thus, as Foucault explained when describing its emergence (Foucault 1969), the author 'serves a regulatory function, converting what we have called the "copiousness" of both mechanical and rhetorical "copy" into personal idiosyncrasy' (de Grazia 1991, 223). This kind of application of Foucault's supposed epistemic shift of 1800 to early modern sexual and literary culture has not gone uncontested (Cady 1992; Egan 2008).

In the mid-1990s there appeared refutations of the claim that Shakespeare revised *King Lear*, partially inflected as reactions against the New Textualism that it gave rise to. Studying the Q/F differences, R. A. Foakes decided that, in art, 'if the basic structure remains roughly the same' then 'versions are rightly considered as variants of one work' and that this is true of *King Lear* (Foakes 1993, 135). Ann R. Meyer argued that non-authorial interference is the likeliest explanation of the most important Q/F differences, especially where the revision seems imperfectly executed (Meyer 1994). On the same tack, Robert Clare thought that the alterations to Edgar's role probably reflect not authorial reconceptualization but someone's quotidian desire to give the actor playing Edgar more, and those playing Albany and Kent less, to do (Clare 1995). According to Richard Knowles, what looks like the substitution of a speech in 3.1 is really only the addition of a few lines and the Q-only lines are absent from F merely by accident (Knowles 1995). Without this, the only example of substantial rewriting, the revision hypothesis theory collapses and Q and F are separated by mere theatrical patching. Sidney Thomas thought the revision hypothesis was driven by theoretical prejudice: 'the two-text theory has flourished because it has lent support to, and been supported by, the deconstructionist emphasis on textual indeterminacy, and the virtual disappearance of the creative autonomy of the author' (Thomas 1995, 584). Clare too detected bias (a 'weighed vocabulary') in the two-version theory: 'The words "ambiguous" and "ambiguity" recur many times in the work of the revisionists, always with a positive spin' (Clare 1995, 45).

Some New Textualist intersections of high French theory and bibliography were unintentionally comic. Discussing the differences between Q (1609) and Folio *Troilus and Cressida*, Karen T. Bjelland wrote that 'Because [Jacques] Lacan is correct in saying that we are "constituted" through language, which we in turn use to further "constitute" our reality' the variants are worth our attention. Before attributing them to someone, Bjelland suggested we pose the questions that 'Foucault might have asked'. Granting herself a precautionary qualification – 'If it is true that texts are created and exist in time and space' – Bjelland framed her key question: 'can we find in the Derridean "trace"/"space" between the two variants some kind of "epistemological shift"?' (Bjelland 1994, 54). She could: Q has 'Neopolitan bone-ache' (Shakespeare 1609, D4^v) where F has just 'bone-ach' (Shakespeare 1623, ¶4^r), showing that the Italophobia of Queen Elizabeth's reign diminished under kings James and Charles (Bjelland 1994, 60). Here Foucault was vulgarized, since his notion of change in the episteme, the mental organization of categories at any given historical moment that limits what individuals can conceive and utter, was more subtle and interesting a concept than mere historical change (as Bjelland understood it), not least because it offered a non-Marxist way to discuss what is otherwise known as ideology (Foucault 1970). By contrast, de Grazia's use of Foucault accurately reflected his ideas about the relationship between power and knowledge and applied them to textual matters. Gary Taylor also understood key aspects of Jacques Derrida's and Foucault's work, and showed their general irrelevance to textual theory and editorial practice, which is at heart the pursuit of something proximate to the absent author, not an effort to make the author utterly present in an edition (Taylor 1993b).

The broad front of New Textualism, from Bjelland's over-enthusiastic adoption of misunderstood theory at one extreme to Taylor's rejection of theory at the other, seemed to Holderness, Loughrey and Andrew Murphy to be coming apart (1995). Taylor's 'new' New Bibliography was for them too close to the conservative old New Bibliography, as evidenced in his analogy between the character Lenny in Harold Pinter's play *The Homecoming* arbitrarily deciding that a woman is diseased and editors arbitrarily deciding that a text is corrupt (Wells *et al.* 1987, 60). For Holderness, Loughrey and Murphy this typified the masculinist culture of New Bibliography as much as Fredson Bowers's rape metaphor of piercing 'the veil of print' that conceals from us the author's manuscript (p. 47 above). Their essay mangled a number of Marxist terms, mistaking commodity fetishism for the ordinary fetishism of objects that Marx thought quite normal and healthy, and perhaps in tacit response Stallybrass shortly after published a supple and accurate account of Marx's notion of commodity fetishism to correct the distortions of it that are rife in literary studies (Stallybrass 1998).

Holderness, Loughrey and Andrew Murphy reported that historical materialists are recognizable by their 'confidence in the reality of matter' and dialectical materialists by their 'acknowledgement of the social and economic structures within which matter is both shaped and defined' (Holderness, Loughrey and Murphy 1995, 106). Distinguishing themselves as 'materialist bibliographers', Holderness, Loughrey and Murphy would accept only the existence of the early editions. Not the least of the problems with this position is the ontological limbo into which it casts lost plays whose former existence and titles are witnessed by unequivocal indirect evidence (Creizenach 1918, 47–9; Sisson 1936). As post-structuralist celebrants of textual multiplicity, de Grazia and Stallybrass might even embrace a conflated modern edition as one of the many forms *King Lear* can take, but Holderness, Loughrey and Murphy dourly advised confining oneself to the early editions alone, readily and cheaply supplied in the Shakespearean Originals series.

AMERICAN MATERIALISM: THE NEW FOLGER LIBRARY SHAKESPEARE

The unediting impulse that drove Graham Holderness and Bryan Loughrey to start Shakespearean Originals prompted Barbara A. Mowat and Paul Werstine to start The New Folger Library Shakespeare series in 1992. This American series shared the British series' disdain for the conflation of early editions but rather than favouring diplomatic reprints its editorial approach was a conservative form of R. B. McKerrow's best-text principle outlined in his *Prolegomena for the Oxford Shakespeare* (pp. 30–7 above). Mowat and Werstine were unconvinced by recent textual scholarship and repeatedly reported that after reading fresh research 'we become more skeptical about ever identifying how the play assumed the forms in which it was [or "came to be"] printed' (Shakespeare 1992b, xlix; 1992c, xlvii; 1993b, lxi). The New Folger Library Shakespeare conveyed multiplicity by surrounding the modernized text with square, pointed and half brackets that showed where early editions differed one from another or the modern editors had interfered. Celebrating the series as the embodiment of New Textualism, Margreta de Grazia likened the typographic system to Jacques Derrida's procedure, derived from Martin Heidegger, of placing words *sous rature* (under erasure), marking the imperfection of signification by printing a cross over a word to reveal the inadequacy of the sign without obliterating it (de Grazia 1995, 249; Derrida 1976, xiii–xix). The aim is honourable compromise, and de Grazia thought it better to put the mediating process on show within each line of dialogue than to confine part of the play to an appendix, as the Oxford *Complete Works* did.

In fact, almost all the editions in the series used half brackets just as in the Oxford *Complete Works* to show disputable emendations to dialogue, speech prefixes and stage directions, and both projects used no marks where the editor was confident of the intervention. De Grazia's analogy with Heideggerian/Derridean erasure implies that any defamiliarizing mark will do, since the point is the inability of language to live up to its duties. It is hard to know where such a process should stop because all emendations are to some degree disputable. The Oxford editors soon regarded their half brackets as a 'mistake', since the entire text is mediated and marking only some of the interventions gives the 'false impression that anything not bracketed is "authentic"' (Wells and Taylor 1990, 15). Recognizing that it was not a practical edition, de Grazia also celebrated the multiplicity of Michael Warren's four-text *King Lear* (Shakespeare 1989a) that offered unbound facsimile leaves of Q1 (1608), Q2 (1619) and F (1623). Leaves from different editions could be combined to give the reader access to 'any number' of new textual patterns (de Grazia 1995, 248). However, Warren's presentation of the material suggested a scepticism of the postmodern delight in all possible combinations being equally valid. For each of the three early editions the loose facsimile leaves had an independent page-numbering sequence and set of running titles, performing the function of a conventional binding in at least indicating (while not insisting upon) the proper order. A strong hint that the reader should put the leaves back in the box in the order in which the publisher had packed them was the inclusion of modern-type title leaves indicating what should follow each one in the unbound sequence. These made sense and told the truth only if the reader restored the unbound leaves to their correct order.

New Textualism's appeal in the 1990s was bolstered by the collapse of the theory of memorial reconstruction (pp. 100–28 above), giving more reason to see early editions of a play as *equal-but-different* versions rather than ranking them according to their accidental deviation from a supposed archetype. The splitting of *King Lear* established the model for such claims, and expanding on an argument first presented orally in 1986, Steven Urkowitz pioneered the application to other plays (1988a). Reproducing the Q1 (1594) and F versions of the opening scene of *The Contention of York and Lancaster*, in which King Henry welcomes his new bride Margaret of Anjou, Urkowitz illustrated their contrasting representations of Margaret's demeanour and Henry's confidence in her, and the accompanying stage business, none of which can sensibly be conflated (Urkowitz 1995). In the scene of Jack Cade's capture, 4.9, Q1 has Iden remark that they are the same size, while in F Iden notes how much smaller Cade is; perhaps the casting of a revival necessitated revision. Although his particular instances were compelling, Urkowitz failed to build the cumulative body of interlocking evidence that irrevocably split *King Lear*. Urkowitz tried again with scene 2.6 in Q1 (1597) and Q2 (1599) *Romeo and Juliet* and scene 5.5 in Q1 (1602) and F *The Merry Wives of Windsor* (Urkowitz 1996). Barbara Kreps joined in for *The Contention of York and Lancaster*, adducing evidence that authorial revision is the reason that 'in F Margaret is more of a virago, Humphrey is more admirable, the king's relationship with Humphrey is cooler, Henry's personal and political inadequacies are more evident, York and his claim to the throne are more politically complex and the cardinal more Machiavellian than they appear in the quarto' (Kreps 2000, 162).

Version-distinguishing reached its logical climax when Leah S. Marcus argued for two *Merry Wives of Windsor*s, more merry and more bourgeois in Q1 than F, two *Shrew*s, less misogynistic and less triumphantly masculinist in *A Shrew* (1594) than F, and two *Hamlet*s, faster paced and less psychological in Q1 (1603) than Q2 (1604–5) (Marcus 1996). Critical reinterpretation as much as bibliography raised the status of the bad quartos as distinct versions. Marcus claimed that the snatches of Christopher Marlowe's work embedded in *The Taming of a Shrew* need not be patchwork indicative of memorial reconstruction, but might be deliberate 'quotations designed to create a ludicrous effect of mock heroic in their new and incongruous setting' (Marcus 1996, 121). Bibliographical arguments are powerless against such critical flexibility, but even Werstine thought Marcus had gone too far: in *The Merry Wives of Windsor* at least, the convergence of Q1 and F at moments connected with the Host's presence onstage proves that whether or not revision separated them, corruption must be at work too (Werstine 1999a, 313 n.9). New Textualists attempting to level the good and bad in Shakespeare were apt to accuse their opponents of historical and cultural bias, as when Marcus decided that Prospero's description of Sycorax as a 'blew ey'd hag' (Shakespeare 1623, A2^v) frightened editors who wanted her to be alien, not alluringly Aryan (Marcus 1996, 1–37).

It is certainly true that historical and cultural bias affects bibliography – how could it not? – but for Peter W. M. Blayney the greatest distortion is our assumption that printed plays were as valuable to early modern literary culture as they are to us (Blayney 1997). Rates of reprinting are the key index of popularity with readers and publishers because second and subsequent editions were not subject to the one-time costs of the first edition, the 'price of the manuscript, authority, license, and registration', for which Blayney provided definitions and estimates (Blayney 1997, 412). Plays, Blayney decided, were an unattractive commercial proposition for publishers, yet because we value Shakespeare's plays we have deluded ourselves that there was a lucrative market for them. Blayney's economic analysis was disputed by Alan B. Farmer and Zachary Lesser, who showed that he miscounted several of the factors involved – including the changing size of the overall book market and the relative success of competing genres – and that plays were considerably more popular than Blayney thought (Farmer and Lesser 2005a; Blayney 2005; Farmer and Lesser 2005b).

Blayney's was the most frequently cited essay of the collection in which it appeared (Cox and Kastan 1997), and Douglas Bruster vividly described the enthusiastic embrace of his numerically incorrect view as an 'orgy of academic self-loathing' (Bruster 2008). Shakespearians, that is, perversely enjoyed believing that his books were not popular. The collection was typically New Textualist. Werstine again attacked W. W. Greg's categorization of play manuscripts, pointing out that it took no account of the holdings of the Folger Shakespeare Library, which was not yet open when Greg was writing *Dramatic Documents from the Elizabethan Playhouses*, nor the Huntington Library in California, which Greg did not bother to visit; so limited a survey was bound only to confirm Greg's prejudices (Werstine 1997). Eric Rasmussen argued that the internal evidence of revision in play manuscripts and editions cannot tell us who was responsible for it (Rasmussen 1997). Folio-only *Hamlet* material is mainly lines missing from the middles of long speeches in Q2 (1604–5), but Folio-only *King Lear* material is mainly lines missing from the ends of speeches in Q1 (1608); if the different procedures indicate different cutters, one was not Shakespeare (Rasmussen 1997, 443–6).

Who else might cut? Omissions marked in the manuscript of *The Second Maiden's Tragedy* (= *The Lady's Tragedy*, British Library Lansdowne 807) are, like those in Folio *Hamlet*, mid-speech cuts, such as a book-keeper might make to shorten speeches without changing their essential meanings, whereas cuts at the ends of speeches (as in *King Lear*) tend to alter meanings. John Kerrigan thought that small-scale and detailed revisions show the author at work, while addition and subtraction of large textual units could be authorial or non-authorial (pp. 135–6 above), but Rasmussen denied this distinction. William Birde and Samuel Rowley's revisions to Marlowe's *Doctor Faustus* introduced a number of single-word substitutions (Marlowe 1604; 1616), and Hand C's rewriting (in Addition 4) of a passage of Anthony Munday's original script in the manuscript of *Sir Thomas More* shows 'numerous small verbal changes' (Rasmussen 1997, 452–3). Rasmussen drew the New Textualist conclusion that in general we cannot attribute revision so an editor can only do what Rasmussen and David Bevington did for *Doctor Faustus* (Marlowe 1993) and edit each version independently. It is salutary to recall that Greg did the same (Marlowe 1950).

New Textualism tended to accord speech prefixes a spurious significance, as when Holderness and Loughrey complained that although based on Folio *The Taming of the Shrew*, where his prefix is consistently *Beg*[*gar*], the Oxford *Complete Works* calls this character 'SLY', which they thought 'a clear instance of modern editors imposing anachronistic values on an early modern text' (Holderness and Loughrey 1993, 191 n.18). (The character identifies himself with 'I am Christophero Sly', Induction 2.5). In fact, speech prefixes might be invented in the printshop, as when Nicholas Okes changed *Alb*[*any*] to *Duke* in Q1 *King Lear* (1608) because his box of upper-case italic *A*s was exhausted (Blayney 1982, 141–2). McKerrow suggested that speech prefix variation might arise because in the heat of composition a dramatist would think in relational rather than absolute terms (pp. 31–3 above), and in its assumption that such variation is meaningful the New Textualism took on trust this suspect claim from New Bibliography.

Examining speech prefix variation in Q1 and Q2 *A Midsummer Night's Dream* (1600 and 1619), Q2 *Titus Andronicus* (1600), Q1 *The Merchant of Venice* (1600), Q2 *1 Henry 4* (1598) and Q2 *Hamlet* (1604–5), Richard F. Kennedy diagnosed type shortage in the printshop (Kennedy 1998). When Q2 *A Midsummer Night's Dream* reprinted Q1 it changed the prefix *Quin*[*ce*] to *Pe*[*ter*] just as the compositor ran out of upper-case italic *Q*s, as witnessed by his setting *quince* in a stage direction. In Q1 itself we see evidence of the compositor running out of upper-case italic *T*s in his use of ones of the wrong size and then altering the prefix *The*[*seus*] to *Duk*[*e*]. Likewise for the change from various forms of *Hippolyta* to various forms of *Dutchesse*, explained by counting how many upper-case italic *H*s were available as judged from the decision to set the wrong size when none were left. Other speech prefix variations Kennedy could not account for so surely, for lack of hard evidence. Although pressure upon a particular sort can be shown by counting what the compositor had recently set (and was likely to still be standing in type), only the consistent resort to desperate measures such as use of wrong fount or size proves the complete exhaustion of a sort-box and provides a baseline from which to count its replenishment by distribution and its subsequent depletion to exhaustion again. By such a rigorous analysis John Jowett conclusively proved that type shortage caused speech prefix variation in Folio *Julius Caesar* (pp. 177–8 above).

As well as the interpretation of speech prefix variation as a sign of the author, another aspect of New Bibliography that New Textualism unconsciously clung to was the idea that bad quartos have an especially close connection to performance, as Werstine pointed out. This arose from the theory of memorial reconstruction and from Greg's book *Two Elizabethan Stage Abridgements* (1922) in which he argued that the first editions of George Peele's *The Battle of Alcazar* (1594) and Robert Greene's *Orlando Furioso* (1594) reflect cut-down versions of the plays witnessed in the extant playhouse plot and actor's part respectively (Werstine 1998b). The boosted status of bad quartos under New Textualism was assisted by this alleged and unproven connection with performance, which was no longer treated by literary scholars as a process corrupting the dramatist's artistic conception. When Holderness and Loughrey defended the bad quarto of *Hamlet* for its theatricality, they unwittingly relied upon another of New Bibliography's weak links (Werstine 1998b, 59). We now know from the Records of Early English Drama (REED) project that touring was a regular part of the London company's activity, not a desperate expedient in times of plague, and that rather than produce a new script requiring fewer men, the companies were obliged to bring their licensed playbooks on tour. In any case, Scott McMillin had worked out that the bad quarto of *Hamlet* requires as many actors as the good, Werstine observed.

New Bibliographers accorded the stage directions of a bad quarto based on memorial reconstruction greater authority than its dialogue because actions are harder to garble than words. Where it witnesses the play after rehearsal, a bad quarto's stage directions could be imported to a modern critical edition. New Textualism carried this idea to an absurd extreme when Holderness and Loughrey straight-facedly defended a literal understanding of Q1 *Hamlet*'s stage direction indicating that the grave-digger 'throwes vp a shouel' (Shakespeare 1603, H4^r) rather than a skull (Holderness and Loughrey 1993, 185–6). As Alan Posener remonstrated, a shovel also means a shovelful (Posener 1994, 264). In at least one case, however, a bad quarto's stage directions seem to have been written in the printshop (Jowett 1998a). The long literary stage directions in Q1 *Romeo and Juliet* (1597) almost all appear in the part of the book printed by Edward Allde in too small a typeface, and they are space-wasters employed to preserve the agreed page-breaks. To judge from verbal parallels, they were probably written by Henry Chettle, perhaps from memory of the play in performance.

Kennedy's and Jowett's New Bibliographical studies re-examined and found wanting New Bibliographical accounts of the origins of speech prefixes and stage directions. This kind of self-examination Marxists call immanent critique (Adorno 1973), meaning the testing of a set of ideas using its own terms and principles in order to probe its inconsistencies and expose its weaknesses. The Oxford *Complete Works* editors decided that for eighteen plays the Folio copy possibly or definitely involved direct or indirect use of a scribal transcript, which conclusion was subsequently bolstered (with more plays added) when Taylor realized that an early edition's use of scene divisions, which neither Shakespeare nor a book-keeper would add though a scribe might, is good evidence that a transcript was involved in its underlying copy. As Taylor noted, this meant that Sidney Lee had been right all along in arguing that transcripts provided copy for most of the Folio (pp. 12–14 above). In response to Lee, Greg began the New Bibliography that nearly a century later was, on this point, 'defeated by the very evidence it taught us to look for' (Taylor 1993a, 243). Because of immanent critique, the New Bibliographical method is more powerful a means of generating knowledge than New Textualism, which passes judgement on textual theory from what its adherents appear to feel are Olympian heights but are really the unexamined constructions of its opponent. A concrete example is Urkowitz's argument that scene 2.6 of *Romeo and Juliet* in Q1, including its stage direction '*Enter* I*uliet somewhat fast, and embraceth Romeo*' (Shakespeare 1597b, E4^r), is a distinct version not to be conflated with its counterpart in Q2 (Urkowitz 1996, 224). The distinctiveness is greater than Urkowitz thought since, as Jowett showed, the stage direction probably was written by Chettle as padding (Jowett 1998a, 71).

The New Textualism's dependence on New Bibliography is easier to discern now that its apogee has passed. In a brilliant critique at the time, Edward Pechter concluded that Holderness, Loughrey and Murphy and de Grazia and Stallybrass's exhortation to look at the pages of early editions rather than through them gave Shakespearians no powerful reasons to do so (Pechter 1997). Pechter doubted that attention to just the marks on the page could be sustained, since all reading is a process of looking beyond the page to something else, some context that makes sense of what is read. De Grazia and Stallybrass themselves looked beyond the page to the paper-makers, compositors and pressmen that made it, which at first seems a democratic manoeuvre. On inspection it is elitist because the scholarly resources for this research are restricted to a privileged few (Pechter 1997, 60–2). This point reruns the debate in the 1960s about the degressive principle in bibliography (pp. 84–6 above), with its disagreements about the very point of studying books. Purists called for bibliographers to study all the books made in one printshop, with no regard to who wrote them, and pragmatists responded that unless one pays greatest attention to the writers one values no useful work can be completed in a lifetime. Mainstream New Bibliography provided a compromise solution to this dilemma in Blayney's comprehensive study of all the books printed in Nicholas Okes's printshop around the time it produced Q1 *King Lear* (1608).

Responding to Pechter, Holderness, Loughrey and Murphy made a frank disclosure of the post-structuralist prejudice that I have been arguing pervades New Textualism. Rather than taking joy in aesthetic coherence, 'we discover more pleasure in the knowledge that our great works of literature disclose, when subjected to materialist textual and historical analysis, a *disorder* and *incoherence* matching the world that produced them' (Holderness, Loughrey and Murphy 1997, 85). In the absence of an argument that the early modern world was essentially disorderly and incoherent this pleasure seems to be no more than a confirmation of prior assumptions. Writing about Shakespeare's history plays, Holderness repeatedly attacked E. M. W. Tillyard's account of early modern ideology for merely reflecting Tillyard's personal preference for order and coherence (Tillyard 1943; 1944; Holderness 1985; 1992); such attacks on Tillyard were a hallmark of the British Cultural Materialism of the 1980s (Drakakis 1985, 14–15; Dollimore and Sinfield 1985, 206–7, 210). Declaring their pleasure at finding in art a confirmation that disorder and incoherence prevailed in the early modern world, Holderness, Loughrey and Murphy were in danger of sounding like a Looking-Glass version of Tillyard himself (or at least the Cultural Materialist caricature of him) with the critical preferences simply reversed.

Preparing an edition of *Richard 3*, Jowett declared himself convinced by parts of the New Textualism and vowed to take its concerns into account without giving up on editing altogether, as Randall McLeod would advocate (Jowett 1998b, 242). Jowett distanced himself from the stemma drawn by Gary Taylor for the Oxford *Complete Works* (Wells *et al.* 1987, 230) because he found in Q1 (1597) not only possible memorial corruption but also improvement upon the version in the Folio edition. Q1 is more economical in staging, cutting Clarence's unnecessary daughter and rearranging the ghosts of the last act to require only four boy actors; it removes a reference to the murder of Rutland that otherwise ties the play to the preceding histories and diminishes its power to stand alone as a tragedy; and it eliminates the ghosts Woodville and Scales caused by Shakespeare's misreading of the chronicles. There were losses to go with the gains, including the sporadic mangling of meaning, and in basing his edition on Q1 Jowett sought 'not to uncover the readings of a lost document, but rather to realise what Q, as a printed text perceived to be close to a performance text, is within reach of being' (Jowett 1998b, 245). Acknowledging that his aim was idealist,

Jowett defended idealizing as a natural function of the human brain: an editor is not 'a photocopier or scanner' and Jowett planned to interpret the play in the process of transmitting it (Jowett 1998b, 245). Holderness and Carol Banks had actually made a defence of the 'radical suggestion' that a photocopier could do just as well as an editor in the transmission of historical documents (Holderness and Banks 1995, 332).

The Shakespearean Originals and The New Folger Library Shakespeare editions that neither fully edited their base texts nor followed them in every significant detail were bound to seem too interventionist to some readers and insufficiently interventionist to others. Urkowitz focussed on a moment that shows the cost of taking the middle road, the entrance of France and Burgundy in the first scene of *King Lear* (Urkowitz 1998, 88–9). Even in New Textualist editions meant to preserve the Q1/F differences the Folio speech prefix that calls for '*Cor.*' (indicating Cordelia or Cornwall) to say 'Heere's France and Burgundy, my Noble Lord' (Shakespeare 1623, qq2^v) is emended to give the line to Gloucester, as in Q1 (Shakespeare 1608, B3^v). The reassignment, justified on the grounds that Gloucester was instructed to fetch in France and Burgundy, was made in the Folio-based New Folger Library Shakespeare edition (Shakespeare 1993b) and on the Folio side of René Weis's parallel-text edition (Shakespeare 1993c). Urkowitz objected that post-structuralist editing here lapses back into the Platonic fallacy of recovering authorial intention when it should be opening up new critical possibilities by encouraging readers to consider what follows from Cornwall or even Cordelia announcing the entry of France and Burgundy. Only a photofacsimile would satisfy Urkowitz, but rather than solving the problem this passes it on to the reader who must decide for herself which peculiarities are error and which art. Among the misinterpretable errors, Q1's scene 20, in which Gloucester's son apparently leads him to the top of a Dover cliff, begins with the arresting stage direction '*Enter Gloster and Edmund*' (Shakespeare 1608, 12^r). The New Folger Library Shakespeare editors corrected errors more minor than this, and Mowat explained their criteria. Their Q2-based *Hamlet* called the queen Gertrude rather than Gertrard (her name in Q2) because the former name 'has existed for nearly three hundred years' (Mowat 1998, 142). Their Folio-based *Othello* used Q1's 'That I did loue the Moore, to liue with him' (Shakespeare 1622, c4^v) in preference to F because of 'the weight of the familiarity of the line as we have inherited it from the editorial tradition'. Mowat complained that it is editorially difficult to 'shake off the eighteenth-century hand of Nicholas Rowe' (Mowat 1998, 143), apparently without realizing that preference for the familiar is the problem.

At the end of the century, Werstine kept up his attack on New Bibliography by showing that Greg's account of foul papers and prompt-books relied upon a priori selection of evidence and categories invented to suit his story. Speech prefixes and stage directions, Werstine argued, simply do not become more regular as plays 'progress in manuscript towards production' (Werstine 1999b, 105). Unlike the anachronistic term prompt-book, the term foul papers occurs in the period, when book-keeper Edward Knight explained where he got material for his transcription of John Fletcher's *Bonduca* (pp. 25–6 above). Since Knight was explaining why two-and-a-bit scenes are missing, these foul papers could hardly be the complete play as it left the author, which was Greg's definition. Werstine re-examined the events of 1916–23 that led to acceptance of A. W. Pollard's claim that Hand D of the *Sir Thomas More* manuscript is Shakespeare's (Werstine 1999c). Pollard wanted to show that the good quartos were printed directly from Shakespeare's papers, and Hand D helped because it shared some of their unusual spellings (pp. 23–4 above). According to Werstine, putting together in one book the individually weak pieces of evidence about Hand D gave them the appearance of solidity (Pollard *et al.* 1923). Where R. W. Chambers saw in Hand D thematic and imagistic parallels with other Shakespeare writing (Pollard *et al.* 1923, 142–87), Werstine saw ideas and image clusters common in others' writing too. The matter has since been settled by MacDonald P. Jackson showing that Hand D contains relatively rare words and phrases that occur in five or fewer plays first performed in the period 1590–1630, overwhelmingly those by Shakespeare (Jackson 2006). Whomever's the handwriting, Shakespeare is the author. If Hand D is, as it appears, authorial first draft then it is also Shakespeare's hand, but not if the writing is a scribal copy (Downs 2007).

The preliminaries to the 1623 Folio repeatedly assert that the book makes up for the man's absence, but New Textualism held that plays originated not with an author but a playing company. John Heminges and Henry Condell meant to create the author Shakespeare but according to Murphy they made a Derridean *supplement* that stands between complete presence and absence, filling the place of the never-existing authorial text (Murphy 1999). Predicated on an absence it cannot fill, such a *supplement* has forever to be remade, hence the never-ending job of editing Shakespeare. New Bibliography idealized what came before the early editions, the authorial manuscripts, and according to Murphy its defenders are stuck in a futile and psychologically naive search for direct communion with the author. Futile because 'Intention can never be fully elevated above the complex dynamic' of textuality (Murphy 1999, 134). The best we can do, Murphy concluded, is give up searching for 'the text as the author finally intended it' and instead explain how 'particular versions of texts functioned within particular historical moments' and 'how such versions and moments differ over time' (Murphy 1999, 136). As we have seen (pp. 146–52 above), D. F. McKenzie proposed this as an extension of Jerome J. McGann's notion of the socialized text and it is no despicable project. Murphy was, of course, right that intention cannot fully be elevated above the complexities of textuality, yet there remains a great deal worth doing (short of 'fully') in distinguishing better from worse representations of intention. My grocery list does not perfectly express what I want to buy, but it comes much closer to that ideal than does my laundry list. To use an elegant phrase articulating the intersection of philosophy and practical politics, the impossibility of utter transcendence should not put us off the 'art of the finite' (Sartre 1986, 238).

Conclusion: the twenty-first century

Our account of editorial theory and practice has almost arrived at the present, so the remaining contributions form essentially the current state of the debate and will be treated thematically. We begin with an examination of how New Textualism has influenced mainstream Shakespeare studies – the new series it spawned having already been discussed (pp. 190–7 above) – and then consider the effect of Lukas Erne's powerful and as yet unanswered argument that Shakespeare was not exclusively a man of the theatre, being concerned also with his growing readership. The closing remarks address the future of the theory and practice of editing Shakespeare, focussing on the problems that arise from Shakespeare's practice of co-authorship, the routine theatrical cutting of his plays, and his being a literary as well as a dramatic author.

THE EFFECTS AND LIMITS OF NEW TEXTUALISM

New Textualism began visibly to encroach upon mainstream New Bibliographical practice when Jill L. Levenson edited *Romeo and Juliet* for a volume in the single-play Oxford Shakespeare series (p. 167 above; Appendix 3 below) by treating Q1 (1597) and Q2 (1599) as distinct versions and giving modernized texts of each (Shakespeare 2000e). New Bibliographers called Q1 a bad or illicit edition because it is short, lacks a Stationers' Register entry, and was poorly printed. Levenson found that only the first of these claims stood up to scrutiny; it is simply a short quarto. The versions underlying Q1 and Q2, she decided, might have been separated by authorial revision that enlarged the former to make the latter or cut the latter to make the former. Q2 has three moments of repetition usually thought to indicate authorial papers, but they might equally represent revision well after original composition, or 'record different versions in different performances' (Shakespeare 2000d, 123). Unable to be certain of the copy for Q1 or Q2, Levenson was not prepared to privilege one of them and felt she had to edit both, just as Eric Rasmussen counselled (pp. 199–200 above).

New Textualism again intersected with New Bibliography when Paul Werstine published a much-delayed article promised as 'forthcoming' in the *Textual Companion* to the Oxford *Complete Works* (Wells *et al.* 1987, 148), in which he argued that the supposed differences of habit between Folio compositors D and F disappear when one takes into account the influence of manuscript copy made by the King's men's scribe Ralph Crane (Werstine 2001). The first four Folio plays, *The Tempest*, *The Two Gentlemen of Verona*, *The Merry Wives of Windsor* and *Measure for Measure* (occupying quires A–G) were printed from Crane transcripts, as shown by the punctuation, spelling and elision matching extant Crane dramatic manuscripts. Charlton Hinman identified five compositors in the Folio and labelled them A, B, C, D and E (pp. 55–7 above), but T. H. Howard-Hill showed that the A working on these first four comedies could not be the same man A that Hinman found working on *The Winter's Tale* and the histories and tragedies, so he called the four men working on these first four comedies B, C, D and F (pp. 91–2 above). John O'Connor showed that there was not much evidence to distinguish this new man F from D so he sought to isolate their spelling habits (pp. 93–5 above). Howard-Hill discriminated D from F by the habit of indenting the second part of an overflowing line and thought the absence of this habit in quires A–E shows D's absence, but Werstine objected that there was no consistent idiosyncratic pattern, only collective ones: when D indented overflows, so did others, and apparently when he refrained others did too. Moreover, D seems influenced by use of indented overflows in his copy, but again not consistently. This negative evidence is not convincing, but positive evidence is: the only overflows in quires A–G come in D's stints, so the single one on G5^v is probably his (Werstine 2001, 318).

O'Connor too rested his argument on weak negative evidence, the absence of other compositors' habits. Four later comedies were set from printed copy, *Much Ado About Nothing*, *Love's Labour's Lost*, *A Midsummer Night's Dream* and *The Merchant of Venice*, and from D's habits in his stints on these (for which his copy can be compared with his setting) O'Connor worked out compositor D's spelling habits, although he admitted that D followed copy spelling so often that it is hard to tell just what his preferences were. O'Connor nonetheless came up with some preferences (setting *-ie* endings where his copy has *-y* endings, and the unusual spellings *sweete*, *meete*, *maide*, *eie* and *praier*) and because these are almost entirely absent from pages of quires A–G not set by B or C, O'Connor deduced that compositor D worked on none of these quires except F. Quires A–G were set from lost manuscript copy, which prevents comparison of copy with setting, but the manuscript was by Crane and his spelling preferences are known (Werstine 2001, 319). Werstine found twelve words – *any*, *beauty*, *body*, *company*, *deny*, *happy*, *heavy*, *pitty*, *presently*, *try*, *very* and *weary* – that compositor D preferred to end with *-ie* endings while compositor F preferred *-y*. However, for ten of these words Crane too preferred the *-y* ending, so compositor D following Crane's copy would look like compositor F. Other supposedly distinct spelling preferences alleged by O'Connor fell to the same objection.

Werstine repeated O'Connor's comparison of compositor D's setting from quarto copy with the quartos themselves, excluding full lines (where spelling might be influenced by the needs of justification), eye-rhymes (like *quay* / *day*) and words for which we do not know Crane's spelling. This left sixty words that ought to reveal compositor F's work in quires A–G by distinctive spellings that are not Crane's spellings nor compositor D's. However, of the 322 times compositor F set one of these 60 test words, 317 times he chose a spelling that was either the same as Crane's, or compositor D's, or both. A failure to show distinctive habits also emerged when compositor D's setting of quires H–V from quarto copy was considered. Thus Werstine was able to announce that 'Exhaustive analysis of Compositor D's habits thus produces almost no evidence to distinguish him from Compositor F, and much to associate him with Compositor F' (Werstine 2001, 333–4). The main Folio compositors (A, B, C, D and E) were still in place, but the peripheral F – and probably H, I and J added by Gary Taylor (pp. 171–2 above) – were not solidly grounded in evidence. For Werstine, this cast yet more gloom on New Bibliography's dream of recovering what Shakespeare wrote.

Werstine's study used standard New Bibliographical techniques to undermine earlier works of New Bibliography, illustrating that the discipline's immanent critique generates knowledge (negative in this case, but knowledge nonetheless), in contrast to the a priori indeterminacy that New Textualism simply inherited from post-structuralism as an article of faith. Hitherto, Werstine's attacks upon New Bibliography treated it as a consensus, but by the turn of the century Werstine saw it as a conflictual field offering two incompatible approaches to editing (Werstine 2000a). R. B. McKerrow's best-text approach described in the *Prolegomena for the Oxford Shakespeare* (pp. 30–7 above) admitted variants from an edition later than the substantive one only *en bloc* and on account of proven authorial revision, while W. W. Greg's eclectic approach, described in

The Editorial Problem in Shakespeare and 'The Rationale of Copy-Text' (pp. 38–47 above) and championed by Fredson Bowers, allowed each variant's merit to be weighed individually. Werstine forgave McKerrow's mistaken 'A Suggestion Regarding Shakespeare's Manuscripts' (pp. 31–3 above) in order to align him with New Textualism's project to edit the early editions that come down to us rather than seeking their underlying copy or the authorial intention. Thus, in his rejection of Greg, Werstine now saw himself like McKerrow, not outside of New Bibliography but squarely within its diverse field (Werstine 2000a, 53).

The New Textualist idea that each early edition has its own integrity continues to generate studies of small differences between quarto and Folio versions of a play. Lois Potter pointed out that Desdemona is innocent yet sexual and that the Q1/F differences can be seen as attempts to get that tricky balance right (Potter 2003). For his stories, Q1 Desdemona gave Othello 'a world of sighs' (Shakespeare 1622, c3^v) – as Brabantio says, a 'maiden never bold' – but in F it is the more sexually active 'world of kisses' (Shakespeare 1623, ss5^v). Editors generally prefer the demure Desdemona of Q1 even when using F as their control text, and Potter detected latent sexual moralism. Awkwardly, though, the evidence can be argued either way. A number of small Q1/F differences (detailed by Potter) show F toning down the sensuality and loquaciousness of Desdemona, yet Cassio's speech on Othello arriving in Cypress and making 'loues quicke pants in *Desdemonaes* Armes' (1623, ss6^v) is stronger in F than Q1's 'swiftly come to *Desdemona's* armes' (1622, D4^r). The trickiest scene is 4.3, which in Q1 lacks Desdemona's song and much of the dialogue, including Emilia's long final speech, while F has Desdemona say, with no prompting, 'This *Lodouico* is a proper man' (1623, vv3^r), perhaps suggesting that she is tempted to infidelity. If the song and Emilia's long speech were cut to make the version underlying Q1, this might again be a sign of embarrassment: women should not talk about infidelity. According to Potter, Q1 and F are distinct attempts to balance the sexuality and innocence of Desdemona, and while the sum of their differences is small, so is Desdemona's part and a few changes greatly alter characterization.

Lawrence Manley applied this methodology to Eleanor Cobham, Duchess of Gloucester, in Q1 *The Contention of York and Lancaster* (1594) and Folio *2 Henry 6* (Manley 2003). Combining close readings of the versions' differences with histories of the acting companies that first performed the play, Strange's men and Pembroke's men, Manley decided that the version underlying F is earlier than the one underlying Q1. As first written (and in F) Eleanor is accused of witchcraft, as was the mother of

Ferdinando Stanley (Lord Strange), but when Pembroke's men adapted the play (as reflected in Q) this became the lesser crime of treason. Manley contextualized the change within contemporary religious and state politics and the complexities of representing the anti-Lollardism from which the historical Eleanor, like her kinsman John Oldcastle, suffered. A few words make all the difference: 'sinne, | Such as by Gods Booke are adiudg'd to death' (Shakespeare 1623, m6^v) and 'Treasons ... committed against vs, our States and Peeres' (Shakespeare 1594, D1^r). Other adjustments resulting in a Q1 that 'follows the government's line' (Manley 2003, 266) include Eleanor actively preparing the conjuring, so that she loses audience sympathy: she has the questions already written, is more eager to get on with it and more devious in taking advantage of the court being away at Saint Albans. F has the bishop of Winchester (as well as Suffolk) behind Hume's temptation of Eleanor, and Hume boasts about deceiving her, making her downfall more of a political conspiracy than it is in Q1. In the conjuring scene, Q1's Eleanor is an active instigator while F's is spectatorially aloft. The paper holding the questions and answers is clearly tracked in Q1 and it constitutes proof of Eleanor's guilt, whereas in F she is condemned by hearsay. All these adjustments showed Manley what Pembroke's men did to the play once it entered their repertory.

Such studies are kept high upon a slippery slope by the frictional force of weighty evidence that revision took place. Without it they slide into subjectivism, as in Pamela Mason's argument that Osric's 'Shall I deliuer you so?' in Q2 *Hamlet* (1604–5, N3^r) became F's 'Shall I redeliuer you ee'n so?' (1623, pp6^v) in order to 'give two more opportunities [*re-* and *ee'n*] to display the character's fussiness' (Mason 2003, 96). Since F's Ophelia uses the word 're-deliuer' to Hamlet (1623, oo5^r) and Horatio says 'E'en so' to Hamlet twice (1623, pp5^v), the fussiness is hard to see. Because F's Osric is called upon to enter twice in the final scene without an intervening exit – once with the royal party (1623, pp6^v) and once to announce the arrival of Fortinbras (1623, qq^r) – editors generally supply the missing exit for him after he has refereed the duel. Mason, however, proposed leaving the text faulty 'so that a reader might experience the shock of the realization that we had not noticed that he had left' (Mason 2003, 97). In truth, the shock would not be that Osric had left (since Mason would deny him an exit) but that the editor produced an unperformable script that actors and readers would have to complete. Similar ideas are close to catching on in mainstream editions: Claire McEachern toyed with the idea of providing multiple-choice stage directions to avoid being prescriptive about the action in her Arden Shakespeare edition of

Much Ado About Nothing (Shakespeare 2006d, 133). Mason also advised editors to leave speech prefixes unnormalized, so that Claudius's wife flits between Queen and Gertrude 'to reflect what we can identify as scenes in which she functions more in her public or private role' (Mason 2003, 97).

New Textualist objections to the regularizing of speech prefixes continue to resurface periodically, as when John Drakakis complained that under the sway of 'some stable conception of dramatic "character"' an editor of *The Merchant of Venice* must use 'either "*Shylock*" or "*Jew*"' rather than 'follow the instability of Q1 (1600) *and* F1 (1623) in representing *both*' (Drakakis 2007, 229–30). Leah S. Marcus lamented that regularizing the early editions' variation of Aaron and Moore in *Titus Andronicus* loses these words' 'subtle interplay between racial and individual identification' (Marcus 2007, 134). Lina Perkins Wilder likewise objected to the regularizing of Bottom's speech prefixes in *A Midsummer Night's Dream*, since this Protean figure should be allowed to break all constraints and be at once lover and tyrant, the company clown inhabiting various roles, and Bottom the artisan. To editorially reduce the multiplicity of *Clowne*, *Pyramus*, and *Bottom* (as in the early editions) to just 'BOTTOM' is to efface the expression at a paratextual level of the phenomenon of changeability that the play is concerned with (Wilder 2008).

As we saw, speech prefix variation emerged in the printshop for purely technical reasons (p. 200 above), and John Jowett pointed out that were it present in manuscripts the practices of actors normalized it. After all, 'it can scarcely be assumed that Shylock would have acted more stereotypically when the prefix was for the Jew, or that the actor of Capulet's wife would have added a shake of flour to his wig when called an old lady, even supposing that the variants survived transcription into the playbook and hence into the actors' parts, which is doubtful' (Jowett 1999, 73). Yet small-scale speech prefix variation has begun to occur in recent editions. Editing *Titus Andronicus* for the Arden Shakespeare, Jonathan Bate switched between '2 SON' and 'QUINTUS' and '3 SON' and 'MARTIUS', according to how far they had become individuated in the dramatist's mind as he wrote the scenes they are in (Shakespeare 1995c), and in the same series John D. Cox and Eric Rasmussen switched between 'WIDOW' and 'LADY GREY' according to how far she has become individuated in the minds of the audience as they watch a performance (Shakespeare 2001a).

Margaret Jane Kidnie took the same line as Mason, arguing that modern editions tidy up and augment stage directions too much and should instead leave readers to face the indeterminacies of early editions (Kidnie 2000). Even if editors want only to help readers get the right virtual performance in their minds, they should not assume that 'the ways we currently make sense of performance would have been shared by early modern practitioners and theatergoers' (Kidnie 2000, 465). Reacting against Stanley Wells's *Re-editing Shakespeare for the Modern Reader* (pp. 182–3 above), Kidnie cautioned against anachronism and posited an unbridgeable gulf between the ways that early modern theatre worked and the solutions that modern practitioners and scholars invent. Kidnie's version of the New Textualist insistence upon the otherness of the past was overstated, since, to use one of Wells's examples, we can in fact be tolerably sure that characters who kneel rise again before exiting (Wells 1991b, 184). Although we cannot be sure how early modern actors staged certain moments, not all possibilities are equally plausible: even exits that call for characters to 'vanish' were not performed by beaming-up à la Star Trek. Kidnie reported that she 'deliberately resisted the temptation' to offer plans for better ways to present stage directions than those suggested by Wells (Kidnie 2000, 469), but in a book-length collection co-edited with Lukas Erne she came up with some (Kidnie 2004).

Kidnie's main suggestion was putting stage directions to one side of the printed page rather than aligning them with particular lines of dialogue; this would indicate indeterminate timing. Strangely, the early modern manuscripts that gave her this idea, which she quoted in support of it, show an abiding concern with determinate timing. *The Second Maiden's Tragedy* brackets the stage directions that Kidnie used as her examples, the brackets' points identifying just when the actions occur. The bracket around '*Enter | Nobles*' (Middleton 1909, 55b) is positioned to point at the dialogue that occasions the entrance, the cry 'my lordes treason'. The same is true of Kidnie's second example: '*Enter | Heluetius*' on the same page is bracketed so that the point identifies exactly where in the dialogue he enters, just before Memphonius says, in response to his entrance, 'heere comes another'. Kidnie's second illustrative manuscript, *Sir Thomas More*, does the same thing by confining the direction '*Enter A messenger*' (Greg 1911, 7b) to a wedge-shaped box whose left vertex presses into the dialogue to indicate precisely when he is needed. Greg's Malone Society edition tidies this wedge into a rectangle, but it is visible in Kidnie's facsimile reproduction (Kidnie 2004, 167). She could not have chosen better illustrations to prove wrong her claim that 'rarely can they [stage directions] be aligned visually with a precise moment in the dialogue' (Kidnie 2004, 165). Kidnie's third example, Q2 *Hamlet* (1604–5), differs from the manuscripts probably because it is fiddly to typeset brackets and boxes around dialogue. Yet a counter-example to Kidnie's claimed ambiguity exists even in print: the marginal direction 'They bow se- | verall wayes: | then advance and stand' is keyed to its precise moment of enactment by an asterisk within Arcite's line 'And me my love: * Is there ought else to say?' in the quarto of *The Two Noble Kinsmen* (Fletcher and Shakespeare 1634, H1ᵛ). Kidnie offered sample texts of *Troilus and Cressida* and *Romeo and Juliet* with their stage directions floating free in a left-side box to indicate her suggestion for editors.

In the same collection, Cox advocated leaving out stage directions altogether, or confining them to the commentary (Cox 2004). He complained that editors who add a stage direction for York to sit because Henry says 'See where the sturdy rebel sits' (*Richard Duke of York*, 1.1.50) are not helping confused readers but just 'yearning for closure' (Cox 2004, 193 n.27). Cox praised Kidnie's perspicacity and resistance to closure, apparently without noticing that in her essay for the collection she added the direction '[Ajax passes money to trumpeter]' to accompany the line 'AJAX Thou trumpet, there's my purse' (4.6.6). Presumably Kidnie feared that a naive reader might otherwise think Ajax simply pointed at his money. Marcus's contribution to Kidnie and Erne's collection argued that Folio *Othello* is more racist than Q1 (1622) and we must concern ourselves with how they became different, not conflate them (Marcus 2004). The argument and evidence were sound – the racism clusters in the 160 lines of F not in Q1 – but were swamped by postmodern illogic. Close reading, her own technique, Marcus called a 'rather clumsy, formalist mode' that prevents us seeing 'how a given text differs from itself' (Marcus 2004, 23). This claim is unintelligible since *differ* and *self* have opposite meanings, but it had become a New Textualist shibboleth. Randall McLeod used 'non-identity with itself' to describe textual multiplicity (McLeod 1991, 246) and Margreta de Grazia and Peter Stallybrass echoed him by calling multi-version editions of *King Lear* and *Hamlet* symptoms of 'the problem of a work's nonidentity with itself' (de Grazia and Stallybrass 1993, 258). Meredith Skura deflated the expression with an apt theatre-historical comparison: 'there are other valid responses to the two texts of *King Lear* besides assuming that there is no *King Lear* or no Shakespeare – just as there are other responses to the two floor plans for the Rose Theater [the original of 1587 and the refurbishment of the 1592] besides assuming that there was no Rose Theater' (Skura 1996, 171).

In his contribution to the Erne and Kidnie collection, Werstine used impeccable scholarship to add a fresh stigma, the apparent false start, to his list of phenomena misread by New Bibliography as evidence that an edition was based on foul papers (Werstine 2004). Crane's transcript of John Fletcher and Philip Massinger's play *Sir John van Olden Barnavelt* contains the line 'I know you love the *Prince* valiant *Prince* and yet' (Fletcher and

Massinger 1980, 7a). The line originally read 'I know you love the *Prince of Orange*, yet' and the censor George Buc deleted two words to make it 'I know you love the *Prince* ~~of Orange~~, yet'. Crane inserted three words above the line so it now reads:

valiant *Prince* and
I know you love the *Prince* ~~of Orange~~, yet

Had this occurred in a print edition (with the deletion omitted), New Bibliography would declare it an authorial false start pointing to foul papers copy, yet it appears here in a scribal transcript. Werstine offered another example of misdiagnosis in Q2 *Romeo and Juliet*'s stage direction '*Enter Will Kemp*' (Shakespeare 1599, K3^v). In *Dramatic Documents from the Elizabethan Playhouses* Greg acknowledged that in all surviving theatrical manuscripts the use of an actor's name instead of a character's was not part of the original composition (Greg 1931, 216), yet he always insisted that Q2 *Romeo and Juliet* was printed from foul papers. True, but Greg's more considered opinion, in *The Shakespeare First Folio*, was that an actor's name appeared in foul papers instead of a character's if the part was being written for a specific actor (as likely here) and appeared in a prompt-book alongside the character's name if the book-keeper wanted to remind himself of minor casting (Greg 1955, 142). Holding his earlier view against Greg was unfair of Werstine.

The most recent mainstream editorial projects have still not seen practical implementation of the wilder proposals of New Textualism, although version-editing has spread from *King Lear* to *Romeo and Juliet* (Shakespeare 2000e) and *Hamlet* (Shakespeare 2006b; 2006c). The existence of the Early Quartos subseries of the New Cambridge Shakespeare, and the third series Arden Shakespeare's provision of appendices giving photofacsimiles of bad quartos, mark the success of the New Textualist argument that early editions cannot hierarchically be organized as departures from a single archetype. Further corollaries of New Textualism are clearly active in the minds of editors but not manifest in mainstream editions, which continue to be edited along essentially New Bibliographical lines, albeit usually with less editorial confidence than at any time since the beginning of the twentieth century.

SHAKESPEARE AS LITERATURE

The stage-centred approach to editing Shakespeare that came to prominence in the 1980s won widespread but not universal assent. N. W. Bawcutt saw the departure from the authority of the author in the 'new' New Bibliography and New Textualism as mistaken because early modern dramatists were as much literary authors as men of the theatre (Bawcutt 2001). They wanted their plays printed without the actors' cuts, as shown by their title-page boasts: Ben Jonson's *Every Man out of His Humour* has '*more than hath been Publickely Spoken or Acted*' (Jonson 1600, A2^r), John Webster's *The Duchess of Malfi* includes 'diuerse things Printed, that the length of the Play would not beare in the Presentment' (Webster 1623, A2^r), and the contents of Barnabe Barnes's *The Devil's Charter* were 'more exactly reuewed, corrected, and augmented since [performance] by the Author, for the more pleasure and profit of the Reader' (Barnes 1607, A1^r). Jonson, Webster and Barnes could be dismissed as bookish exceptions to the rule, but Richard Brome cannot and his *The Antipodes* ends with a note saying that the book includes all the bits left out in performance, 'inserted according to the allowed *Original*' (Brome 1640, L4^v). The address of 'The Printers to the Reader' in Thomas Urquhart's *Epigrams: Divine and Moral* shows that, contrary to the New Textualists' claim, printers idealized the final, perfected text even though, for reasons of economy, they could not achieve it. The printers explain that they include a full list of errors even though (because of press correction) not every copy will have every error, for they were 'willing rather to insert the totall, where the parts are wanting in their distinguish't places, then by omitting any thing of the due count, to let an errour slip uncorrected' (Urquhart 1641, 13^r). Equally aimed at perfection were the requests in many books that the reader go through and write necessary corrections in pen. Early modern dramatists, Bawcutt concluded, would be amazed at the modern veneration of printing errors in their books and at notions of the socialized text overthrowing 'two centuries of patient and disinterested efforts to purify and clarify texts' that Renaissance authors would have thanked us for (Bawcutt 2001, 20).

Bawcutt saw Shakespeare and John Fletcher as un-bookish exceptions, and as G. E. Bentley pointed out, dramatists attached to playing companies (as they were) seem not to have been permitted to sell their work for print publication (Bentley 1971, 264–92). Richard Dutton suggested that being a Chamberlain's/King's man, Shakespeare left publication of his work to the company rather than getting involved in it himself: the plays were collective not individual property. But what if, Dutton wondered, Shakespeare considered manuscript circulation an acceptable alternative means of disseminating his plays as writing (Dutton 1996)? Perhaps their excessive length is an indication that he foresaw a readership for whom this would not present the problem it presented for actors. We have evidence that Jonson, Webster and Beaumont and Fletcher wrote plays longer than could be performed. This might explain why so many good Shakespeare quartos were printed from authorial papers or transcripts closely reflecting them: non-theatrical versions were circulating as manuscripts outside the actors' control. Plays published in the 1623 Folio with no preceding quarto editions such as *Macbeth* and *The Tempest* are short enough to be performable, which would make sense if the company's manuscripts were usually shorter than the literary versions in circulation.

Bawcutt and Dutton imagined a Shakespeare who considered himself a literary author as well as a dramatist, but was uninterested in print. Lukas Erne made the entirely unexpected suggestion that in fact Shakespeare was not indifferent to the print publication of his plays and consciously cultivated his readership. Erne's argument appeared first as an article and then in expanded form as a book, and at its core was a fresh arrangement of long-established facts (Erne 2002; 2003). By the end of 1600, fourteen of Shakespeare's plays – a significant portion of his output – had been printed. Confining himself to just the plays we can confidently say were written for the Chamberlain's men (leaving aside his pre-1594 work), Erne sought explanations for the plays' appearance in print. One frequently offered explanation is that when an unauthorized bad quarto appeared the company felt obliged to put a good version on the market for the sake of their reputation. Thus the bad quarto *Romeo and Juliet* (1597) was superseded by a good (1599), a bad quarto *Love's Labour's Lost* of an unknown date and now lost was superseded by a good (1598), and the bad quarto *Hamlet* (1603) was superseded by a good (1604–5). To disable this argument that the company released its plays to publishers only to force bad versions off the market, Erne argued that in each case the company sold a good manuscript of the play to a publisher before the bad quarto appeared.

James Roberts, who printed Q2, entered *Hamlet* in the Stationers' Register on 26 July 1602, before Q1 – printed by Valentine Simmes for Nicholas Ling and John Trundell, without a Stationers' Register entry – appeared in 1603. Roberts did not publish Q2 but rather was its printer when Ling published it, which curious state of affairs Erne explained by supposing that when Ling and Trundell published Q1 in 1603 they were unaware of Roberts' entry of a different version the previous year. Roberts decided that instead of making a fuss about Ling and Trundell's breach of company rules he should compel them to buy his good manuscript and pay him to print it as Q2 (Erne 2002, 7). In this ingenious narrative, the copy Roberts registered in 1602 was good and hence Shakespeare or his fellows sold a good manuscript before (and therefore not in reaction to) the appearance of the bad quarto. For *Romeo and Juliet* Erne could construct no such narrative, but argued that it is at least possible that Cuthbert Burby bought the good manuscript (which he published as Q2 in 1599) before John Danter published the bad one (Q1) in 1597. Regarding *Love's Labour's Lost*, Paul Werstine argued that Q1 reprinted a lost Q0, which therefore must also have been good (Werstine 1978b), and hence 'in each case the Lord Chamberlain's Men sold a "good" manuscript before the publication of the first edition' (Erne 2002, 8). Erne's argument slipped a gear here. The existence of a now lost edition of *Love's Labour's Lost* is attested by discovery of a private library catalogue from 1640 that includes 'Loves Labours Lost by W: Sha: 1597' (Freeman and Grinke 2002), but if Werstine is right then this 1597 edition was as good as its reprint in 1598.

The bad quartos dealt with, Erne turned to the six Chamberlain's men's plays by Shakespeare appearing in good quartos by the end of 1600: Q1 *Richard 2* (1597), Q1 and Q2 *1 Henry 4* (1598), Q1 *A Midsummer Night's Dream* (1600), Q1 *The Merchant of Venice* (1600), Q *2 Henry 4* (1600) and Q *Much Ado About Nothing* (1600). Notwithstanding critiques of New Bibliography that undermined the determinations, the underlying copy in each case seems to be authorial papers or a faithful transcript of them, and hence there is nothing to 'contradict the interpretation that any one of them [the manuscripts] may (though not necessarily all of them must) have been in the possession of the Lord Chamberlain's Men and/or their playwright before being sold to a stationer' (Erne 2002, 10). Looking at likely dates of composition and entrance in the Stationers' Register, Erne found roughly a two-year wait in each case. Leaving aside the bad quartos, only two more of Shakespeare's plays were printed in his lifetime – Q *Troilus and Cressida* (1609) and Q1 *King Lear* (1608) – and again there was a two-year gap between composition (1601 and 1605, respectively) and Stationers' Register entry (1603 and 1607, respectively). Erne saw the danger of circularity in his method: some of the datings are dependent on the assumption that the players would fear publication harming attendance at the theatre. For *A Midsummer Night's Dream* 'there's nothing beyond style to suggest a particular date' (Erne 2002, 11), which caveat Erne was forced to introduce because the usual dating of 1595 is fully five years before the Stationers' Register entry and Q1. To explain this, Erne wondered if its being written for a private wedding and not publicly performed until some time later solves the problem. There is, in fact, no evidence that the play was written for a private wedding.

Erne summed up crisply: 'of Shakespeare's first dozen or so plays written for the Lord Chamberlain's Men, not a single one that could legally have been printed remained unprinted by 1602' (Erne 2002, 12) and the typical vector was the company selling a manuscript to a publisher two years after first performance. Why wait two years? Because that was about the time between first performance and revival, and publication would promote the latter. For some reason the printing of Shakespeare's plays fell off after 1600: thirteen plays in twenty-four editions from 1594 to 1600 were followed by five plays in nineteen editions from 1601 to 1616. Peter W. M. Blayney had suggested that perhaps the market was glutted around 1600, with twenty-seven plays entered in the Stationers' Register between May 1600 and October 1601, and publishers were finding that they did not sell as hoped. Gary Taylor had a simpler answer: after *Hamlet* Shakespeare hit a run of relatively unsuccessful plays until, pulling himself out of a mid-life crisis, he collaborated with George Wilkins on their spectacularly successful *Pericles* in 1607 (Taylor 2004a).

In the book-length version of this argument, Erne developed reasons for believing that Shakespeare was conscious of his readership and wrote for them, showing that the moral case for authors owning their work was widely accepted in the period even though publishers had the upper hand. Usually Jonson is named as the first man to insist that plays were literature, either in his collection *Workes* (1616) or in more tentative ways in editions of *Every Man Out of His Humour* (1600) and *Sejanus* (1605) that mark a gap between performance and printed book. According to Erne this gap opened around 1590, and plays became literary artefacts part-way through Shakespeare's career, not at the playwrights' behest but at the publishers' (Erne 2003, 31–3). Pushing back to 1590 the date when printed plays began to legitimize themselves by stressing their non-theatrical features and their authorial as opposed to theatrical origins makes these developments coincide with the beginning of Shakespeare's career. Editions of commercial theatre plays remained mostly anonymous until the 1590s, but by the 1610s it was the norm to name the dramatist, the gradual transition being co-extensive with Shakespeare's career. The Jonsonian distinction between great dramatic matter to be studied in print by the learned and the dross that the actors threw in to please the multitude was already apparent in the preface to the reader in the first edition of Christopher Marlowe's *Tamburlaine* that 'left out some fond and friuolous Iestures' that ignorant audiences enjoyed (Marlowe 1590, A2^r). For the first edition of Thomas Kyd's *The Spanish Tragedy* the multilingual inset play was turned into English to benefit readers (hence it is not a record of performance), apparently by Kyd himself who thus wrote the same matter twice, once for the stage and once for the page (Kyd 1592).

It is odd, almost unique in fact, that in Shakespeare's case anonymous first editions of Q1 *Richard 2* (1597), Q1 *Richard 3* (1597) and Q2 *1 Henry 4* (1598) – Q1 of the last surviving only fragmentarily so we cannot tell what it read – were replaced by ones that named the author in 1598, 1598 and 1599 respectively (Erne 2003, 57–8). In 1598 Shakespeare was invented as an author and by the turn of the century other dramatists were too, their names appearing on their title pages. Shakespeare led the way, having been canonized by Francis Meres among the acknowledged greats in *Palladis Tamia* (Meres 1598, Nn8^r, Oo1^v–Oo2^r; Erne 2003, 66–7). After Meres, Shakespeare's name sold books and thus 'the social *cachet* of printed playbooks increased well before the advent of Ben Jonson and the publication of his *Workes* in folio in 1616' (Erne 2003, 71). Robert Allott's selection for his collection *England's Parnassus* (1600) was strongly influenced by non-anonymous publication: most excerpts were from printed plays with named authors. Identifiable playwrights already qualified as 'the choicest flowers of our modern poets', as the collection's subtitle calls them, as they did in the compilation *Bel-vedére or the Garden of the Muses* (Bodenham 1600), in which plays are given place amongst literature and Shakespeare's most of all. According to Erne, we must stop saying that before the big dramatic folios appeared plays were considered sub-literary, and stop thinking of publishers as the dramatists' enemies. Rather, to a considerable extent, the publishers made the dramatic authors. By 1600, Shakespeare had a substantial body of published work and must have expected that what he wrote next would also appear in print. The surprise is that mostly it did not and only five more plays – *The Merry Wives of Windsor*, *Hamlet*, *King Lear*, *Troilus and Cressida* and *Pericles* – were published in his lifetime. This Erne admitted he could not explain.

Erne detected irony in modern performance-centred approaches to early modern drama, since they are only possible because early moderns did not agree that scripts exist primarily to be performed (Erne 2003, 131). Made in defiance of the view that drama belongs in the theatre, the early editions are scarcely promising material for stage-centred research now. The considerable gap between performance and printing is apparent in the excessive length of many Shakespeare editions. Alfred Hart's counts in the 1930s (pp. 112–13 above) showed that Shakespeare (alongside Jonson) was unusual in writing such long plays, his comedies averaging 2,500 lines, performable in about two hours, his histories and tragedies averaging

3,000 lines. Humphrey Moseley's address to the reader in the Beaumont and Fletcher folio (Fletcher and Beaumont 1647, A4^r–A4^v) claims that whole scenes were cut in performance, and since that collection's plays are on average already 15 per cent shorter than those in the 1623 Folio of Shakespeare, his must have been cut all the more. That Moseley was telling the truth is suggested by the fact that the plays he did not initially enter in the Stationers' Register, presumably because he did not have manuscript copies, are indeed shorter than the others, presumably because printed from the private, post-cutting transcripts he refers to (Erne 2003, 153). Erne's line-counts from manuscript playbooks from 1576 to 1642 confirmed the general picture that plays over 2,500 lines were cut to around that length (Erne 2003, 158–64).

What does this all mean for editors? At the height of author-centred New Bibliography, Erne's conclusions would have mattered little, but for a stage-centred 'new' New Bibliography attempting to recover the play as performed, Shakespeare's use of print to convey to readers material that could not be performed would be devastating. The Oxford *Complete Works* editors argued that in several cases the Folio version shows theatrical improvement over the good quarto of a play printed from authorial papers (pp. 184–5 above). Erne would see such a Folio version as only a preliminary abridgement. Folio *Hamlet*, he acknowledged, reflects some of the cuts that made the play performable, shown by omissions it shares with Q1 (1603). On a couple of occasions, F omits things that are in Q2 (1604–5) and at that point Q2 seems to have lost half a line, suggesting that the cut realized in F was marked in the authorial papers but misread by the compositor as only a half-line excision. Because compositors generally ignored deletion marks, 'no printed text allows us to recover how much would have been marked for omission in its copy-text and, consequently, would have been cut in performance' (Erne 2003, 180–1). In this view, neither Q2 nor F *Hamlet* nor any modern edition derived from them shows us the play as performed. Being 160 lines shorter than F, Q1 *Othello* (1622) might reflect a preliminary abridgement, but more would have to go to make it performable. Folio *Macbeth* is roughly 2,000 lines and since it probably reflects posthumous theatrical adaptation we should accept that the other long tragedies also lost about a third of their lines in performance. Those who do not blanch at the thought that he revised his work should be able to accept an artistically self-conscious Shakespeare not driven solely by the exigencies of live performance (Erne 2003, 189). Regarding the bad quartos, there are two possibilities (Erne 2003, 192–219). If they are memorial reconstructions the aim was to reproduce the texts as cut by the usual amount for the London theatres, not abridgements for regional performance. If not memorial reconstructions, they are simply performance texts and should be called the short quartos, and their longer companions are essentially literary works not meant for performance.

Writing independently of Erne and only glancing at his work, Edward Pechter made a parallel argument about 'new' New Bibliography and New Textualism overvaluing the theatrical *vis-à-vis* the literary, finding that although it was meant to be anti-elitist this attitude towards theatre suppresses the truly radical aspects of literary creativity (Pechter 2003). Taking a different line from Erne on the short quartos, Pechter argued that seeing shortness itself as a theatrical quality – the loss of unnecessary, wordy stuff, a sign of cutting for pace – arises from an impoverished sense of what theatre can do. The fourth acts of Shakespeare plays often contain reflective, female scenes whose loss in shortened versions alters the gender balance. We should not be afraid to laud the plays' literary qualities, but we are told to reject the literary as conservative and elitist and the theatrical as radical and demotic. Yet in many cases, a short quarto is less radical than its counterpart(s). Compared to F, Q1 *Henry 5* (1600) is shorn of the politically interesting ambiguities about the king's reputation for heroism, and in Q1 *Othello* (1622) the parallel loss is an exploration of the gender double standard. Pechter located some of the trouble in our modern misreading of the Romantics, who are held responsible for the apotheosis of the lone authorial genius, which forms by reaction the modern preference for the socialized over the authorial text and collective over individual labour. In fact, he argued, Romantic notions of creativity were more complex and politically radical than they are given credit for (Pechter 2001; Pechter 2010).

THE FUTURE: CUTTING, COLLABORATION, LITERARY AUTHORSHIP AND THE LEGACY OF NEW BIBLIOGRAPHY

At the end of the twentieth century, Andrew Gurr published an argument that drew together accepted points of theatre history to produce a startling new editorial principle. Surveying records of the playing companies, Gurr had established that two hours was said to be the standard running time of an early modern performance across the period (Gurr 1996, 78–83). Editing Q1 *Henry 5* (1600) he became convinced that it represented the play as performed in two hours during Shakespeare's lifetime (Shakespeare 2000a). Q1 lacks the Folio edition's choruses and the sophisticated political material that puts Henry to sceptical scrutiny, and Gurr decided that F represents the maximal text, an intentionally overlong version of each play that Shakespeare wrote for the purpose of securing the Master of the Revels' licence and that his fellow actors would routinely cut heavily for performance (Gurr 1999). Elements of this argument had been made before: Stephen Orgel pointed out the two-hour problem and assumed that Shakespeare wrote more than was needed, letting the actors pick out what they wanted (Orgel 1988, 6–7; 1994). Like N. W. Bawcutt (pp. 215–17 above), Gurr cited evidence from printed plays by Ben Jonson, John Webster and Richard Brome that actors routinely cut the scripts they received, but he did not agree with Bawcutt and Lukas Erne that an overlong play was a literary extravagance; rather the explanation lies in the value placed upon the Master of the Revels' licence.

No play could be performed in London without the censor's licence, and on tour local authorities checked for it, so the licensed playscript stayed with the actors at all times. This document was too valuable to be marked up with cuts or alterations or to be given to a printer for publication. The players kept the licensed maximal text unsullied and drew from it a selection of scenes and speeches for individual performances and runs, giving themselves the flexibility to adapt to variable conditions of performance and the changing political and cultural climate without needing to seek a fresh licence. To produce a performance of around two hours, speeches were cut in their middles; Gurr did not mention it, but this would usefully preserve the speech-end cues. The routine practices of the company – casting, rehearsal, revision, revival, adaptation and publication – were done using transcripts of the maximal, licensed book. William B. Long showed that there was no such thing as a prompt-book in the sense New Bibliography understood it (see pp. 155–8 above), and according to Gurr only one licensed maximal play manuscript survives, Thomas Middleton's *The Second Maiden's Tragedy* with George Buc's licence written at its end. All other manuscripts pored over by scholars are transcripts. (As we have seen, p. 202 above, Gary Taylor now thinks Sidney Lee was right and much of the 1623 Shakespeare Folio was put together from transcripts, so there were more of them around than most New Bibliographers realized.) When performance caused political trouble, as with Middleton's *A Game at Chess*, the licensed playbook manuscript was checked by the authorities and in that case it saved the players from censure. Although he did not deny that the bad quartos contain elements of memorial reconstruction, along with other causes of shortness and badness, Gurr (like Erne) thought they were based on a minimal performed text for which, except in the case of *Pericles*, we also have the maximal text.

As Gurr pointed out, his hypothesis would make the 'new' New Bibliography entirely misconceived, since editors aiming to recover the words of the first performances need to look to the bad quartos rather than the good quartos or Folio. We should, he argued, return to the New Bibliographical recovery of the script as it was received by players, for this they licensed and this formed the superset of all the things said and done in performances. Added weight was given to the New Bibliographical privileging of the author's papers by Gurr's pointing out that as a sharer in his playing company, and as part-owner of its two London theatres, Shakespeare had an especially good sense of what could be achieved in performance (Gurr 2004, 72). Other dramatists' relative ignorance of what the players could do gives the rehearsed and performed versions of their plays (the ones improved by the actors) greater authority than the writers' naive ideals, but not so with Shakespeare. His close relationship with his company means that departures from his ideals caused by colleagues overruling him should count as interference in his art and not be validated by modern editors. By far the commonest source for early editions was a version of the author's papers – the licensed playbook never being allowed out of the company's possession – so the old New Bibliographical principles work quite well for respecting the writer's ideal version. The 'new' New Bibliographical aim to recover the words of the first performance is unattainable since this was only ever a subset of the writer's relatively stable ideal and it varied over time.

Gurr's theory requires that early modern theatre people did not consider, as we do, that cutting a script is a process of interpreting it. If Gurr is right, the Master of the Revels must have agreed with the actors that because the maximal script was authorized in its entirety, any subset of it was also thereby authorized. Either they thought that leaving bits out did not change a play's meanings, or else the censor did not see it as his job to judge the meaning of the whole, only to censure local readings (words, phrases, actions) that were ribald, religiously heterodox or seditious. This fits rather well with the pragmatism that emerges as a central feature of how Edmund Tilney, George Buc and Henry Herbert understood their jobs (Dutton 1991). It follows as a consequence of Gurr's theory that revision of a play was not undertaken lightly: any significant departure from the licensed script would require relicensing and hence would be undertaken as a thoroughgoing exercise. Allowing small tweaks would invite trouble.

Gurr was not the first to suggest that we have long misread the manuscript evidence because in general we do not have licensed playbooks, only intermediate states and transcripts. T. H. Howard-Hill (pp. 165–6 above) thought that Fredson Bowers took the proliferation of manuscripts too far, but like Bowers he rejected the foul papers/prompt-book binarism of W. W. Greg and could see the theatrical utility of documents representing various states of preparedness for performance, with John Fletcher and Philip Massinger's *Sir John van Olden Barnavelt* the key witness (Howard-Hill 1988). Gurr's approach shows that accepting the proliferation of documents does not disable a conceptual model in which writers and players idealized their endeavours, and it provides a particularly appealing narrative for those who see the exercise of power as central to cultural labour, for the idealized script embodied in the licensed playbook was a negotiated settlement between authorial wishes and the censorious power of the early modern state. Contrary to the post-structuralist notions of New Textualism, idealization need not be a conservative habit of thought to be contrasted to a supposedly radical dispersal of authority. Rather, idealization is what artists do in response to centralized power. When plays gave offence, their writers rather than the players were usually held culpable. For all that the script circulated in fragments such as actors' parts, it also presented a singularity when authorized by the censor. State power rendered the dispersed, fragmentary, unstable and plural text into something unitary for which the writer was responsible, just as pre-structuralist models of authorship always supposed.

Tiffany Stern uses actors' parts to stress the fragmented textual nature of early modern drama (2000; 2004; Palfrey and Stern 2007), and an insistence on the integrity and value of the licensed playbook acts as a counterweight to her view. According to Stern, the script was a singularity seldom or never seen by the actor, who knew only his own piece of the dramatic jigsaw puzzle in the form of a part containing just the speeches for one character (or group of minor characters), each preceded by its cue, the two or three final words of the previous speaker. Stern's approach is postmodern in its anti-authoriality and dispersal of textual authority, dismissing the complete script as less than the whole story because certain effects – such as cues deliberately given too early to make characters talk over one another – are invisible until the script becomes a collection of parts employed by actors. Ironically, Stern's approach diminishes the singularity and isolation of the dramatic author by precisely the degree to which it enhances the singularity and isolation of the dramatic character. In the script-centred model a character is a personality inferred from its social engagement in dialogues with others, but in Stern's part-centred model it is instantiated in a singular document containing one speaker's words held apart from those of its interlocutors, which is studied ('conned') largely in private. Postmodern anti-humanism aims to diminish the authority of the human author and of the invented human characters at the same time, but it can diminish one only at the cost of bolstering the other. As if conforming to a principle of conservation, it seems that lone human agency can be dispersed to, or condensed in, different places but not done away with altogether. Counterbalancing Stern's emphasis on the parts with Gurr's emphasis on the licensed playbook, a more complete picture of the relative integrity of early modern drama emerges.

The collaborative rehearsal and acting practices of the playing company do not detract from the lone authorial agency of Shakespeare, but his collaborative writing habits do. It is generally agreed that he voluntarily collaborated when writing *Titus Andronicus* (with George Peele), *1 Henry 6* (with Thomas Nashe and others), *Sir Thomas More* (with Anthony Munday and others), *Edward 3* (with persons unknown), *Timon of Athens* (with Middleton), *Pericles* (with George Wilkins) and *All is True* and *The Two Noble Kinsmen* (with Fletcher), and in a sense he involuntarily collaborated on *Macbeth* and *Measure for Measure* because Middleton adapted them after Shakespeare's death (Vickers 2002; Taylor and Lavagnino 2007, 681–703). Collaborative authorship can be detected by the presence of incompatible linguistic habits that vary between different writers no matter what they are working on, and in the little that has been written on how collaboratively composed early modern drama should be edited two views emerge. From a New Textualist and queer-theory angle, Jeffrey Masten thinks it hopeless to try to disentangle the various labours that make a collaborative play, for whether working side-by-side or alone the collaborators are likely to have influenced one another at every verbal level (Masten 1997b; 2001). According to Masten, even when not overtly sexualized the collaborative writing union synthesized participants' personalities to make a composite irreducible to its parts. In contrast to Masten, two of the founders of 'new' New Bibliography, Taylor and John Jowett, adjust rather than dispense with their editorial methods when editing collaborative drama. They think that individual authorial agencies can sometimes be distinguished and must, when discovered, be respected (Jowett 2004, 182–83; Taylor 2004b, 267–9).

For five of Shakespeare's plays, collaboration is so extensive that they appear within the collected works of his co-authors: *All is True* (as *Henry 8*) and *The Two Noble Kinsmen* (Beaumont and Fletcher 1989) and *Timon of Athens*, *Macbeth* and *Measure for Measure* (Middleton 2007). These editions, described in Appendix 3, distinguish the contributors' parts, and in the case of *Macbeth* and *Measure for Measure* they attempt to represent typographically the pre- and post-adaptation states of the texts. Masten's conviction that collaborative authorial labours cannot be disentangled arises from the theoretical predisposition of New Textualism rather than practical experience. Having once agreed with him, Suzanne Gossett went on to address the practical editorial problems created by collaboration's complication of authorial intention (Gossett 2002; 2006). Editing scenes, or smaller units, in relation to the habits of their particular writers foregrounds the discontinuities that editing generally tries to smooth by modernizing and regularizing. Yet not attending to each dramatist's habits and treating the script as homogeneous effaces discontinuities it readily displays. Both approaches risk distorting the work.

Rewriting an earlier argument about editing collaborative plays (1996), Gordon McMullan began with Michel Foucault and ended with Derridean supplementarity in trying to establish the terms for a reasonable compromise between authorial agency, as preferred by the New Bibliographers and the reading public, and socially dispersed agency, as preferred by postmodern New Textualism (Shakespeare 2000b, 180–99). As a theorist McMullan found that collaboration highlights 'the inadequacy of the paradigm of the "solo" author' (McMullan 1996, 437) – inadequate even for sole-authored works, let alone collaborations – yet as an editor of *All is True* he was obliged to say which parts are Shakespeare's and which Fletcher's. Forced to treat them as distinct agencies, McMullan was able to accommodate socialization by using Jonathan Hope's socio-historical linguistics that looks at writers' backgrounds (where brought up, where educated) to determine how quickly they are likely to have adopted linguistic alternates such as the auxiliary *do* – our modern 'what do you say?' instead of the early modern 'what say you?' – and then looks for these in the collaborative writing. The strength of this approach is that it treats writers as 'products of their linguistic environment rather than autonomous agents' (Shakespeare 2000b, 195).

McMullan's approach to *All is True* was attacked by Brian Vickers, who saw a distinction between collaboration, which applies to many theatrical practices, and co-authorship as a specific mode of writing with known ground rules (Vickers 2002, 333–432). The Diary of theatre impresario Philip Henslowe shows that in co-authorship the labour was divided by acts even before 1609 when intervals spread from the indoor hall playhouses to the open-air amphitheatres (Vickers 2002, 27–34; Taylor 1993c). Grace Ioppolo independently reached the same conclusion (2006, 110), although aside from *Pericles* the Shakespearian co-authoring was done in smaller units, scenes or parts of them. McMullan followed Hope in giving *All is*

True 1.1, 1.2, 2.3, 2.4, 3.2a and 5.1 to Shakespeare and the rest to Fletcher (Shakespeare 2000b, 187 n.1). Surprisingly, Vickers dedicated his book to Hope, McMullan's one-time co-author (McMullan and Hope 1992) and the deviser of the socio-historical linguistic tests that McMullan used to disperse authorial agency.

Thomas Merriam also criticized McMullan's edition for blurring of the authorial boundaries and complained that the postmodern insistence upon authorial undecidability is a revival of the Romantic idea that Shakespeare was so much the artist that his personality disappeared, denying us a clear view of his opinions (Merriam 2005). Whereas McMullan thought that *All is True* relativizes truth by having people of opposed views believe they are telling it, Merriam held that 'Katherine's judgment as to what is true is, without irony, that of the playwright' Shakespeare and that parts of the play lacking sympathy for Katherine are by Fletcher (Merriam 2005, 27). Using sound stylometric techniques, Merriam moved Hope's boundaries between the Shakespeare and Fletcher shares in the play, and found that each then speaks with a distinct voice and takes a coherent moral and politico-theological line on the historical material that simply differs from his partner's. In other words, by failing correctly to divide the play into its respective shares, we have mistaken the two writers' disagreements on points of principle for a kind of polysemous multi-vocality. Misguided postmodern criticism, Merriam argued, copies the Romanticism of S. T. Coleridge's delight in '*myriad-minded* Shakespear' (Coleridge 1907, 13) but is really celebrating its own, not Shakespeare's, self-contradictions.

Taking his title from Foucault's classic essay 'What is an Author?' (1969) and Orgel's responses 'What is a Text?' (1981) and 'What is an Editor?' (1996), Jeffrey Knapp attempted an historical answer to the question 'What is a Co-Author?' (2005). Knapp found that, contrary to recent arguments, sole authorship was not an emergent paradigm in the seventeenth century, but had long been the dominant paradigm. After summarizing the mountain of evidence that there were authors, including dramatic ones, in the sixteenth century, Knapp asked why people have thought otherwise and found his answer in the pernicious influence of Foucault, aided by G. E. Bentley's guess, in *The Profession of Dramatist in Shakespeare's Time*, that half of all plays were co-authored (Bentley 1971, 197–234). Knapp acknowledged Vickers's work and the discovery that in title-page naming there was an increasing tendency to recognize co-authorship rather than suppress it under single authorship. Yet truly collaborative writing, such as in the plays attributed to Beaumont and Fletcher but actually written with or by other dramatists, could not be properly acknowledged, Knapp argued, because the single-author paradigm, or at most the dual-authorship one, remained dominant.

The increasing evidence for Shakespeare's co-authorship and Erne's claims about his literary consciousness present two challenges not yet fully addressed by editors, although their effects are beginning to be apparent. The latest Arden Shakespeare editor of *As You Like It*, Juliet Dusinberre, was convinced by Erne and edited the play on the assumption that it is literary as well as theatrical (Shakespeare 2006a, 113–20). This encouraged her to pay more than the usual attention to its courtly context and less to early performances at open-air amphitheatres. With only the Folio edition to work from, Dusinberre had no opportunity to see how a presumed literariness would affect editorial choices regarding the readings of multiple authoritative early editions. Erne's ideas may one day be dismissed, although in the eight years (to date) since he announced them no-one has attempted a comprehensive refutation. Perhaps we have been conceiving the problem in the wrong terms. From a comprehensive study of how title pages pitched printed plays to prospective readers, Alan B. Farmer and Zachary Lesser dismissed as overly simplistic a binarism that pits authoriality against theatricality (Farmer and Lesser 2000). Dramatic authorship emerged as a distinct phenomenon in the early seventeenth century as part of the theatre industry, not separate from it. Even when title pages used status-conscious devices such as Latin tags and boasted of the dramatists' university degree qualifications, these 'helped to create the dramatic author *within* the context of the commercial theater; indeed, to a great extent, the emerging dramatic author *was* an author of the commercial theater' (Farmer and Lesser 2000, 101). Becoming a literary figure need not have changed Shakespeare's practices but only made him keep one eye on readers as additional consumers of his material.

If Gurr and Erne are right, the principles of high New Bibliography (prior to the 'new' New Bibliography's stage-centred adjustments) suit our present state of knowledge. According to both, the long versions of his plays do not reflect what got performed either because much was cut for any particular performance (Gurr) or much had been written specifically for readers to enjoy (Erne). Acceptance of these hypotheses does not entail a rejection of theatre, for, as George Walton Williams remarked, all productions of a play, from the first to the present day, are potentially valuable and interesting and all spring from the author's pre-theatrical script, interpreted and reinterpreted afresh by actors over the centuries. Editing a play to present that originary document rather than the first performance shows not a disdain for theatrical art but rather a celebration of writing's capacity to generate so much of it (Williams 1989, 107). The price paid in this approach is that for several plays readers would have to accept scripts that are manifestly incomplete in certain details.

As Stanley Wells and John Kerrigan concluded in respect of the incomplete theatricalization witnessed in Folio *Love's Labour's Lost* (pp. 169–70 above), the desire to show the performed version can bring editors hard up against the surviving materials' failure as evidence. In such a case the editor may reasonably retreat to the pre-theatrical version or push on to the theatrical version by making informed guesses about what Shakespeare and his fellows would have done. Fidelity to the partially theatricalized early edition (as New Textualism counsels) would be mistaken for the same reason that partially modernizing spelling is mistaken: the result would represent no particular stage in the history of the work of art, only a stage in the history of a document. The new arguments about actors' cuts and Shakespeare's literary consciousness need not return us to the state of relative pessimism about his texts that obtained before the rise of New Bibliography in the early twentieth century. Contrary to the thrust of most of the New Textualism, the struggle for Shakespeare's texts has not been pointless. There remains fundamental bibliographical work to do, for example in the comprehensive collation and explanation of press variants in the early editions, for the treatment of which editorial theory currently has no coherent criteria. In both senses of the title of this book – the Herculean (admittedly, at times, Sisyphean) and the combatorial senses – the struggle for Shakespeare's texts is not over.

APPENDIX I

How early modern books were made: a brief guide

The standard primers on how early modern books were made are R. B. McKerrow's *An Introduction to Bibliography for Literary Students* (1927) and Philip Gaskell's *A New Introduction to Bibliography* (1972). The former has significant errors of fact discussed above (pp. 63, 73), which are worth encountering in order to understand how the corrections to McKerrow influenced the debates in the middle of the twentieth century. The latter covers the mechanics of printing well into the twentieth century and only its first half, covering the period of the hand-press, is relevant. For readers who do not wish to pursue these matters in close detail, what follows is the minimum information about early modern printing necessary to follow the narrative of this book. The important details of the manufacture of type and paper are covered by Gaskell but for our purposes these may be left aside and we may start with the early modern compositor standing or sitting in front of two typecases comprising boxes of various sizes containing pieces of type. The typecases are supported on a frame that angles them towards the compositor and stacks one upon another so that the upper case contains the capital letters (still commonly called upper-case letters) and the lower case the small letters. The compositor reads his copy (either handwritten manuscript or an existing book) and one-by-one he selects individual pieces of type representing what he reads and places them into his composing stick, a small hand-held tray set to the width (called the measure) of the page he wishes to print. Most of the pieces of type represent one letter, number, space or piece of punctuation, although certain common combinations (such as *ss*) are formed as ligatures on a single body. Each piece of type is a long thin rectangular prism of metal, on the top face of which the shape it will print when inked stands in relief as a mirror image. The line of type in the stick reads from left to right (as does the copy) but each one is placed upside down so that a new line may sit upon its predecessor as the page is built up.

If the matter being printed is verse, the gap between the end of the last word on the line and the end of the stick is filled with spaces of differing width that the compositor selects to exactly fill out the measure. For all the type to stay firmly in the press during printing each line has to be the same width as the others on the page because the lines will be held in place by strips of wood called furniture. If the matter being printed is prose, the conventions of printing require that the right edge of the page is, like the left edge, perfectly straight (as they are on this page) and this requirement puts the compositor to additional trouble. To produce a straight right edge to the type page, the last letter of the last word must abut the right edge of the composing stick, so when he sees that he can get no more words into the line the compositor pushes the last word to the right and fills with extra, small spaces the inter-word gaps earlier in the line. This process is called justification and if it cannot be achieved with spaces of various sizes the compositor is at liberty to alter the spellings of words in order to make the line of type fit tightly into his stick. (Strictly speaking, the adding of spaces to the ends of verse lines is justification too – the word simply means making the type fill the measure – although the term is usually reserved for the more complex task needed when setting prose.) After the compositor has set perhaps six lines of type, his composing stick is full and he moves the type, carefully held as one block by the fingers, from the stick into a tray called a galley. The compositor repeats this process until the galley holds all the type for one page of the book, and then he ties the page of type with cord to keep it together until it is ready to be imposed.

Imposition is the bringing together of two or more pages to make what is known as a forme, which consists of the type pages (topped and tailed by such things as running titles, page numbers and catchwords) held in frame called a chase. Rather than being made page-by-page, early modern books were printed on large sheets capable of holding two or more pages on each side so that when folded the sheet made a collection of leaves with the pages in the correct reading order. The commonest formats of book were the folio in which the sheet was folded once (giving a vertical crease) to make two leaves holding four pages and the quarto in which a sheet was folded twice (once horizontally and once vertically) to make four leaves holding eight pages. The four-leaf gathering of a quarto was assigned an alphabetic letter known as its signature and as these are more reliable than page-numbers (which in many books are absent or inconsistent) the pages in early modern books are referred to by the signature, leaf number and side. Looking at the book in its usual reading position, a quarto gathering begins with a right-hand page on the first leaf (say, signature A1 recto, abbreviated to A1ʳ) and overleaf is the left-hand page on the reverse of that leaf (so, A1 verso, abbreviated to A1ᵛ). The next right-hand page is A2ʳ, and the fourth page is A2ᵛ. The remaining four pages, occupying the second half of the gathering, are A3ʳ, A3ᵛ, A4ʳ and A4ᵛ. If the book has more than eight pages, the next eight are printed on a new gathering (again made from one sheet) so the sequence repeats with B1ʳ, B1ᵛ, B2ʳ, B2ᵛ and so on. After sixteen pages a third gathering would start with C1ʳ. Because they were used to these sequences, early modern printers abbreviated them and in most early quartos the 'r' for recto is assumed (not printed) and the versos are not marked at all, nor is the fourth leaf. If we use square brackets to show the information that one has to infer when reading a quarto, the sequence seen typically is A1⁽ʳ⁾, [A1ᵛ], A2⁽ʳ⁾, [A2ᵛ], A3⁽ʳ⁾, [A3ᵛ], [A4ʳ] and [A4ᵛ].

A quarto gathering based on one sheet makes a convenient four-leaf unit. When printing in folio, however, printers usually brought together several sheets to make such a unit, tucking one folded two-leaf sheet inside another, a process known as quiring. A common combination, the folio-in-sixes, quired three two-leaf sheets to make a six-leaf gathering with twelve pages. This was the format used for the Shakespeare Folio of 1623 and it produces signatures that typically run A1⁽ʳ⁾, [A1ᵛ], A2⁽ʳ⁾, [A2ᵛ], A3⁽ʳ⁾, [A3ᵛ], [A4ʳ], [A4ᵛ], [A5ʳ], [A5ᵛ], [A6ʳ] and [A6ᵛ]. In the 1623 Folio these first twelve pages hold the text of *The Tempest* up to the end of scene 3.2, with the scenes from 3.3 to the end occupying B1ʳ–B4ʳ and the next play, *The Two Gentlemen of Verona*, occupying B4ᵛ–D1ᵛ. Where there were more gatherings than letters in the alphabet, printers would continue by doubling up letters (Aa, Bb and so on) and where matter was inserted out of sequence various symbols such as *, ¶ and ♣ could be employed in place of letters. In order to make the pages of a book appear in the correct reading order after the printed sheet had been folded, the process of imposition – putting the type pages for one side of a sheet into their correct positions and locking them together to make a printable forme – required careful planning.

If the reader would care to take a blank sheet of A4 or Letter (8½ by 11 inch) paper and place it in portrait (that is, tall and narrow) orientation on the table before her, the imposition of pages can be visualized, although early modern printers used sheets rather larger than this. To see how a quarto gathering was imposed, first grasp the top edge of the sheet and, without lifting the whole sheet off the table, bring it down to meet the bottom edge of the sheet and by applying pressure make a light horizontal fold using a single swipe of the fingernail so that the top half does not spring back upon release. Next take the left edge of the folded sheet and, again without lifting the whole off the table, bring it right to meet the right edge of the sheet and make a light vertical fold. The resulting four-leaf booklet is a quarto gathering and, opening it only slightly, the pages should now be numbered A1^r to A4^v from beginning to end in reading order without tearing the two top-edge joins called bolts. (These were usually left for the book-buyer to cut.) With the pages numbered, the sheet may now be opened to show the imposition of type pages necessary for the text to appear in the correct reading order.

The opened sheet has two sides. The side that has three valley-shaped creases and one mountain-ridge crease would be printed from four type pages brought together to make what is known as the inner forme: the type for A1^v and beside it the type for A4^r and opposite these two (and upside down in relation to them) the type for A2^r and A3^v. The other side of the sheet has one valley-shaped crease and three mountain-ridge creases and is printed from the outer forme containing the type for A4^v (on the back of A4^r) beside the type for A1^r (on the back of A1^v) and opposite these two (and upside down in relation to them) the type for A3^r (backed by A3^v) and A2^v (backed by A2^r). Thus to make the inner forme the compositors had to bring together the type for pages A1^v, A4^r, A2^r and A3^v, and to make the outer forme they had to bring together the type for pages A4^v, A1^r, A3^r and A2^v. Although these sides of the sheet are commonly referred to as the inner and outer formes, the term forme strictly refers to the locked-together pages of type from which the inked impression was taken. The type forme is a mirror image of the inked impression that it leaves on the sheet, as the reader may easily see by mocking up a second sheet of paper (representing the type itself) onto which the first sheet (the paper to be printed) must be pressed to make the ink image transfer.

The imposition of type for the three quired sheets that make a gathering in a folio-in-sixes may be demonstrated by putting a pile of three sheets of paper on the table, in landscape (that is, short and wide) orientation this time, and bringing the left edge of the pile to meet the right edge as before (without lifting the whole pile off the table) and making a vertical fold. The reader will now have a six-leaf, twelve-page gathering and the pages should be numbered in reading order from A1^r to A6^v. The required formes of type (which again will be mirror images of the ink impressions they leave on the paper) will bring together as pairs the type pages A1^r beside A6^v, A1^v beside A6^r, A2^r beside A5^v, A2^v beside A5^r, A3^r beside A4^v and A3^v beside A4^r. Bibliographers refer to two type pages (and their resulting impressions) that are beside one another like this as forme-mates and represent the relationship with a colon, so that the forme 'A1^r beside A6^v' is abbreviated to A1^r:6^v.

The foregoing description of how type was set, how pages were brought together to make gatherings and gatherings brought together to make books are all that is needed to follow the arguments described in this book. We have here omitted other possible formats (apart from quarto and folio-in-sixes) that were well known, such as octavo (with eight pages per forme) and duodecimo (with twelve pages per forme); these were seldom used for the early editions of Shakespeare. Until about the middle of the twentieth century so little was known about how early books were put together that misconceptions abounded regarding such elementary matters as whether the compositors proceeded through a book setting the pages of type in reading order (1^r, 1^v, 2^r, 2^v and so on), called seriatim setting, or instead chose to set pages in a discontinuous sequence in order to fill a forme as quickly as possible. Only a completed forme (four pages for quarto, two for folio) could be loaded into the printing press, and the reader may enjoy working out for herself how many pages had to be set in type before printing could commence if compositors worked seriatim through a gathering starting at page 1^r. The answer (which happens to be the same for a quarto and a folio-in-sixes) is given and explained in Chapter 2 (pp. 73–4 above), at the point in our narrative when certain ideas about printshop efficiency became important to bibliographers in the 1950s.

Two final complications are to be borne in mind. The first is that once the press was ready to print one side of a sheet the process of inking the type and impressing the paper was repeated as many times as there were to be copies of the book in the print run. (The word *exemplar* is here used instead of *copy*, so the latter can be reserved for what the compositors read when typesetting.) That is to say, if one thousand exemplars of the book were required then one thousand impressions of one side of a sheet were made – say, 3^v:4^r for the inner forme of the inner sheet of a gathering of a folio-in-sixes – and then these one thousand sheets were perfected, as it is called, by being impressed on the other side by forme 4^v:3^r. These thousand sheets were then kept aside waiting to be united with the other sheets in the processes of gathering and binding that produced a complete book. When printing a folio-in-sixes such as the 1623 Shakespeare Folio, the usual procedure was to print from the inside of the quire out, so the inner forme of the inner sheet of the quire (3^v:4^r) was printed first, followed by the outer forme of that sheet (4^v:3^r), then the middle sheet's inner and outer formes (2^v:5^r and 5^v:2^r) and then the outer sheet's inner and outer forme (1^v:6^r and 6^v:1^r). The last complication is that a printing press could be stopped in the middle of a run and corrective changes made to the type. This could be done as part of routine proof correction, or because something had gone wrong during the run, such as type shifting in the press. Once the correction was made, the uncorrected sheets were usually not discarded but rather were mixed with the corrected sheets so that an average early modern book is likely to contain certain pages (or more precisely, the pages on certain formes) in the uncorrected state and other pages in the corrected state.

APPENDIX 2

Table of Shakespeare editions up to 1623

Abbreviations of play titles: 1H4 1 Henry 4; 2H4 2 Henry 4; ADO Much Ado About Nothing; CYL The Contention of York and Lancaster (= 2 Henry 6); E3 Edward 3; H5 Henry 5; LLL Love's Labour's Lost; LR The History of King Lear; MND A Midsummer Night's Dream; MV The Merchant of Venice; OTH Othello; PER Pericles; R2 Richard 2; R3 Richard 3; RDY Richard Duke of York (= 3 Henry 6); ROM Romeo and Juliet; WIV The Merry Wives of Windsor; TIT Titus Andronicus; TRO Troilus and Cressida. Editions widely accepted as bad quartos for most of the twentieth century are italicized. Parenthetical names after titles are publishers unless separated by 'for' in which case they are printer(s) for publisher(s). All the Shakespeare editions before the 1623 Folio were made in the quarto format (abbreviated to Q), with the exception of Richard Duke of York (1595) printed in octavo (O).

Year	First editions	Subsequent editions
1594	Q1 TIT (John Danter)	
	Q1 CYL (Thomas Creede for Thomas Millington)	
1595	*O RDY (Peter Short for Thomas Millington)*	
1596	Q1 E3 (Thomas Scarlet for Cuthbert Burby)	
1597	*Q1 ROM (Edward Allde and John Danter for John Danter)*	
	Q1 R2 (Valentine Simmes for Andrew Wise)	
	Q1 R3 (Valentine Simmes and Peter Short for Andrew Wise)	
1598	Q1 1H4 (Peter Short for Andrew Wise)	Q2 1H4 (Peter Short for Andrew Wise)

(*cont.*)

237

Year	First editions	Subsequent editions
	Q1 LLL (William White for Cuthbert Burby)	Q2 R2 (Valentine Simmes for Andrew Wise)
		Q3 R2 (Valentine Simmes for Andrew Wise)
		Q2 R3 (Thomas Creede for Andrew Wise)
1599		Q2 E3 (Simon Stafford for Cuthbert Burby)
		Q2 ROM (Thomas Creede for Cuthbert Burby)
		Q3 1H4 (Simon Stafford for Andrew Wise)
1600	Q1 H5 (Thomas Creede for Thomas Millington and John Busby)	Q2 CYL (Valentine Simmes for Thomas Millington)
	Q 2H4 (Valentine Simmes for Andrew Wise and William Aspley)	Q2 RDY (William White for Thomas Millington)
	Q ADO (Valentine Simmes for Andrew Wise and William Aspley)	Q2 TIT (James Roberts for Edward White)
	Q1 MND (Richard Bradock for Thomas Fisher)	
	Q1 MV (James Roberts for Thomas Heyes)	
1602	Q1 WIV (Thomas Creed for Arthur Johnson)	Q2 H5 (Thomas Creede for Thomas Pavier)
		Q3 R3 (Thomas Creede for Andrew Wise)
1603	Q1 HAM (Valentine Simmes for Nicholas Ling and John Trundell)	
1604		Q2 HAM (James Roberts for Nicholas Ling; some exemplars dated 1605)
		Q4 1H4 (Valentine Simmes for Matthew Law)
1605		Q4 R3 (Thomas Creede for Matthew Law)
1608	Q1 LR (Nicholas Okes for Nathaniel Butter)	Q4 R2 (William White for Matthew Law)
		Q5 1H4 (John Windet for Matthew Law)
1609	Q1 PER (William White and Thomas Creede for Henry Gosson)	Q2 PER (William White for Henry Gosson)
	Q TRO (George Eld for Richard Bonian and Henry Walley)	Q3 ROM (John Windet for John Smethwick)

Table of Shakespeare editions up to 1623

Year	First editions	Subsequent editions
1611		Q3 TIT (Edward Allde for Edward White)
		Q3 HAM (George Eld for John Smethwick)
		Q3 PER (Simon Stafford)
1612		Q5 R3 (Thomas Creede for Matthew Law)
1613		Q6 1H4 (William White for Matthew Law)
1615		Q5 R2 (Thomas Purfoot for Matthew Law)
1619		*Q3 CYL (William Jaggard for Thomas Pavier)*
		Q3 RDY (William Jaggard for Thomas Pavier)
		Q4 PER (William Jaggard for Thomas Pavier)
		Q2 WIV (William Jaggard for Thomas Pavier)
		Q3 H5 ([William Jaggard] for Thomas Pavier)
		Q2 MV (William Jaggard for Thomas Pavier)
		Q2 MND (William Jaggard for Thomas Pavier)
		Q2 LR (William Jaggard for Nathaniel Butter)
1622	Q1 OTH (Nicholas Okes for Thomas Walkley)	Q6 R3 (Thomas Purfoot for Matthew Law)
		Q7 1H4 (Thomas Purfoot for Matthew Law)
1623		Q4 ROM (William Stansby for John Smethwick)

APPENDIX 3

Editorial principles of the major twentieth-century Shakespeare editions

The following are significant Shakespeare editions since 1899 with descriptions of their editorial approaches, cross-referenced to discussions of the editions or their ideas in the main body of this book. Only editions that stimulated debate about what editors should do or that helped establish Shakespeare's texts are included, so for example the New Variorum Shakespeare (1936–55), most facsimiles and a number of best-selling complete works editions are omitted. David Bevington's complete works was made by successive revisions of Hardin Craig's lightly corrected version of the Victorian Globe text, which iteratively narrowed the differences between itself and twentieth-century editions made from first principles (Shakespeare 1951a; 1973; 1980a; 1992a; 1997a). Thus, from a bibliographical point of view Bevington's edition is only belatedly theorized. The source for publication information is Andrew Murphy's *Shakespeare in Print* or the books themselves where they disagree (Murphy 2003, 367–86). Series are deemed to end when the final volume is published for the first time. The absence of an edition or series recorded by Murphy indicates that it made no significant contribution to the editorial tradition.

Comparing the development of theory and practice in Shakespeare editing across the century, the starkest fact is how seldom people at the heart of the former were engaged in the latter. A. W. Pollard and W. W. Greg produced no significant editions of Shakespeare, and aside from certain proof pages (Wells 1984, v) neither did R. B. McKerrow. Some members of the Virginian school produced relatively unambitious editions (with little documentation of their interventions) for the Pelican Shakespeare, described below, and Charlton Hinman's Folio facsimile is noticed because of the debates it stimulated. Two figures on the periphery of New Bibliography, John Dover Wilson and Peter Alexander, edited Shakespeare, but only Alexander made a substantial contribution to textual scholarship, in his work on memorial reconstruction (pp. 104–7 above). This contribution was in any case a weak point in the New Bibliography and his edition was of little significance. Another minor exception is Alice Walker, who edited a couple of the New Shakespeare volumes. Not until the end of the century did theory and practice fully coincide. Only after the 'new' New Bibliography was manifested in the 1986 Oxford *Complete Works* did a mainstream New Bibliographer, Fredson Bowers, publish editions of Shakespeare's plays. Ironically, since New Bibliography was largely driven by the desire to recover Shakespeare's plays, they were *All is True* and *The Two Noble Kinsmen* undertaken by Bowers as part of his project to edit the dramatic canon of John Fletcher.

THE ARDEN SHAKESPEARE FIRST SERIES, GENERALLY EDITED BY EDWARD DOWDEN, W. J. CRAIG AND R. H. CASE (1899–1924)

The first of the Arden Shakespeares was *Hamlet* edited by Edward Dowden (1899). Preceding the impact of the first fruits of New Bibliography, this volume is typical of editing in the wake of the Cambridge–Macmillan edition of 1863–6, which supplied the base texts via its second edition (Shakespeare 1891–3), a fact not readily discerned from the volumes themselves but mentioned by Una Ellis-Fermor when the second Arden series began (Shakespeare 1951c, ix). From their descriptions of their work, the editors appear to have been permitted minor departures from the Cambridge–Macmillan text. Dowden thought Q1 *Hamlet* (1603) surreptitious, made by a stenographic record of the dialogue that was perhaps fleshed out by referring to the theatre's copy of the script, and he rejected the idea that behind Q1 lay an old *Hamlet* play, perhaps by Thomas Kyd. The Folio edition of *Hamlet* Dowden thought 'cut for the purpose of stage representation', so 'more theatrical, but less literary' (Shakespeare 1899, xx) than Q2 (1604–5). Dowden decided that the customary act intervals were misplaced and he would have corrected them 'but for the inconvenience' of disturbing standardized references (Shakespeare 1899, xxii). He apparently did not suppose that the Arden Shakespeare series might initiate new and better standards for referencing.

Dowden resigned as general editor of the series after publication of his *Hamlet* edition, to be replaced by W. J. Craig (Murphy 2003, 207), but he continued as editor of particular volumes. The second in the series was his *Romeo and Juliet* based on Q2 (1599) but with 'the corrections of the later Quartos and of the Folio' used as 'valuable aids towards ascertaining the text, while in not a few passages Q1 lends assistance which cannot elsewhere be found' (Shakespeare 1900, xi). This eclecticism illustrates the prevailing assumption that all early editions are distant from Shakespeare's papers yet between them they may provide a reasonable approximation of those papers. Series editor Craig's *King Lear* (1901) was hampered by his not knowing – the discovery was made seven years later (Greg 1908a; 1908b) – that Q2 dated 1608 was in fact published in 1619. Craig spotted that Nathaniel Butter and John Busby's Stationers' Register entry for *King Lear* in 1607 has George Buc's authority behind it – 'Entred for their copie vnder th[e h]andes of Sir GEORGE BUCK knight and Th[e]wardens A booke called …' (Arber 1876, 366) – and yet the Folio preliminaries, Craig knew, characterize the preceding quartos as stolen and surreptitious. A. W. Pollard had not yet made his innovative argument that the Folio preliminaries refer only to certain preceding quartos, not including *King Lear* (pp. 12–15 above). Craig debated just what form Buc's authority took and could not settle the matter; it is an intriguing point not pursued in the much longer introductions to recent scholarly editions (Shakespeare 1997b; 2000c). The Q1/F differences he thought were authorial or non-authorial revision and although it was 'impossible to say with any certainty' which is the original, the 'superiority of the Folio' was beyond doubt (Shakespeare 1901, xiii). In choosing between Q1/F readings, 'fitness and positive superiority, or what in my judgment I deem to be such, are the only guides' (Shakespeare 1901, xv). Craig remarked that it was not surprising that his text was like other editions, since 'the ground has been too exhaustively worked by preceding editors to admit of any new discoveries of importance' (Shakespeare 1901, xv). Thus he seems to have felt himself to be working near the end of a long and fruitful tradition, with only the tidying up left to do, rather than setting out to develop a new tradition that would break fresh ground.

Michael Macmillan reported that he had not 'the temerity to suggest many new readings' (Shakespeare 1902b, v) in *Julius Caesar* and the same year Morton Luce's *The Tempest* contained nothing on matters textual (Shakespeare 1902c). Dowden's final contribution to the series was his conservatively edited *Cymbeline* (Shakespeare 1903a). He came up with Imogen's (as he named her) 'Think that you are upon a lock, and now | Throw me again' (his 5.5.262–3) to improve on F's awkward 'vpon a Rocke' (Shakespeare 1623, bbb5^r), supporting this from the *New English Dictionary* (later the *Oxford English Dictionary*). Yet Dowden did not adopt this reading in his text. Being certain on the basis of strong evidence to support an emendation apparently was not enough to warrant interference in the text. Likewise, although he thought the ghosts' speeches were invented by the actors, Dowden kept them in: his 'Idle conjectures' were 'harmless' because 'not insisted on' (Shakespeare 1903a, xl).

H. C. Hart's edition of *Othello* was the first to mention press variants, in respect of Q1 (Shakespeare 1903c, ix n.2), which he thought printed from 'an independent MS., which had been an early acting copy' since the non-deletion of oaths showed that it predated the 1606 Act to Restrain Abuses of Players (Shakespeare 1903c, x). We have to trust the Folio preliminaries' claim that it contains the 'true original copies' and hence it is our authority 'unless the Quarto can establish a prior claim' (Shakespeare 1903c, xi); Hart thought it could not. Herbert Arthur Evans's *Henry 5* quickly and deeply immersed its reader in consideration of the textual situation (Shakespeare 1903b). Evans called Thomas Millington and John Busby 'two piratical booksellers [who] had succeeded in getting hold of a garbled version' to make Q1 (1600) which is 'a very imperfect and clumsy representation of the text of the play as curtailed for some particular performance' (Shakespeare 1903b, xii). He devoted an entire section of his introduction to the Q1/F relationship, noting that the idea of Q1 being Shakespeare's first version of the play was exploded by P. A. Daniel in his introduction to the New Shakspere Society parallel text edition (p. 103 above). The textual basis of Evans's edition was the Folio modernized in spelling and punctuation and 'not ... departed from without reason' (Shakespeare 1903b, xlvii). 'For any apparatus criticus of the text', he wrote, 'the Cambridge[–Macmillan] Shakespeare remains the fountainhead' (Shakespeare 1903b, xlvii–xlviii).

Editing *All's Well that Ends Well*, W. Osborne Brigstocke assured the reader that 'I have throughout endeavoured to be as conservative of the original folio text as possible' even though this is 'one of the worst printed plays in the volume' (Shakespeare 1904a, ix). For *The Merry Wives of Windsor*, Hart reasoned that when John Heminges and Henry Condell complained of 'stolne, and surreptitious copies, maimed, and deformed' that had been foisted on the reading public, they had the quarto of *The Merry Wives of Windsor* in mind, and so 'the Folio may be accepted as the text of the play in its entirety' (Shakespeare 1904c, xi). However, Hart decided that Q1's omission of lines about Windsor Castle and the Order of the Garter, replaced by lines that 'sound pure London' (Shakespeare 1904c, xix), is due to Q1 being the script for London performance and F the script for performance at Windsor. Leah S. Marcus made precisely this argument more than ninety years later (p. 190 above). Because the text underlying the Folio was marked up for theatrical cuts and joins, there are unfortunate anomalies in it, especially around Falstaff's meeting with Mistress Ford at the end of act three. However, wrote Hart, 'These can only be set right by the alteration of words in the text. This is not, happily, the province of an editor, for it is a complicated and unpleasant investigation'

(Shakespeare 1904c, xiv). 'Nothing', he wrote, 'but an unswerving reverence for the Folio text enables one to withstand the temptation' to insert quarto-only passages in one's edition, but alas that reverence 'did not', he complained, 'belong to the early commentators' (Shakespeare 1904c, xxiv).

One editor upon whom imposition of the Cambridge–Macmillan text seems to have rankled was Henry Cuningham, who set out to produce a text of *A Midsummer Night's Dream* 'in advance of anything that has hitherto been published' because exactly what Shakespeare wrote is 'by no means "fixed and settled." Far from it' (Shakespeare 1905, ix, x). Cuningham anticipated Pollard (pp. 19–20 above) in declaring that the use of the definite article in the Folio stage direction '*Enter Piramus with the Asse head*' (Shakespeare 1623, N4^v) indicates knowledge that the property stock contained only one such head (hence the direction was written by a prompter and not Shakespeare) and that a musician's name in the direction '*Tawyer with a Trumpet before them*' (1623, O2^v) confirms that F's copy was theatrical. The parallels of thought are so aligned that Pollard probably took this claim from Cuningham without realizing it. Cuningham's edition was the first in the series to include an index to his notes. He began the introduction to his *Macbeth* with the words 'The Editor is not responsible for the text of this play as printed in this edition' (Shakespeare 1912, vii) and went on to complain of editors failing to mark off the parts of the play not by Shakespeare, and of his being constrained to make the discrimination only via commentary notes. Cuningham thought that the non-Shakespearian interpolations include the first two-and-a-quarter scenes of the play as well as the oft-suspected meeting of Hecate and the witches, and parts of the Apparitions scene.

A useful illustration of the muddled logic of pre-New Bibliographical editions appears in Hart's *Love's Labour's Lost*. On the basis of his comparison of Q1 (1598) and F, Hart decided that where they indifferently disagree, he would favour F on the assumption that Heminges and Condell knew what they were about. To make 'a full test of their respective merits' he offered a pair of lists of 'where the Folio corrects the Quarto and *vice versa*', which he thought showed F to be 'the more carefully printed' (Shakespeare 1906a, lii, liv) and that both derive from theatrical copy. Hart failed to distinguish the quality of a printing from the reliability of the copy underlying it, and his comparison overlooked the dozens of agreements-in-error that prove F to be a reprint of Q, a fact that leapt out at John Dover Wilson when he repeated the comparison (Shakespeare 1923a, 186–91). Throughout the early Arden Shakespeares there are textual decisions and practices that seem incomprehensible now, such as the collation of unadopted readings from the Second, Third and Fourth Folios even when not remotely possible. A typical example appears in R. Warwick Bond's *The Two Gentlemen of Verona*: 'Her eyes are grey as glass' with the collation '*glass*] F1, *grasse* Ff 2–4' (Shakespeare 1906b, 4.4.197).

Towards the end of the first decade of the century, just as the New Bibliography was emerging, the Arden Shakespeare introductions became increasingly concerned with matters textual. Whereas the introductions to early volumes mainly or wholly confined themselves to themes, characters, sources and related literary topics, the new ones started to devote ever greater space to the textual problems. For *Pericles*, K. Deighton admitted the stylometric evidence that for most of the twentieth century was to be ignored: 'metrical tests ... prove almost the whole of the first two Acts to be by some other author' (Shakespeare 1907, xxv). Deighton dealt at length with the authorship, leaving room in his introduction for nothing else, and his was the best concise summary of the textual situation of *Pericles* available until the 1980s (Wells *et al.* 1987, 556–60), and the best account of the debate about the evidence until the monographs *Shakespeare, Co-Author* (Vickers 2002) and *Defining Shakespeare:* Pericles *as Test Case* (Jackson 2003).

The New Bibliography was first acknowledged when J. W. Holme edited *As You Like It* (Shakespeare 1914), dating it from its Stationers' Register entry, which he explained using the narrative given in Pollard's *Shakespeare Folios and Quartos* (pp. 12–15 above). The general editor R. H. Case, who took over in 1909, was quickly convinced by the new thinking, as is clear from his additions to reprints of the early volumes and his own edition of *Coriolanus* co-edited with W. J. Craig (Shakespeare 1922a). Case and Craig explicitly agreed with Pollard's continuous copy theory from *Shakespeare's Fight with the Pirates* (pp. 15–23 above): 'the author's autograph copies of his plays became the prompt-copies' and 'the text of many of the plays, both of those printed in quarto and those which first appeared in the folio, were set up from them' (Shakespeare 1922a, xxv). For *2 Henry 4*, R. P. Cowl, under the sway of the new optimism, wrote of 'the excellencies of the text of *2 Henry IV* as transmitted to us in the authorised stage version published by Wise and Aspley in 1600, and in the completer version of the Folio' (Shakespeare 1923b, xv). Optimism did not instantly boost editorial self-confidence, however. Convinced that F's 'The vertuous Sweetes' (Shakespeare 1623, gg4^v), absent in Q, is an un-Shakespearian interpolation, Cowl nonetheless felt he could not cut a reading that 'time has invested with authority' (Shakespeare 1923b, vii).

Arden Shakespeare editorial practices gradually changed in response to the new theories. The last volume in the series, Grace R. Trenery's

Much Ado About Nothing (1924), began with the play's Stationers' Register entry and Pollard's interpretation of it, which she entirely accepted. The 1600 quarto, she agreed, was based on 'theatrical prompt copy' (Shakespeare 1924b, ix) and she was almost convinced by Pollard's argument that the copy was in Shakespeare's hand. If that were proven, she wrote, we should hold the quarto 'in still greater reverence and the alterations and emendations of the later editors in rather less respect' (Shakespeare 1924b, x). The Arden series took twenty-five years to edit all the plays, and the early volumes were reprinted with revisions, some of them two or three times, before the final volume appeared. The commonest kind of revision was for general editor Case to add extra footnotes that amplified, corrected or flatly contradicted the editor whose volume was being reprinted. Thus in his edition of *1 Henry 6*, H. C. Hart explained that the Henry 6 trilogy was the collective writing of Shakespeare, Christopher Marlowe, George Peele and Robert Greene, which is why *The Contention of York and Lancaster* (printed in 1594) and *Richard Duke of York* (printed in 1595) have the distinctive words and phrases of all four men (Shakespeare 1909). Revising the volume for a second edition, Case added a footnote referring the reader to Peter Alexander's alternative explanation that the 1590s editions are based on memorial reconstruction (pp. 104–6 above), which 'seriously damages the case for attributing these plays in whole or part to other authors than Shakespeare' and thus 'The whole of this Introduction should now be read in the light of' Alexander's work (Shakespeare 1930, vii n.1). This was not an isolated incident: throughout the reprinted introduction Case inserted new footnotes disagreeing with Hart's main text.

The intellectual force of the New Bibliography was so strong that Case clearly felt it his duty to modify as far as he could the editions first printed before its benefits were available. That force also made its adherents adjust their positions so as to join and bolster the advancing front. Alexander's memorial reconstruction explanation aligned perfectly with E. K. Chambers's desire, expressed in his British Academy lecture 'The Disintegration of Shakespeare' (1924–5), to dispel the idea that Shakespeare co-authored plays. The unified front was achieved at the cost of a certain reinvention of previous scholarship. In his Warwick Shakespeare edition of *Macbeth* Chambers marked off the passages he thought were Thomas Middleton's (Shakespeare 1893). When he came to write his British Academy lecture, however, Chambers described the idea that Middleton had a hand in the play as a 'heresy' of S. T. Coleridge's elaborated by Victorian editors (Chambers 1924–5, 92).

THE NEW SHAKESPEARE, EDITED BY ARTHUR QUILLER-COUCH AND JOHN DOVER WILSON (1921–1966)

Early editors of the first Arden Shakespeare series seem to have conceived of themselves nestling in the pockets, rather than standing on the shoulders, of the giants who established the text of Shakespeare in the Cambridge–Macmillan edition of 1863–6. Only towards the end of the series did they seek to build upon fresh discoveries that were arising from what was becoming known as the New Bibliography. The New Shakespeare, begun by Arthur Quiller-Couch and John Dover Wilson, by contrast was meant to establish new knowledge. No moment since 1623 was 'more favourable in auspicating a text of the plays and poems' with the aim of 'cutting Shakespeare free from the accretions of a long line of editors', wrote Quiller-Couch in the inaugurating volume, *The Tempest* (Shakespeare 1921b, vii). The heavy lifting on matters textual was to be work for Wilson alone, and he identified three recent discoveries that transformed his task: A. W. Pollard had shown that the early editions (especially the quartos) are much better than had been thought (pp. 12–23 above), Hand D in the manuscript of *Sir Thomas More* had been identified as Shakespeare's (pp. 23–4 above), and Percy Simpson (1911) had shown that the punctuation of the early editions reliably represents playhouse practice (Shakespeare 1921b, xxix). Simpson's idea did not survive closer investigation and had no lasting impact.

Having outlined the foundations of the New Bibliography, Wilson set out upon investigations owing something to its principles and much to his own brilliant but erratic logic. Wilson's texts gave as little indication as possible of the act and scene breaks, since Shakespeare 'did not work in acts and scenes' (Shakespeare 1921b, xxxv), but for the sake of compatibility with 'glossaries, concordances, etc' Wilson retained the inauthentic breaks (1921b, xxxvii). Wilson's willingness to invent stage directions has been much commented upon (for example, Wells 1984, 66–7) and one illustration, showing that his mind's eye pictured modern rather than early modern theatres, may stand for hundreds: '"*A tempestuous noise of thunder and lightning heard.*" *The waist of a ship is seen, seas breaking over it*' (1921b, 1.1.0.1–2). Wherever Wilson saw verse mislined he took it as a 'sure sign of marginal alteration in a good text' (1921b, 79) and, on the assumption that copy could be continuous even from a preceding version of the play, he read the several expositions (of Prospero's usurpation, of Sycorax's exile, of Claribel's African marriage) as signs that scenes depicting these events in an earlier version had been cut; the masque too he thought an interpolation. In his *The Two Gentlemen of Verona*, Wilson decided that copy for the Folio edition had been put together from the actors' parts (guided by the plot), which would explain why there were few stage directions and entrances are massed at the beginnings of scenes (Shakespeare 1921c, 77–8). For the realization that Q1 *The Merry Wives of Windsor* (1602) could not be an early version but must be a corruption of the play better represented by F, Wilson credited P. A. Daniel (Shakespeare 1881) and he pointed to the moments where an omission or corruption in F can be rectified from Q1 (Shakespeare 1921a, x–xii). Wilson's co-authored essay with Pollard of two years earlier established his view that, like *The Two Gentlemen of Verona*, Folio *The Merry Wives of Windsor* was put together from actors' parts (Pollard and Wilson 1919d).

A sense of how such new thinking was received and what it was measured against can be gained from E. K. Chambers's remark that 'we are faced with a reopening of the textual questions, which a generation of Shakespearians has regarded with complacency as substantially disposed of by the labours of the Cambridge[–Macmillan] editors' (Chambers 1923c, 253). Reviewing the first six volumes in the series, Chambers found the continuous copy theory (pp. 15–23 above) to be disabling because it multiplies the agents and processes by which a textual phenomenon might be explained, so that the chances of finding the correct ones (and undoing them) approaches zero. An editor working under such conditions can compensate only by overstating the certainties, and this Chambers found Wilson doing, being 'apt to arrive at revolutionary conclusions on the basis of quite small disturbances in the text' (Chambers 1923c, 254).

Wilson's forte was locating and explaining dislocations in dramatic writing that disrupt metre or meaning, or that render the plot, time scheme or characterization imperfect; from what seemed to him awkward joins Wilson diagnosed revision. Detecting most of the problems found by the latest editors of *Measure for Measure*, Wilson rightly diagnosed adaptation and 'additions by a post-Shakespearian reviser' (Shakespeare 1922b, 110), while sticking to his entirely implausible idea that F was put together from actors' parts (1922b, 113). For a reprint-with-revisions of his edition, Wilson maintained this line on the actors' parts (Shakespeare 1950) long after Chambers and W. W. Greg had shown its virtual impossibility (Chambers 1930, 153–5; Greg 1942, 134–8), the latter supplying the explanation that Ralph Crane's habits (such as the massing of stage directions) caused the features Wilson was trying to account for. This indicates Wilson's distance from mainstream New Bibliography, and even from the ordinary interaction of scholarship. He simply did not engage with the developing field.

Only one of Wilson's discoveries had a lasting impact. The first eighty-four lines of the last act of Q1 *A Midsummer Night's Dream* (1600) contain a series of mislined verse passages, three to six lines long, that are interlarded in speeches otherwise properly lined. With the mislined passages removed, the dialogue retains perfect sense. Asking himself how a compositor could make such a peculiar set of errors, Wilson hit upon the passages being additions to the scene crammed into the margins of a manuscript with their lineation not marked. Inserting the passages in their rightful places, the compositor had only his wits to guide him on lineation (Shakespeare 1924a, 80–6). Editors found Wilson's explanation convincing, although his confidence in detecting the style of early Shakespeare in the properly lined material and late Shakespeare in the marginal material (indicating revision long after first composition) was not universally shared. Even if we leave aside the unconvincing claim about stylistic difference, Wilson had established that Shakespeare revised his writing, which was a substantial achievement not widely appreciated until the 1980s (pp. 133–46 above).

Wilson's *Hamlet* (Shakespeare 1934) contained no discussion of the textual situation, which was instead published as a pair of monographs (Wilson 1934a; 1934b). He had by this time abandoned the theory of continuous copy – he later wrote that he could not recall holding it (Shakespeare 1952b, 118) – and found that Q2 (1604–5) was based on authorial papers, available because the company 'had gone to the trouble of making out a clean prompt-book from Shakespeare's draft'. Part of the evidence that Q2's copy was an authorial manuscript was its very availability: it 'must have existed at some time or other; [so] what became of it' if it was not used (Wilson 1934a, 89)? Wilson's study was flawed by such lapses of logic, yet full of primary evidence gleaned from extensive close study of the early editions. For example, he provided the first collation of Q2's press variants (Wilson 1934a, 121–34) and his explanations of them, including the determination of the corrected and uncorrected states and which corrections are really miscorrections, appear largely unaltered in the latest edition (Shakespeare 2006b, 524–5). Wilson's main conclusions that Q2 was set from authorial papers and F from a transcript of the prompt-book are also largely accepted by modern editors, their differences from him focussing on the means – infidelity to copy or authorial revision – by which Q2 and F came to be so different and the possibility that the former influenced the latter, perhaps via its reprint Q3. As George Ian Duthie noted for a foreword to a 1963 reprint of Wilson's monographs on *Hamlet*, the bibliographical landscape had changed in the preceding three decades, with the Virginian school (pp. 54–80 above) rendering much of Wilson's work obsolete (Wilson 1963, xiv).

The last nine plays in the series were produced in collaboration with Duthie, J. C. Maxwell and Alice Walker. Before they officially became editors on the project, Maxwell and Walker helped with *Richard 3*, as seen in the discussion of the copy for Q1 and F (Shakespeare 1954f, 140–60). Compared to its predecessors, the three Henry 6 plays, this *Richard 3* edition was less idiosyncratic and more engaged with the current state of bibliographical knowledge. After the arrival of Duthie, Maxwell and Walker, the phrases 'I suggest' and 'I believe' that had become characteristic of the series' textual discussions were used less frequently, and citations of authorities went beyond the main works of Greg and Chambers to include recent articles. Discussing the authorship of *Pericles*, Maxwell concluded that acts three, four and five are by Shakespeare and the first two by someone else, perhaps George Wilkins (Shakespeare 1956, xii–xxv), and helping Wilson with *Othello* (Shakespeare 1957a, 121–35) Walker provided up-to-date engagement with research on compositor identification and habits, including advance access to Charlton Hinman's discoveries (pp. 74–5 above). Walker's own *Troilus and Cressida* used analyses of compositorial habits in Q (1609) and F and represents a high-point of contact between editorial practice and the development of theories and methodologies (Shakespeare 1957c, 122–34). The contact did not rub off on Wilson: his 1960 *Coriolanus* essentially reprinted an account of the textual situation he had given thirty-two years earlier (Shakespeare 1928, Introduction; 1960a, 130–7), and his disengagement from textual studies is apparent in the last play he worked on, *King Lear*, for which his contribution was almost entirely confined to the explanatory notes (Shakespeare 1960c, vii).

THE COMPLETE WORKS, EDITED BY PETER ALEXANDER (1951)

Peter Alexander was the first New Bibliographer to produce an edition of all the plays of Shakespeare. This is not the same as editing all the plays, for Alexander merely revised a Victorian text provided by his publisher (Murphy 2003, 237–43). That his edition was not the thorough revaluation that readers might have hoped for is clear from Alexander's decision to present the plays in the order in which they appeared in the 1623 Folio and to use line numbers from the Cambridge–Macmillan edition of 1863–6 rather than give fresh counts based on his own edition's typesetting (Shakespeare

1951b, v). Because he used two narrow text columns, Alexander's edition contains blocks of prose whose stated line numbers differ, often greatly, from a count of the lines before the reader's eyes. The edition contained only the scantest of surveys of the textual situation of Shakespeare's plays, with no account of Alexander's editorial procedures nor a collation or explanatory notes. Only an exhaustive manual comparison of each play against each early edition would reveal just how Alexander worked. The edition's influence on textual studies was marginal despite its popularity.

THE ARDEN SHAKESPEARE SECOND SERIES, GENERALLY EDITED BY UNA ELLIS-FERMOR, HAROLD F. BROOKS, HAROLD JENKINS AND BRIAN MORRIS (1951–1982)

The second series of the Arden Shakespeare was launched specifically in response to a feeling that much of the first series had appeared too early to benefit from 'the immense body of scholarship which the first half of the twentieth century has contributed to the field' (Shakespeare 1951d, vii). Yet the original plan was to reuse the texts of the first series by stereotyping, confining the editors to minor alterations that did not demand extensive resetting. This plan was abandoned after the first two volumes (Shakespeare 1952a, vii), which describe themselves as 'based on' the texts of the first series (Shakespeare 1951c, iii; 1951d, iii). From Kenneth Muir's *King Lear* onwards, the editors were responsible for their texts, although they were free to borrow from their predecessors. M. R. Ridley, for example, used not only R. H. Case's text of *Antony and Cleopatra*, with altered punctuation, but his introduction too (Shakespeare 1954a). J. H. Walter elected to write his own introduction to *Henry 5*, with a three-page sketch of the textual situation, but got his text directly from the 1891–3 second edition of Cambridge–Macmillan (Shakespeare 1954d). The second Arden Shakespeare series, then, was initially conceived as a reprinting-with-revisions of the first rather than a fresh attempt to establish Shakespeare's texts. Throughout the 1950s, each volume began with a summary by the editor of its relation to the predecessor in the first series; by the end of the decade this was most often used to disavow the original plan and assert editorial independence.

The new scholarship that made the first series obsolete was foregrounded in the extended introductions to the plays, which took on a relatively uniform style of beginning with the facts of the early editions' publication, the provenance of their copy, dating the composition and reporting records of first performance. These facts were articulated using the latest research and with New Bibliography much in evidence; only with these matters out of the way did editors feel free to address the literary merits of their plays. The introductions were given roman numeral pagination despite being much too long for its convenient use, until Philip Brockbank broke with the convention to use arabic numbers (Shakespeare 1976). As a guide to editorial practice, R. B. McKerrow's *Prolegomena for the Oxford Shakespeare* remained dominant until the ramifications of W. W. Greg's 'The Rationale of Copy-Text' were fully absorbed (pp. 30–46 above). Thus, as 'a devoted disciple of McKerrow', Richard David promised a *Love's Labour's Lost* that 'kept to the only primary text we have, the 1598 Quarto, wherever a conceivable explanation can be made out for its reading' (Shakespeare 1951c, li).

In choice of copy-text, the clearest consequence of New Bibliography that set the second series apart from the first was the newly enfranchised editors' willingness to base their editions on good quartos in preference to their Folio counterparts, as Wilson had been doing for some time in the New Shakespeare. General editor Una Ellis-Fermor did not impose uniformity on the series, so in his *Cymbeline* J. M. Nosworthy was allowed to make no mention of the textual situation, remarking only his intention to preserve as much of F's distinctiveness (including its 'picturesque ... use of brackets') as modern reading conventions would permit (Shakespeare 1955a, ix). In general, though, even editors not much concerned with matters textual took pains to show that they were up-to-date. T. S. Dorsch reported that Shakespeare's spellings, as discovered by the New Bibliographers in Hand D of *Sir Thomas More* and good quartos (pp. 23–4 above), are absent in Folio *Julius Caesar* so it presumably was not printed from authorial papers (Shakespeare 1955b, xxiii). Dorsch also sketched Charlton Hinman's latest findings from collation of Folger Shakespeare Library First Folios (pp. 74–5 above), as did Frank Kermode when given a chance to revise his edition of *The Tempest* (Shakespeare 1958, lxxxix–xciii).

The first of the Arden Shakespeares to be edited by a groundbreaking New Bibliographer was John Russell Brown's *The Merchant of Venice* (Shakespeare 1955c), in which the textual situation was explained by reference to the latest scholarship, including Brown's publications on the compositors of the 1600 quarto (pp. 56–7 above), whose edition formed the basis of his. Knowing these men's habits to be conservative, Brown emended little; this was the first time such a consideration bore directly upon editorial practice. As if to prove, however, that the New Bibliographical methodology could be dangerously misused, Andrew S. Cairncross 'deduced' that Folio *2 Henry 6* and *3 Henry 6* were printed in part from Q3 (1619) because they occasionally agreed against Q1 and Q2 (Shakespeare

1957b; 1964). Cairncross's blindness to the principle that only agreements-in-error are strong evidence drew heavy fire from other researchers (pp. 33–4 above). G. K. Hunter shared the new interest in looking at the early editions as physical objects, and from the first page of his introduction to *All's Well that Ends Well* (Shakespeare 1959a) he attempted to account for the patterns of Folio speech prefix variation in terms of the order of printing of particular gatherings as indicated by headline reuse. In a similar vein, H. J. Oliver reported recent bibliographical analysis of *Timon of Athens*'s anomalous position in the 1623 Folio (included initially to fill a gap meant for *Troilus and Cressida*), and added to it a consideration, in the light of Folio compositor B's habits, of the play's many oddities and contradictions (Shakespeare 1959b). Only with the ground thus surveyed was he prepared to give a tentative opinion on the nature of the underlying copy.

A. R. Humphreys's introduction to his *1 Henry 4* was the first to offer a section devoted to 'Editorial Methods' that reported what he did and conveyed to the reader the complexity of certain problems (Shakespeare 1960b). 'Modernization of proper names is not easy', nor is it clear what to do with words like Hotspur's 'Parmacitie' (Shakespeare 1598a, B2^v; 1960b, lxxvii). By the early 1960s certain pronouncements typical of New Bibliography became routine in Arden Shakespeare editions, such as R. A. Foakes's interpretation of inconsistencies in the speech prefixes of Folio *The Comedy of Errors* as signs of authorial copy, since the book-keeper 'would need to regularize them' (Shakespeare 1962, xii). The early results of collation of exemplars of the 1623 Folio and the identification of compositors and their habits (pp. 54–75 above) began to appear in editors' introductions, as with J. H. P. Pafford's *The Winter's Tale* (Shakespeare 1963) and J. W. Lever's *Measure for Measure* (Shakespeare 1965). Indeed, editions that did not go into details thrown up by the new approaches began to look exceptional. Reliance upon Greg's simple rules (pp. 38–54 above) for telling authorial papers from theatrical copy (in this case as the copy for a transcript), which is dangerous in the absence of corroborating evidence, is apparent in the *Twelfth Night* of J. M. Lothian and T. W. Craik (Shakespeare 1975, xix–xxii): they found directions such as '*and other Lords*', '*and Saylors*' and '*and Attendants*' (Shakespeare 1623, Y2^r, Y3^r) to be too imprecise for theatrical copy.

Depending on who was editing it, a second series Arden Shakespeare might say nothing about the play in performance or as much as fifteen pages (in an introduction of eighty-nine pages), as in Brockbank's *Coriolanus* (Shakespeare 1976). Not until almost the completion of the series did one of its general editors contribute an edition, when Harold F. Brooks edited *A Midsummer Night's Dream* (Shakespeare 1979). We have seen that the high-water mark New Bibliography of Brian Gibbons's *Romeo and Juliet* (Shakespeare 1980b) was critiqued by Randall McLeod (pp. 132–3 above). As late as 1981, twelve years after D. F. McKenzie showed it to be untrue, Antony Hammond insisted that seriatim setting of a quarto would prevent any piece of type recurring within a gathering (that is, a sheet) and hence that such recurrence proves setting by formes (Shakespeare 1981, 21–22). Since printing of the inner forme (1^v, 2^r 3^v, 4^r) may proceed after seven of the sheet's eight pages have been set, there is nothing to prevent pieces of type from these four pages appearing on 4^v (the page that completes the outer forme) if the inner forme were first distributed. In the event, Hammond found recurrence on pages other than 4^v, so setting by formes was in this case proven, but his failure to indicate that this was the clinching evidence (it was buried in a footnote, its significance unremarked) is characteristic of the slow uptake of McKenzie's warnings (pp. 81–97 above). As befits his play, *Richard 3*, Hammond used nearly half of his 45,000-word introduction to describe the textual situation. The inflation of introductions as the series approached its end was marked: Harold Jenkins needed nearly 70,000 words for his *Hamlet* (Shakespeare 1982a). The end of the series overlapped with publications by the Oxford *Complete Works* editors and the first volume in the Oxford Shakespeare single-play series. Stanley Wells's work on modernizing spelling (pp. 167–8) clearly persuaded the Arden Shakespeare general editors, who openly regretted the early volumes in their series retaining archaic spellings such as *murther* for *murder* and *vild* for *vile* (Shakespeare 1982a, 77).

THE PELICAN SHAKESPEARE, GENERALLY EDITED BY ALFRED HARBAGE (1956–1969)

This series came about because of protective contractual arrangements between the owners of the imprints Penguin Books and Pelican Books (Shakespeare 1969d, ix; Wells 2006, 40–2). Between 1956 and 1967, it produced individual volumes of thirty-seven plays (those in the Folio plus *Pericles*) and two of poetry, each edited by one of a team of scholars including the New Bibliographers Madeleine Doran, Brents Stirling, Fredson Bowers, Charlton Hinman, Robert K. Turner Junior and George Walton Williams, as well as leading critics of the day such as Northrop Frye and Jonas A. Barish. Yet the series was noticeably underpowered in its theoretical bases. None of the plays shows a systematic rethinking of the textual situation, although Alfred Harbage later assured readers that each text had been 'constructed from that of the original quartos and folio in the light of the new principles of bibliographical study that have evolved in recent years' (Shakespeare 1969d, ix). Few of the volumes contained complete collations and most offered no more than a sentence or two about the early editions. In all cases the editing principle was essentially R. B. McKerrow's best-text approach (pp. 30–7 above) with no overt responses to the complexities arising from W. W. Greg's theorizing of authority being split between editions (pp. 44–6 above).

When the series was complete, the texts were combined as three volumes (comedies and romances, histories and poems, tragedies) and a single-volume complete works (Shakespeare 1969a; 1969b; 1969c; 1969d). For the latter Cyrus Hoy supplied an essay on 'The Original Texts' and Harbage one on 'Editions and Current Variant Readings' (Shakespeare 1969d, 40–4, 44–50). Both were up-to-date accounts of the state of knowledge and discussed in abstract terms the problems of editing Shakespeare, but neither was able to move directly from theory to practice by showing what had been done in the Pelican Shakespeare, evidently because of the series' lack of a coherent editorial rationale. Thus Hoy's discussion of Charlton Hinman's identification of compositorial stints in the 1623 Folio ended with 'some knowledge of the habits and degree of competence of particular compositors is useful to the modern editor' (1969d, 43) but he gave no examples from the edition, and Harbage's table of variants was only an 'illustrative sampling ... with no indication of those preferred by the Pelican editors' (1969d, 46). Given the calibre of the editorial team, this project appears to have missed a considerable opportunity.

THE DRAMATIC WORKS IN THE BEAUMONT AND FLETCHER CANON, GENERALLY EDITED BY FREDSON BOWERS (1966–1996)

In the ten volumes of this old-spelling series, individual plays were edited by a team comprising Fredson Bowers, George Walton Williams, Robert K. Turner Junior, Hans Walter Gabler, L. A. Beaurline and Cyrus Hoy, each taking a few plays. In the first volume Bowers outlined the team's textual approach, explicitly reliant on W. W. Greg's theorizing of authority being split between two early editions. Press variants resulting from proof correction were not automatically admitted since, as Bowers had long argued, there is often no evidence that copy was consulted (Beaumont and Fletcher 1966, x–xi) and hence the uncorrected setting, made with the copy in sight, has greater authority (p. 76 above). The editors were conservative in altering punctuation and attempted 'to avoid finical or sophisticating emendation' of substantives (Beaumont and Fletcher 1966, xi–xii). In every regard, the edition represented high New Bibliography and had the project sooner got around to *All is True* and *The Two Noble Kinsmen*, Shakespeare's collaborations with John Fletcher, it would have been in the vanguard of Shakespeare editions. Both plays were edited by Bowers (Beaumont and Fletcher 1989), the former under the 1623 Folio's title *Henry VIII* and incorporating Hoy's groundbreaking linguistic and stylometric research to determine which author wrote which parts (Hoy 1962). Hoy's work took into account the known spelling habits of Folio compositors in order to settle on authorial preferences that could reliably distinguish Shakespeare and Fletcher, and Bowers refined the methodology (Beaumont and Fletcher 1989, 5–6) in the light of Gary Taylor's claimed discovery of further compositors H, I and J, unknown in 1962 (pp. 171–2 above). Bowers edited *The Two Noble Kinsmen* with much the same concerns, but interpreted the marginal readying notes and stage directions in the 1634 quarto (our only authority) as evidence of theatrical annotation in the printer's copy, either a prompt-book or more likely one of the intermediate transcripts that he thought would be created as a play was being readied for performance (pp. 65–6 above; Beaumont and Fletcher 1989, 149–56). Bowers removed the theatricalizing marginalia that were merely reminders to prepare properties – such as '2 Hearses ready ...' (Fletcher and Shakespeare 1634, c3^v) – but left in 'calls for trumpets, cornets, and the like ... as useful guides to production even though not authorial' (1989, 163).

THE NEW PENGUIN SHAKESPEARE, GENERALLY EDITED BY T. J. B. SPENCER AND STANLEY WELLS (1967–2005)

The genesis and logic of this series is described in Wells 2006. In guidance to editors, Stanley Wells wrote that 'The scholarship ... should be immaculate, but this edition is not intended to rival the new [that is, second series] Arden'; rather, editors should aim to answer 'questions that the reader of a Pelican book is likely to put' (Wells and Wardman [1965], Section 'A. General'). The editions have become popular with theatre practitioners because the pages on which the script appears are clean: notes and collations are confined to the end of the book. As well as avoiding distraction, this enables theatre directors to dismantle two copies and paste the leaves into a scrapbook, giving plenty of room for directorial notes around the dialogue. Many prompt-books in the archives of the Royal Shakespeare Company were made this way. The layout of textual material was consistent across the series, every volume containing a brief 'Account of the Text'. Even where these reported substantial original research by the editor, as in Peter Davison's *1 Henry 4*, the account was kept to fewer than 4,000 words (Shakespeare 1968a, 243–52), and most were scarcely a quarter of that length. Denied the use of references to significant bodies of research (other than via a list of 'Further Reading'), these accounts necessarily read like statements of uncontested facts rather than engagements with the ongoing textual debates, and New Bibliographical certainties appeared in their least qualified forms. For *Richard 3*, E. A. J. Honigmann reduced the complexities of Q1 (1597) to a '[memorially] reconstructed text … perhaps for provincial performance' and the debate about the copy for F to 'Some think … others, that … others, that' (Shakespeare 1968c, 242, 243). Showing just what can be done in under 2,000 words, John Kerrigan's account of the textual situation of *Love's Labour's Lost* (Shakespeare 1982c, 241–7) was a masterpiece of concise expression. By contrast, G. K. Hunter unwisely attempted to convey W. W. Greg's account (pp. 61–4 above) of the proofing of Q1 *King Lear* (1608), compressing it to near unintelligibility (Shakespeare 1972, 316–17).

Editions made by those active in bibliographical research such as Davison, Wells and E. A. J. Honigmann were typically New Bibliographical albeit without giving detailed explanations of their textual principles. For *Richard 2*, Wells incorporated into his edition based on Q1 (1597) those elements of theatricalization such as trumpet calls that appear only in F, on the grounds that they must have been supplied for performance, but otherwise he was 'conservative in adopting Folio readings where Quarto ones are acceptable' because we do not know that F's alterations were 'authoritatively' made (Shakespeare 1969e, 270). In such a case, where a quarto reprint was annotated by consultation of the theatrical manuscript to make copy for F, Wells's Oxford *Complete Works* took a markedly different line on F's authority, the theorizing of which is here identified as 'new' New Bibliography (pp. 173–6 above). R. L. Smallwood was unexceptionally reflective of mainstream New Bibliography in finding speech prefix and stage direction irregularities 'irrelevant to the conditions of the Elizabethan stage' (Shakespeare 1974a, 352) and indicative of authorial papers forming the Folio copy for *King John*. After an initial flurry of nineteen plays in the late 1960s, the series slowed, producing eleven in the 1970s, six in the 1980s and none in the 1990s. The series was completed early in the new millennium by Sonia Massai and Jacques Berthoud's *Titus Andronicus* (Shakespeare 2001b) and John Pitcher's *Cymbeline* (Shakespeare 2005a). With few editions completed between 1980 and 2000, there is little evidence from which to gauge the effect of New Textualism. Massai and Berthoud's edition (like several others) was justly criticized by Brian Vickers for ignoring the considerable evidence that George Peele wrote the first act of *Titus Andronicus* (Vickers 2002, 210). Coinciding with the completion of the initial series, a fresh one was started by reprinting the old texts with newly written introductions and commentaries.

THE NORTON FACSIMILE, EDITED BY CHARLTON HINMAN, 1968, SECOND EDITION WITH A NEW INTRODUCTION BY PETER W. M. BLAYNEY (1996)

Upon returning from the Korean War, Charlton Hinman announced his intention to collate all seventy-nine exemplars of the 1623 First Folio at the Folger Shakespeare Library in Washington DC (Hinman 1953, 280 n.2, 282 n.4), which project, although not completed, led to a monumental book (Hinman 1963a; 1963b). The logical corollary was publication of an idealized facsimile of the Folio: who better to show readers what it would have looked like if its makers had been able to work to the very best of their capability? The Norton facsimile became the standard means for pursuing research on the Folio, displacing Sidney Lee's (Shakespeare 1902a), and its Through Line Numbering is widely used for referencing. New Textualists in the 1980s and 1990s complained that Hinman misrepresented the material reality of the Folio and the labour that went into it (pp. 192–4 above). Of all possible targets for this accusation, Hinman was the least deserving: he spent more time studying the differences between exemplars than anyone before or since. The objections were based on critical and philosophical prejudices transposed into the field of bibliography.

In 1996, Peter W. M. Blayney's new introduction contradicted Hinman on key points. For example, rather than falling into the binate distinction of foul papers/prompt-book, Blayney described surviving theatrical manuscripts as showing great variety, including authorial papers annotated for theatrical purposes, scribal transcripts with authorial annotations and copies made as gifts for patrons. Hinman believed in pursuing each play in its final form as intended by Shakespeare, but Blayney saw them as works forever in motion, altered by Shakespeare and others for various purposes at various times. Hinman thought that the 1623 Folio was relatively poorly printed – the compositors were not faithful to their copy and the proofreading and correction were scant – but Blayney argued that it was well made. Hinman had overstated the number of press variants in the exemplars he collated, wrongly treating imperfect inking and slippage of type during machining as equivalent to conscious alterations made during stop-press correction. As D. F. McKenzie pointed out (p. 83 above), all rounds of proofreading and correction prior to the printing run leave no trace in the final book, and Blayney thought Hinman had underestimated the labour spent on getting the text of the Folio right. In all, Blayney reckoned that Hinman's collation uncovered just one press variant that matters to editors, there being four others of this kind already known. Hinman was wrong, Blayney insisted, in thinking he could calculate the size of the print run from the need to balance compositing and presswork: concurrent printing (pp. 81–4 above) invalidates such calculations. Blayney updated Hinman's table showing which compositor set which part of the Folio, using the studies that appeared after Hinman's research ceased (pp. 89–97 above).

THE RIVERSIDE SHAKESPEARE, EDITED BY G. BLAKEMORE EVANS (1974)

This was the first single-volume complete works edition executed entirely along New Bibliographical lines, although others had been influenced by the new thinking at certain points. Rather than adopt an existing text (as Peter Alexander had done, pp. 250–1 above), G. Blakemore Evans started with 'a new collation and study of the early substantive editions' (Shakespeare 1974b, 39). After sketching the development of New Bibliography, Evans indicated that his approach was McKerrowian best-text editing (pp. 30–7 above) rather than eclectic editing: 'an editor today, having chosen for what he considers sound reasons a particular copy-text, will adhere to that copy-text unless he sees substantial grounds for departing from it' (Shakespeare 1974b, 37). However, where the authority of the early editions is disputable, Evans used typography to show variants. Using examples from *King Lear*, Evans demonstrated how an editor might represent the decision that F reflects a theatrical cut where Q1 (1608) shows the original authorial writing before the cut was made. Necessarily, according to Evans, an edition based on F would undo the theatrical cut, and he put the restored words in square brackets: '*Glou*. He cannot be such a monster – | [*Edm*. Nor is not, sure. | *Glou*. To his father, that so tenderly and entirely loves him. Heaven and earth!] Edmund, seek him out' (Shakespeare 1974b, *King Lear*, 1.2.94–7). Thus without turning to the collation, a reader can see that F (when modernized) reads '*Glou*. He cannot be such a monster – Edmund, seek him out' (Shakespeare 1608, c2^r; 1623, qq3^v). Fifty lines later, Edmund's Q1-only account of the prediction he has read, 'as of unnaturalness between the child and the parent ... Come, come' (1608, C2^v), was likewise marked off with square brackets by Evans. For extensive differences such as the mock trial in 3.6, Evans's unobtrusive square brackets are easily missed, especially where further pairs are nested within the main pair.

In marking his edition this way, Evans anticipated the New Textualist desire to keep the reader aware of the differences between the early editions (pp. 196–7 above). Evans was also innovative in breaking from the line-numbering of the Cambridge–Macmillan edition and its derivatives, and he adopted Charlton Hinman's Through Line Numbering (from his Folio facsimile of 1968) within the running headers of his modernized text. Unlike rival single-volume complete works, Evans's provided textual notes registering his emendations (including those of punctuation where it affects meaning) and readings not adopted from substantive early editions. Evans's edition was used for the first modern-spelling computer-made concordance of Shakespeare (Spevack 1965–80). The distinction between syllabic and non-syllabic *-ed* word-endings Evans maintained in verse (by printing *-ed* and *-'d* respectively) but for prose all were represented as *-'d*. Unfortunately Evans's opinion of whether single-line speeches are verse or prose cannot be determined because he printed the speech prefix on the same line as the start of the speaker's dialogue. (Other editions maintain for single-line speeches the general distinction of printing the prefix on the same line as the speech for prose and on a line of its own above the speech for verse.) Evans retained 'a selection of Elizabethan spelling forms that reflect, or may reflect, a distinctive contemporary pronunciation' (Shakespeare 1974b, 39); Wells's criticism of this practice has since won almost universal assent (pp. 167–8 above), with only David Bevington maintaining a public demurral (Bevington 2004).

THE OXFORD SHAKESPEARE, GENERALLY EDITED BY STANLEY WELLS (1982–PRESENT)

The Oxford Shakespeare series of one-play-per-volume editions began to appear as editing of the Oxford *Complete Works*, also led by Stanley Wells, was under way. The first volume was *Henry 5* by Wells's assistant (later, co-editor) on the Oxford *Complete Works*, Gary Taylor (Shakespeare 1982b). Building on his essays in Wells's book *Modernizing Shakespeare's Spelling* (pp. 170–1 above), Taylor's edition was the first fruits of the 'new' New Bibliography. But there was no programme to make the series follow the Oxford *Complete Works* in its principles or execution; Wells gave individual editors considerable freedom. In his edition, Kenneth Muir accepted Taylor's new argument that Q *Troilus and Cressida* (1609) derives from foul papers and F from the prompt-book (p. 172 above), but did not accept 'all the conclusions that Taylor derives from it' (Shakespeare 1982d, 3). Although he used the 'new' New Bibliography's term control text (the authority for substantive readings, as opposed to the copy-text, the authority for accidentals), Muir chose Q to be his, while the Oxford *Complete Works*, from the same argument of Taylor's, chose F (Wells *et al.* 1987, 426). A number of the early editors for the Oxford Shakespeare, such as H. J. Oliver, T. W. Craik and David Bevington, had extensive previous experience with other series and publishers, and did not embrace Wells and Taylor's 'new' New Bibliography. Editing *Hamlet*, however, G. R. Hibbard collaborated extensively with the Oxford *Complete Works*'s editors and their approaches were essentially the same (Shakespeare 1987, 131; Wells *et al.* 1987, 402).

This, then, is a diverse and heterogeneous series and little can be generalized about it. The three decades of its production span the rise of the New Textualism, and in general the series has resisted that movement's pressure, manifest in rival series, to accord a place to each of the competing early editions. However, for *Romeo and Juliet* (Shakespeare 2000e) Jill L. Levenson insisted on including a fully edited and modernized Q1 version to supplement her main Q2-based text, and Wells's *King Lear* (Shakespeare 2000c) was based on the 1608 quarto, which he treated as distinct from the 1623 Folio edition. Peter Holland's *A Midsummer Night's Dream* (Shakespeare 1994) was singled out by Paul Werstine for its reiteration of the New Bibliographical saw that variant speech prefixes and imprecise or permissive stage directions are indicative of authorial copy (Werstine 1998a). An indication of how different approaches bear on editorial results can be had by comparing Jay L. Halio's *All is True* (edited as *Henry 8*), which devoted just half a paragraph to the copy for F (citing W. W. Greg and John Dover Wilson as authorities) and nothing to the special problems of editing a collaborative play, with Gordon McMullan's rival Arden Shakespeare edition, which explored these matters at length (pp. 227–8 above; Shakespeare 1999a; Shakespeare 2000b). John Jowett's exemplary handling of the difficulties of editing *Richard 3* usefully illustrates the refinement of 'new' New Bibliography since 1986 (Shakespeare 2000d). To contrast the afterlives of 'new' New Bibliography and New Textualism one may compare Roger Warren's *Pericles* (Shakespeare 2004b), which takes even further the Oxford *Complete Works*'s reconstruction of the play using George Wilkins's novelization, with Suzanne Gossett's Arden

Shakespeare edition (Shakespeare 2004a), which is less interventionist and more concerned with the theoretical difficulties arising from collaboration.

THE NEW CAMBRIDGE SHAKESPEARE, GENERALLY EDITED BY PHILIP BROCKBANK, BRIAN GIBBONS, A. R. BRAUNMULLER AND ROBIN HOOD (1984–PRESENT), INCLUDING THE EARLY QUARTOS SUBSERIES (1994–PRESENT)

Had the original publication schedule been kept to, this series would have preceded the Oxford Shakespeare series into print. Brockbank's editorial guidelines indicate aims close to those of the rival Oxford Shakespeare, although the intention to combine the individual New Cambridge Shakespeare volumes to make a complete works necessitated greater uniformity within the series (Brockbank 1979). By contrast, the Oxford *Complete Works* edition was independent of the Oxford series, sharing only the name and Stanley Wells as general editor. In its editorial aims the New Cambridge Shakespeare stands halfway between the second Arden Shakespeare series and the Oxford *Complete Works*. Like the Arden, the New Cambridge Shakespeare drew upon the latest work of New Bibliography: when dealing with a Folio-only play, editors were enjoined to begin with the printing and give 'A description of the compositors' stints' (Brockbank 1979, 22). Unlike the Arden, the series would be explicitly 'attentive ... to the realisation of the plays on the stage' and 'the experience and needs of actors and directors [would] be taken into account' (Brockbank 1979, 1). The editorial guidelines were written just as Brockbank was appointed Director of the Shakespeare Institute to replace T. J. B. Spencer (1961–78), the general editor of the New Penguin Shakespeare. Spencer had relocated the Institute from Stratford-upon-Avon to Birmingham and Brockbank succeeded in relocating it back, 'to restore and promote a closer relationship with the theatre' (Dobson and Wells 2001, 'Shakespeare Institute'). Although the theatre would be explicitly a concern of editors in the series, there was no redefinition of the editorial process to accommodate it, which development marks off the 'new' New Bibliography as a distinct practice.

The New Cambridge Shakespeare editorial guidelines preceded Wells's systematic rethinking of modernization (pp. 167–8) and were vague: 'inconsequentially archaic and quaint' spellings were to be modernized but the 'expressive and characteristically Shakespearean' were to be retained (Brockbank 1979, 1). Editors were free to 'dislodge an accepted scene division ... if the grounds are judged sufficient' (Brockbank 1979, 10) and if the name Imogen (from *Cymbeline*) were thought a misreading then the editor 'should not be deterred by tradition from restoring *Innogen*' (Brockbank 1979, 14). The evidence of Hand D of *Sir Thomas More* would count in respect of punctuation, and since it showed Shakespeare pointing lightly it was hoped editors would do so too (Brockbank 1979, 15). The plan was to have just 'A select collation' at the end of the book with 'no apparatus ... to appear on the page' (Brockbank 1979, 1, 18), but this layout was abandoned before the appearance of the first volume, R. A. Foakes's *A Midsummer Night's Dream* (Shakespeare 1984a), which represents mature New Bibliography at its best. Foakes pondered how far Shakespeare himself was behind the theatricalizations – the advances upon the apparently authorial Q1 (1600) – that are reflected in the Folio edition, such as Egeus replacing Philostrate as the manager of mirth in the last act. Although there is 'no reason to doubt' that such changes 'came from the prompt-book', the 'half-hearted' way that F's copy, Q2 (1619), was annotated from the prompt-book dissuaded Foakes from adopting the changed readings (Shakespeare 1984a, 143). Fulfilling the series' aims of taking performance seriously, Foakes included twelve half and full-page pictures of the play in performance, including two sketches of ways to stage certain moments.

The ample warnings of uncertainty about the reuse of skeletons, the identification of compositors, and the complexities of stop-press correction that were available by the mid-1980s (pp. 158–62 above) did not deter Norman Sanders from pronouncing confidently on these matters, and even giving a version of W. W. Greg's account of proofing (pp. 61–4 above), in his *Othello* (Shakespeare 1984b, 194). However, Sanders's handling of the Q1/F differences was nuanced and brought him to the conclusion that each might well derive from a distinct Shakespearian manuscript and hence they are separated by revision (Shakespeare 1984b, 206–7). In this case, Sanders decided, the revision was not extensive and Q1/F could be conflated without great harm so long as the interventions were properly recorded. Editing *Hamlet*, Philip Edwards accepted that the Folio reflects the theatricalized version and Q2 (1604–5) the authorial, but thought that preparations for performance were 'going forward without his [Shakespeare's] cooperation' (Shakespeare 1985, 24). The bulk of the Q2/F differences arose after Shakespeare handed the script to the actors and his engagement with it ended:

The play then became the property of these colleagues who began to prepare it for the stage. At this point what one can only call degeneration began, and it is at this point that we should arrest and freeze the play, for it is sadly true that the nearer we get to the stage, the further we are getting from Shakespeare. (Shakespeare 1985, 32)

Edwards was lamenting what he saw as the debasement of the text, and he dispensed with the series' usual brief section on 'Textual Analysis' in order to treat the subject at length near the start of his introduction. He was by no means opposed to the theatre in principle, as selective quotation of him (as in Shakespeare 2006b, 493) occasionally suggests: his edition was as lavishly illustrated as any other in the series with pictures of actors at work and suggestions of possible staging.

Michael Hattaway's *1 Henry 6* was up-to-date on everything, his 'Textual Analysis' section heavily footnoted with the latest research (Shakespeare 1990a); likewise his editions of the other two Henry 6 plays. By contrast, L. A. Beaurline was still telling readers of *King John* that speech prefix variation ruled out a prompt-book as Folio copy and that with setting by formes 'the balance between composition and press work was easier to achieve' than it would otherwise have been (Shakespeare 1990b, 184, 188). Taking over as General Editor upon Brockbank's death, Brian Gibbons edited *Measure for Measure* without serious consideration of the ample evidence that it survives only in the form of an adaptation by Thomas Middleton (Shakespeare 1991). In 1994 a new subseries, Early Quartos, began with plays not easily conflated, *King Lear*, *Richard 3* and *Hamlet*, and those for which the early editions' relationship to performance and to F is uncertain, *The Taming of a Shrew* (1594) and Q1 *Henry 5*. Under the influence of New Textualism, the series provided modernized edited texts of the quartos together with reconsideration of the textual and theatrical theories constructed to account for them. Andrew Gurr's key contributions to the current debates about theatrical documents and the editing of Shakespeare (pp. 222–5 above) emerged directly from his work preparing the volume on Q1 *Henry 5* for this series (Shakespeare 2000a).

It is peculiar that Doreen DelVecchio and Antony Hammond's *Pericles* appeared in the main series rather than the Early Quartos subseries, for their conservative approach suited the latter (Shakespeare 1998). Rather than correcting the manifest errors of Q1 (1609) by reference to George Wilkins's prose novelization and their own judgement, DelVecchio and Hammond retained every reading that had the slightest purchase upon meaning, and many more that had none. Another misstep of the series was the reprinting after ten years of Janis Lull's *Richard 3* (Shakespeare 1999b) in an 'Updated Edition' that solemnly evaluated the evidence for Q1 (1597) being based on a memorial reconstruction, using exactly the words of her original edition and concluding that 'Without evidence external to the two texts, however, nothing can be proved' (Shakespeare 2009, 222). Jowett had in the meantime disproved the memorial reconstruction hypothesis for this play, solely on internal evidence (pp. 125–6 above).

THE COMPLETE WORKS, EDITED BY STANLEY WELLS, GARY TAYLOR, JOHN JOWETT AND WILLIAM MONTGOMERY (1986)

The Oxford *Complete Works* comprised an original-spelling edition, a modernized edition, a *Textual Companion* and an electronic version of the modernized edition distributed in ASCII format on $5^{1}/_{4}$-inch floppy disks for the IBM personal computer (and compatibles). The project's major innovation was the displacement of the editorial goal from an idealized version of the last pre-rehearsal script (a fair copy of the authorial papers) to the script of the first performances, as refined and revised in rehearsal. In line with standard New Bibliography, this idealized script was to be recovered in a form as close as possible to the author's spellings, so its corresponding document in the real world would be a first performance prompt-book made by marking up authorial fair copy. The hope of coming close to such an ideal for the accidentals (or as the project called them, incidentals) was not held to be great, but for the substantives the stage-centred approach made the Oxford editors prefer many readings from the Folio over good quartos based on authorial papers. This was true even where the Folio essentially reprinted a quarto if that quarto were first annotated by consultation of a manuscript later than authorial papers, such as a prompt-book or transcript of it. Also arising from the new stage-centred approach was a willingness to incorporate details from bad quartos where these reflected performance decisions later than those in another edition. Thus Q1 *Henry 5* (1600) seems to reflect a decision, made later than the authorial papers behind F, to give the Dauphin's actions at Agincourt to Bourbon (Wells and Taylor 1979, 102–5). Another notable aspect of the stage-centred approach to editing was to give plays and characters the names they had at the first performances, even where this overturned long-standing and familiar nomenclature. Oldcastle was the edition's new name for Falstaff in *1 Henry 4*, Innogen for Imogen in *Cymbeline*, *The Contention of York and Lancaster* for *2 Henry 6*, *Richard Duke of York* for *3 Henry 6* and *All is True* for *Henry 8*. The development and implementation of this stage-centred approach to editing, here called the 'new' New Bibliography, is discussed on pp. 167–89 above. A second edition (Shakespeare 2005b) added *Edward 3* to the canon and included all of *Sir Thomas More* where the first edition gave only the lines written by Shakespeare.

THE COMPLETE KING LEAR, EDITED BY MICHAEL WARREN (1989)

In response to the wide acceptance of his claim that *King Lear* exists as two distinct plays, Michael Warren produced a parallel-text edition of Q1 and F and a much more expensive 'complete' version using unbound facsimile leaves (Shakespeare 1989a; Shakespeare 1989c). The logic and limitations of this innovative publication, and responses to it, are discussed on p. 197 above.

SHAKESPEAREAN ORIGINALS: FIRST EDITIONS, GENERALLY EDITED BY GRAHAM HOLDERNESS AND BRYAN LOUGHREY (1992–1996)

This series offered cheap diplomatic reprints of each play by Shakespeare in the form in which it first reached the book-buying public. For some plays such as *Henry 5* this was a bad quarto (Shakespeare 1993a), for others such as *A Midsummer Night's Dream* a good quarto (Shakespeare 1996a), and for others again such as *Antony and Cleopatra* the Folio (Shakespeare 1995d). Except for turnovers, the lineation of the first edition was followed, but the pagination and columnation were not, and press variants were ignored. The series ended after publishing fifteen of the plays. The rationale of the series, the debates excited by it and its place in arguments about the editing of Shakespeare are discussed on pp. 191–6 above.

THE NEW FOLGER LIBRARY SHAKESPEARE, EDITED BY BARBARA A. MOWAT AND PAUL WERSTINE (1992–PRESENT)

This series shares something of the Shakespearean Originals series' approach to the materiality of dramatic writing arising from the conviction that we know so little about how the early editions were made and the provenance of their copy that editorial intervention ought to be minimized. However, Barbara A. Mowat and Paul Werstine knew more about textual matters than Graham Holderness and Bryan Loughrey and were more willing to use their knowledge to correct obvious errors. They saw no reason to fixate on the first edition and for some plays they thought a composite made from different early editions the best way to present the complexities of the case to the modern reader. All the plays except *The Two Noble Kinsmen* (which is forthcoming) have been published. The rationale of the series and its place in the debates about editing Shakespeare are discussed on pp. 197, 204 above.

THE ARDEN SHAKESPEARE THIRD SERIES, GENERALLY EDITED BY
RICHARD PROUDFOOT, DAVID SCOTT KASTAN, ANN THOMPSON AND
H. R. WOUDHUYSEN (1995–PRESENT)

This series can fairly be called a post-New Bibliography project: from the outset it embodied key aspects of the rejection of New Bibliography in the 1980s and 1990s. Whereas the second Arden Shakespeare series contained texts made by adjusting an existing edition, the third series' general editors promised editions 'Newly edited from the original quarto and folio editions' (Shakespeare 1995a, x). The general editors' preface made a firm commitment that editors would consider the plays in performance, which was an aspect left to the individual editors' preference in the first two series. (Notoriously, the introduction to Harold Jenkins's *Hamlet* of 1982, the longest in the second series, had no section on the stage history and a critical section attending to literary matters – poetic imagery, narrative structure, characterization – but not dramatic ones.) The general editors also made an explicit commitment to a principle of literary criticism that became prominent in the 1980s with the ascendancy of anti-elitism: that meaning is made equally by readers and writers (engaged with one another at the point of reception) and hence each 'new generation's encounter with Shakespeare' is unique and of its time (Shakespeare 1995a, x).

The first volume in the series, John Wilders's *Antony and Cleopatra*, had old school New Bibliography in it – authorial copy was diagnosed by, amongst other things, imprecise stage directions (Shakespeare 1995a, 78) – and refinements of what started as the Virginian school. T. H. Howard-Hill's detection of Folio compositor E by his comma-spacing habits was described as 'particularly strong because it relies not simply on spelling, which could be influenced by the manuscript copy, but on habits which are distinctively personal' (Shakespeare 1995a, 79). Such tests had been shown to be unreliable in the mid-1980s (pp. 159–60 above) and because Wilders applied directly the tests' results – in greater willingness to emend compositor E's pages than compositor B's – the risk of unwarranted intervention was real. Wilders used Charlton Hinman's discovery that Folio copy was cast off for setting by formes to explain, by space shortage, the mislineation of Pompey's speech 'No, Antony take the lot ... with feasting there' (Shakespeare 1623, xx5^r). Since this occurs in the second half of the gathering, where Hinman assumed seriatim setting, any necessary compression could be spread over this and the next three pages, which in this case show considerable spare room in the form of wide spacing around stage directions. Paul Werstine argued that where three compositors worked together, the second half of the quire might also have to be cast off (as well as the first) to enable two men to work on it at once (Werstine 1982), but this does not apply here since Wilders accepted the presence of just two compositors.

Editing *Henry 5*, T. W. Craik responded with parody to the 'new' New Bibliographical use of the bad quarto as indirect evidence of the final completion of Shakespeare's intention in performance (pp. 170–1 above): 'imagine Burbage as Bottom: "There are things in this history of Henry the Fifth that will never please"' (Shakespeare 1995b, 31). Craik found it implausible that Shakespeare was responsible for changes evident in the differences between the essentially authorial F and the performance-derived Q1. A third Arden Shakespeare edition to appear in this first year of the new series was Jonathan Bate's *Titus Andronicus*, which rejected the considerable evidence that George Peele was Shakespeare's co-author. Bate reported second-hand Andrew Q. Morton's conclusion that the odds of Peele's involvement are less than one in ten thousand million (Shakespeare 1995c, 83) even though his source, G. Harold Metz, mentioned this conclusion in order to distance himself from 'such unqualified statements' (Metz 1985, 155). Bate marked with brackets parts of the play that look like authorial false starts, preferring not to delete them or relegate them to appendices (as in the Oxford *Complete Works*) because he 'would like to see readers and directors trying out the alternatives and deciding for themselves' (Shakespeare 1995c, 103). Another editorial practice apparently responsive to the New Textualism was Bate's use of variable speech prefixes: Quintus and Martius are identified only as '2 SON' and '3 SON' in the first act because Shakespeare had not, at that point, developed them as individuals (Shakespeare 1995c, 95 n.1). For the scene of the killing of a fly in *Titus Andronicus* (3.2), which first appeared in the 1623 Folio, Bate's text switched to a different typeface to show that it is a later addition to the play.

Editing *King Lear*, R. A. Foakes had much larger textual differences to signal and he settled on conflating Q1 and F and using typographic notation that enclosed in superscripted '^{Q}...^{Q}' and '^{F}...^{F}' words appearing only in one of them (Shakespeare 1997b). But what about words that are subtly different rather than simply present/absent in each edition? Strictly, each such variant comprises a word that is present in Q1 and absent in F and a word that is absent in Q1 and present in F. Foakes did not treat the problem this way, but instead allowed certain variants to go unmarked other than in the collation because they are alternatives. For example, the Q1 line 'Sir I am made of the selfe same mettall that my sister is' (Shakespeare 1608, B2^r) has as its Folio counterpart 'I am made of that selfe-mettle as my Sister' (Shakespeare 1623, qq2^r). Without the principle that alternatives remain unmarked, Foakes's notation would have to show the line as '^{Q}Sir^Q I am made of ^{Q}the^{QF}that^F self ^{Q}same^Q mettle ^{Q}that^{QF}as^F my sister ^{Q}is^Q'. However, some words are clearly alternatives (*the* / *that* and *that* / *as*) and following Foakes's preference for F in such cases (Shakespeare 1997b, 149) would make the line '^{Q}Sir^Q I am made of that self ^{Q}same^Q mettle as my sister ^{Q}is^Q'. Foakes, however, gave the line as '^{Q}Sir^Q I am made of that self mettle as my sister' (Shakespeare 1997b, 1.1.69), confining to his collation all Q1/F differences except the appearance of 'Sir' only in Q1. That is, he treated whole phrases (*selfe same* / *self-* and *sister is* / *sister*) as alternatives for which he could prefer F. This approach required subjective judgement about verbal equivalence, which tugged against the impulse to show Q1 and F together at once. Readers who do not check the collation might gain the impression that Q1 and F differ only on the first word in this line, while readers who check the collation are left, as they are in other editions, to reconstruct the full extent of the difference for themselves.

Foakes's solution to the problem of two-text plays is, to date, unique in the series and recalls the typographic solutions invented by Barbara A. Mowat and Paul Werstine for their New Folger Library Shakespeare (pp. 196–7 above). For plays with a bad quarto, the Arden Shakespeare third series responded to the textual multiplicity by reproducing, at the back of the book, a photofacsimile of an exemplar of the early edition not used as the basis of the modern one. This has the considerable merit of presenting to readers unfamiliar versions of the plays that they would otherwise be unlikely to see, and the high quality of the reproductions make more expensive facsimile editions redundant for many purposes. On the other hand, the policy can seem like a refusal to commit oneself to the editorial task of turning a multiplicity of textual witnesses into a single piece of writing: if the bad quartos really are so different, do they not deserve their own editions, as the existence of the New Cambridge Shakespeare Early Quartos subseries suggests?

E. A. J. Honigmann's *Othello* was accompanied by a monograph on the textual problems of the play (Shakespeare 1996c; Honigmann 1996). The monograph was the subject of a vituperative review by Werstine (2000b) for its vestigial New Bibliography and, more fairly, for Honigmann's reliance upon Alice Walker's characterization of Folio compositor B's unreliability, which Werstine had long since overturned (pp. 96–7 above). Some Arden editors reconsidered the judgements embodied in the Oxford *Complete Works*, as when David Scott Kastan decided that Folio *1 Henry 4* merely reprints Q6 (1613), since its departures from it 'need not have resulted from anything more than an aggressive editorial hand and do not clearly imply access to an alternative authority for the text itself' (Shakespeare 2002, 115). The significance of Gordon McMullan's approach to collaborative drama in his edition of *All is True* is discussed on pp. 227–8 above. The influence of New Textualist thinking upon this series – manifest, for example, in the desire to leave stage directions imprecise and speech prefixes variable – is discussed on pp. 207–15 above. The limitations of Ann Thompson and Neil Taylor's policy of editing each of Q1 (1603), Q2 (1604–5) and Folio *Hamlet* independently, as if the others did not exist, are discussed on pp. 181–2 above. In general (and excluding Foakes's *King Lear* and Honigmann's *Othello*), the series is witness to the new orthodoxy that an editor cannot make an edition of the play itself conceived as a Platonic Form but only an edition of an extant early material embodiment of the play.

THOMAS MIDDLETON: THE COLLECTED WORKS, GENERALLY EDITED BY GARY TAYLOR AND JOHN LAVAGNINO (2007)

Three plays in the Thomas Middleton canon are partly or mainly by Shakespeare: *Timon of Athens*, *Measure for Measure* and *Macbeth*. The first of these was a collaboration between the two dramatists, and the others are adaptations of Shakespeare plays (of which the originals are lost) made by Middleton after Shakespeare's death. For the adapted plays, the editors Gary Taylor and John Jowett attempted to reconstruct the lost, pre-adaptation versions using their knowledge of Middleton's and Shakespeare's habits and characteristic phrasings. Taylor and Jowett were central figures in the 'new' New Bibliography and although their procedures here were not the same – a number of assumptions inherited from New Bibliography were dropped as no longer tenable – their extensive interventions in the received texts of the adaptations (both from the 1623 Shakespeare Folio) were as bold as their work on the 1986 Oxford *Complete Works*. Their views on the distinctive problems of editing collaborative drama are discussed on pp. 178, 226 above.

For what we might call the involuntary collaborations when Middleton adapted Shakespeare after the latter's death, Taylor and Jowett used typographic conventions to represent the script before and after the adaptation. This sounds like, but is distinct from, the typographic signals in The New Folger Library Shakespeare and R. A. Foakes's Arden Shakespeare edition of *King Lear* (pp. 196–7, 268–9 above) that represented the differences between early editions. Barbara A. Mowat and Paul Werstine's and Foakes's symbols indicated editorial reluctance to choose between readings, preferring a composite in which the joins remain visible, but Taylor and Jowett wished to display two layers of writing at once, breaking the composite into its parts. Instead of symbols, Taylor and Jowett varied the density of the ink on the page so that passages added or moved to their present location by Middleton are emboldened and passages he cut or moved from their present location are in grey rather than black ink. Thus, relocated passages appear twice, in grey where they used to be and in bold where they ended up. These editions were offered as genetic texts, named from the new field of genetic criticism that studies the processes of composition and revision by which literary works come into being (Bowman 1990; Deppman, Ferrer and Groden 2004). The means by which the plays' transformations were discerned and the pre-adaptation versions inferentially recovered were highly speculative, and Taylor and Jowett's departures from the only substantive early editions, in the 1623 Shakespeare Folio, are extensive. The departures were fully explained and the principles justified (Taylor and Lavagnino 2007, 383–98, 417–21, 681–703). As both editors pragmatically pointed out, there exist numerous editions of *Macbeth* and *Measure for Measure* that follow the Folio closely, so their experiments deprived no-one of access to the plays edited by conventional means, as they might if the same were tried with obscure plays in the Middleton canon.

Works cited

Adams, John Cranford. 1942. *The Globe Playhouse: Its Design and Equipment*. Cambridge MA. Harvard University Press.
Adorno, Theodor. 1973. *Negative Dialectics*. Trans. E. B. Ashton. London. Routledge.
Albright, Evelyn May. 1928. '*Dramatic Publication in England, 1580–1640*: A Reply [to W. W. Greg's Review].' *Review of English Studies*. o.s. 4. 193–202.
Alexander, Peter. 1924a. '*2 Henry VI* and the Copy for *The Contention* (1594).' *Times Literary Supplement* Number 1186 (9 October). 629–30.
  1924b. '*3 Henry VI* and *Richard, Duke of York*.' *Times Literary Supplement* Number 1191 (13 November). 730.
  1926. '*The Taming of a Shrew*.' *Times Literary Supplement* Number 1285 (16 September). 614.
  1928. '*The Taming of a Shrew*: A Letter to the Editor.' *Times Literary Supplement* Number 1375 (7 June). 430.
  1929. *Shakespeare's* Henry VI *and* Richard III. Introd. Alfred W. Pollard. Shakespeare Problems 3. Cambridge University Press.
Allott, Robert. 1600. *Englands Parnassus: Or the Choysest Flowers of Our Moderne Poets*. STC 378. London. N[icholas] L[ing], C[uthbert] B[urby] and T[homas] H[ayes].
Anonymous. 1594. *A Pleasant Conceited Historie, Called The Taming of a Shrew*. STC 23667 BEPD 120a. London. Peter Short sold by Cuthbert Burbie.
Anonymous. 1929. *The First Part of the Reign of King Richard the Second, or Thomas of Woodstock*. Ed. Wilhelmina P. Frijlinck. Malone Society Reprints. London. Malone Society.
Anonymous. 1938 for 1937. *Charlemagne, or the Distracted Emperor*. Ed. John Henry Walter. Malone Society Reprints. London. Malone Society.
Anonymous. 1972. '"Texts and Editors": Review of *Proof: The Yearbook of American Bibliographical and Textual Studies* volume 1 (1971) and *Studies in Bibliography* volume 25 (1972).' *Times Literary Supplement* Number 3666 (2 June). 640.
Arber, Edward (ed.). 1876. *A Transcript of the Registers of the Company of Stationers of London 1554–1640 AD*. Vol. 3: Text. Entries of Books to 11 July 1620; Entries of Freemen to 31 December 1640; Succession of Master Printers in London 1586–1636. 5 vols. London. Privately printed.

Baender, Paul. 1969. 'The Meaning of Copy-Text.' *Studies in Bibliography* 22. 311–18.

Bald, R. C. 1942. 'Evidence and Inference in Bibliography.' *English Institute Annual* volume for 1941. 159–81.

Barnes, Barnabe. 1607. *The Divils Charter: A Tragaedie Conteining the Life and Death of Pope Alexander the Sixt*. STC 1466 BEPD 252a(i). London. G[eorge] E[ld] for John Wright.

  1904. *The Devil's Charter*. Ed. R. B. McKerrow. Materialien zur kunde des alteren englischen Drama 6. Louvain. A. Uystpruyst.

Barthes, Roland. 1968. 'La Mort de l'auteur' ('The Death of the Author'). *Mantéia* 5. 12–17.

  1977. *Image–Music–Text*. Trans. Stephen Heath. London. Fontana.

Bateson, F. W. 1935. '"The Genuine Text": A Letter to the Editor.' *Times Literary Supplement* Number 1736 (9 May). 301.

Bawcutt, N. W. 2001. 'Renaissance Dramatists and the Texts of Their Plays.' *Research Opportunities in Renaissance Drama* 40. 1–24.

Bayfield, M. A. 1919a. 'Shakespeare's Hand in the Play of "Sir Thomas More": A Letter to the Editor.' *Times Literary Supplement* Number 904 (15 May). 265.

  1919b. 'Shakespeare's Hand in the Play of "Sir Thomas More": A Letter to the Editor.' *Times Literary Supplement* Number 906 (29 May). 295.

Beaumont, Francis and John Fletcher. 1966. *The Dramatic Works in the Beaumont and Fletcher Canon*. Ed. Fredson Bowers. Vol. 1: *The Knight of the Burning Pestle*; *The Masque of the Inner Temple and Gray's Inn*; *The Woman Hater*; *The Coxcomb*; *Philaster*; *The Captain*. 10 vols. Cambridge University Press.

  1989. *The Dramatic Works in the Beaumont and Fletcher Canon*. Ed. Fredson Bowers. Vol. 7: *Henry VIII*; *The Two Noble Kinsmen*; *Wit at Several Weapons*; *The Nice Valour*; *The Night Walker*; *A Very Woman*. 10 vols. Cambridge University Press.

Bentley, Gerald Eades. 1971. *The Profession of Dramatist in Shakespeare's Time, 1590–1642*. Princeton University Press.

Berger, Thomas L. 1979. 'The Printing of *Henry V*, Q1.' *The Library* (= *Transactions of the Bibliographical Society*). 6th series (=4th of *Transactions of the Bibliographical Society*) 1. 114–25.

  1989. 'Review of William Shakespeare, *The Complete Works*, ed. Stanley Wells, Gary Taylor, John Jowett and William Montgomery (Oxford: Clarendon Press, 1986) and William Shakespeare, *The Complete Works: Original Spelling Edition*, ed. Stanley Wells, Gary Taylor, John Jowett and William Montgomery (Oxford: Clarendon Press, 1986) and Stanley Wells, Gary Taylor, John Jowett and William Montgomery, *William Shakespeare: A Textual Companion* (Oxford: Clarendon Press, 1987).' *Analytical and Enumerative Bibliography*. New Series 3. 139–70.

Bertram, Paul. 1981. *White Spaces in Shakespeare: The Development of the Modern Text*. Cleveland OH. Bellflower.

Bevington, David. 1987. '"Determining the Indeterminate": Review of William Shakespeare, *The Complete Works*, ed. Stanley Wells, Gary Taylor, John Jowett and William Montgomery (Oxford: Clarendon Press, 1986) and Stanley Wells, Gary Taylor, John Jowett and William Montgomery, *William Shakespeare: A Textual Companion* (Oxford: Clarendon Press, 1987).' *Shakespeare Quarterly* 38. 501–19.

2004. 'Modern Spelling: The Hard Choices.' In Erne and Kidnie (eds.). 143–57.

Binns, James. 1977. 'STC Latin Books: Evidence for Printing-house Practice.' *The Library* (=*Transactions of the Bibliographical Society*). 5th series (=3rd of *Transactions of the Bibliographical Society*) 32. 1–27.

1979a. '"STC Latin Books: Evidence for Printing-house Practice": A Letter to the Editor.' *The Library* (=*Transactions of the Bibliographical Society*). 6th series (=4th of *Transactions of the Bibliographical Society*) 1. 171.

1979b. 'STC Latin Books: Further Evidence for Printing-house Practice.' *The Library* (=*Transactions of the Bibliographical Society*). 6th series (=4th of *Transactions of the Bibliographical Society*) 1. 347–54.

Bjelland, Karen T. 1994. 'Variants as Epistemological Shifts: A Proposed Methodology for Recovering the Two Texts of Shakespeare's *Troilus and Cressida*.' *Papers of the Bibliographical Society of America* 88. 53–78.

Blayney, Peter W. M. 1972. '"Compositor B" and the Pavier Quartos: Problems of Identification and Their Implications.' *The Library* (=*Transactions of the Bibliographical Society*). 5th series (=3rd of *Transactions of the Bibliographical Society*) 27. 179–206.

1982. *The Texts of* King Lear *and their Origins*. Vol. 1: Nicholas Okes and the First Quarto. 2 vols. New Cambridge Shakespeare Studies and Supplementary Texts. Cambridge University Press.

1997. 'The Publication of Playbooks.' In Cox and Kastan (eds.). 383–422.

2005. 'The Alleged Popularity of Playbooks.' *Shakespeare Quarterly* 56. 33–50.

Bodenham, John. 1600. *Bel-vedére or the Garden of the Muses* [*Edited By*] (A[nthony]? M[unday])?. STC 3189. London. F[elix] K[ingston] for Hugh Astley.

Bond, William H. 1948. 'Casting Off Copy by Elizabethan Printers: A Theory.' *Papers of the Bibliographical Society of America* 42. 281–91.

Bowers, Fredson. 1938–9. 'Notes on Running-titles as Bibliographical Evidence.' *The Library* (=*Transactions of the Bibliographical Society*). 4th series (=2nd of *Transactions of the Bibliographical Society*) 19. 315–38.

1942. 'The Headline in Early Books.' *English Institute Annual Volume for 1941*. 185–205.

1947–8. 'An Examination of the Method of Proof Correction in *Lear*.' *The Library* (=*Transactions of the Bibliographical Society*). 5th series (=3rd of *Transactions of the Bibliographical Society*) 2. 20–44.

1948. 'Elizabethan Proofing.' *Joseph Quincy Adams: Memorial Studies*. Ed. James G. McManaway, Giles E. Dawson and Edwin E. Willoughby. Washington DC. Folger Shakespeare Library. 571–86.

1949–50. 'Bibliographical Evidence from the Printer's Measure.' *Studies in Bibliography* 2. 153–67.

1950–1. 'Some Relations of Bibliography to Editorial Problems.' *Studies in Bibliography* 3. 37–62.

1952. 'The Problem of the Variant Forme in a Facsimile Edition.' *The Library* (=*Transactions of the Bibliographical Society*). 5th series (=3rd of *Transactions of the Bibliographical Society*) 7. 262–72.

1955a. 'McKerrow's Editorial Principles for Shakespeare Reconsidered.' *Shakespeare Quarterly* 6. 309–24.

1955b. *On Editing Shakespeare and the Elizabethan Dramatists*. Philadelphia. University of Pennsylvania Library.

1955c. 'The Yale Folio Facsimile and Scholarship.' *Modern Philology* 53. 50–7.

1956. 'The Textual Relation of Q2 to Q1 *Hamlet* (I).' *Studies in Bibliography* 8. 39–66.

1959. *Textual and Literary Criticism: The Sandars Lectures in Bibliography 1957–58*. Cambridge University Press.

1964. *Bibliography and Textual Criticism: The Lyell Lectures at Oxford, Trinity Term 1959*. Oxford. Clarendon Press.

1966. *On Editing Shakespeare*. 2nd edn. Charlottesville. University Press of Virginia.

1969. 'Bibliography Revisited.' *The Library* (=*Transactions of the Bibliographical Society*). 5th series (=3rd of *Transactions of the Bibliographical Society*) 24. 89–128.

1973. '"McKerrow Revisited": A Review of Philip Gaskell, *A New Introduction to Bibliography* (Oxford: Oxford University Press, 1972).' *Papers of the Bibliographical Society of America* 67. 109–24.

1975. 'Remarks on Eclectic Texts.' *Proof: The Yearbook of American Bibliographical and Textual Studies* 4. 31–76.

1978. 'The Copy for Shakespeare's *Julius Caesar*.' *South Atlantic Bulletin* 43.4. 23–36.

Bowman, Frank Paul. 1990. 'Genetic Criticism.' *Poetics Today* 11. 627–46.

Bradley, David. 1992. *From Text to Performance in the Elizabethan Theatre*. Cambridge University Press.

Brockbank, Philip. 1979. *The New Cambridge Shakespeare: Editorial Guide and Specimen Pages*. Unpublished Pamphlet Deposited at the Library of the Shakespeare Institute of the University of Birmingham, Shelfmark 'P/Box 200'.

Brome, Richard. 1640. *The Antipodes: A Comedie*. STC 3818 BEPD 586a. London. John Okes for France Constable.

Brown, John Russell. 1955. 'The Compositors of *Hamlet* Q2 and *The Merchant of Venice*.' *Studies in Bibliography* 7. 17–40.

1960. 'The Rationale of Old-spelling Editions of the Plays of Shakespeare and His Contemporaries.' *Studies in Bibliography* 13. 49–67.

Bruster, Douglas. 2008. 'Reading Shakespeareans': Paper Delivered on 4 August at the 33rd International Shakespeare Conference at the Shakespeare Institute, Stratford-upon-Avon, on 'Close Encounters with the Text of Shakespeare', 3–8 August.

Cady, Joseph. 1992. '"Masculine Love", Renaissance Writing, and the "New Invention" of Homosexuality.' *Homosexuality in Renaissance and Enlightenment*

England: Literary Representations in Historical Context. Ed. Claude J. Summers. New York. Haworth Press. 9–40.

Cairncross, Andrew S. 1956. 'Quarto Copy for Folio *Henry V*.' *Studies in Bibliography* 8. 67–93.

1957. 'The Quartos and the Folio Text of *Richard III*.' *Review of English Studies*. n.s. 8. 225–33.

1971. 'Compositors C and D of the Shakespeare First Folio.' *Papers of the Bibliographical Society of America* 65. 41–52.

1972. 'Compositors E and F of the Shakespeare First Folio.' *Papers of the Bibliographical Society of America* 66. 369–406.

Cantrell, Paul L. and George Walton Williams. 1956. 'Roberts' Compositors in *Titus Andronicus* Q2.' *Studies in Bibliography* 8. 27–38.

1957. 'The Printing of the Second Quarto of *Romeo and Juliet* (1599).' *Studies in Bibliography* 9. 107–28.

Carter, John. 1966a. '"The Degressive Principle": A Letter to the Editor.' *Times Literary Supplement* Number 3362 (4 August). 716.

1966b. '"The Degressive Principle": A Letter to the Editor.' *Times Literary Supplement* Number 3363 (11 August). 732.

Cauthen Junior, I. B. 1952–3. 'Compositor Determination in the First Folio *King Lear*.' *Studies in Bibliography* 5. 73–80.

Chambers, E. K. 1923a. *The Elizabethan Stage*. Vol. 3. 4 vols. Oxford. Clarendon Press.

1923b. *The Elizabethan Stage*. Vol. 4. 4 vols. Oxford. Clarendon Press.

1923c. 'The First Folio.' *Times Literary Supplement* Number 1109 (19 April). 253–4.

1924–5. '"The Disintegration of Shakespeare": The British Academy Annual Shakespeare Lecture Read 12 May 1924.' *Proceedings of the British Academy* 11. 89–108.

1930. *William Shakespeare: A Study of Facts and Problems*. Vol. 1. 2 vols. Oxford. Clarendon Press.

Clare, Robert. 1995. '"Who is it that Can Tell Me Who I Am?": The Theory of Authorial Revision between the Quarto and Folio Texts of *King Lear*.' *The Library* (=*Transactions of the Bibliographical Society*). 6th series (=4th of *Transactions of the Bibliographical Society*) 17. 34–59.

Clayton, Thomas. 1983. '"Is This the Promis'd End?": Revision in the Role of the King.' In Taylor and Warren (eds.). 121–41.

(ed.). 1992. *The Hamlet First Published (Q1, 1603): Origins, Forms, Intertextualities*. Newark. University of Delaware Press.

Coghill, Nevill. 1964. *Shakespeare's Professional Skills*. Cambridge University Press.

Coleridge, S[amuel] T[aylor]. 1907. *Biographia Literaria, and Aesthetical Essays*. Ed. J. Shawcross. Vol. 2: *Biographia Literaria* Chapters 14 to 24; *Aesthetical Essays*. 2 vols. Oxford. Clarendon Press.

Congreve, William. 1710a. *The Works*. Vol. 1: *The Old Bachelor*; *Double Dealer*; *Love for Love*. London. Jacob Tonson.

1710b. *The Works*. Vol. 2: *The Mourning Bride*; *The Way of the World*; *The Judgment of Paris*; *Semele*. London. Jacob Tonson.

1710c. *The Works.* Vol. 3: *Poems Upon Special Occasions.* London. Jacob Tonson.

Cox, John D. 2004. 'Open Stage, Open Page? Editing Stage Directions in Early Dramatic Texts.' In Erne and Kidnie (eds.). 178–93.

Cox, John D. and David Scott Kastan (eds.). 1997. *A New History of Early English Drama.* Foreword by Stephen J. Greenblatt. New York. Columbia University Press.

Craven, Alan E. 1971. 'The Compositors of the Shakespeare Quartos Printed by Peter Short.' *Papers of the Bibliographical Society of America* 65. 393–7.

1973a. 'Simmes' Compositor A and Five Shakespeare Quartos.' *Studies in Bibliography* 26. 37–60.

1973b. 'Two Valentine Simmes Compositors.' *Papers of the Bibliographical Society of America* 67. 161–71.

1974. 'Proofreading in the Shop of Valentine Simmes.' *Papers of the Bibliographical Society of America* 68. 361–72.

Creizenach, Wilhelm. 1918. 'Verloren gegangene englische Dramen aus dem Zeitalter Shakespeares.' *Shakespeare Jahrbuch* 54. 42–9.

Dam, B[astiaan] A[driaan] P[ieter] van. 1924. *The Text of Shakespeare's* Hamlet. London. John Lane.

Davidson, Adele. 1992. 'Shakespeare and Stenography Reconsidered.' *Analytical and Enumerative Bibliography.* n.s. 6. 77–100.

1996. '"Some by Stenography?": Stationers, Shorthand, and the Early Shakespearean Quartos.' *Papers of the Bibliographical Society of America* 90. 417–49.

1999. 'King Lear in an Age of Stenographical Reproduction or "On Sitting Down to Copy *King Lear* Again".' *Papers of the Bibliographical Society of America* 92. 297–324.

Davis, Tom. 1977. 'The CEAA and Modern Textual Editing.' *The Library* (=*Transactions of the Bibliographical Society*). 5th series (=3rd of *Transactions of the Bibliographical Society*) 32. 61–74.

Davis, William. 2006. '"Now, Gods, Stand Up for Bastards": The 1603 "Good Quarto" *Hamlet.*' *Textual Cultures: Texts, Contexts, Interpretations* 1.2. 60–89.

Davison, Peter. 1970. 'Marry, Sweet Wag.' *The Elizabethan Theatre II: Papers Given at the Second International Conference on Elizabethan Theatre Held at the University of Waterloo, Ontario, in July 1969.* Ed. David Galloway. London. Macmillan. 134–43.

1972. 'Science, Method, and the Textual Critic.' *Studies in Bibliography* 25. 1–28.

1977. 'The Selection and Presentation of Bibliographical Evidence.' *Analytical and Enumerative Bibliography* 1. 101–36.

Day, John, William Rowley and George Wilkins. 1607. *The Travailes of the Three English Brothers.* STC 6417 BEPD 248a(i). London. [George Eld] for John Wright.

de Grazia, Margreta. 1988. 'The Essential Shakespeare and the Material Book.' *Textual Practice* 2. 69–86.

1991. *Shakespeare Verbatim: The Reproduction of Authenticity and the 1790 Apparatus.* Oxford. Clarendon Press.

1993. 'What is a Work? What is a Document?' *New Ways of Looking at Old Texts: Papers of the Renaissance English Text Society, 1985–1991.* Ed. W. Speed Hill. Medieval and Renaissance Texts and Studies 107. Binghamton NY. Center for Medieval and Early Renaissance Studies at the State University of New York. 199–207.

1995. 'The Question of the One and the Many: The Globe Shakespeare, *The Complete King Lear*, and The New Folger Library Shakespeare.' *Shakespeare Quarterly* 46. 245–51.

de Grazia, Margreta and Peter Stallybrass. 1993. 'The Materiality of Shakespeare's Text.' *Shakespeare Quarterly* 44. 255–83.

Deppman, Jed, Daniel Ferrer and Michael Groden (eds.). 2004. *Genetic Criticism: Texts and Avant-textes*. Philadelphia. University of Pennsylvania Press.

Derrida, Jacques. 1976. *Of Grammatology*. Trans. Gayatri Chakrovorty Spivak. Baltimore MD. Johns Hopkins University Press.

DiPietro, Cary. 2006. 'The Shakespeare Edition in Industrial Capitalism.' *Shakespeare Survey* 59: Editing Shakespeare. 147–56.

Dillon, Janette. 1994. 'Is There a Performance in the Text?' *Shakespeare Quarterly* 54. 74–88.

Dobson, Michael. 1990. 'The Design of the Oxford Shakespeare: An Ever Writer to a Never Reader?' *Analytical and Enumerative Bibliography* 4. 91–7.

Dobson, Michael and Stanley Wells (eds.). 2001. *The Oxford Companion to Shakespeare*. Oxford University Press.

Dollimore, Jonathan and Alan Sinfield. 1985. 'History and Ideology: The Instance of *Henry V.*' *Alternative Shakespeares*. Ed. John Drakakis. New Accents. London. Methuen. 206–27.

Doran, Madeleine. 1928. Henry VI, *Parts II and III: Their Relation to the* Contention *and the* True Tragedy. University of Iowa Humanistic Studies 4.4. Iowa City. University of Iowa.

1931. *The Text of* King Lear. Stanford University Publications University Series: Language and Literature 4.2. Stanford University Press.

Downs, Gerald. 2007. 'A Question (Not) to be Askt: Is Hand D a Copy?' *The Shakespeare Apocrypha*. Ed. Douglas A. Brooks. The Shakespeare Yearbook 16. Ceredigion. Edwin Mellen. 241–66.

Drakakis, John. 1985. 'Introduction.' *Alternative Shakespeares*. Ed. John Drakakis. New Accents. London. Methuen. 1–25.

2007. 'Afterword.' *Shakespeare and the Text*. Ed. Andrew Murphy. Concise Companions to Literature and Culture. Oxford. Blackwell. 221–38.

Duthie, George Ian. 1941. *The 'Bad' Quarto of* Hamlet: *A Critical Study*. Shakespeare Problems 6. Cambridge University Press.

1943. '*The Taming of a Shrew* and *The Taming of the Shrew.*' *Review of English Studies*. o.s. 19. 337–56.

1949. *Elizabethan Shorthand and the First Quarto of* King Lear. Oxford. Basil Blackwell.

Dutton, Richard. 1991. *Mastering the Revels: The Regulation and Censorship of English Renaissance Drama*. London. Macmillan.

1996. 'The Birth of the Author.' In Parker and Zitner (eds.). 71–92.

Edwards, Philip. 1952. 'An Approach to the Problem of *Pericles.*' *Shakespeare Survey* 5. 25–49.
  1982. 'Review of Steven Urkowitz, *Shakespeare's Revision of "King Lear"* (Princeton University Press, 1980) and P. W. K. Stone, *The Textual History of "King Lear"* (London: Scolar Press, 1980).' *Modern Language Review* 77. 694–8.
Egan, Gabriel. 2006. *Green Shakespeare: From Ecopolitics to Ecocriticism.* Accents on Shakespeare. London. Routledge.
  2008. 'Foucault's Epistemic Shift and Verbatim Repetition in Shakespeare.' *Shakespeare's Book.* Ed. Richard Meek, Jane Rickard and Richard Wilson. Manchester University Press. 123–39.
Erne, Lukas. 2002. 'Shakespeare and the Publication of His Plays.' *Shakespeare Quarterly* 53. 1–20.
  2003. *Shakespeare as Literary Dramatist.* Cambridge University Press.
Erne, Lukas and Margaret Jane Kidnie (eds.). 2004. *Textual Performances: The Modern Reproduction of Shakespeare's Drama.* Cambridge University Press.
Farmer, Alan B. and Zachary Lesser. 2000. 'Vile Arts: The Marketing of English Printed Drama, 1512–1660.' *Research Opportunities in Renaissance Drama* 39. 77–165.
  2005a. 'The Popularity of Playbooks Revisited.' *Shakespeare Quarterly* 56. 1–32.
  2005b. 'The Structures of Popularity in the Early Modern Book Trade.' *Shakespeare Quarterly* 56. 206–13.
Ferguson, W. Craig. 1959. 'The Compositors of *Henry IV Part 2, Much Ado About Nothing, The Shoemakers' Holiday,* and the *First Part of the Contention.*' *Studies in Bibliography* 13. 19–29.
  1989. 'Compositor Identification in *Romeo* Q1 and *Troilus.*' *Studies in Bibliography* 42. 211–18.
  1966a. '"The Degressive Principle": Response to John Carter's Letter to the Editor.' *Times Literary Supplement* Number 3362 (4 August). 716.
  1966b. '"Impressions of Burke": Review of William B. Todd, *A Bibliography of Edmund Burke* (London: Hart-Davis, 1964).' *Times Literary Supplement* Number 3358 (7 July). 604.
Fletcher, John. 1951. *Bonduca.* Ed. W. W. Greg. Malone Society Reprints. London. Malone Society.
Fletcher, John and Francis Beaumont. 1647. *Comedies and Tragedies.* Wing B1581. London. For Humphrey Robinson and Humphrey Mosely.
Fletcher, John and Philip Massinger. 1980 (for 1979). *Sir John van Olden Barnavelt.* Ed. T. H. Howard-Hill. Malone Society Reprints. London. Malone Society.
Fletcher, John and William Shakespeare. 1634. *The Two Noble Kinsmen.* STC 11075 BEPD 492a. London. Tho[mas] Cotes for John Waterson.
Foakes, R. A. 1958. 'On the First Folio Text of *Henry VIII.*' *Studies in Bibliography* 11. 55–60.
  1993. *Hamlet* Versus Lear: *Cultural Politics and Shakespeare's Art.* Cambridge University Press.

Foucault, Michel. 1969. 'Qu'est-ce qu-un auteur?' ('What is an Author?'). *Bulletin de la Societé francaise de philosophie* 63.3. 73–104.

1970. *The Order of Things: An Archeology of the Human Sciences*. World of Man: A Library of Theory and Research in the Human Sciences. London. Tavistock.

1994. 'What is an Author?' Trans. Josue V. Harari. *Contemporary Literary Criticism: Literary and Cultural Studies*. 3rd edn. Ed. Robert Con Davis and Ronald Schleifer. New York. Longman. 341–53.

Franzén, Torkel. 2005. *Gödel's Theorem: An Incomplete Guide to Its Use and Abuse*. Wellesley MA. A. K. Peters.

Freeman, Arthur and Paul Grinke. 2002. 'Four New Shakespeare Quartos?: Viscount Conway's Lost English Plays.' *Times Literary Supplement* Number 5166 (5 April). 17–18.

Gaskell, Philip. 1969. '"Depth Analysis": Review of Fredson Bowers (ed.), *Studies in Bibliography* Volume 22 (1969) and D. F. McKenzie and J. C. Ross (eds.), *A Ledger of Charles Ackers* (London: Oxford University Press, 1968).' *Times Literary Supplement* Number 3508 (22 May). 564.

1972. *A New Introduction to Bibliography*. Oxford. Clarendon Press.

Glapthorne, Henry. 1959. *The Lady Mother*. Ed. Arthur Brown. Malone Society Reprints. Oxford. Malone Society.

Godshalk, W. L. 1994. '"Shakespeare's Bad Quarto": A Letter to the Editor.' *Times Literary Supplement* Number 4759 (17 June). 17.

Goldberg, Jonathan. 1986. 'Issues: Textual Properties.' *Shakespeare Quarterly* 37. 213–17.

Gossett, Suzanne. 2002. 'Major/minor, Main Plot/subplot, Middleton/and.' *The Elizabethan Theatre XV: Papers Given at the Fifteenth (1993) and Sixteenth (1997) International Conferences on Elizabethan Theatre Held at the University of Waterloo, Waterloo, Ontario*. Ed. C. E. McGee, A. L. Magnusson, Valerie Creelman and Todd Pettigrew. Toronto. P. D. Meany. 21–38.

2006. 'Editing Collaborative Drama.' *Shakespeare Survey* 59. 213–24.

Grady, Hugh. 1991. *The Modernist Shakespeare: Critical Texts in a Material World*. Oxford. Clarendon Press.

Gray, Henry David. 1915. 'The First Quarto *Hamlet*.' *Modern Language Review* 10. 171–80.

Greene, Robert. 1594. *The Historie of Orlando Furioso*. STC 12265 BEPD 123a. London. John Danter for Cuthbert Burbie.

Greg, W. W. 1902. 'Bacon's Biliteral Cipher and Its Applications.' *The Library*. n.s. (=2nd series) 3. 51–3.

1903a. 'The Bibliographical History of the First Folio.' *The Library*. n.s. (=2nd series) 4. 258–85.

1903b. 'Facts and Fancies in Baconian Theory.' *The Library*. n.s. (=2nd series) 4. 47–62.

1908a. 'On Certain False Dates in Shakespearian Quartos [Part I].' *The Library*. n.s. (=2nd series) 9. 113–31.

1908b. 'On Certain False Dates in Shakespearian Quartos [Parts II and III].' *The Library*. n.s. (=2nd series) 9. 381–409.
1909. 'Another Baconian Cipher.' *The Library*. n.s. (=2nd series) 10. 418–42.
1910. 'The *Hamlet* Quartos, 1603, 1604.' *Modern Language Review* 5. 196–7.
1913. 'Autograph Plays By Anthony Munday.' *Modern Language Review* 8. 89–90.
1919a. '"Bad" Quartos Outside Shakespeare – *Alcazar* and *Orlando*.' *The Library*. 3rd series 9. 193–222.
1919b. 'The *Hamlet* Texts and Recent Work in Shakespearian Bibliography.' *Modern Language Review* 14. 380–5.
1919c. '*Titus Andronicus*.' *Modern Language Review* 14. 322–3.
1922. *Two Elizabethan Abridgements:* The Battle of Alcazar *and* Orlando Furioso. Malone Society Reprints. Extra Volume. London. Malone Society.
1925. 'The Evidence of Theatrical Plots for the History of the Elizabethan Stage.' *Review of English Studies*. o.s. 1. 257–74.
1925–6. 'Prompt Copies, Private Transcripts, and the "Playhouse Scrivener".' *The Library* (=*Transactions of the Bibliographical Society*). 4th series (=2nd of *Transactions of the Bibliographical Society*) 6. 148–56.
1928a. '*Dramatic Publication in England, 1580–1640*: A Response to Evelyn May Albright's Reply [to W. W. Greg's Review].' *Review of English Studies*. o.s. 4. 202–4.
1928b. 'Review of Evelyn May Albright, *Dramatic Publication in England, 1580–1640: A Study of Conditions Affecting Content and Form of Drama* (London: Oxford University Press, 1927).' *Review of English Studies*. o.s. 4. 91–100.
1933. 'The Function of Bibliography in Literary Criticism Illustrated in a Study of the Text of *King Lear*.' *Neophilologus* 18. 241–62.
1935. '"The Genuine Text": A Letter to the Editor.' *Times Literary Supplement* Number 1740 (6 June). 364.
1936–7. '*King Lear* – Mislineation and Stenography.' *The Library* (=*Transactions of the Bibliographical Society*). 4th series (=2nd of *Transactions of the Bibliographical Society*) 17. 172–83.
1940. *The Variants in the First Quarto of* King Lear: *A Bibliographical and Critical Inquiry*. Supplements to the Bibliographical Society's Transactions 15. London. The Bibliographical Society.
1941. 'McKerrow's "Prolegomena" Reconsidered.' *Review of English Studies*. o.s. 17. 139–49.
1942. *The Editorial Problem in Shakespeare: A Survey of the Foundations of the Text*. Oxford. Clarendon Press.
1950–1. 'The Rationale of Copy-Text.' *Studies in Bibliography* 3. 19–36.
1952. Jonson's Masque of Gipsies *in the Burley, Belvoir, and Windsor Versions: An Attempt at Reconstruction*. London. British Academy.
1955. *The Shakespeare First Folio: Its Bibliographical and Textual History*. Oxford. Clarendon Press.
(ed.). 1907. *Henslowe Papers: Being Documents Supplementary to Henslowe's Diary*. London. Bullen.

(ed.). 1908c. *Henslowe's Diary*. Vol. 2: Commentary. 2 vols. London. Bullen.

(ed.). 1911. *The Book of Sir Thomas More*. Malone Society Reprints. Oxford. Malone Society.

(ed.). 1931. *Dramatic Documents from the Elizabethan Playhouses: Stage Plots, Actors' Parts, Prompt Books*. Vol. 1: Commentary. 2 vols. Oxford. Clarendon Press.

Gurr, Andrew. 1996. *The Shakespearian Playing Companies*. Oxford. Clarendon Press.

1999. 'Maximal and Minimal Texts: Shakespeare v. the Globe.' *Shakespeare Survey* 52. 68–87.

2004. 'A New Theatre Historicism.' *From Script to Stage in Early Modern England*. Ed. Peter Holland and Stephen Orgel. Redefining British Theatre History. Basingstoke. Palgrave Macmillan. 71–88.

Hammond, Antony. 1984. 'Review of Peter W. M. Blayney, *The Texts of "King Lear" and Their Origins*. Vol. 1: Nicholas Okes and the First Quarto (Cambridge University Press, 1982).' *The Library* (=*Transactions of the Bibliographical Society*). 6th series (=4th of *Transactions of the Bibliographical Society*) 6. 89–93.

Harbage, Alfred. 1964. *Annals of English Drama 975–1700: An Analytical Record of All Plays, Extant or Lost, Chronologically Arranged and Indexed By Authors, Titles, Dramatic Companies, Etc*. Rev. S. Schoenbaum. Philadelphia. University of Pennsylvania Press.

Harrison, G. B. 1948. 'A Note on *Coriolanus*.' *Joseph Quincy Adams: Memorial Studies*. Ed. James G. McManaway, Giles E. Dawson and Edwin E. Willoughby. Washington DC. Folger Shakespeare Library. 239–52.

Hart, Alfred. 1932a. 'The Length of Elizabethan and Jacobean Plays.' *Review of English Studies*. o.s. 8. 139–54.

1932b. 'The Time Allotted for Representation of Elizabethan and Jacobean Plays.' *Review of English Studies*. o.s. 8. 395–413.

1942. *Stolne and Surreptitious Copies: A Comparative Study of Shakespeare's Bad Quartos*. Melbourne University Press.

Hasker, Richard E. 1952–3. 'The Copy of the First Folio *Richard II*.' *Studies in Bibliography* 5. 53–72.

Heywood, Thomas. 1637. *Pleasant Dialogues and Dramma's*. STC 13358. London. R[ichard] O[ulton] for R[ichard] H[earne] to be sold by Thomas Slater.

1639. *If You Know Not Me, You Know no Bodie: Or, the Troubles of Queen Elizabeth*. STC 13335 BEPD 215h. London. J[ohn] Raworth for N[athaniel] Butter.

Hinman, Charlton. 1940–1. 'Principles Governing the Use of Variant Spellings as Evidence of Alternate Setting by Two Compositors.' *The Library* (=*Transactions of the Bibliographical Society*). 4th series (=2nd of *Transactions of the Bibliographical Society*) 21. 78–94.

1942a. 'New Uses for Headlines as Bibliographical Evidence.' *English Institute Annual* volume for 1941. 207–22.

1942b. 'A Proof-sheet in the First Folio of Shakespeare.' *The Library* (=*Transactions of the Bibliographical Society*). 4th series (=2nd of *Transactions of the Bibliographical Society*) 23. 101–7.

1947. 'Mechanized Collation: A Preliminary Report.' *Papers of the Bibliographical Society of America* 41. 99–106.

1950. 'Mark III: New Light on the Proof-reading for the First Folio of Shakespeare.' *Studies in Bibliography* 3. 145–53.

1953. 'Variant Readings in the First Folio of Shakespeare.' *Shakespeare Quarterly* 4. 279–88.

1953–4. 'The Proof-reading of the First Folio Text of *Romeo and Juliet*.' *Studies in Bibliography* 6. 61–70.

1955. 'Cast-off Copy for the First Folio of Shakespeare.' *Shakespeare Quarterly* 6. 259–73.

1957. 'The Prentice Hand in the Tragedies of the Shakespeare First Folio: Compositor E.' *Studies in Bibliography* 9. 3–20.

1963a. *The Printing and Proof-reading of the First Folio of Shakespeare*. Vol. 1. 2 vols. Oxford. Clarendon Press.

1963b. *The Printing and Proof-reading of the First Folio of Shakespeare*. Vol. 2. 2 vols. Oxford. Clarendon Press.

Holderness, Graham. 1985. *Shakespeare's History*. New York. St Martin's Press.

1994. '"Shakespeare's Bad Quarto": A Letter to the Editor.' *Times Literary Supplement* Number 4749 (8 April). 17.

2003. *Textual Shakespeare: Writing and the Word*. Hatfield. University of Hertfordshire Press.

Holderness, Graham and Carol Banks. 1995. 'Mimesis: Text and Reproduction.' *Critical Survey* 7. 332–8.

Holderness, Graham and Bryan Loughrey. 1993. 'Text and Stage: Shakespeare, Bibliography, and Performance Studies.' *New Theatre Quarterly* 9. 179–91.

1994. '"Shakespeare's Bad Quarto": A Letter to the Editor.' *Times Literary Supplement* Number 4740 (4 February). 15.

Holderness, Graham, Bryan Loughrey and Andrew Murphy. 1995. '"What's the Matter?": Shakespeare and Textual Theory.' *Textual Practice* 9. 93–119.

1997. 'Busy Doing Nothing: A Response to Pechter.' *Textual Practice* 11. 81–7.

Holderness, Graham (ed.). 1992. *Shakespeare's History Plays:* Richard II *to* Henry V. New Casebooks. Basingstoke. Macmillan.

Honigmann, E. A. J. 1965. *The Stability of Shakespeare's Text*. London. Edward Arnold.

1996. *The Texts of* Othello *and Shakespearian Revision*. London. Routledge.

2001. 'Harold Jenkins 1909–2000.' *Proceedings of the British Academy* 111: [Year] 2000 Lectures and Memoirs. 553–72.

Hoppe, Harry R. 1948. *The Bad Quarto of* Romeo and Juliet: *A Bibliographical and Textual Study*. Cornell Studies in English 36. Ithaca NY. Cornell University Press.

Howard, Jean E. 2003. 'Material Shakespeare/Materialist Shakespeare.' *Shakespeare Matters: History, Teaching, Performance.* Ed. Lloyd Davis. Newark. University of Delaware Press. 29–45.

Howard-Hill, T. H. 1960. 'Spelling-analysis and Ralph Crane: A Preparatory Study of His Life, Spelling, and Scribal Habits'. Unpublished Ph.D. thesis, Victoria University of Wellington (New Zealand).

   1963. 'Spelling and the Bibliographer.' *The Library* (=*Transactions of the Bibliographical Society*). 5th series (=3rd of *Transactions of the Bibliographical Society*) 18. 1–28.

   1969. 'The Oxford Old-spelling Shakespeare Concordances.' *Studies in Bibliography* 22. 143–64.

   1971. 'Ralph Crane and Five Shakespeare First Folio Comedies.' Unpublished D.Phil. thesis, University of Oxford.

   1972. *Ralph Crane and Some Shakespeare First Folio Comedies.* Charlottesville. University Press of Virginia.

   1973. 'The Compositors of Shakespeare's Folio Comedies.' *Studies in Bibliography* 26. 61–106.

   1976. *Compositors B and E in the Shakespeare First Folio and Some Recent Studies.* Columbia SC. Published privately by the author.

   1977. *A Reassessment of Compositors B and E in the First Folio Tragedies.* Columbia SC. Published privately by the author.

   1980. 'New Light on Compositor E of the Shakespeare First Folio.' *The Library* (=*Transactions of the Bibliographical Society*). 6th series (=4th of *Transactions of the Bibliographical Society*) 2. 156–78.

   1982. 'The Problem of Manuscript Copy for Folio *King Lear*.' *The Library* (=*Transactions of the Bibliographical Society*). 6th series (=4th of *Transactions of the Bibliographical Society*) 4. 1–24.

   1985. '"The Challenge of *King Lear*": Review of Gary Taylor and Michael Warren (eds.), *The Division of the Kingdoms: Shakespeare's Two Versions of "King Lear"* (Oxford University Press, 1983).' *The Library* (=*Transactions of the Bibliographical Society*). 6th series (=4th of *Transactions of the Bibliographical Society*) 7. 161–79.

   1986. 'Q1 and the Copy for Folio *Lear*.' *Papers of the Bibliographical Society of America* 80. 419–35.

   1988. 'Crane's 1619 "Promptbook" of *Barnavelt* and Theatrical Processes.' *Modern Philology* 86. 146–70.

   2006. 'Early Modern Printers and the Standardization of English Spelling.' *Modern Language Review* 101. 16–29.

Hoy, Cyrus. 1962. 'The Shares of Fletcher and His Collaborators in the Beaumont and Fletcher Canon ([Part] VII [of VII]).' *Studies in Bibliography* 15. 71–90.

Ioppolo, Grace. 2006. *Dramatists and Their Manuscripts in the Age of Shakespeare, Jonson, Middleton and Heywood: Authorship, Authority and the Playhouse.* Routledge Studies in Renaissance Literature and Culture. London. Routledge.

Irace, Kathleen O. 1994. *Reforming the 'Bad' Quartos: Performance and Provenance of Six Shakespearean First Editions.* Newark. University of Delaware Press.

Jackson, MacDonald P. 1974. 'Compositor C and the First Folio Text of *Much Ado About Nothing.*' *Papers of the Bibliographical Society of America* 68. 414–18.

　1975. 'Punctuation and the Compositors of Shakespeare's *Sonnets,* 1609.' *The Library* (=*Transactions of the Bibliographical Society*). 5th series (=3rd of *Transactions of the Bibliographical Society*) 30. 1–24.

　1978. 'Compositors B, C, and D, and the First Folio Text of *Love's Labour's Lost.*' *Papers of the Bibliographical Society of America* 72. 61–5.

　1982. 'Two Shakespeare Quartos: *Richard III* (1597) and *1 Henry IV* (1598).' *Studies in Bibliography* 35. 173–90.

　1983. 'Fluctuating Variation: Author, Annotator, or Actor?' In Taylor and Warren (eds.). 313–49.

　1987. 'Compositors' Stints and the Spacing of Punctuation in the First Quarto (1609) of *Pericles.*' *Papers of the Bibliographical Society of America* 81. 17–23.

　1989. 'Review of William Shakespeare, *The Complete Works,* ed. Stanley Wells, Gary Taylor, John Jowett and William Montgomery (Oxford: Clarendon Press, 1986) and William Shakespeare, *The Complete Works: Original Spelling Edition,* ed. Stanley Wells, Gary Taylor, John Jowett and William Montgomery (Oxford: Clarendon Press, 1986) and Stanley Wells, Gary Taylor, John Jowett and William Montgomery, *William Shakespeare: A Textual Companion* (Oxford: Clarendon Press, 1987).' *Shakespeare Survey* 41. 228–41.

　2001a. 'Finding the Pattern: Peter Short's Shakespeare Quartos Revisited.' *Bibliographical Society of Australia and New Zealand Bulletin* 25. 67–86.

　2001b. 'Shakespeare's *Richard II* and the Anonymous *Thomas of Woodstock.*' *Medieval and Renaissance Drama in England* 14. 17–65.

　2003. *Defining Shakespeare:* Pericles *as Test Case.* Oxford University Press.

　2006. 'The Date and Authorship of Hand D's Contribution to *Sir Thomas More*: Evidence from "Literature Online".' *Shakespeare Survey* 59. 69–78.

Jenkins, Harold. 1994. '"Shakespeare's Bad Quarto": A Letter to the Editor.' *Times Literary Supplement* Number 4750 (15 April). 17.

Johnson, Francis R. 1946. 'Press Corrections and Presswork in the Elizabethan Printing Shop.' *Papers of the Bibliographical Society of America* 40. 276–86.

Jones, Millard T. 1974. 'Press-variants and Proofreading in the First Quarto of *Othello.*' *Studies in Bibliography* 27. 177–84.

Jonson, Ben. 1600. *The Comicall Satyre of Every Man Out of His Humor.* STC 14767 BEPD 163a. London. [Adam Islip] for William Holme.

　1605. *Sejanus His Fall.* STC 14782 BEPD 216a. London. George Eld for Thomas Thorpe.

　1616. *The Workes of Benjamin Jonson.* STC 14751. London. William Stansby.

Jowett, John. 1983. 'New Created Creatures: Ralph Crane and the Stage Directions in *The Tempest.*' *Shakespeare Survey* 36. 107–20.

　1984. 'Ligature Shortage and Speech-prefix Variation in *Julius Caesar.*' *The Library* (=*Transactions of the Bibliographical Society*). 6th series (=4th of *Transactions of the Bibliographical Society*) 6. 244–53.

1987. 'The Thieves in *1 Henry IV*.' *Review of English Studies*. n.s. 38. 325–33.

1989. 'Cuts and Casting: Author and Book-keeper in the Folio Text of *2 Henry IV*.' *AUMLA: Journal of the Australasian Universities Language and Literature Association* 72. 275–95.

1998a. 'Henry Chettle and the First Quarto of *Romeo and Juliet*.' *Papers of the Bibliographical Society of America* 92. 53–74.

1998b. '*Richard III* and the Perplexities of Editing.' *TEXT: An Interdisciplinary Annual of Textual Studies* (formerly *TEXT: Transactions of the Society for Textual Scholarship*) 11. 224–45.

1999. 'After Oxford: Recent Developments in Textual Studies.' *Shakespearean International Yearbook* 1. 65–86.

2000. '"Derby", "Stanley", and Memorial Reconstruction in Quarto *Richard III*.' *Notes and Queries* 245. 75–9.

2004. 'The Pattern of Collaboration in *Timon of Athens*.' *Words that Count: Essay on Early-modern Authorship in Honor of MacDonald P. Jackson*. Ed. Brian Boyd. Newark. University of Delaware Press. 181–205.

2007. *Shakespeare and Text*. Oxford Shakespeare Topics. Oxford University Press.

Jowett, John and Gary Taylor. 1985. 'Sprinklings of Authority: The Folio Text of *Richard II*.' *Studies in Bibliography* 38. 151–200.

1987. 'The Three Texts of *2 Henry IV*.' *Studies in Bibliography* 40. 31–50.

Kable, William S. 1967. 'The Influence of Justification on Spelling in Jaggard's Compositor B.' *Studies in Bibliography* 20. 235–9.

1968. 'Compositor B, the Pavier Quartos, and Copy Spellings.' *Studies in Bibliography* 21. 131–61.

Kastan, David Scott. 1998. 'Killed with Hard Opinions: Oldcastle, Falstaff, and the Reformed Text of *1 Henry IV*.' In Maguire and Berger (eds.). 211–27.

Kennedy, Richard F. 1998. 'Speech Prefixes in Some Shakespearean Quartos.' *Papers of the Bibliographical Society of America* 92. 177–209.

Kenney, E. J. 1974. *The Classical Text: Aspects of Editing in the Age of the Printed Book*. Sather Classical Lectures 44. Berkeley. University of California Press.

Kerrigan, John. 1983. 'Revision, Adaptation, and the Fool in *King Lear*.' In Taylor and Warren (eds.). 195–243.

Kidnie, Margaret Jane. 2000. 'Text, Performance, and the Editors: Staging Shakespeare's Drama.' *Shakespeare Quarterly* 51. 456–73.

2004. 'The Staging of Shakespeare's Drama in Print Editions.' In Erne and Kidnie (eds.). 158–77.

King, Edmund. 2006. 'Narratives About Collaborating Playwrights: The New Bibliography, "Disintegration", and the Problem of Multiple Authorship in Shakespeare': A Paper for the Seminar 'Sa(l)vaging the New Bibliography: The New World of Editing' on 21 July at the 8th World Shakespeare Congress in Brisbane, 16–21 July.

King, Rosalind and Nigel Alexander. 1994. '"Shakespeare's Bad Quarto": A Letter to the Editor.' *Times Literary Supplement* Number 4741 (11 February). 15.

Kirschbaum, Leo. 1938. 'A Census of Bad Quartos.' *Review of English Studies*. o.s. 14. 20–43.
   1946. 'Author's Copyright in England Before 1640.' *Papers of the Bibliographical Society of America* 40. 43–80.
Knapp, Jeffrey. 2005. 'What is a Co-Author?' *Representations* 89. 1–29.
Knowles, Richard. 1995. 'Revision Awry in Folio *Lear* 3.1.' *Shakespeare Quarterly* 46. 32–46.
Kreps, Barbara. 2000. 'Bad Memories of Margaret?: Memorial Reconstruction versus Revision in *The First Part of the Contention* and *2 Henry VI*.' *Shakespeare Quarterly* 51. 154–80.
Kumar, Manjit. 2008. *Quantum: Einstein, Bohr and the Great Debate About the Nature of Reality*. London. Icon.
Kyd, Thomas. 1592. *The Spanish Tragedie*. STC 15086 BEPD 110a. London. Edward Allde for Edward White.
   1602. *The Spanish Tragedie… Newly Corrected, Amended, and Enlarged*. STC 15089 BEPD 110d. London. W[illiam] W[hite] for T[homas] Pavier.
Lawrence, W. J. 1935a. '"The Genuine Text": A Letter to the Editor.' *Times Literary Supplement* Number 1738 (23 May). 313.
   1935b. '"The Genuine Text": A Letter to the Editor.' *Times Literary Supplement* Number 1740 (6 June). 364.
Lewis, C[live] S[taples]. 1935a. '"The Genuine Text": A Letter to the Editor.' *Times Literary Supplement* Number 1735 (2 May). 288.
   1935b. '"The Genuine Text": A Letter to the Editor.' *Times Literary Supplement* Number 1738 (23 May). 313.
Loewenstein, Joseph F. 1998. 'Authentic Reproductions: The Material Origins of the New Bibliography.' In Maguire and Berger (eds.). 23–44.
Long, William B. 1985a. '"A Bed / for Woodstock": A Warning for the Unwary.' *Medieval and Renaissance Drama in England* 2. 91–118.
   1985b. 'Stage-directions: A Misinterpreted Factor in Determining Textual Provenance.' *TEXT: Transactions of the Society for Textual Scholarship* 2. 121–37.
   1989. '*John a Kent and John a Cumber*: An Elizabethan Playbook and Its Implications.' *Shakespeare and Dramatic Tradition: Essays in Honor of S. F. Johnson*. Ed. W. R. Elton and William B. Long. Newark. University of Delaware Press. 125–43.
Lumet, Sidney. 1982. *The Verdict*. Motion Picture. Twentieth Century-Fox Film.
Maguire, Laurie E. 1996. *Shakespearean Suspect Texts: The 'Bad' Quartos and Their Contexts*. Cambridge University Press.
Maguire, Laurie E. and Thomas L. Berger (eds.). 1998. *Textual Formations and Reformations*. Newark: University of Delaware Press.
Manilius, Marcus. 1903. *Astronomicon*. Ed. A. E. Housman. Vol. 1. 5 vols. London. Grant Richards.
Manley, Lawrence. 2003. 'From Strange's Men to Pembroke's Men: *2 Henry VI* and *The First Part of the Contention*.' *Shakespeare Quarterly* 54. 253–87.
Marcus, Leah S. 1991. 'Levelling Shakespeare: Local Customs and Local Texts.' *Shakespeare Quarterly* 42. 168–78.

1996. *Unediting the Renaissance: Shakespeare, Marlowe, Milton.* London. Routledge.

2004. 'The Two Texts of *Othello* and Early Modern Constructions of Race.' In Erne and Kidnie (eds.). 21–36.

2007. 'Editing Shakespeare in the Postmodern Age.' *Shakespeare and the Text.* Ed. Andrew Murphy. Concise Companions to Literature and Culture. Oxford. Blackwell. 128–44.

Marlowe, Christopher. 1590. [*1 and 2 Tamburlaine*] *Tamburlaine the Great... Deuided Into Two Tragicall Discourses.* STC 17425 BEPD 94a, 95a. London. Richard Jones.

1604. *The Tragicall History of D[octor] Faustus.* STC 17429 BEPD 205a. London. Valentine Simmes for Thomas Bushell.

1616. *The Tragicall History of the Life and Death of Doctor Faustus.* STC 17432 BEPD 205d. London. John Wright.

1950. *Doctor Faustus 1604–1616: Parallel Texts.* Ed. W. W. Greg. Oxford. Clarendon Press.

1993. *Doctor Faustus.* Ed. David Bevington and Eric Rasmussen. The Revels Plays. Manchester University Press.

Mason, Pamela. 2003. '"... and Laertes": The Case against Tidiness.' *Stage Directions in Hamlet: New Essays and New Directions.* Ed. Hardin L. Aasand. Madison NJ. Fairleigh Dickinson University Press. 92–8.

Massai, Sonia. 2007. *Shakespeare and the Rise of the Editor.* Cambridge University Press.

Masten, Jeffrey. 1997a. 'Pressing Subjects; Or, the Secret Lives of Shakespeare's Compositors.' *Language Machines: Technologies of Literary and Cultural Production.* Ed. Jeffrey Masten, Peter Stallybrass and Nancy Vickers. Essays from the English Institute. New York. Routledge. 75–107.

1997b. *Textual Intercourse: Collaboration, Authorship, and Sexualities in Renaissance Drama.* Cambridge Studies in Renaissance Literature and Culture 14. Cambridge University Press.

2001. 'More or Less: Editing the Collaborative.' *Shakespeare Studies* 29. 109–31.

McGann, Jerome J. 1983. *A Critique of Modern Textual Criticism.* University of Chicago Press.

(ed.). 1985. *Textual Criticism and Literary Interpretation.* University of Chicago Press.

McKenzie, D. F. 1959a. 'Compositor B's Role in *The Merchant of Venice* Q2 (1619).' *Studies in Bibliography* 12. 75–90.

1959b. 'Shakespearian Punctuation – A New Beginning.' *Review of English Studies.* n.s. 10. 361–70.

1969. 'Printers of the Mind: Some Notes on Bibliographical Theories and Printing-house Practices.' *Studies in Bibliography* 22. 1–75.

1981. 'Typography and Meaning: The Case of William Congreve.' *Buch und Buchhandel in Europa im achtzehnten Jahrhundert: fünftes Wolfenbütteler Symposium vom 1 bis 3 November 1977* [= *The Book and the Book Trade in Eighteenth-century Europe: Proceedings of the Fifth Wolfenbütteler*

Symposium 1–3 November 1977]. Ed. Giles Barber and Bernhard Fabian. Hamburg. Hauswedell. 81–125.

1984. 'Stretching a Point: Or, the Case of the Spaced-out Comps.' *Studies in Bibliography* 37. 106–21.

1986. *Bibliography and the Sociology of Texts: The Panizzi Lectures for 1985*. London. The British Library.

McKerrow, R. B. 1921–2. 'The Use of the Galley in Elizabethan Printing.' *The Library* (=*Transactions of the Bibliographical Society*). 4th series (=2nd of *Transactions of the Bibliographical Society*) 2. 97–108.

1924–5. 'Elizabethan Printers and the Composition of Reprints.' *The Library* (=*Transactions of the Bibliographical Society*). 4th series (=2nd of *Transactions of the Bibliographical Society*) 5. 357–64.

1927. *An Introduction to Bibliography for Literary Students*. Oxford. Clarendon Press.

1931–2. 'The Elizabethan Printer and Dramatic Manuscripts.' *The Library* (=*Transactions of the Bibliographical Society*). 4th series (=2nd of *Transactions of the Bibliographical Society*) 12. 253–73.

1935. 'A Suggestion Regarding Shakespeare's Manuscripts.' *Review of English Studies*. o.s. 11. 459–65.

1937. 'A Note on the "Bad Quartos" of *2* and *3 Henry VI* and the Folio Text.' *Review of English Studies*. o.s. 13. 64–72.

1939. *Prolegomena for the Oxford Shakespeare: A Study in Editorial Method*. Oxford. Clarendon Press.

McLeod, Randall. 1979. 'Spellbound: Typography and the Concept of Old-spelling Editions.' *Renaissance and Reformation / Renaissance et Réforme* 3.1. 50–65.

[as Random Cloud]. 1982a. 'The Marriage of Good and Bad Quartos.' *Shakespeare Quarterly* 33. 421–31.

1982b. 'UNEditing Shak-speare.' *Sub-stance* 33–4. 26–55.

1983. '*Gon*. No More, the Text is Foolish.' In Taylor and Warren (eds.). 153–93.

1984. 'Spellbound.' *Play-texts in Old Spelling: Papers from the Glendon Conference*. Ed. G. B. Shand and Raymond C. Shady. AMS Studies in the Renaissance. New York. AMS. 81–96.

[as Random Clod]. 1991. 'Information on Information.' *TEXT: Transactions of the Society for Textual Scholarship* 5. 241–81.

McMillin, Scott. 1970. '*The Book of Sir Thomas More*: A Theatrical View.' *Modern Philology* 68. 10–24.

1972. 'Casting for Pembroke's Men: The *Henry VI* Quartos and *The Taming of a Shrew*.' *Shakespeare Quarterly* 23. 141–59.

McMullan, Gordon. 1996. '"Our Whole Life is Like a Play": Collaboration and the Problem of Editing.' *Textus: English Studies in Italy* 9.2: 'Shakespeare's Text(s)' guest-edited by Ann Thompson and Keir Elam. 437–60.

McMullan, Gordon and Jonathan Hope (eds.). 1992. *The Politics of Tragicomedy: Shakespeare and After*. London. Routledge.

Meres, Francis. 1598. *Palladis Tamia: Wits Treasury Being the Second Part of Wits Common Wealth*. STC 17834. London. P[eter] Short for Cuthbert Burbie.

Merriam, Tom. 2005. *The Identity of Shakespeare in* Henry VIII. Renaissance Monographs 32. Tokyo. The Renaissance Institute of Sophia University.

Metz, G. Harold. 1985. 'Disputed Shakespearean Texts and Stylometric Analysis.' *TEXT: Transactions of the Society for Textual Scholarship* 2. 149–71.

Meyer, Ann R. 1994. 'Shakespeare's Art and the Texts of *King Lear*.' *Studies in Bibliography* 47. 128–46.

Middleton, Thomas. 1909. *The Second Maiden's Tragedy, 1611*. Ed. W. W. Greg. Malone Society Reprints. Oxford. Malone Society.

    1990. *A Game at Chess*. Ed. T. H. Howard-Hill. Malone Society Reprints. London. Malone Society.

    2007. *Thomas Middleton: The Collected Works*. Gen. ed. Gary Taylor and John Lavagnino. Oxford. Clarendon Press.

Mommsen, Tycho. 1857. '*Hamlet*, 1603 and *Romeo and Juliet*, 1597.' *The Athenaeum* 29. 182.

Montgomery, William. 1985. '*The Contention of York and Lancaster*: A Critical Edition.' Unpublished D.Phil. thesis, University of Oxford.

Mountfort, Walter. 1933. *The Launching of the Mary, or The Seaman's Honest Wife*. Ed. John Henry Walter. Malone Society Reprints. Oxford. Malone Society.

Mowat, Barbara A. 1998. 'The Problem of Shakespeare's Text(s).' In Maguire and Berger (eds.). 131–48.

Moxon, Joseph. 1683. *Mechanick Exercises, Or, The Doctrine of Handy-works*. Wing M3014. Vol. 2: Applied to the Art of Printing. 2 vols. London. Joseph Moxon.

Munro, Lucy. 2005. *Children of the Queen's Revels: A Jacobean Theatre Repertory*. Cambridge University Press.

Murphy, Andrew. 1999. '"Came Errour Here By Mysse of Man": Editing and the Metaphysics of Presence.' *Yearbook of English Studies* 29. 118–37.

    2003. *Shakespeare in Print: A History and Chronology of Shakespeare Publishing*. Cambridge University Press.

Nashe, Thomas. 1904. *The Works*. Ed. Ronald B. McKerrow. Vol. 1: Note on the Treatment of the Text; *The Anatomie of Absurditie*; *A Countercuffe Giuen to Martin Iunior*; *The Returne of Pasquill*; *The First Parte of Pasquils Apologie*; *Pierce Penilesse His Supplication to the Diuell*; *Strange News, or the Intercepting Certaine Letters*; *The Terrors of the Night*. 5 vols. London. A. H. Bullen.

Nathan, Norman. 1957. 'Compositor Haste in the First Folio.' *Shakespeare Quarterly* 8. 134–5.

O'Connor, John [S]. 1975. 'Compositors D and F of the Shakespeare First Folio.' *Studies in Bibliography* 28. 81–117.

    1977. 'A Qualitative Analysis of Compositors C and D in the Shakespeare First Folio.' *Studies in Bibliography* 30. 57–74.

Orgel, Stephen. 1981. 'What is a Text?' *Research Opportunities in Renaissance Drama* 24. 3–6.

    1988. 'The Authentic Shakespeare.' *Representations* 21. 1–25.

    1994. 'Acting Scripts, Performing Texts.' *Crisis in Editing: Texts of the English Renaissance: Papers Given at the Twenty-fourth Annual Conference on Editorial*

Problems, University of Toronto, 4–5 November 1988. Ed. Randall McLeod. New York. AMS Press. 251–94.

1996. 'Forum on Editing Early Modern Texts: What is an Editor?' *Shakespeare Studies* 14. 23–9, 75–8.

Palfrey, Simon and Tiffany Stern. 2007. *Shakespeare in Parts*. Oxford University Press.

Parker, R. B. and S. P. Zitner (eds.). 1996. *Elizabethan Theater: Essays in Honor of S. Schoenbaum*. Newark. University of Delaware Press.

Parrott, T. M. 1919. 'Shakespeare's Revision of *Titus Andronicus*.' *Modern Language Review* 19. 16–37.

Patrick, David Lyall. 1936. *The Textual History of* Richard III. Stanford University Publications University Series: Language and Literature 6.1. Stanford University Press.

Pechter, Edward. 1997. 'Making Love to Our Employment; Or, the Immateriality of Arguments About the Materiality of Shakespearean Text.' *Textual Practice* 11. 51–67.

2001. 'Romanticism Lost: Bloom and the Twilight of Literary Shakespeare.' *Harold Bloom's Shakespeare*. Ed. Christy Desmet and Robert Sawyer. New York. Palgrave. 145–66.

2003. 'What's Wrong with Literature?' *Textual Practice* 17. 505–26.

2010. *Shakespeare Studies Today: Romanticism Lost*. New York. Palgrave, 2010.

Peele, George. 1594. *The Battell of Alcazar*. STC 19531 BEPD 127a. London. Edward Allde for Richard Bankworth.

Pendleton, Thomas A. 1990. '"This is Not the Man": On Calling Falstaff Falstaff.' *Analytical and Enumerative Bibliography* 4. 59–71.

Pettitt, Thomas. 2001. 'The Living Text: The Play, the Players, and Folk Tradition.' *Porci Ante Margaritam: Essays in Honour of Meg Twycross*. Ed. Sarah Carpenter, Pamela King and Peter Meredith. Leeds Studies in English n.s. 32. Leeds. School of English, University of Leeds. 413–29.

Pitcher, John. 1993. 'Names in *Cymbeline*.' *Essays in Criticism* 43. 1–16.

Pollard, A. W. 1909. *Shakespeare Folios and Quartos: A Study in the Bibliography of Shakespeare's Plays*. London. Methuen.

1916a. 'Authors, Players, and Pirates in Shakespeare's Day.' *The Library*. 3rd series 7. 73–101.

1916b. 'The Improvers of Shakespeare.' *The Library*. 3rd series 7. 265–90.

1916c. 'The Manuscripts of Shakespeare's Plays.' *The Library*. 3rd series 7. 198–226.

1916d. 'The Regulation of the Book Trade in the Sixteenth Century.' *The Library*. 3rd series 7. 18–43.

1917. *Shakespeare's Fight with the Pirates and the Problems of the Transmission of His Text*. London. Moring.

1919a. 'Shakespeare's Hand in the Play of "Sir Thomas More".' *Times Literary Supplement* Number 901 (24 April). 222.

1919b. 'Shakespeare's Hand in the Play of "Sir Thomas More": A Letter to the Editor.' *Times Literary Supplement* Number 905 (22 May). 279.

1923–4. 'Elizabethan Spelling as a Literary and Bibliographical Clue.' *The Library* (=*Transactions of the Bibliographical Society*). 4th series (=2nd of *Transactions of the Bibliographical Society*) 4. 1–8.

Pollard, A. W. and John Dover Wilson. 1919a. 'The "Stolne and Surreptitious" Shakespearian Texts, Part One: Why Some of Shakespeare's Plays Were Pirated.' *Times Literary Supplement* Number 886 (9 January). 18.

1919b. 'The "Stolne and Surreptitious" Shakespearian Texts, Part Two: How Some of Shakespeare's Plays Were Pirated.' *Times Literary Supplement* Number 887 (16 January). 30.

1919c. 'The "Stolne and Surreptitious" Shakespearian Texts, *Henry V* (1600).' *Times Literary Supplement* Number 895 (13 March). 134.

1919d. 'The "Stolne and Surreptitious" Shakespearian Texts, *Merry Wives of Windsor* (1602).' *Times Literary Supplement* Number 916 (7 August). 420.

1919e. 'The "Stolne and Surreptitious" Shakespearian Texts: *Romeo and Juliet*, 1597.' *Times Literary Supplement* Number 917 (14 August). 434.

1920. 'What Follows if Some of the Good Quarto Editions of Shakespeare's Plays were Printed from his Autograph Manuscripts: Summary.' *Transactions of the Bibliographical Society*. 2nd series 15. 136–9.

Pollard, A. W., W. W. Greg, E. Maunde Thompson, John Dover Wilson and R. W. Chambers. 1923. *Shakespeare's Hand in the Play of* Sir Thomas More. Shakespeare Problems 2. Cambridge University Press.

Posener, Alan. 1994. '"Materialism", Dialectics, and Editing Shakespeare.' *New Theatre Quarterly* 10. 263–6.

Potter, Lois. 2003. 'Editing Desdemona.' In *Arden: Editing Shakespeare: Essays in Honour of Richard Proudfoot*. Ed. Ann Thompson and Gordon McMullan. The Arden Shakespeare. London. Thomson Learning. 81–94.

Povey, Kenneth. 1955. 'Variant Formes in Elizabethan Printing.' *The Library* (=*Transactions of the Bibliographical Society*). 5th series (=3rd of *Transactions of the Bibliographical Society*) 10. 41–8.

1960. 'The Optical Identification of First Formes.' *Studies in Bibliography* 13. 189–90.

Price, George R. 1978. 'The Printing of *Love's Labour's Lost* (1598).' *Papers of the Bibliographical Society of America* 72. 405–34.

Price, Hereward T. 1920. *The Text of* Henry V. Newcastle-under-Lyme. Mandley and Unett.

Ragg, Edward. 2001. 'The Oxford Shakespeare Re-visited: An Interview with Professor Stanley Wells.' *Analytical and Enumerative Bibliography* 12. 73–101.

Rasmussen, Eric. 1991. 'Setting Down What the Clown Spoke: Improvisation, Hand B, and *The Book of Sir Thomas More*.' *The Library* (=*Transactions of the Bibliographical Society*). 6th series (=4th of *Transactions of the Bibliographical Society*) 13. 126–36.

1997. 'The Revision of Scripts.' In Cox and Kastan (eds.). 441–60.

Reid, S. W. 1985. 'B and "J": Two Compositors in Two Plays of the Shakespeare First Folio.' *The Library* (=*Transactions of the Bibliographical Society*). 6th series (=4th of *Transactions of the Bibliographical Society*) 7. 126–36.

Rhodes, R. Crompton. 1923. *Shakespeare's First Folio: A Study*. Oxford. Basil Blackwell.

Rider, Philip R. 1977. 'The Concurrent Printing of Shirley's *The Wittie Faire One* and *The Bird in a Cage*.' *Papers of the Bibliographical Society of America* 71. 328–33.

Ridley, M. R. 1935. '"The Genuine Text": A Letter to the Editor.' *Times Literary Supplement* Number 1739 (30 May). 348.

Sartre, Jean-Paul. 1986. *What is Literature?* Trans. Bernard Frechtman. Introd. David Caute. London. Methuen.

Satchell, Thomas. 1920. '"The Spelling of the First Folio": A Letter to the Editor.' *Times Literary Supplement* Number 959 (3 June). 352.

Saussure, Ferdinand de. 1916. *Cours de Linguistique Générale* (*Course in General Linguistics*). Ed. Charles Bally, Albert Sechehaye and Albert Riedlinger. Paris. Payot.

Schäfer, Jürgen. 1970. 'The Orthography of Proper Names in Modern-spelling Editions of Shakespeare.' *Studies in Bibliography* 23. 1–19.

Shaaber, M. A. 1947. 'Problems in the Editing of Shakespeare: Text.' *English Institute Essays*. 97–116.

Shakespeare, William. 1594. [*The Contention of York and Lancaster*] *The First Part of the Contention Betwixt the Two Famous Houses of Yorke and Lancaster*. STC 26099 BEPD 119a (Q1). London. Thomas Creede for Thomas Millington.

    1595. [*Richard Duke of York*] *The True Tragedie of Richard Duke of Yorke, and the Death of Good King Henrie the Sixt*. STC 21006 BEPD 138a (O). London. P[eter] S[hort] for Thomas Millington.

    1597a. [*Richard 2*] *The Tragedie of King Richard the Second*. STC 22307 BEPD 141a (Q1). London. Valentine Simmes for Andrew Wise.

    1597b. [*Romeo and Juliet*] *An Excellent Conceited Tragedie of Romeo and Juliet*. STC 22322 BEPD 143a (Q1). London. [Edward Allde and John Danter] for John Danter.

    1598a. [*1 Henry 4*] *The Historie of Henrie the Fourth*. STC 22279a BEPD 145a (Q1). London. [Peter Short for Andrew Wise].

    1598b. [*1 Henry 4*] *The Historie of Henrie the Fourth*. STC 22280 BEPD 145b (Q2). London. P[eter] S[hort] for Andrew Wise.

    1599. [*Romeo and Juliet*] *The Most Excellent and Lamentable Tragedie, of Romeo and Juliet*. STC 22323 BEPD 143b (Q2). London. Thomas Creede for Cuthbert Burby.

    1600a. [*2 Henry 4*] *The Second Part of Henrie the Fourth*. STC 22288 BEPD 167a(i) (Q). London. V[alentine] S[immes] for Andrew Wise and William Aspley.

    1600b. [*Henry 5*] *The Cronicle History of Henry the Fift*. STC 22289 BEPD 165a (Q1). London. Thomas Creede for Thomas Millington and John Busby.

    1600c. [*Much Ado About Nothing*] *Much Adoe About Nothing*. STC 22304 BEPD 168a (Q). London. V[alentine] S[immes] for Andrew Wise and William Aspley.

1603. [*Hamlet*] *The Tragicall Historie of Hamlet Prince of Denmarke*. STC 22275 BEPD 197a (Q1). London. [Valentine Simmes] for N[icholas] L[ing] and John Trundell.

1604–5. [*Hamlet*] *The Tragicall Historie of Hamlet, Prince of Denmarke*. STC 22276 BEPD 197b (Q2). London. J[ames] R[oberts] for N[icholas] L[ing].

1608. [*King Lear*] [*The*] *True Chronicle Historie of the Life and Death of King Lear and His Three Daughters*. STC 22292 BEPD 265a (Q1). London. [Nicholas Okes] for Nathaniel Butter.

1609. [*Troilus and Cressida*] *The Historie of Troylus and Cresseida*. STC 22331 BEPD 279a(i) (Qa). London. G[eorge] Eld for R[ichard] Bonian and H[enry] Walley.

1619. [*King Lear*] [*The*] *True Chronicle Historie of the Life and Death of King Lear and His Three Daughters*. STC 22293 BEPD 265b (Q2). London. [William Jaggard] for Nathaniel Butter.

1622. [*Othello*] *The Tragoedy of Othello, the Moore of Venice*. STC 22305 BEPD 379a (Q1). London. N[icholas] O[kes] for Thomas Walkley.

1623. *Comedies, Histories & Tragedies*. STC 22273 (F1). London. Isaac and William Jaggard for Edward Blount, John Smethwick, Isaac Jaggard and William Aspley.

1765. *The Plays*. Ed. Samuel Johnson. Vol. 1: Preliminary Matter; *The Tempest*; *A Midsummer-Night's Dream*; *The Two Gentlemen of Verona*; *Measure for Measure*; *The Merchant of Venice*. 8 vols. London. J. and R. Tonson [etc.].

1821. *The Plays and Poems*. Ed. Edmond Malone and James Boswell. Vol. 18: *Henry VI Part I*; *Henry VI Part II*; *Henry VI Part III*; Mr Malone's Dissertation. 21 vols. London. F. C. and Rivington [etc.].

1863. *The Works*. Ed. William George Clark and John Glover. Vol. 1: *The Tempest*; *The Two Gentlemen of Verona*; *The Merry Wives of Windsor*; *Measure for Measure*; *The Comedy of Errors*. 9 vols. Cambridge. Macmillan.

1866. *The Works*. Ed. William George Clark, John Glover and William Aldis Wright. Vol. 8: *Hamlet*; *King Lear*; *Othello*. 9 vols. Cambridge. Macmillan.

1877. *King Henry V: Parallel Texts of the First Quarto (1600) and First Folio (1623) Editions*. Ed. Brinsley Nicholson. Introd. P. A. Daniel. New Shakspere Society Publications Series 2: Plays 9. London. Trübner.

1881. *The Merry Wives of Windsor, 1602: A Photo-facsimile*. Introd. P. A. Daniel. London. Griggs.

1891–3. *The Works*. Ed. William Aldis Wright. 2nd edn. 9 vols. London. Macmillan.

1893. *Macbeth*. Ed. E. K. Chambers. The Warwick Shakespeare. London. Blackie and Son.

1899. *Hamlet*. Ed. Edward Dowden. The Arden Shakespeare. London. Methuen.

1900. *Romeo and Juliet*. Ed. Edward Dowden. The Arden Shakespeare. London. Methuen.

1901. *King Lear*. Ed. W. J. Craig. The Arden Shakespeare. London. Methuen.

1902a. *Comedies, Histories, and Tragedies: A Reproduction in Facsimile of the First Folio Edition 1623 from the Chatsworth Copy.* Introd. Sidney Lee. Oxford University Press.
1902b. *Julius Caesar.* Ed. Michael Macmillan. The Arden Shakespeare. London. Methuen.
1902c. *The Tempest.* Ed. Morton Luce. The Arden Shakespeare. London. Methuen.
1903a. *Cymbeline.* Ed. Edward Dowden. The Arden Shakespeare. London. Methuen.
1903b. *The Life of King Henry the Fifth.* Ed. Herbert Arthur Evans. The Arden Shakespeare. London. Methuen.
1903c. *Othello.* Ed. H. C. Hart. The Arden Shakespeare. London. Methuen.
1904a. *All's Well That Ends Well.* Ed. W. Osborne Brigstocke. The Arden Shakespeare. London. Methuen.
1904b. *Love's Labour's Lost.* Ed. Horace Howard Furness. New Variorum 14. Philadelphia. Lippincott.
1904c. *The Merry Wives of Windsor.* Ed. H. C. Hart. The Arden Shakespeare. London. Methuen.
1905. *A Midsummer Night's Dream.* Ed. Henry Cuningham. The Arden Shakespeare. London. Methuen.
1906a. *Love's Labour's Lost.* Ed. H. C. Hart. The Arden Shakespeare. London. Methuen.
1906b. *The Two Gentlemen of Verona.* Ed. R. Warwick Bond. The Arden Shakespeare. London. Methuen.
1907. *Pericles.* Ed. K. Deighton. The Arden Shakespeare. London. Methuen.
1909. *The First Part of King Henry the Sixth.* Ed. H. C. Hart. The Arden Shakespeare. London. Methuen.
1910. *The Merry Wives of Windsor, 1602.* Ed. W. W. Greg. Oxford. Clarendon Press.
1912. *Macbeth.* Ed. Henry Cuningham. The Arden Shakespeare. London. Methuen.
1914. *As You Like It.* Ed. J. W. Holme. The Arden Shakespeare. London. Methuen.
1916. *King Richard II: A New Quarto.* Ed. and Introd. Alfred W. Pollard. London. Bernard Quaritch.
1921a. *The Merry Wives of Windsor.* Ed. Arthur Quiller-Couch and John Dover Wilson. The New Shakespeare. Cambridge University Press.
1921b. *The Tempest.* Ed. Arthur Quiller-Couch and John Dover Wilson. The New Shakespeare. Cambridge University Press.
1921c. *The Two Gentlemen of Verona.* Ed. Arthur Quiller-Couch and John Dover Wilson. The New Shakespeare. Cambridge University Press.
1922a. *Coriolanus.* Ed. W. J. Craig and R. H. Case. The Arden Shakespeare. London. Methuen.
1922b. *Measure for Measure.* Ed. Arthur Quiller-Couch and John Dover Wilson. The New Shakespeare. Cambridge University Press.

1923a. *Love's Labour's Lost*. Ed. Arthur Quiller-Couch and John Dover Wilson. The New Shakespeare. Cambridge University Press.
1923b. *The Second Part of King Henry the Fourth*. Ed. R. P. Cowl. The Arden Shakespeare. London. Methuen.
1924a. *A Midsummer Night's Dream*. Ed. Arthur Quiller-Couch and John Dover Wilson. The New Shakespeare. Cambridge University Press.
1924b. *Much Ado About Nothing*. Ed. Grace R. Trenery. The Arden Shakespeare. London. Methuen.
1928. *Coriolanus: A Facsimile of the First Folio Text*. Introd. John Dover Wilson. Facsimiles of the First Folio Texts. London. Faber and Gwyer.
1930. *The First Part of King Henry the Sixth*. Ed. H. C. Hart. 2nd edn revised by R. H. Case. The Arden Shakespeare. London. Methuen.
1934. *Hamlet*. Ed. John Dover Wilson. The New Shakespeare. Cambridge University Press.
1950. *Measure for Measure*. Ed. John Dover Wilson. 2nd edn. The New Shakespeare. Cambridge University Press.
1951a. *The Complete Works*. Ed. Hardin Craig. Chicago. Scott, Foresman.
1951b. *The Complete Works*. Ed. Peter Alexander. London. Collins.
1951c. *Love's Labour's Lost*. Ed. Richard David. The Arden Shakespeare. London. Methuen.
1951d. *Macbeth*. Ed. Kenneth Muir. The Arden Shakespeare. London. Methuen.
1952a. *King Lear*. Ed. Kenneth Muir. The Arden Shakespeare. London. Methuen.
1952b. *The Third Part of King Henry VI*. Ed. John Dover Wilson. The New Shakespeare. Cambridge University Press.
1954a. *Antony and Cleopatra*. Ed. M. R. Ridley. The Arden Shakespeare. London. Methuen.
1954b. *Comedies, Histories, and Tragedies: A Facsimile Edition*. Ed. Helge Kökeritz. Introd. Charles Tyler Prouty. New York. Yale University Press.
1954c. *The Complete Works*. Ed. Charles Jasper Sisson. London. Odhams.
1954d. *King Henry V*. Ed. J. H. Walter. The Arden Shakespeare. London. Methuen.
1954e. *King John*. Ed. E. A. J. Honigmann. The Arden Shakespeare. London. Methuen.
1954f. *Richard III*. Ed. John Dover Wilson. The New Shakespeare. Cambridge University Press.
1955a. *Cymbeline*. Ed. J. M. Nosworthy. The Arden Shakespeare. London. Methuen.
1955b. *Julius Caesar*. Ed. T. S. Dorsch. The Arden Shakespeare. London. Methuen.
1955c. *The Merchant of Venice*. Ed. John Russell Brown. The Arden Shakespeare. London. Methuen.
1956. *Pericles*. Ed. J. C. Maxwell. The New Shakespeare. Cambridge University Press.

1957a. *Othello*. Ed. Alice Walker and John Dover Wilson. The New Shakespeare. Cambridge University Press.
1957b. *The Second Part of King Henry VI*. Ed. Andrew S. Cairncross. The Arden Shakespeare. London. Methuen.
1957c. *Troilus and Cressida*. Ed. Alice Walker. The New Shakespeare. Cambridge University Press.
1958. *The Tempest*. Ed. Frank Kermode. Rev. edn. The Arden Shakespeare. London. Methuen.
1959a. *All's Well That Ends Well*. Ed. G. K. Hunter. The Arden Shakespeare. London. Methuen.
1959b. *Timon of Athens*. Ed. H. J. Oliver. The Arden Shakespeare. London. Methuen.
1960a. *Coriolanus*. Ed. John Dover Wilson. The New Shakespeare. Cambridge University Press.
1960b. *The First Part of King Henry IV*. Ed. A. R. Humphreys. The Arden Shakespeare. London. Methuen.
1960c. *King Lear*. Ed. George Ian Duthie and John Dover Wilson. The New Shakespeare. Cambridge University Press.
1962. *The Comedy of Errors*. Ed. R. A. Foakes. The Arden Shakespeare. London. Methuen.
1963. *The Winter's Tale*. Ed. J. H. P. Pafford. The Arden Shakespeare. London. Methuen.
1964. *The Third Part of King Henry VI*. Ed. Andrew S. Cairncross. The Arden Shakespeare. London. Methuen.
1965. *Measure for Measure*. Ed. J. W. Lever. The Arden Shakespeare. London. Methuen.
1966. *Richard II, 1597*. Ed. Charlton Hinman. Shakespeare Quarto Facsimiles 13. Oxford. Clarendon Press.
1968a. *Henry IV Part One*. Ed. P. H. Davison. New Penguin Shakespeare. London. Penguin.
1968b. *The Norton Facsimile of the First Folio of Shakespeare*. Ed. Charlton Hinman. New York. Norton.
1968c. *Richard III*. Ed. E. A. J. Honigmann. New Penguin Shakespeare. London. Penguin.
1969a. *The Complete Pelican Shakespeare: The Comedies and Romances*. Gen. ed. Alfred Harbage. 3 vols. Harmondsworth. Penguin.
1969b. *The Complete Pelican Shakespeare: The Histories and the Non-Dramatic Poetry*. Gen. ed. Alfred Harbage. 3 vols. Harmondsworth. Penguin.
1969c. *The Complete Pelican Shakespeare: The Tragedies*. Gen. ed. Alfred Harbage. 3 vols. Harmondsworth. Penguin.
1969d. *The Complete Works*. Gen. ed. Alfred Harbage. The Pelican Shakespeare. Baltimore MD. Penguin.
1969e. *Richard II*. Ed. Stanley Wells. New Penguin Shakespeare. London. Penguin.
1972. *King Lear*. Ed. G. K. Hunter. New Penguin Shakespeare. London. Penguin.

1973. *The Complete Works*. Ed. Hardin Craig and David Bevington. Rev. edn. Glenview IL. Scott, Foresman.

1974a. *King John*. Ed. Robert Smallwood. New Penguin Shakespeare. London. Penguin.

1974b. *The Riverside Shakespeare*. Ed. G. Blakemore Evans. Boston. Houghton Mifflin.

1975. *Twelfth Night*. Ed. J. M. Lothian and T. W. Craik. The Arden Shakespeare. London. Methuen.

1976. *Coriolanus*. Ed. Philip Brockbank. The Arden Shakespeare. London. Methuen.

1979. *A Midsummer Night's Dream*. Ed. Harold F. Brooks. The Arden Shakespeare. London. Methuen.

1980a. *The Complete Works*. Ed. David Bevington. 3rd edn. Glenview IL. Scott, Foresman.

1980b. *Romeo and Juliet*. Ed. Brian Gibbons. The Arden Shakespeare. London. Methuen.

1981. *King Richard III*. Ed. Antony Hammond. The Arden Shakespeare. London. Methuen.

1982a. *Hamlet*. Ed. Harold Jenkins. The Arden Shakespeare. London. Methuen.

1982b. *Henry V*. Ed. Gary Taylor. The Oxford Shakespeare. Oxford University Press.

1982c. *Love's Labour's Lost*. Ed. John Kerrigan. New Penguin Shakespeare. London. Penguin.

1982d. *Troilus and Cressida*. Ed. Kenneth Muir. The Oxford Shakespeare. Oxford. Clarendon Press.

1984a. *A Midsummer Night's Dream*. Ed. R. A. Foakes. The New Cambridge Shakespeare. Cambridge University Press.

1984b. *Othello*. Ed. Norman Sanders. The New Cambridge Shakespeare. Cambridge University Press.

1985. *Hamlet*. Ed. Philip Edwards. The New Cambridge Shakespeare. Cambridge University Press.

1986. *William Shakespeare: The Complete Works: Original Spelling Edition*. Ed. Stanley Wells, Gary Taylor, John Jowett and William Montgomery. Oxford. Clarendon Press.

1987. *Hamlet*. Ed. G. R. Hibbard. The Oxford Shakespeare. Oxford. Clarendon Press.

1989a. *The Complete King Lear, 1608–1623: Texts and Parallel Texts in Photographic Facsimile*. Ed. Michael Warren. Berkeley. University of California Press.

1989b. *The Complete Works*. Ed. Stanley Wells, Gary Taylor, John Jowett and William Montgomery. Electronic edition prepared by William Montgomery and Lou Burnard. Oxford University Press.

1989c. *The Parallel King Lear 1608–1623*. Ed. Michael Warren. Berkeley. University of California Press.

1990a. *The First Part of King Henry VI*. Ed. Michael Hattaway. The New Cambridge Shakespeare. Cambridge University Press.

1990b. *King John*. Ed. L. A. Beaurline. The New Cambridge Shakespeare. Cambridge University Press.
1991. *Measure for Measure*. Ed. Brian Gibbons. The New Cambridge Shakespeare. Cambridge University Press.
1992a. *The Complete Works*. Ed. David Bevington. 4th edn. New York. HarperCollins.
1992b. *The Tragedy of Hamlet*. Ed. Barbara A. Mowat and Paul Werstine. The New Folger Library Shakespeare. New York. Washington Square Press.
1992c. *The Tragedy of Romeo and Juliet*. Ed. Barbara A. Mowat and Paul Werstine. The New Folger Library Shakespeare. New York. Washington Square Press.
1993a. *The Cronicle History of Henry the Fift*. Ed. Graham Holderness and Bryan Loughrey. Shakespearean Originals: First Editions. Hemel Hempstead. Harvester Wheatsheaf.
1993b. *King Lear*. Ed. Barbara A. Mowat and Paul Werstine. The New Folger Library Shakespeare. New York. Simon and Schuster.
1993c. *King Lear: A Parallel Text Edition*. Ed. René Weis. Longman Annotated Texts. London. Longman.
1994. *A Midsummer Night's Dream*. Ed. Peter Holland. The Oxford Shakespeare. Oxford University Press.
1995a. *Antony and Cleopatra*. Ed. John Wilders. The Arden Shakespeare. London. Routledge.
1995b. *King Henry V*. Ed. T. W. Craik. The Arden Shakespeare. London. Routledge.
1995c. *Titus Andronicus*. Ed. Jonathan Bate. The Arden Shakespeare. London. Routledge.
1995d. *The Tragedie of Anthonie, and Cleopatra*. Ed. John Turner. Shakespearean Originals: First Editions. Hemel Hempstead. Harvester Wheatsheaf.
1996a. *A Midsommer Night's Dreame*. Ed. T. O. Treadwell. Shakespearean Originals: First Editions. Hemel Hempstead. Harvester Wheatsheaf.
1996b. *The Norton Facsimile of the First Folio of Shakespeare*. Ed. Charlton Hinman. 2nd edn with a new introduction by Peter W. M. Blayney. New York. Norton.
1996c. *Othello*. Ed. E. A. J. Honigmann. The Arden Shakespeare. Walton-on-Thames. Thomas Nelson.
1997a. *The Complete Works*. Ed. David Bevington. Updated 4th edn. New York. Longman.
1997b. *King Lear*. Ed. R. A. Foakes. The Arden Shakespeare. Walton-on-Thames. Thomas Nelson.
1998. *Pericles, Prince of Tyre*. Ed. Doreen DelVecchio and Antony Hammond. The New Cambridge Shakespeare. Cambridge University Press.
1999a. *King Henry VIII or All is True*. Ed. Jay L. Halio. The Oxford Shakespeare. Oxford University Press.
1999b. *King Richard III*. Ed. Janis Lull. The New Cambridge Shakespeare. Cambridge University Press.

2000a. *The First Quarto of King Henry V*. Ed. Andrew Gurr. The New Cambridge Shakespeare: The Early Quartos. Cambridge University Press.

2000b. *King Henry the Eighth*. Ed. Gordon McMullan. The Arden Shakespeare. London. Thomson Learning.

2000c. *King Lear*. Ed. Stanley Wells. The Oxford Shakespeare. Oxford University Press.

2000d. *Richard III*. Ed. John Jowett. The Oxford Shakespeare. Oxford University Press.

2000e. *Romeo and Juliet*. Ed. Jill L. Levenson. The Oxford Shakespeare. Oxford University Press.

2001a. *King Henry VI Part 3*. Ed. John D. Cox and Eric Rasmussen. The Arden Shakespeare. London. Thomson Learning.

2001b. *Titus Andronicus*. Ed. Sonia Massai and Jacques Berthoud. New Penguin Shakespeare. London. Penguin.

2002. *King Henry IV Part 1*. Ed. David Scott Kastan. The Arden Shakespeare. London. Thomson Learning.

2004a. *Pericles*. Ed. Suzanne Gossett. The Arden Shakespeare. London. Thomson Learning.

2004b. *Pericles, Prince of Tyre*. Ed. Roger Warren. The Oxford Shakespeare. Oxford University Press.

2005a. *Cymbeline*. Ed. John Pitcher. New Penguin Shakespeare. London. Penguin.

2005b. *William Shakespeare: The Complete Works*. Ed. Stanley Wells, Gary Taylor, John Jowett and William Montgomery. 2nd edn. Oxford. Clarendon Press.

2006a. *As You Like It*. Ed. Juliet Dusinberre. The Arden Shakespeare. London. Thomson Learning.

2006b. *Hamlet*. Ed. Ann Thompson and Neil Taylor. The Arden Shakespeare. London. Thomson Learning.

2006c. *Hamlet: The Texts of 1603 and 1623*. Ed. Ann Thompson and Neil Taylor. The Arden Shakespeare. London. Thomson Learning.

2006d. *Much Ado About Nothing*. Ed. Claire McEachern. The Arden Shakespeare. London. Thomson Learning.

2009. *King Richard III*. Ed. Janis Lull. Updated edn. The New Cambridge Shakespeare. Cambridge University Press.

Shakespeare, William and George Wilkins. 1609. [*Pericles*] *The Late, and Much Admired Play Called Pericles, Prince of Tyre*. STC 22334 BEPD 284a (Q1). London. [William White and Thomas Creede] for Henry Gosson.

Shapiro, I. A. 1948. 'The Bankside Theatres: Early Engravings.' *Shakespeare Survey* 1. 25–37.

1978. '"Accidentals or Incidentals"?: A Letter to the Editor.' *The Library* (=*Transactions of the Bibliographical Society*). 5th series (=3rd of *Transactions of the Bibliographical Society*) 33. 335.

Sharpham, Edward. 1607. *The Fleire*. STC 22384 BEPD 255a. London. [Edward Allde for] F[rancis] B[urton].

Shirley, James. 1633a. *The Bird in a Cage.* STC 22436 BEPD 479a. London. Bernard Alsop and Thomas Fawcett for William Cooke.

    1633b. *The Wittie Fair One.* STC 22462 BEPD 477a. London. Bernard Alsop and Thomas Fawcett for William Cooke.

Simpson, Percy. 1911. *Shakespearian Punctuation.* Oxford. Clarendon Press.

    1919. '"The First Quarto of Hamlet": Review of John Dover Wilson' *The Copy for "Hamlet", 1603, and the "Hamlet" Transcript, 1593* ([London: Alexander] Moring[, 1918]).' *Times Literary Supplement* Number 912 (10 July). 374.

Sisson, C. J. 1936. *Lost Plays of Shakespeare's Age.* Cambridge University Press.

    1942. 'Shakespeare Quartos as Prompt-copies.' *Review of English Studies.* o.s. 18. 129–43.

Skura, Meredith. 1996. 'Is there a Shakespeare after the New New Bibliography?' In Parker and Zitner (eds.). 169–83.

Smart, John Semple. 1928. *Shakespeare: Truth and Tradition. With a memoir by W. Macneile Dixon.* London. Edward Arnold.

Smith, John Hazel. 1963. 'The Composition of the Quarto of *Much Ado About Nothing.*' *Studies in Bibliography* 16. 9–26.

    1964. 'The Cancel in the Quarto of *2 Henry IV* Revisited.' *Shakespeare Quarterly* 15.3. 173–8.

Sokal, Alan and Jean Bricmont. 1998. *Intellectual Impostures: Postmodern Philosophers' Abuse of Science.* London. Profile.

Spevack, Marvin. 1965–80. *A Complete and Systematic Concordance to the Works of Shakespeare.* 9 vols. Hildesheim. Georg Olms Verlag.

Spinner, Jonathan H. 1977. 'The Compositor and Presswork of *Henry V*, Q1.' *The Library* (=*Transactions of the Bibliographical Society*). 5th series (=3rd of *Transactions of the Bibliographical Society*) 32. 37–44.

Sprinchorn, Evert. 1994a. '"Shakespeare's Bad Quarto": A Letter to the Editor.' *Times Literary Supplement* Number 4738 (21 January). 15.

    1994b. '"Shakespeare's Bad Quarto": A Letter to the Editor.' *Times Literary Supplement* Number 4748 (1 April). 19.

Stallybrass, Peter. 1998. 'Marx's Coat.' *Border Fetishisms: Material Objects in Unstable Spaces.* Ed. Patricia Spyer. Zones of Religion. New York. Routledge. 183–207.

Steele, Robert. 1919. 'Shakespeare's Hand in the Play of "Sir Thomas More": A Letter to the Editor.' *Times Literary Supplement* Number 906 (29 May). 295.

Stern, Tiffany. 2000. *Rehearsal from Shakespeare to Sheridan.* Oxford. Clarendon Press.

    2004. *Making Shakespeare: From Stage to Page.* Accents on Shakespeare. London. Routledge.

Stirling, Brents. 1962. '*Julius Caesar* in Revision.' *Shakespeare Quarterly* 13. 187–205.

Stone, P. W. K. 1980. *The Textual History of* King Lear. London. Scolar Press.

Stopes, C. C. 1919. 'Shakespeare's Hand in the Play of "Sir Thomas More": A Letter to the Editor.' *Times Literary Supplement* Number 906 (29 May). 295–6.

Tanselle, G. Thomas. 1987. *Textual Criticism Since Greg: A Chronicle, 1950–1985.* Charlottesville. University Press of Virginia.

1989. *A Rationale of Textual Criticism*. Philadelphia. University of Pennsylvania Press.

1993. 'The Life and Work of Fredson Bowers.' *Studies in Bibliography* 46. 1–154.

1994. 'Editing Without a Copy-text.' *Studies in Bibliography* 47. 1–22.

Taylor, Gary. 1981a. 'Copy-text and Collation (with Special Reference to *Richard III*).' *The Library* (=*Transactions of the Bibliographical Society*). 6th series (=4th of *Transactions of the Bibliographical Society*) 3. 33–42.

1981b. 'The Shrinking Compositor A of the Shakespeare First Folio.' *Studies in Bibliography* 34. 96–117.

1982a. 'Four New Readings in *King Lear*.' *Notes and Queries* 227. 121–3.

1982b. '*Troilus and Cressida*: Bibliography, Performance, and Interpretation.' *Shakespeare Studies* 15. 99–136.

1983a. 'The Folio Copy for *Hamlet*, *King Lear*, and *Othello*.' *Shakespeare Quarterly* 34. 44–61.

1983b. '*King Lear*: The Date and Authorship of the Folio Version.' In Taylor and Warren (eds.). 351–468.

1983c. 'Monopolies, Show Trials, Disaster, and Invasion: *King Lear* and Censorship.' In Taylor and Warren (eds.). 75–119.

1985a. 'Folio Compositors and Folio Copy: *King Lear* and its Context.' *Papers of the Bibliographical Society of America* 79. 17–74.

1985b. 'The Fortunes of Oldcastle.' *Shakespeare Survey* 38. 85–100.

1985–6. 'Some Manuscripts of Shakespeare's Sonnets.' *Bulletin of the John Rylands Library* 6. 210–46.

1986a. 'Inventing Shakespeare.' *Deutsche Shakespeare-Gesellschaft West Jahrbuch*. 26–44.

1986b. 'The Transmission of *Pericles*.' *Papers of the Bibliographical Society of America* 80. 193–217.

1993a. 'Post-script.' *Shakespeare Reshaped, 1606–1623*. Ed. Gary Taylor and John Jowett. Oxford Shakespeare Studies. Oxford. Clarendon Press. 237–43.

1993b. 'The Renaissance and the End of Editing.' *Palimpsest: Editorial Theory in the Humanities*. Ed. George Bornstein and Ralph G. Williams. Editorial Theory and Literary Criticism 1. Ann Arbor. University of Michigan Press. 121–49.

1993c. 'The Structure of Performance: Act-Intervals in the London Theatres, 1576–1642.' *Shakespeare Reshaped, 1606–1623*. Ed. Gary Taylor and John Jowett. Oxford Shakespeare Studies. Oxford. Clarendon Press. 3–50.

2004a. 'Shakespeare's Midlife Crisis.' *The Guardian* (newspaper) 3 May. 11.

2004b. 'Thomas Middleton, *The Spanish Gypsy*, and Collaborative Authorship.' *Words That Count: Essay on Early-modern Authorship in Honor of MacDonald P. Jackson*. Ed. Brian Boyd. Newark. University of Delaware Press. 241–73.

Taylor, Gary and Michael Warren. 1983a. 'Preface.' In Gary Taylor and Warren (eds.). v–x.

Taylor, Gary and John Lavagnino (eds.). 2007. *Thomas Middleton and Early Modern Textual Culture: A Companion to the Collected Works*. Oxford. Clarendon Press.

Taylor, Gary and Michael Warren (eds.). 1983b. *The Division of the Kingdoms: Shakespeare's Two Versions of* King Lear. Oxford Shakespeare Studies. Oxford. Clarendon Press.

Thomas, Sidney. 1995. 'The Integrity of *King Lear*.' *Modern Language Review* 90. 572–84.

Thompson, Edward Maunde. 1916. *Shakespeare's Handwriting: A Study*. Oxford. Clarendon Press.

Thorpe, James. 1972. *Principles of Textual Criticism*. San Marino CA. Huntington Library.

Tillyard, E. M. W. 1943. *The Elizabethan World Picture*. London. Chatto and Windus.

1944. *Shakespeare's History Plays*. London. Chatto and Windus.

Todd, William B. 1966. '"The Degressive Principle": A Letter to the Editor.' *Times Literary Supplement* Number 3366 (1 September). 781.

Tronch-Pérez, Jesús. 2002. 'A Comparison of the Suspect Texts of Lope de Vega's La Dama Boba and Shakespeare's *Hamlet*.' *Shakespeare Yearbook* 13: Shakespeare and Spain. 30–57.

2004. 'Playtext Reporters and Memoriones: Suspect Texts in Shakespeare and Spanish Golden Age Drama.' *Shakespeare and the Mediterranean: The Selected Proceedings of the International Shakespeare Association World Congress at Valencia 2001*. Ed. Tom Clayton, Susan Brock and Vicente Fores. Newark. University of Delaware Press. 270–85.

Trousdale, Marion. 1986. 'Issues: A Trip Through the Divided Kingdoms.' *Shakespeare Quarterly* 37. 218–23.

1990. 'A Second Look at Critical Bibliography and the Acting of Plays.' *Shakespeare Quarterly* 41. 87–96.

Turner Junior, Robert K. 1962. 'Printing Methods and Textual Problems in *A Midsummer Night's Dream* Q1.' *Studies in Bibliography* 15. 33–55.

1966. 'Reappearing Types as Bibliographical Evidence.' *Studies in Bibliography* 19. 198–209.

Urkowitz, Steven. 1980. *Shakespeare's Revision of* King Lear. Princeton University Press.

1986a. 'Reconsidering the Relationship of Quarto and Folio Texts of *Richard III*.' *English Literary Renaissance* 16. 442–66.

1986b. '"Well-sayd Olde Mole": Burying Three *Hamlets* in Modern Editions.' *Shakespeare Study Today: The Horace Howard Furness Memorial Lectures*. Ed. Georgianna Ziegler. AMS Studies in the Renaissance 13. New York. AMS Press. 37–70.

1988a. 'Five Women Eleven Ways: Changing Images of Shakespearean Characters in the Earliest Texts.' *Images of Shakespeare: Proceedings of the Third Congress of the International Shakespeare Association in Berlin, 1–6 April 1986*. Ed. Werner Habicht, D. J. Palmer and Roger Pringle. Newark. University of Delaware Press. 292–304.

1988b. '"If I Mistake in those Foundations which I Build Upon": Peter Alexander's Textual Analysis of *Henry VI Parts 2 and 3*.' *English Literary Renaissance* 18. 230–56.

 1995. '"Brother, Can You Spare a Paradigm?": Textual Generosity and the Printing of Shakespeare's Multiple-text Plays by Contemporary Editors.' *Critical Survey* 7. 292–8.

 1996. 'Two Versions of *Romeo and Juliet* 2.6 and *Merry Wives of Windsor* 5.5.215–45: An Invitation to the Pleasures of Textual/sexual Di(per)versity.' In Parker and Zitner (eds.). 222–38.

 1998. 'Preposterous Poststructuralism: Editorial Morality and the Ethics of Evidence.' *New Ways of Looking at Old Texts II: Papers of the Renaissance English Text Society, 1992–1996*. Ed. W. Speed Hill. Medieval and Renaissance Texts and Studies 188. Temple. Arizona State University. 83–90.

Urquhart, Thomas. 1641. *Epigrams: Divine and Moral*. Wing U135. London. Barnard Alsop and Thomas Fawcett.

Vickers, Brian. 1993. '"*Hamlet* by Dogberry": Review of Graham Holderness and Bryan Loughrey (eds.), *The Tragicall Historie of Hamlet Prince of Denmark*, The Shakespearean Originals: First Editions (Hemel Hempstead: Harvester Wheatsheaf, 1993).' *Times Literary Supplement* Number 4734 (24 December). 5–6.

 1994a. '"Shakespeare's Bad Quarto": A Letter to the Editor.' *Times Literary Supplement* Number 4740 (4 February). 15.

 1994b. '"Shakespeare's Bad Quarto": A Letter to the Editor.' *Times Literary Supplement* Number 4744 (4 March). 15.

 1994c. '"Shakespeare's Bad Quarto": A Letter to the Editor.' *Times Literary Supplement* Number 4752 (29 April). 19.

 1994d. '"Shakespeare's Bad Quarto": A Letter to the Editor.' *Times Literary Supplement* Number 4765 (29 July). 15.

 2002. *Shakespeare, Co-Author: A Historical Study of Five Collaborative Plays*. Oxford University Press.

Walker, Alice. 1951. 'The Textual Problem of *Hamlet*: A Reconsideration.' *Review of English Studies*. n.s. 2. 328–38.

 1953. *Textual Problems of the First Folio:* Richard III, King Lear, Troilus and Cressida, 2 Henry IV, Hamlet, Othello. Shakespeare Problems 7. Cambridge University Press.

 1954. 'The Folio Text of *1 Henry IV*.' *Studies in Bibliography* 6. 45–59.

 1955a. 'Collateral Substantive Texts (with Special Reference to *Hamlet*).' *Studies in Bibliography* 7. 51–67.

 1955b. 'Compositor Determination and Other Problems in Shakespearian Texts.' *Studies in Bibliography* 7. 3–15.

 1956. 'Some Editorial Principles (with Special Reference to *Henry V*).' *Studies in Bibliography* 8. 95–111.

Walton, J. K. 1959. 'The Quarto Copy for Folio *Richard III*; and Dr Cairncross's Answer.' *Review of English Studies*. n.s. 10. 127–40.

 1971. *The Quarto Copy for the First Folio of Shakespeare*. Dublin University Press.

Warren, Michael. 1978. 'Quarto and Folio *King Lear* and the Interpretation of Albany and Edgar.' *Shakespeare, Pattern of Excelling Nature: Shakespeare Criticism in Honor of America's Bicentennial from the International Shakespeare

Association Congress, Washington DC, April 1976. Ed. David Bevington and Jay L. Halio. Newark. University of Delaware Press. 95–107.

Warren, Roger. 1983. 'The Folio Omission of the Mock Trial: Motives and Consequences.' In Taylor and Warren (eds.). 44–57.

2000. 'The Quarto and Folio Texts of *2 Henry VI*: A Reconsideration.' *Review of English Studies*. n.s. 51. 193–207.

Webster, John. 1623. *The Tragedy of the Duchesse of Malfy*. STC 25176 BEPD 389a. London. Nicholas Okes for John Waterson.

Weingust, Don. 2006. *Acting from Shakespeare's First Folio: Theory, Text, and Performance*. London. Routledge.

Wells, Stanley. 1980. 'Editorial Treatment of Foul-paper Texts: *Much Ado About Nothing* as Test Case.' *Review of English Studies*. n.s. 31. 1–16.

1982. 'The Copy for the Folio Text of *Love's Labour's Lost*.' *Review of English Studies*. n.s. 33. 137–47.

1984. *Re-editing Shakespeare for the Modern Reader*. Oxford. Clarendon Press.

1991a. *The Oxford Shakespeare Editorial Procedures*. Unpublished typescript deposited at the library of the Shakespeare Institute of the University of Birmingham, Shelfmark 'r q PR 2754.W3'.

1991b. 'Theatricalizing Shakespeare's Text.' *New Theatre Quarterly* 7. 184–6.

2006. 'On Being a General Editor.' *Shakespeare Survey* 59: Editing Shakespeare. 39–48.

2009. 'Charles Jasper Sisson': private correspondence to the author, 7 September.

Wells, Stanley and Gary Taylor. 1979. *Modernizing Shakespeare's Spelling, with Three Studies in the Text of* Henry V. Oxford. Clarendon Press.

1990. 'The Oxford Shakespeare Re-viewed.' *Analytical and Enumerative Bibliography*. n.s. 4. 6–20.

Wells, Stanley, Gary Taylor, John Jowett and William Montgomery. 1987. *William Shakespeare: A Textual Companion*. Oxford University Press.

Wells, Stanley and Judith Wardman. [1965]. *Editorial Procedures for the New Penguin Shakespeare*. Undated, unpublished and currently uncatalogued typescript deposited at the library of the Shakespeare Institute of the University of Birmingham, with its date inferred from surrounding dated drafts and commentaries.

Werstine, Paul. 1978a. 'Compositor B of the Shakespeare First Folio.' *Analytical and Enumerative Bibliography* 2. 241–63.

1978b. 'Editorial Uses of Compositor Study.' *Analytical and Enumerative Bibliography* 2. 153–65.

1982. 'Cases and Compositors in the Shakespeare First Folio Comedies.' *Studies in Bibliography* 35. 206–34.

1983. 'Folio Editors, Folio Compositors, and the Folio Text of *King Lear*.' In Taylor and Warren (eds.). 247–312.

1984. 'Line Division in Shakespeare's Dramatic Verse: An Editorial Problem.' *Analytical and Enumerative Bibliography* 8. 73–125.

1985a. '"An Important but Imperfect Study of the *Lear* Texts": A Review of Steven Urkowitz, *Shakespeare's Revision of "King Lear"* (Princeton University Press, 1980).' *Shakespeare Quarterly* 36. 368–70.

1985b. '"An Important New Textual Study": A Review of Peter W. M. Blayney, *The Texts of "King Lear" and their Origins*. Vol. 1: Nicholas Okes and the First Quarto (Cambridge University Press, 1982).' *Shakespeare Quarterly* 36. 120–5.

1988a. '"Foul Papers" and "Prompt Books": Printer's Copy for Shakespeare's *Comedy of Errors*.' *Studies in Bibliography* 41. 232–46.

1988b. 'McKerrow's "Suggestion" and Twentieth-Century Shakespeare Textual Criticism.' *Renaissance Drama*. n.s. 19. 149–73.

1988c. 'The Textual Mystery of *Hamlet*.' *Shakespeare Quarterly* 39. 1–26.

1990. 'Narratives About Printed Shakespeare Texts: "Foul Papers" and "Bad" Quartos.' *Shakespeare Quarterly* 41. 65–86.

1995. 'Shakespeare.' *Scholarly Editing: A Guide to Research*. Ed. D. C. Greetham. New York. The Modern Language Association of America. 253–82.

1997. 'Plays in Manuscript.' In Cox and Kastan (eds.). 481–97.

1998a. 'Hypertext and Editorial Myth.' 2.1–19. Online (http://purl.oclc.org/emls/). Internet. 17 May 1998. *Early Modern Literary Studies* 3.3. n. pag.

1998b. 'Touring and the Construction of Shakespeare Textual Criticism.' In Maguire and Berger (eds.). 45–66.

1999a. 'A Century of "Bad" Shakespeare Quartos.' *Shakespeare Quarterly* 50. 310–33.

1999b. 'Post-Theory Problems in Shakespeare Editing.' *Yearbook of English Studies* 29. 103–17.

1999c. 'Shakespeare, More or Less: A. W. Pollard and Twentieth-Century Shakespeare Editing.' *Florilegium* 16. 125–45.

2000a. 'Editing Shakespeare and Editing Without Shakespeare: Wilson, McKerrow, Greg, Bowers, Tanselle, and Copy-text Editing.' *TEXT: An Interdisciplinary Annual of Textual Studies* 13. 27–53.

2000b. 'Review of E. A. J. Honigmann, *The Texts of "Othello" and Shakespearian Revision* (London and New York: Routledge, 1996).' *Shakespeare Quarterly* 51. 240–4.

2001. 'Scribe or Compositor: Ralph Crane, Compositors D and F, and the First Four Plays in the Shakespeare First Folio.' *Papers of the Bibliographical Society of America* 95. 315–39.

2004. 'Housmania: Episodes in Twentieth-century "Critical" Editing of Shakespeare.' In Erne and Kidnie (eds.). 49–62.

West, Anthony James. 2002. *The Shakespeare First Folio: The History of the Book*. Vol. 2: A New World Census of First Folios. Oxford University Press.

Wilde, A. D. 1919a. 'Shakespeare's Hand in the Play of "Sir Thomas More": A Letter to the Editor.' *Times Literary Supplement* Number 902 (1 May). 237.

1919b. 'Shakespeare's Hand in the Play of "Sir Thomas More": A Letter to the Editor.' *Times Literary Supplement* Number 905 (22 May). 279.

Wilder, Lina Perkins. 2008. 'Changeling Bottom: Speech Prefixes, Acting, and Character in *A Midsummer Night's Dream*.' *Shakespeare* 4. 45–64.

Wilkins, George. 1608. *The Painfull Adventures of Pericles Prince of Tyre*. STC 25638.5. London. T[homas] P[urfoot] for Nat[haniel] Butter.

Williams, George Walton. 1949–50. 'A Note on *King Lear*, III.ii.1–3.' *Studies in Bibliography* 2. 175–82.
   1958. 'Setting By Formes in Quarto Printing.' *Studies in Bibliography* 11. 39–53.
   1989. 'Review of William Shakespeare, *The Complete Works*, ed. Stanley Wells, Gary Taylor, John Jowett and William Montgomery (Oxford: Clarendon Press, 1986) and William Shakespeare, *The Complete Works: Original Spelling Edition*, ed. Stanley Wells, Gary Taylor, John Jowett and William Montgomery (Oxford: Clarendon Press, 1986) and Stanley Wells, Gary Taylor, John Jowett and William Montgomery, *William Shakespeare: A Textual Companion* (Oxford: Clarendon Press, 1987).' *Cahiers Élisabéthains* 35. 103–17.
Williams, Philip. 1948–9. 'The Compositor of the "Pied Bull" *Lear*.' *Studies in Bibliography* 1. 61–8.
   1956. 'New Approaches to Textual Problems in Shakespeare.' *Studies in Bibliography* 8. 3–14.
Willis, John. 1602. *The Art of Stenographie*. STC 25744a. London. [William White] for Cuthbert Burby.
Willoughby, Edwin Eliott. 1932. *The Printing of the First Folio of Shakespeare*. Oxford. Oxford University Press for the Bibliographical Society.
Wilson, F. P. 1945. 'Shakespeare and the "New Bibliography".' *The Bibliographical Society, 1892–1942: Studies in Retrospect*. Ed. F. C. Francis. Bibliographical Society Publications in Large Quarto 4: For the year 1942. London. The Bibliographical Society. 76–135.
Wilson, John Dover. 1918a. 'The Copy for *Hamlet*, 1603.' *The Library*. 3rd series 9. 153–85.
   1918b. *The Copy for* Hamlet, *1603, and the* Hamlet Transcript, *1593*. London. Alexander Moring.
   1918c. 'The *Hamlet* Transcript, 1593.' *The Library*. 3rd series 9. 217–47.
   1919a. 'Shakespeare's Hand in the Play of "Sir Thomas More": A Letter to the Editor.' *Times Literary Supplement* Number 903 (8 May). 251.
   1919b. 'Shakespeare's Hand in the Play of "Sir Thomas More": A Letter to the Editor.' *Times Literary Supplement* Number 906 (29 May). 295.
   1934a. *The Manuscript of Shakespeare's* Hamlet *and the Problems of its Transmission: An Essay in Critical Bibliography*. Vol. 1: The Texts of 1605 and 1623. 2 vols. Shakespeare's Problems 4. Cambridge University Press.
   1934b. *The Manuscript of Shakespeare's* Hamlet *and the Problems of its Transmission: An Essay in Critical Bibliography*. Vol. 2: Editorial Problems and Solutions. 2 vols. Shakespeare's Problems 4. Cambridge University Press.
   1935a. '"The Genuine Text": A Letter to the Editor.' *Times Literary Supplement* Number 1737 (16 May). 313.
   1935b. '"The Genuine Text": A Letter to the Editor.' *Times Literary Supplement* Number 1739 (30 May). 348.
   1935c. '"The Genuine Text": A Letter to the Editor.' *Times Literary Supplement* Number 1741 (13 June). 380.
   1963. *The Manuscript of Shakespeare's* Hamlet *and the Problems of its Transmission: An Essay in Critical Bibliography*. Reprinted with a new foreword by

George Ian Duthie. Vol. 1: The Texts of 1605 and 1623. 2 vols. Cambridge University Press.
Wimsatt, W. K. and M. C. Beardsley. 1946. 'The Intentional Fallacy.' *Sewanee Review* 54. 468–88.
Wolf, Edwin. 1942. 'Press Correction in Sixteenth- and Seventeenth-Century Quartos.' *Papers of the Bibliographical Society of America* 36. 187–98.
Zimmerman, Susan. 1985. 'The Uses of Headlines: Peter Short's Shakespearian Quartos *1 Henry IV* and *Richard III*.' *The Library* (=*Transactions of the Bibliographical Society*). 6th series (=4th of *Transactions of the Bibliographical Society*) 7. 218–55.

Index

All plays that Shakespeare had a hand in are indexed under his name alone and where he is believed to have collaborated on a play his co-authors' contributions are separately indexed under their names. Early editions with uncertain relationships to Shakespeare plays (such as *The Taming of a Shrew*) are indexed under the names of their related Shakespeare plays.

accidentals 44–6, 67, 72, 88, 96, 138, 147, 150, 151, 171, 172, 174, 183, 261, 265
   distinction from substantives 44, 45, 131, 171
   philosophical meaning of 45
Act to Restrain Abuses of Players 1606 42, 53, 178, 243
actors' names
   in printed texts 28–9, 215
   in theatrical manuscripts 49, 52, 215
actors' parts 23, 24, 39, 54, 109, 165, 212, 225–6, 248
Adams, John Cranford, his Globe playhouse reconstruction 34
agreement-in-error as evidence of textual descent 33–5, 138, 142, 170, 244, 253
Alexander, Nigel 191
Alexander, Peter 108, 240, 246
   his *Complete Works* edition of Shakespeare 250–1, 259
   on the origins of the bad quartos of *The Contention of York and Lancaster* and *Richard Duke of York* 103, 104–6, 111, 113, 116
   on the origins of *The Taming of a Shrew* 106–7, 123
Allde, Edward 201
Alleyn, Edward 105, 108
Allott, Robert
   England's Parnassus 220
Alsop, Bernard 96
anti-theatrical bias of editors, alleged 41–2, 43, 65, 99, 112, 129, 181, 262, 263–4
Arden Shakespeare series 5, 115, 132, 181, 192, 211, 212, 215, 229, 241–6, 247, 251–4, 256, 261, 262, 267–70

Ariosto, Ludovico, *I Suppositi* 106
Aristotle, *Metaphysics* 45
Aspley, William 245
Auden, W. H. 149
authorial papers 9, 14, 16, 17, 18, 19, 20, 21, 22, 23, 31, 37, 38, 39, 40, 41, 43, 44, 53, 54, 65, 66, 70, 88, 96, 112, 123, 132, 135, 139, 140, 143, 145, 146, 154, 155, 164, 165, 171, 172, 174, 176, 177, 178, 180, 181, 185, 186, 187, 188, 192, 205, 207, 217, 218, 221, 224, 245, 249, 252, 253, 257, 258, 261, 265
   Greg's characterization of 25–8
   signs of in printed texts 47–50, 162, 168–70, 172, 200, 214–15
   treatment in the theatre of 14, 30–1, 32–3, 48, 50–3, 205, 263–4

bad quartos xi, 14–16, 33, 46, 99, 100, 101, 102, 103, 106, 109, 110, 111, 112, 113, 114, 116, 117, 118, 119, 121, 123, 127, 147, 164, 182, 185, 188, 190, 192, 198, 201, 215, 217, 218, 221, 223, 224, 237, 265, 266, 268, 269
Baender, Paul 87, 88, 131, 146, 148
Bald, R. C. 63
Banks, Carol 204
Barish, Jonas A. 254
Barnes, Barnabe, *The Devil's Charter* 77, 216
Barthes, Roland 151
   'La mort de l'auteur' ('The Death of the Author') 79, 84, 149
Bate, Jonathan 212, 268
Bawcutt, N. W. 215–16, 223
Beaumont, Francis 8, 26, 119, 217, 221, 228, 255–6

309

Beaurline, L. A. 255, 264
Bentley, G. E. 216
    The Profession of Dramatist in Shakespeare's Time 130, 228
Berger, Thomas L. 94, 95, 183, 184
Berthoud, Jacques 257, 258
Bertram, Paul 184
Bevington, David 178, 184, 200, 240, 260, 261
Binns, James 77, 96, 122, 131
Birde, William 136, 199
Bjelland, Karen 195
Blake, William 149
Blayney, Peter W. M. 75, 89, 90, 134, 193, 203, 219, 258
    on the popularity of playbooks 198–9
        refuted 199
    revised Introduction to *The Norton Facsimile of the First Folio of Shakespeare* 258–9
    The Texts of King Lear *and Their Origins* 158–9
Bodenham, John, *Bel-vedére or the Garden of the Muses* 220
Bond, R. Warwick 245
Bond, William H. 73
Bonian, Richard 183
book-keeper. *See* prompter
Bowers, Fredson 8, 38, 47, 54, 58, 60, 61, 62, 63, 64, 65, 68, 69, 70, 71, 75, 76, 81, 82, 83, 85, 86, 87, 147, 149, 150, 152, 153, 158, 159, 166, 177, 195, 210, 225, 241, 254
    Dramatic Works in the Beaumont and Fletcher Canon, The 255–6
    his edition of Thomas Dekker 167
    his review of Philip Gaskell, *A New Introduction to Bibliography* 89
    On Editing Shakespeare and the Elizabethan Dramatists 65–8
    Studies in Bibliography 54–8
Braunmuller, A. R. 262
Bricmont, Jean 87
Brigstocke, W. Osborne 243
Brockbank, Philip 252, 253, 262–3, 264
Brome, Richard 119, 223
    The Antipodes 216
Brooks, Harold F. 251, 253
Brown, Arthur 18
Brown, John Russell 56, 167, 168, 252
Bruster, Douglas 199
Buc, George 135, 215, 223, 224, 242
Bulwer-Lytton, Edward, *Pelham* 149
Burke, Edmund 85
Busby, John 242, 243
Butter, Nathaniel 183, 242
Byron, George Gordon 149

Cairncross, Andrew S. 93, 98, 117, 170, 252–3
    disregarding importance of agreement-in-error 34
Cambridge University Press 4, 10, 82, 85, 89, 159, 192
Cambridge–Macmillan Shakespeare edition of 1863–6 6–8, 9, 13, 241, 243, 244, 247, 248, 250, 251, 260
Cantrell, Paul L. 56, 57
Carter, John 85
Case, R. H. 241, 245, 246, 251
casting off manuscript copy 68, 90, 94, 97, 191, 267, 268
    the advantages and disadvantages of doing so 73–5
Cauthen Junior, I. B. 56
Chamberlain's/King's men playing company 14, 54, 91, 102, 103, 110, 122, 179, 208, 216, 217, 218, 219
Chambers, E. K. 10, 17, 64, 110, 114, 124, 158, 248, 250
    'Disintegration of Shakespeare, The' 108, 246
    Elizabethan Stage, The 154
    William Shakespeare: A Study of Facts and Problems 109
Chambers, R. W. 205
Chapman, George 119, 140, 157
Charlemagne (anonymous) 156–8
Chaucer, Geoffrey 98
Chettle, Henry 127, 201, 202
Chinese Whispers, the children's game 1, 2, 4
Clare, Robert 194
Clark, W. G. 6
Clayton, Thomas 135
co-authorship. *See* collaborative authorship of plays
Coghill, Nevill 130
Coleridge, S. T. 228, 246
collaborative authorship of plays 226–9
Columbia University 54
compositors
    Folio apprentice identified as 'E' 57, 92, 93, 98, 136, 138, 141, 142, 143, 145, 160, 208, 267
    Folio man identified as 'A' 55, 56, 57, 92, 93, 96, 160, 171, 172, 173, 208
    Folio man identified as 'B' 55, 57, 59, 67, 79, 80, 89, 90, 92, 93, 95, 98, 138, 141, 142, 143, 144, 145, 160, 175, 187, 208, 253, 267
        his alleged carelessness 56, 58
            disproved 96–7, 136, 269
    Folio man identified as 'C' 57, 92, 93, 95, 160, 208

Folio man identified as 'D' 57, 92, 93, 95, 160, 208–9
Folio man identified as 'F' 92, 93, 208–9
Folio men identified as 'H', 'I', and 'J' 160, 171–2, 209, 256
  identified by their psycho-mechanical habits 84, 92, 93, 95, 98, 159–62, 171, 267
  identified by their spelling preferences. *See* spelling, used to identify compositors
  man identified as Valentine Simmes's 'A' 92, 93, 95, 175
  men identified as George Eld's 'A' and 'B' 94
  men identified as James Roberts's 'X' and 'Y' 56–7, 68
concurrent printing of multiple books in a printshop 82, 84, 85, 89, 95, 96, 98, 159, 259
Condell, Henry 13, 14, 15, 19, 66, 69, 79, 205, 243, 244
Congreve, William 131
  The Way of the World 151
continuous copy, the theory of 17, 18, 19, 22, 23, 25, 26, 52, 53, 65, 155, 156, 245, 248, 249
control text 40, 68, 172, 185, 210, 261
  defined 171
Cooke, William 96
Copenhagen Interpretation of quantum mechanics 87
copyright 12, 96, 183
Cowl, R. P. 245
Cox, John D. 212, 214
Craig, Hardin 240
Craig, W. J. 241–2, 245
Craik, T. W. 253, 261, 268
Crane, Ralph 91, 92, 122, 165, 208–9, 214–15, 248
  writing stage directions for *The Tempest* 176–7
Craven, Alan E. 92, 93, 95, 175
Creede, Thomas 161
Cuningham, Henry 244
cutting of plays 18, 106, 113, 170, 203, 207, 221, 222–5

Daborne, Robert 16
  letters to Philip Henslowe 26–7, 65
  The Owl 27
Dam, B. A. P. van 104
Daniel, P. A. 243, 248
  proving order of composition of Q1/F *Henry 5* 103
Danter, John 218
David, Richard 252
Davidson, Adele 127
Davis, William 127
Davison, Peter 160, 257

responding to D. F. McKenzie's 'Printers of the Mind' 86–7, 95
Day, John, George Wilkins and William Rowley
  The Travels of the Three English Brothers 20
de Grazia, Margreta 6, 163, 192–4, 195, 196, 197
  'Essential Shakespeare and the Material Book, The' 154–5
  Shakespeare Verbatim 194
de Grazia, Margreta and Peter Stallybrass, 'The Materiality of Shakespeare's Text' 192–4, 202, 214
degressive principle 85, 202
Deighton, K. 245
Dekker, Thomas 51, 119, 167
  The Welsh Ambassador 51
DelVecchio, Doreen 264
Derrida, Jacques 153, 164, 195, 196, 197, 205, 227
Dick of Devonshire (anonymous) 51
Dickens, Charles 140
Dillon, Janette 191
DiPietro, Cary 10
division of *King Lear* into two plays. *See* William Shakespeare, *King Lear*
Dobson, Michael 189, 191
Doran, Madeleine 107–8, 109, 110, 114, 115, 138, 254
Dorsch, T. S. 252
Dowden, Edward 241, 242
Drakakis, John 203, 212
Dusinberre, Juliet 229
Duthie, George Ian 111, 113, 127, 191, 249, 250
Dutton, Richard 216–17

Early English Books Online (EEBO) database of printed book facsimiles xi, 192
Edmond Ironside (anonymous) 49
Edwards, Philip 161, 263–4
Einstein, Albert, his Theory of Relativity 87
Eld, George 94
Ellis-Fermor, Una 241, 251, 252
Erne, Lukas 119, 207, 213, 223, 229
  'Shakespeare and the Publication of his Plays' 217–19
  Shakespeare as Literary Dramatist 219–22
Evans, G. Blakemore 259–60
Evans, Herbert Arthur 243

Faithful Friends, The (anonymous) 39
false starts as signs of the author 47, 48, 52, 214–15, 268
Farmer, Alan B. 199, 229
Fawcett, Thomas 96
Febvre, Lucien 9
Ferguson, W. Craig 92, 161
Field, Nathan 140

Fleeman, J. D. 85
Fletcher, John 8, 26, 119, 140, 216, 217, 221, 226, 227, 228, 241, 255–6
  Bonduca 25–6, 66, 205
  The Honest Man's Fortune 49
Fletcher, John and Philip Massinger, *Sir John van Olden Barnavelt* 49, 165–6, 214–15, 225
Foakes, R. A. 57, 167, 194, 253, 268–9, 270
Folger Shakespeare Library, Washington DC 35, 38, 73, 75, 78, 193, 196–7, 199, 252, 258
forme of type. See type, forme of, defined
Foucault, Michel 29, 151, 163, 164, 193, 194, 195, 227
  'Qu'est-ce qu-un auteur?' ('What is an Author?') 79, 84, 85, 149, 228
foul papers. See authorial papers
Fourth Folio of Shakespeare 1685 2, 6, 8
Frijlinck, Wilhelmina P. 157
Frye, Northrop 254
Furness, Horace Howard 8

Gabler, Hans Walter 255
Gaskell, Philip 146, 148
  A New Introduction to Bibliography 88–9, 94, 231
'ghost' characters as signs of the author 48, 70, 122, 188, 203
Gibbons, Brian 132, 133, 254, 262, 264
Glapthorne, Henry, *The Lady Mother* 17, 18, 19, 29, 51
Globe playhouse 34, 172
  fire at the 13, 102, 183
Globe Shakespeare edition of 1864 8, 178, 240
Glover, John 6
Gödel, Kurt, his Incompleteness Theorems 87
Godshalk, W. L. 191
Goldberg, Jonathan 153, 154, 190
good quartos 15, 21, 22, 23, 24, 121, 164, 180, 182, 205, 218, 221, 224, 252, 265, 266
Gossett, Suzanne 227, 261
Gray, Henry David 100, 101
Greene, Robert 26, 105, 108, 116, 119, 167, 246
  John of Bordeaux 49
  Orlando Furioso 106, 108, 201
Greg, W. W. 8, 12, 16, 17, 18, 22, 31, 32, 33, 37, 38, 58, 59, 61, 62, 63, 64, 65, 66, 67, 69, 75, 86, 88, 92, 95, 98, 101, 102, 103, 104, 106, 108, 110, 111, 112, 113, 115, 123, 124, 129, 131, 132, 133, 136, 137, 138, 142, 146, 149, 152, 155, 156, 162, 165, 166, 167, 168, 169, 174, 177, 178, 181, 188, 200, 202, 205, 213, 225, 240, 248, 250, 253, 255, 257, 261, 263
  baiting anti-Stratfordian Baconians 97–8
  discovering memorial reconstruction in Q1 *The Merry Wives of Windsor* 15, 100–1, 109, 124, 164–5
  Dramatic Documents from the Elizabethan Playhouses 24–30, 39, 51, 164, 199, 215
  Editorial Problem in Shakespeare, The 38–47, 52, 111–12, 164, 210
  'Rationale of Copy-Text, The' 40, 44–6, 47, 88, 147, 153, 171, 183, 210, 252
  Shakespeare First Folio, The 44, 47–54, 215
  Two Elizabethan Stage Abridgements 201
Gurr, Andrew 222–5, 226, 229, 264

Halio, Jay L. 261
Hammond, Antony 115, 159, 254, 264
Harbage, Alfred 254–5
  Annals of English Drama 158
Harrison, G. B. 184
Hart, Alfred 112, 191, 220
Hart, H. C. 243–4, 246
Hasker, Richard E. 55, 173, 174
Hawthorne, Nathaniel, *The House of Seven Gables* and *The Blithedale Romance* 147
headline analysis. See skeleton formes
Heidegger, Martin 196, 197
Heisenberg, Werner, his Uncertainty Principle 86, 87
Heminges, John 13, 14, 15, 19, 66, 69, 79, 205, 243, 244
Henslowe, Philip 16, 65, 66, 69, 130, 227
Herbert, Henry 156, 224
  demanding fair copy 17–18, 27
Hercules, mythical God 3, 230
Heywood, Thomas 26, 49, 70, 119
  The Captives 28, 39, 47, 49, 51, 52, 70
  Play of Queen Elizabeth (= *If You Know Not Me You Know Nobody*) 15
Hibbard, G. R. 180, 181, 261
Hinman, Charlton 3, 38, 54, 55, 57, 58, 59, 60, 63, 68, 72, 73, 79, 80, 84, 85, 87, 91, 92, 93, 95, 98, 136, 153, 159, 160, 171, 177, 193, 208, 240, 250, 252, 254, 255, 260, 267
  deducing print run from headline reuse 62, 82, 259
  discovering that the First Folio was set by formes 74–5
  Norton Facsimile of the First Folio of Shakespeare, The 12, 76–9, 258–9
  on the absence of proofreading and correction 56, 76, 83, 89
  Printing and Proof-reading of the First Folio of Shakespeare, The 57, 72–5, 258
Holderness, Graham 47, 190, 191, 200, 201, 204, 266

Holderness, Graham, Bryan Loughrey and
    Andrew Murphy
  'Busy Doing Nothing' 203
  'What's the Matter?' 195–6, 202
Holinshed, Raphael 70
Holland, Peter 261
Holme, J. W. 245
Honigmann, E. A. J. 123, 167, 181, 257, 269, 270
  The Stability of Shakespeare's Text 66, 69–72,
    86, 130, 133, 175, 181
Hope, Jonathan 227, 228
Hoppe, Harry R. 113, 124
Housman, A. E. 11
Howard, Jean F. 155
Howard-Hill, T. H. 59, 84, 91, 92, 93, 94, 98,
    136, 138, 141, 142, 145, 159, 160, 165–6,
    171, 172, 208, 224, 267
  his concordances to the early editions of
    Shakespeare 91–2, 168, 187
  his discovery of Folio compositor F 92
  resisting the theory that *King Lear* was revised
    141, 142, 143, 145–6
Hoy, Cyrus 255, 256
Hubler, Edwin 110
Humphreys, A. R. 253
Hunter, G. K. 253, 257
Huntington Library, San Marino CA 17, 70, 71,
    199

idealism, philosophical theory of 4, 45, 152–5,
    192, 203
immanent critique 202, 209
imposition. *See* type, imposition of, explained
incidentals as alternative name for accidentals
    44, 265
Inklings club 130
Inns of Court 172
Irace, Kathleen, *Reforming the 'Bad' Quartos* 113,
    117–19, 125

Jackson, MacDonald P. 93, 94, 159, 161–2, 182,
    188, 205
  Defining Shakespeare 245
  on revision of *King Lear* 137
Jaggard, William and Isaac 57, 58, 59, 76, 79, 89,
    90, 174
James I 135, 140
Jenkins, Harold 181, 191, 251, 254
Johnson, Francis R. 63
Johnson, Samuel 2, 23
Jones, Millard T. 94
Jonson, Ben 44, 112, 119, 136, 140, 179, 217, 220,
    223
  adding to Kyd's *The Spanish Tragedy* 135
  Every Man Out of His Humour 216, 219

Gypsies Metamorphosed, The 44
Sejanus His Fall 219
Workes 219, 220
Jowett, John xi, 178, 181, 182, 185–7, 200, 201,
    202, 203–4, 212, 226, 261, 265, 270–1
  disproving the presence of memorial
    reconstruction in Q1 *Richard 3* 125–6,
    264
  on stage directions in *The Tempest* by Ralph
    Crane 176–7
  on the doubly told death of Portia in *Julius
    Caesar* 177–8
Jowett, John and Gary Taylor on *Richard 2*
    173–6
Joyce, James 140

Kable, William S. 79, 80, 89, 90
Kastan, David Scott 173, 267, 269
Keats, John 151
Kennedy, Richard F. 200, 201
Kermode, Frank 252
Kerrigan, John 169, 170, 230, 257
  on distinguishing authorial from
    non-authorial revision 135–6, 140,
    178
  repudiated 199–200
Kidnie, Margaret Jane 212–14
King Leir (anonymous) 115
King, Rosalind 191
King's men playing company. *See* Chamberlain's/
    King's men playing company
Kirschbaum, Leo 46, 110, 111, 123, 124
Knapp, Jeffrey 228–9
Knight, Edward 25, 66, 205
Knowles, Richard 194
Korean War 258
Kreps, Barbara 198
Kuhn, Thomas 86
Kyd, Thomas 101, 119, 241
  The Spanish Tragedy 135, 219

Lacan, Jacques 195
Lachmann, Karl 7, 11, 34
Lavagnino, John 270
Law, Matthew 183
Lawrence, W. J. 129
Lee, Sidney, *Facsimile of the First Folio* 12, 13–14,
    76, 92, 202, 223, 258
Lesser, Zachary 199, 229
Levenson, Jill L. 207–8, 261
Lever, W. J. 253
Lewis, C. S. 129, 130
Library, The 12, 15, 97
Ling, Nicholas 217
Lodge, Thomas 119

Long, William B. 51, 155–8, 162, 163, 164, 165–6, 178, 223
Lothian, J. M. 253
Loughrey, Bryan 47, 190, 191, 200, 201, 266
Luce, Morton 242
Lull, Janis 264–5
Lydgate, John 98
Lyly, John 119

Macalister, J. Y. W. 12
Macmillan, Michael 242
Maguire, Laurie E., *Shakespearean Suspect Texts* 103, 119–23, 165
Malone, Edmond, his Shakespeare edition of 1790 6, 108, 194
Manilius, Marcus, *Astronomica* 11
Manley, Lawrence 210–11
Marcus, Leah S. 190, 212, 243
  Unediting the Renaissance 154, 190, 198
Marlowe, Christopher 8, 107, 116, 119, 130, 198, 246
  Doctor Faustus 136, 146, 199
  Massacre at Paris, The 39, 47
  Tamburlaine 219
Marshe, Thomas 73
Marston, John 119
Martin, Henri-Jean 9
Marx, Karl 86, 195, 196
Marxism 155, 191, 192, 195
Mason, Pamela 211–12
Massai, Sonia 6, 257, 258
Massinger, Philip 140
  Believe as You List 17, 49, 51
Masten, Jeffrey 9, 47, 226, 227
Master of the Revels 17–18, 27, 39, 135, 156, 215, 223, 224, 242
materialism, philosophical theory of 10, 45, 77, 78, 153, 154, 155, 190–206
Maxwell, J. C. 250
McEachern, Claire 211
McGann, Jerome J. 151, 152, 206
  A Critique of Modern Textual Criticism 146–50, 178
  Textual Criticism and Literary Interpretation 150–1
McKenzie, D. F. 59, 79, 98, 133, 148, 206, 259
  Bibliography and the Sociology of Texts 151–2
  'Printers of the Mind' 57, 62, 64, 79, 81–4, 158, 254
    responses to it 84–96
  'Stretching a Point' 159–60, 161, 172
McKerrow, R. B. 7, 8, 22, 39, 42, 43, 44, 46, 54, 64, 65, 73, 77, 88, 89, 91, 117, 181, 188, 255, 259
  his edition of Thomas Nashe 167

Introduction to Bibliography for Literary Students 63, 231
Prolegomena for the Oxford Shakespeare 30–7, 40, 64, 167, 196, 209, 252
'Suggestion Regarding Shakespeare's Manuscripts, A' 31–3, 37, 39, 64, 200, 210
McLeod, Randall 3, 4, 131–3, 135, 151, 153, 154, 163, 178, 188, 203, 214, 254
McMillin, Scott 99, 115, 116, 201
  finding theatrical refinements in bad quartos 113–14, 127
McMullan, Gordon 227–8, 261, 270
memorial reconstruction 11, 15, 99, 100–28, 132, 135, 138, 139, 145, 164, 170, 182, 185, 191, 197, 198, 201, 223, 240, 246, 264
Meres, Francis, *Palladis Tamia* 220
Merriam, Thomas 228
Metz, G. Harold 268
Meyer, Anne R. 194
Middleton, Thomas 119, 140, 180, 226, 246, 264
  A Game at Chess 70–1, 223
  Oxford *Collected Works* edition 178, 270–1
  The Second Maiden's Tragedy (= *The Lady's Tragedy*) 199, 213, 223
Millington, Thomas 108, 243
Mommsen, Tycho 100, 101
Montgomery, William xi, 175, 265
Moore, Marianne 149
Morris, Brian 251
Morton, Andrew Q. 268
Moseley, Humphrey 26, 221
Mountfort, Walter, *The Launching of the Mary* 17, 18, 19, 27, 51, 156, 158
Mowat, Barbara A. 196, 204, 266, 269, 270
Moxon, Joseph, *Mechanick Exercises* 63, 73, 76, 83, 96, 122
Muir, Kenneth 251, 261
Munday, Anthony 119
  his contribution to *Sir Thomas More* 17, 226
  John a Kent and John a Cumber 17, 24, 50, 51, 157, 165
Munro, Lucy, *Children of the Queen's Revels* 158
Murphy, Andrew 4, 6, 8, 47, 205–6
  Shakespeare in Print 240

Nashe, Thomas 8, 119, 167, 226
Nathan, Norman 81
New Cambridge Shakespeare series 192, 265
  Early Quartos sub-series 192, 215, 262, 264, 269
New Folger Library Shakespeare series 196–7, 204, 266, 269, 270
New Historicism 153, 190, 192

'new' New Bibliography 42, 99, 134, 154, 158, 167–89, 195, 216, 221, 222, 224, 226, 229, 241, 257, 260, 261, 262, 265, 268, 270
New Penguin Shakespeare series 167, 169, 174, 256–8, 262
New Shakespeare series 4–5, 247–50
New Textualism 3, 29, 33, 53, 87, 127, 129, 147, 153–8, 162–6, 178, 188, 190, 192, 193, 194, 195, 196, 197, 199, 200, 201, 202, 203, 204, 205, 207–15, 216, 222, 225, 226, 227, 230, 258, 260, 261, 264, 268, 270
New Variorum Shakespeare series 240
Newton, Isaac 87
Nicoll, Allardyce 167
Norden, John, *Civitas Londini* (1600) 34
Norton Facsimile of the First Folio of Shakespeare, The 258–9
Nosworthy, J. M. 252

O'Connor, John 93, 95, 208–9
Okes, Nicholas 55, 158, 159, 200, 203
Oldcastle (Lord Cobham), John, the historical figure 211
Oldcastle/Falstaff naming problem. *See* Shakespeare, William, *1 Henry 4*
Oliver, H. J. 253, 261
Orgel, Stephen 223, 228
  on routine revision of plays 130–1
Oxford *Collected Works* edition of Middleton 178, 270–1
Oxford *Complete Works* edition of Shakespeare xi, xii, 11, 36, 92, 95, 167–89, 191, 197, 200, 202, 203, 208, 221, 241, 254, 257, 260, 261, 262, 265, 268, 269, 270
  Gary Taylor's 'Introduction' to its *Textual Companion* 178–80
  its use of appendices 180
  reviews of 183–4, 187, 189
Oxford English Dictionary 242
Oxford Shakespeare series 207, 254, 260–2
Oxford University Press 12, 30, 91, 167

Pafford, J. H. P. 253
Parrott, T. M. 102
Patrick, David Lyall 110, 112, 115
Pavier, Thomas 90
Pechter, Edward 3, 202–3, 222
Peele, George 108, 116, 119, 226, 246, 258, 268
  The Battle of Alcazar 201
Pelican Shakespeare series 240, 254–5
Pembroke's men playing company 114, 210
Pendleton, Thomas A. 173
Pettitt, Thomas 104
Pinter, Harold, *The Homecoming* 195

piracy of plays 15–16, 19
Pitcher, John 257
plague closing the theatres 102, 201
Plato 152, 153, 192, 204, 270
playhouse plots 24, 39, 50
Pollard, A. W. 12, 25, 26, 27, 28, 31, 35, 37, 39, 46, 49, 52, 59, 64, 65, 66, 100, 103, 108, 109, 110, 123, 124, 155, 205, 240, 242, 244, 246, 247, 248
  collaboration with John Dover Wilson 10, 23–4, 33, 52, 102, 124
  Shakespeare Folios and Quartos 12–15, 245
  Shakespeare's Fight with the Pirates 15–23, 245
Pope, Alexander, his Shakespeare edition of 1723–5 6, 36
Posener, Alan 201
postmodernism 87, 163, 189, 197, 214, 225, 227, 228
post-structuralism 130, 133, 153–8, 163, 165, 190, 203, 209
Potter, Lois 210
Povey, Kenneth 63, 83
  his lamp for detecting which side of a sheet was printed first 69
press variants. *See* type, correction of
Price, George R. 94
Price, Hereward T. 103
prompt-book xi, 12, 14, 17, 18, 19, 20, 21, 22, 23, 24, 25, 26, 27, 28, 37, 39, 41, 44, 47, 48, 49, 50, 51, 52, 53, 54, 65, 66, 102, 112, 138, 139, 140, 141, 142, 143, 145, 146, 155, 157, 158, 162, 164, 165, 166, 168, 169, 170, 172, 173, 174, 175, 176, 177, 178, 180, 185, 205, 215, 223, 225, 249, 256, 258, 261, 263, 264, 265
prompter 17, 19, 22, 24, 28, 29, 32, 48, 49, 50, 51, 52, 155, 157, 165, 199, 202, 205, 215, 244, 253
  prompting from printed plays 21, 22
  signs of in printed plays 19–21
proofreading and correction 38, 61–4, 76–8, 79, 89, 93, 258
Proudfoot, Richard 267
punctuation 23, 31, 37, 40, 43, 44, 71, 72, 88, 117, 120, 122, 131, 146, 160, 168, 180, 208, 231, 243, 247, 251, 255, 260, 263

quantum mechanics 87
Quiller-Couch, Arthur 247

Rasmussen, Eric 208, 212
  on revision of plays 199–200
Records of Early English Drama (REED) 201
Reid, S. W. 160
Remírez, Luís 127

reprinting xi, 6, 7, 13, 15, 20, 21, 31, 36, 40, 41,
    56, 59, 64, 77, 90, 91, 93, 102, 133, 170,
    172, 181, 183, 191, 200, 218, 244, 245, 246,
    248, 249, 250, 251, 264
  accumulation of errors in 1–2
  as indicator of popularity 198
  diplomatic 65, 191, 196, 266
    defined 65
  with additional authority from a manuscript
    7, 20, 21, 23, 35, 41, 46, 53, 126, 137, 168,
    179, 185, 257, 265, 270
  revision of plays 14, 18, 22, 23, 41, 46, 69–72,
    102, 108, 110, 112, 114, 115, 117, 123, 124,
    125, 127, 129–31, 133–46, 163, 167, 169,
    172, 176, 177, 178, 179, 180, 181, 182, 185,
    191, 194, 198, 199–200, 207, 209, 211, 221,
    223, 224, 242, 248, 249, 263, 265, 271
Rhodes, R. Compton 103, 104, 124
Rider, Philip R. 96
Ridley, M. R. 251
Riverside Shakespeare edition 259–60
Roberts, James 56, 217
Romantics, literary movement 3, 147, 222,
    228
Rose playhouse 214
Rowe, Nicholas, his Shakespeare edition of 1709
    6, 204
Rowley, Samuel 136, 199
Rowley, William 20
Royal Holloway, University of London 10
Royal Shakespeare Company 167, 256

Sanders, Norman 263
Satchell, Thomas 55, 56, 57, 92
Saussure, Ferdinand de 153, 165
Schäfer, Jürgen 168
scribal transcripts 14, 23, 24, 32–3, 37, 54, 58, 101,
    165, 185, 202, 215
Second Folio of Shakespeare 1632 2, 8
Shakespeare as literary author 215–22
Shakespeare Institute, Stratford-upon-Avon 167,
    181, 262
Shakespeare Quarto Facsimiles series xi
Shakespeare Survey 11, 34
Shakespeare, William
  All is True xii, 6, 183, 226, 227–8, 241, 256,
    261, 265, 270
  All's Well that Ends Well 32, 243, 253
  Antony and Cleopatra 251, 266, 267–8
  As You Like It 229, 245
  Comedy of Errors, The 31, 162, 253
  Contention of York and Lancaster, The xii, 19,
    34, 46, 103, 104, 107–9, 111, 113–14, 115,
    116–17, 125, 127, 175, 179, 183, 184, 185,
    190, 197, 198, 210–11, 246, 252, 265

Coriolanus 139, 245, 250, 253
Cymbeline 139, 140, 183, 242, 252, 257, 262,
    265
Edward 3 125, 226, 265
Hamlet 7, 15, 33, 41, 46, 56, 65, 67, 68, 92,
    100, 101, 102, 103, 104, 109, 111, 115, 117,
    118, 123, 124, 127, 141, 145, 162–3, 179,
    180–1, 184, 185, 191, 198, 199, 200, 201,
    204, 211–12, 213, 214, 215, 217, 219, 220,
    221, 241, 249–50, 254, 261, 263–4, 267,
    270
1 Henry 4 xii, 56, 86, 96, 97, 136, 145, 160, 161,
    183, 184, 185–6, 200, 218, 220, 253, 257,
    269
  the name Oldcastle/Falstaff 173, 183, 185,
    186, 265
2 Henry 4 53, 68, 92, 173, 178, 179, 184, 185,
    186–7, 218, 245
Henry 5 15, 34, 46, 94, 100, 102, 103, 104, 109,
    111, 112, 117, 118, 123, 124, 125, 170–1, 179,
    184, 185, 222, 243, 251, 260, 264, 265,
    266, 268
1 Henry 6 52, 226, 246, 264
Julius Caesar 6, 177–8, 200, 242, 252
King John 6, 257, 264
King Lear xii, 21, 46, 47, 55, 56, 61, 62, 65,
    109, 110, 111, 112, 113, 115, 127, 131, 146,
    147, 158–9, 178, 179, 180, 183, 184, 185,
    190, 196, 197, 199, 200, 203, 204, 214,
    215, 218, 220, 242, 250, 251, 257, 259–60,
    261, 264, 266, 268–9, 270
  divided into two plays 114–15, 133–46, 153,
    154, 163, 181–2, 188, 197, 198
  division into two plays repudiated 194
Love's Labour's Lost 8, 32, 93, 94, 96, 169, 184,
    208, 217, 230, 244, 252, 257
Macbeth 6, 55, 70, 178, 179, 217, 221, 226,
    244, 246, 270, 271
Measure for Measure 91, 178, 179, 180, 208,
    226, 248, 253, 264, 270, 271
Merchant of Venice, The 56, 57, 59, 96, 179,
    184, 200, 208, 212, 218, 252
Merry Wives of Windsor, The 15, 46, 91, 100,
    101, 102, 103, 104, 109, 111, 113, 117, 118,
    123, 127, 164–5, 185, 188, 190, 198, 208,
    220, 243–4, 248
Midsummer Night's Dream, A 20, 68, 90, 96,
    179, 180, 184, 200, 208, 212, 218, 244,
    249, 254, 261, 263, 266
Much Ado About Nothing 20, 48, 68, 70, 92,
    93, 96, 168, 170, 179, 184, 188, 208, 212,
    218, 246
Othello 65, 72, 94, 130, 141, 145, 178, 179, 184,
    185, 204, 210, 214, 221, 222, 243, 250, 263,
    269, 270

Pericles 15, 20, 46, 100, 111, 123, 161, 182, 184, 185, 218, 219, 220, 223, 226, 227, 245, 250, 254, 261, 264
Rape of Lucrece, The 8
Richard 2 22, 55, 92, 110, 111, 173–6, 179, 180, 183, 184, 218, 220, 257
Richard 3 34, 46, 47, 92, 110, 111, 112, 113, 115, 125, 126, 145, 160, 161, 171, 179, 183, 184, 203–4, 220, 250, 254, 257, 261, 264–5
Richard Duke of York xii, 34, 47, 105, 107–9, 111, 113–14, 115, 116–17, 180, 183, 184, 185, 190, 214, 246, 252, 265
Romeo and Juliet 15, 19, 32, 46, 48, 56, 58, 66, 91, 96, 100, 102, 103, 109, 111, 113, 117, 118, 123, 124, 132, 133, 180, 184, 188, 198, 201, 202, 207–8, 214, 215, 217, 218, 241, 254, 261
Sir Thomas More 17, 18, 23, 24, 31, 39, 47, 50, 52, 53, 88, 121, 122, 166, 181, 199, 205, 213, 226, 247, 252, 263, 265
Sonnets 8, 94, 173
Taming of the Shrew, The 106, 107, 111, 113, 114, 123, 198, 200, 264
Tempest, The 6, 91, 176–7, 208, 217, 233, 242, 247, 252
Timon of Athens 6, 49, 66, 226, 253, 270
Titus Andronicus 56, 96, 102, 112, 123, 145, 184, 185, 200, 212, 226, 257, 258, 268
Troilus and Cressida 65, 94, 145, 172, 179, 183, 184, 195, 214, 218, 220, 250, 253, 261
Twelfth Night 253
Two Gentlemen of Verona, The 31, 91, 121, 208, 233, 245, 248
Two Noble Kinsmen, The 214, 226, 241, 256, 266
Venus and Adonis 8
Winter's Tale, The 91, 208, 253
Shakespearean Originals series 190–2, 196, 204, 266
Shapiro, I. A. 34, 44
Sharpham, Edward, *The Fleire* 136
Shelley, Mary 149
Shirley, James 119
  The Bird in a Cage 96
  The Court Secret 39
  The Wittie Faire One 96
Short, Peter 86, 160, 161
Simmes, Valentine 68, 92, 160, 161, 217
Simpson, Percy 101, 247
Sisson, Charles Jasper 181
Sisyphus, a king in Greek myth 230
skeleton formes
  defined 60, 159
  identified by headline reuse 60, 67, 94, 263

  revealing order/rate of composition or presswork 38, 67, 68, 81, 83, 86, 89, 94
Skura, Meredith 214
Smallwood, R. L. 257
Smart, John Semple 107
Sokal, Alan 87
speech prefixes 70, 160, 179, 205
  variation of names in 31–3, 37, 39, 126, 162, 200–1, 212, 257, 264, 268, 270
spelling 23, 30, 31, 36, 40, 43, 44, 53, 65, 70, 71, 72, 79, 80, 88, 89, 91, 131, 132, 141, 142, 143, 144, 145, 146, 148, 171, 173, 177, 180, 183, 187, 191, 255, 260, 265
  altered to justify a line of type 58–9, 209, 232
  modernizing 45, 167–8, 230, 243, 254, 262
  Shakespeare's own 23, 24, 39, 53, 205, 252
  used to identify compositors 38, 55–9, 67, 68, 80, 92, 93, 94, 98, 160–1, 171, 208–9, 263, 267
Spencer, T. J. B. 167, 256, 262
Spinner, Jonathan H. 94
Sprinchorn, Evert 191
stage directions
  anticipatory 19, 29–30, 51
  indefinite 50, 51, 162, 211, 212–14, 257, 267, 270
Stallybrass, Peter 195, 196
Stallybrass, Peter and Margreta de Grazia
  'The Materiality of Shakespeare's Text' 192–4, 202, 214
Stanley (Lord Strange), Ferdinando 211
Star Trek, television and film series 213
Stationers' Company 16
Stationers' Register 16, 108, 207, 217, 218, 219, 221, 242, 245, 246
stenography 15, 101, 102, 103, 104, 109, 110, 111, 112, 113, 119, 127, 241
Stern, Tiffany 39, 225–6
Stirling, Brents 177–8, 254
Stone, P. W. K. 97, 133, 137, 138, 140, 143
Strange's men playing company 210
Studies in Bibliography 38, 47, 54–8, 68, 69, 91
substantive
  a class of variant 40, 44, 45, 46, 67, 68, 71, 72, 76, 131, 151, 170, 171, 172, 174, 183, 256, 261, 265
  editions 33, 35, 40, 41, 42, 46, 91, 179, 180, 190, 209, 259, 260, 271
  definition of 31

Tanselle, G. Thomas 148, 149, 150, 152–3
Taylor, Gary xi, 2, 40, 125, 136, 154, 159, 160, 162, 163, 171–3, 181, 182, 186–7, 188, 195, 202, 203, 209, 219, 223, 226, 256, 260, 261, 265, 270–1

Taylor, Gary (*cont.*)
  dividing *King Lear* 135, 137–46
  'Introduction' to the Oxford *Complete Works*'s *Textual Companion* 178
Taylor, Gary and John Jowett on *Richard 2* 173–6
Taylor, Gary and Stanley Wells, *Modernizing Shakespeare's Spelling* 167–8, 170–1, 260
Taylor, Neil 270
Telephone, the children's game. *See* Chinese Whispers
Tennyson, Alfred 86, 149
The Verdict, motion picture 1
Third Folio of Shakespeare 1663–4 2, 8
Thomas of Woodstock (anonymous, probably by Samuel Rowley) 49, 51, 156–8
Thomas, Sidney 194
Thompson, Ann 267, 270
Thompson, Edward Maunde 23, 39
Thorpe, James 146, 148, 149
  Principles of Textual Criticism 88
Through Line Numbering xi, 258, 260
Tillyard, E. M. W. 203
Tilney, Edmund 17, 224
Times Literary Supplement 23, 55, 85, 87, 129, 191
Todd, William B. 85
Tonson, Jacob 6, 131
Tourneur, Cyril 119
Trenery, Grace R. 245–6
Trinity College, Cambridge 38, 70
Tronch-Pérez, Jesús 127
Troublesome Reign Parts One and Two (anonymous) 123
Trousdale, Marion 153, 154, 164, 193
Trundle, John 217
Turner Junior, Robert K. 68, 80, 82, 254, 255
Two Noble Ladies, The (anonymous) 49
type
  correction of 38, 61, 75, 76–7, 83, 102, 138, 159, 180, 230, 236, 243, 249, 255, 258, 263, 266
  forme the unit of 43, 77
  forme of, defined 232
  imposition of, explained 232–4
  reuse
    as evidence for compositorial stints 80, 93, 159, 160, 161
    as evidence of order of composition or press-work 38, 57, 68, 73, 83, 95, 159, 160, 161
  shortage of shown by substitutions 38, 177–8
  revealing order of setting 60, 68, 73

unediting 132–3, 178, 190–206
University College London 181

University of Virginia 38, 54
Urkowitz, Steven 134, 141, 154, 188, 190, 191, 197–8, 202, 204
  attacking the theory of memorial reconstruction 115–17, 125, 127
Urquhart, Thomas, *Epigrams: Divine and Moral* 216

Vega, Lope de 127
veil of print, stripping or piercing it 47, 55, 195
Vickers, Brian 10, 131, 191, 227–8, 258
  Shakespeare, Co-Author 245
Visscher, J. C., *View of London* (1616?) 34–5

Walker, Alice 47, 56, 58, 81, 91, 94, 96, 136, 167, 241, 250, 269
  Textual Problems of the First Folio 10, 53
Walley, Andrew 183
Walter, J. H. 251
Walton, J. K. 34, 179
Warren, Michael 116, 154, 163, 266
  dividing *King Lear* 114–15, 133, 134
  his four-text edition of *King Lear* 197
Warren, Roger 125, 127, 135, 261
Warwick Shakespeare series 246
Watts, John 131
Webster, John 119, 140, 217, 223
  The Duchess of Malfi 216
Weis, René 204
Wells, Stanley xi, 2, 11, 95, 167, 168–70, 174, 178, 181, 187, 188, 230, 254, 256, 257, 260–2, 265
  Re-editing Shakespeare for the Modern Reader 182–3, 212
Wells, Stanley and Gary Taylor
  Modernizing Shakespeare's Spelling 167–8, 170–1, 260
Werstine, Paul 2, 3, 52, 80, 154, 159, 162–3, 164–5, 184, 188, 196, 198, 199, 201, 205, 214–15, 218, 261, 266, 267, 269, 270
  disproving Folio compositor B's carelessness 96–7, 136, 269
  his rapprochement with New Bibliography 209–10
  on indistinguishability of Folio compositors 'D' and 'F' 208–9
  on Q/F *King Lear* differences 136–7, 155
  rejecting the theory of memorial reconstruction 123–5, 127
Wilder, Lina Perkins 212
Wilders, John 267–8
Wilkins, George 20, 182, 185, 219, 226, 250, 264
Williams, George Walton 38, 56, 59, 60, 68, 73, 229, 254, 255

Williams, Philip 55
Willoughby, Edwin Eliott 55, 57, 92
Wilson, John Dover 39, 53, 64, 101, 103, 111, 124, 155, 169, 180, 240, 244, 261
   collaboration with A. W. Pollard 10, 23–4, 33, 52, 102, 124
   New Shakespeare series 4–5, 10, 52, 241, 247–50, 252
Wimsatt, W. K. and M. C. Beardsley, 'The Intentional Fallacy' 151

Wise, Andrew 245
Wolf, Edwin 62–3
Woudhuysen, H. R. 267
Wright, W. Aldis 6

Yale University Elizabethan Club 75
Year's Work in English Studies 11
Yeats, William Butler 151

Zimmerman, Susan 160–1